# Praise for *Agentic GraphRAG*

*Agentic GraphRag* is a great starting point for understanding how major frameworks in the space implement this idea in production. Despite the technical complexity, Anthony and Sam start from first principles and guide the user toward a full understanding of the implementation.

*—Vasilije Markovic, Founder and CEO, Cognee*

More than a GraphRAG book, this is a blueprint for production-ready AI agents. The authors expertly connect knowledge graphs, memory, governance, and tooling to help practitioners build trustworthy, context-aware AI systems.

*—Ashok Singamaneni, Principal Engineer, Nike*

Alcaraz and Julien deliver the definitive guide for moving beyond RAG proof-of-concepts. This book offers a practical, production-ready framework for building agentic systems capable of handling complex, real-world enterprise datasets.

*—Jorge Reyes, Cloud Security Consultant*

Agents don't fail because of the LLM or the harness. They fail because of how the information they have access to is represented: the data, the knowledge. I've spent a good part of my career arguing that, both before and during the generative AI era, and I love to see Alcaraz and Julien make the case better than most of us have—they dissect exactly how the failure happens and give each mode a name: context amnesia, relationship blindness, temporal ignorance, reasoning paralysis, tool chaos. The dual-graph architecture is their refreshing answer, and they don't just propose it, they build it: ontologies, entity resolution, bitemporal modeling, provenance, the separation of what you trust from what you merely extracted. Articulating that framing across eight pillars is something every practitioner will learn from. The industry's default answer to a failing agent is more tokens. This book offers a serious alternative. A great read.

*—Jesus Barrasa, AI Field CTO, Neo4j*

# Agentic GraphRAG

*Integrating Knowledge Graphs, Reasoning, and Agency for Enterprise AI*

*Anthony Alcaraz and Sam Julien*

O'REILLY®

**Agentic GraphRAG**

by Anthony Alcaraz and Sam Julien



Published by O'Reilly Media, Inc., 141 Stony Circle, Suite 195, Santa Rosa, CA 95401.

O'Reilly books may be purchased for educational, business, or sales promotional use. Online editions are also available for most titles (*http://oreilly.com*). For more information, contact our corporate/institutional sales department: 800-998-9938 or *corporate@oreilly.com*.

**Acquisitions Editor:** Nicole Butterfield
**Development Editor:** Corbin Collins
**Production Editor:** Beth Kelly
**Copyeditor:** Paula L. Fleming
**Proofreader:** Laura K. Miller
**Indexer:** Potomac Indexing, LLC
**Cover Designer:** Susan Brown
**Cover Illustrator:** José Marzan, Jr.
**Interior Designer:** David Futato
**Interior Illustrator:** Kate Dullea

August 2026: First Edition

**Revision History for the First Edition**

2026-08-19: First Release

See *http://oreilly.com/catalog/errata.csp?isbn=9798341623170* for release details.



979-8-341-62317-0

[LSI]

# Table of Contents

Preface.... xiii

Part I. Foundations of Graph-Based Agentic Systems

1. The Crisis of Enterprise Agentic AI.... 3
   - Defining Agentic AI 5
     - What Is an Agent, Anyway? 6
     - Classifying Agentic Systems: The Workflow-Agent Spectrum 8
     - The Agent Constraint Triangle 9
     - Agent Architecture 10
   - The Limitations of Vector-Based Retrieval 12
     - A Brief Overview of Vector Retrieval 12
     - Where Vector RAG Succeeds and Fails 13
   - GraphRAG: The Evolution of Contextual Retrieval Systems 18
     - A Brief Overview of GraphRAG Architecture 18
     - Where GraphRAG Succeeds and Struggles 21
     - Hybrid GraphRAG 24
     - Learned Graph Reasoning Models 25
   - Summary 26

2. Agentic Graph Architecture Foundations.... 27
   - From Strings to Things 28
   - The Dual-Graph Architecture 30
     - The Vertical Knowledge Graph 31
     - The Horizontal Workflow Graph 33
     - Where the Two Graphs Meet 38

A Note on Context Graphs 40
The Eight Pillars of Agentic Graph Architecture 42
Setup: Building the Digital Twin of a Tech Stack (Part II) 43
Action: From Firefighting to Foresight (Part III) 44
Production: Creating a Self-Healing System (Part IV) 47
The Autonomous DevOps Agent 48
The Initial State 49
The Transformation Arc 50
A Real-World Parallel 52
What the Completed Agent Looks Like 53
Summary 53

## Part II. Setup: Building the Digital Twin of a Tech Stack

**3. Graph-Based Knowledge Modeling for Agentic Systems. . . . . . . . . . . . . . . . . . . . . . . . . 57**
Knowledge Graph Foundations 58
Components of GraphRAG Systems 58
Building Versus Buying a GraphRAG System 60
Graph Data Models 61
Types of Graph Data Models 62
Evaluating Graph Models 63
Graph Design Principles for Agentic Systems 71
The Three-Graph Architecture for Agent Knowledge 71
Schema Design Patterns 75
Homoiconic Knowledge Representation 80
Integrating with Existing Systems 82
Knowledge Organization and Ontology Fundamentals 83
Creating a Unified Semantic Foundation 86
Entity Resolution: The Foundation of Agent Knowledge 91
Building the Knowledge Graph 95
Extraction Approaches for Heterogeneous Sources 95
Automating Knowledge Graph Construction with Multi-Agent Systems 100
Entity Resolution and Linking Across Graphs 100
Knowledge Representation in Practice: DevOps Agent 101
Context Engineering for DevOps Automation 102
The DevOps Knowledge Representation Challenge 102
Designing the DevOps Ontology 102
Populating the Knowledge Graph: Building the Digital Twin 105
Homoiconic Knowledge Representation for Agent Adaptability 108
Querying the Knowledge Graph: Making the Digital Twin Useful 108

Entity Resolution for Infrastructure Identity 110
Measuring Context Quality: Ensuring the Digital Twin Stays Accurate 110
Summary 111

**4. Agentic Graph Memory Systems.............................................. 113**
Architecting Graph Memory Systems 113
The Problem: Why Your Current Memory Approach Fails 114
The Solution: Graph Memory 117
Representing Memory as Graphs 121
Understanding the Architecture Evolution 121
Essential Graph Components 123
Temporal Awareness: Making Memory Evolve 126
Implementation: Building Your First Graph Memory System 128
Four Essential Memory Operations 131
Consolidation: From Experience to Knowledge 132
Indexing: Organizing for Speed 133
Updating: Handling Change Gracefully 134
Retrieval: Finding What Matters 134
Production Patterns and Architectures 135
The Letta (MemGPT) Approach: Hierarchical Memory 135
The A-Mem Pattern: Evolving Knowledge Networks 137
The Graphiti Pattern: Real-Time Performance 138
Comparing Production Systems 139
Cognee 139
Mem0 141
Zep 142
Choosing Your Approach 143
Production-Ready Features and Operations 144
Reasoning and Recommendations 144
Use Case Optimizations 148
Training Your Agents to Use Memory 149
The MEM1 Revelation: Let Them Learn, Not Follow Rules 149
From Static Rules to Learned Strategies 150
The Three Phases of Training 150
Dynamic Memory Without Dynamic Schemas 152
Practical Training Strategies 152
Evolving Your Memory System 154
Moving Beyond Traditional Training 154
Adding Memory to the DevOps Agent 155
Designing the DevOps Memory Schema 155
Implementing Memory for Operational Context 156

Temporal Queries for Root Cause Analysis 156
Consolidation: Learning Patterns from Incidents 157
Training Memory Behavior with Reinforcement Learning 157
Production Considerations 159
Future-Proofing Your Implementation 160
Neurosymbolic Integration 160
Distributed Scaling 160
Continual Learning 160
Summary 161


## Part III. Action: From Firefighting to Foresight


**5. Reasoning and Planning.................................................... 165**
Foundations: Why Graph-Based Reasoning Matters for Agent Development 167
The Two Graph Types: Horizontal and Vertical 169
Ontological Grounding: Keeping Your Agent in Reality 173
Retrieval Mechanisms 174
The Distracting Effect: Why Your Agents Get Misled 175
PathRAG: Structural Protection Against Distractions 176
R3-RAG: Teaching Your Agents When and How to Retrieve 177
GraphRAG Pattern Taxonomy 180
Reasoning and Generation 181
Interleaved Thinking: Real-Time Adaptive Reasoning 181
Structured Generation: The Keystone of Reliable Communication 184
Pipeline Architectures 186
Sequential Pipeline: Linear Execution 186
Loop Pipeline: Iterative Refinement 187
Tree Pipeline: Parallel Exploration 187
Production Implementation Patterns 188
Hybrid Architectures 190
Event-Driven Orchestration: The Production Scaling Layer 193
Planning and Coordination 196
Why Planning Deserves Architectural Separation 196
Hierarchical Planning 197
Constraint-Guided Planning 198
Dynamic DAG Construction 199
Empirical Evidence: Graph Planning at Repository Scale 200
From Architecture to Daily Practice: Task Graphs at Developer Scale 201
The Multi-Agent Debate: Reconciling Parallel Execution 202
DevOps Diagnostic Agent: Pulling It All Together 204

Building the Horizontal Workflow Graph 205
Integrating the Knowledge Graph for Grounded Hypotheses 207
Constructing the Investigation DAG 207
A Production Incident Walkthrough 209
Why the Architecture Matters 210
Summary 211

**6. Agentic Graph-Based Tool Orchestration. . . . . . . . . . . . . . . . . . . . . . . . . . . . . . . . . . . . . 215**
MCP: The Protocol That Changes the Game 216
Securing the Foundation: MCP Authentication 216
Agents as Tools: A Powerful Pattern 217
The Prompt Bloat Crisis: When More Tools Mean Less Intelligence 218
From Listing to Finding: The RAG Way 218
The Gateway Pattern 219
Skills: The Judgment Layer 223
Choosing the Right Primitive: CLIs, MCPs, and Skills 227
The Knowledge Graph Necessity: Tools That Understand Each Other 230
Tools as Graph Nodes 231
Tool Dependencies and Type Matching 232
Securing Data Flow with Information Flow Control 233
Evolving Tool Ecosystems 234
Ontology-Driven Evolution: When Tools Define Themselves 234
The Trust Problem: When Tools Game the System 236
Metatooling: When Tools Create Tools 238
Orchestration at Scale 239
The Intelligent Orchestrator: Modernizing Classical SaaS 240
Hierarchical Orchestration: When Scale Demands Structure 241
Functional Clustering: Resilience Through Redundancy 243
The Enterprise AI OS Layer: Infrastructure for the Synthetic Workforce 244
Learning and Advanced Patterns 246
The Memory Layer: Learning from Every Interaction 246
Advanced Patterns: The Nested Execution Challenge 249
Performance at Scale: Making It Real 250
Context Governance: The Missing Layer in Tool Orchestration 250
Tool Orchestration in Practice: The DevOps Agent 253
Registering Tools in the Knowledge Graph 253
Structured Output for API Integration 254
The Latency Investigation, Continued 257
Summary 260

# Part IV. Production: Creating a Self-Healing System


**7. Self-Evolution and Evaluation. . . . . . . . . . . . . . . . . . . . . . . . . . . . . . . . . . . . . . . . . 265**
The Foundation of Self-Awareness 266
The Execution Graph: The Agent's Autobiography 266
The Multi-Layered Evaluation Framework: A Cognitive Autopsy 268
A Taxonomy for Self-Evolution 280
Targeted Self-Improvement 282
Choosing the Right Intervention: Prompt, Fine-Tune, or Constrain? 282
Semantic Backpropagation: Coherent Evolution Across the Graph 284
A Suite of Self-Improvement Frameworks 285
Safe Evolution in Production 294
The Full Evolutionary Loop 294
The RPO and Graduated Validation Protocol 295
Persistent Self-Learning Without Entropy Collapse 297
The DevOps Agent: Predictive Outage Detection in Practice 299
The Scenario: A Library Update Triggers a Prediction 300
Generating the Execution Graph 301
The Cognitive Autopsy 302
Semantic Backpropagation to the Causal Attribution Node 303
The Improvement and Its Effect 304
Inference-Time Knowledge Augmentation: Learning Without Retraining 305
Skills as Self-Improving Graph Objects 308
Common Pitfalls 310
Summary 313

**8. Optimization. . . . . . . . . . . . . . . . . . . . . . . . . . . . . . . . . . . . . . . . . . . . . . . . . . . 315**
Selective Intelligence 316
The Case for Model Specialization 317
Routing Strategies 317
Measuring Cost-Performance Trade-Offs 320
Data Governance and Access Control 323
Subgraph-Level Access Control 323
PII and Data Retention 324
The Execution Graph as a Compliance Artifact 325
Production Systems and Maintenance 326
Schema Evolution 326
Node and Edge Lifecycle Management 327
Incremental Updates 328
Deployment Patterns 330

Hardware Acceleration 332
GPU-Accelerated Graph Operations 332
Inference Acceleration for Specialist Model Fleets 334
Latency Budgets 336
The DevOps Agent: From Prototype to Production 337
Applying Selective Intelligence 337
Hardware Acceleration for Dependency Analysis 339
Governance for Infrastructure Data 340
The Completed Agent 340
Common Pitfalls 343
Summary 344
Conclusion 345
Where the Field Is Heading 346
Choosing the Right Architecture for Your System 347
Building What Comes Next 348

**Index. . . . . . . . . . . . . . . . . . . . . . . . . . . . . . . . . . . . . . . . . . . . . . . . . . . . . . . . . . . . . 349**

# Preface

The gap between a polished agent demo and a production system you'd stake a service-level agreement on is wider than most teams realize. A single-shot chatbot looks fine in a screenshare but lacks production-level capability. A prompt-chained agent hits a wall the moment it has to carry state across a dozen steps, reconcile information from conflicting sources, or act inside a system where the wrong API call costs real money.

We wrote this book because we kept watching capable engineers run into the same wall and reach for the same tools: more context, a bigger model, a longer prompt, or another framework. The scaffolding gets taller; the failure modes just shift up a floor.

Graph-based architectures cut through that loop, not because graphs are magic (they aren't) but because they make the two things agents most often get wrong inspectable: *what the agent knows* and *what the agent is doing*. Once you see those as distinct structures instead of a blob of tokens streaming through a prompt window, a lot of agent reliability problems start looking like plain process design problems. Those, as a field, we do know how to solve.

This is a genuinely exciting moment to be building in this space. The underlying models keep improving. Knowledge graph tooling has matured past its academic phase and into something you can actually deploy. The integration patterns that bind them together, such as GraphRAG, the dual-graph architecture, and semantic backpropagation, are finally concrete enough to write production code against. If you've been waiting for the field to settle down enough to build something real, it has.

## Who Should Read This Book

We wrote this for senior software engineers and architects who are already building with large language models (LLMs) and have bumped into the ceiling of prompt-only approaches. If you've shipped a vector retrieval-augmented generation (RAG) pipeline and watched it struggle the moment a question required joining information across three documents, you're the reader we have in mind. The same goes if you've wired up an agent that works beautifully for three steps and then forgets why it started.

You'll get the most out of this book if you're comfortable with the following:

- Python and its common data tooling, which we use for every code example
- LLM APIs and basic prompt engineering, including tool-calling and system prompts
- RAG at a working level: embeddings, vector stores, top-k search
- SQL or another query language (we teach the graph query parts as we go)

You don't need a background in graph databases, knowledge representation research, or formal planning systems. We build those up from the ground, and we always introduce a concept with a concrete problem before bringing in the theory.

This is a practitioner's book rather than a survey. If you're a researcher or a technical leader looking for a landscape read, the first two chapters will give you a clear mental model of the field. Then from Chapter 3 onward, we're shoulder-deep in implementation.

## Why We Wrote This Book

We've spent the first years of the agentic era of software shipping systems into environments where the stakes were higher than a demo. During this time, we've watched team after team pour effort into prompt scaffolding, multi-agent choreography, and ever-longer context windows—only to hit the same wall again and again.

The wall has five recognizable cracks. We call them the five flaws of traditional architectures: context amnesia, relationship blindness, temporal ignorance, reasoning paralysis, and tool chaos. Each traces back to treating an agent as a model wrapped in a prompt rather than as a process running on top of a model.

Graph-based architectures address all five, but the existing literature is fragmented across Google's 2012 "strings to things" pivot, Microsoft's GraphRAG paper, Neo4j's design patterns, and a growing body of research on planners and self-evolving systems. Each piece is valuable, but together they fail to add up to a coherent blueprint that a team can pick up on a Monday morning and start building from.

This book is that blueprint. We introduce the dual-graph architecture, which pairs a vertical knowledge graph for what the agent knows with a horizontal workflow graph for how the agent acts, and then we build out the eight pillars that make the architecture work in production. We show the pattern coming together in a single running example: an autonomous DevOps agent that starts as a pile of disconnected monitoring tools and, chapter by chapter, becomes a proactive, self-healing system.

When you close this book, we want you to walk away with three things: a mental model that explains why the agents you've seen in the wild behave the way they do, a concrete architectural pattern you can point to in your next design review, and enough working code to stand up a first version of a graph-based agent in your own stack.

## Navigating This Book

The book is organized in four parts that move from foundations to production.

Part I (Chapters 1 and 2) sets up the problem and the architecture:

- Chapter 1 explains why vector RAG falls apart when you push it into agentic territory, walks through the five flaws in detail, and introduces GraphRAG as the architectural answer.
- Chapter 2 introduces the dual-graph architecture and the eight pillars of GraphRAG architecture, then kicks off the autonomous DevOps agent example that we carry through the rest of the book.

Part II (Chapters 3 and 4) builds the agent's brain and memory:

- Chapter 3 covers knowledge representation, including graph models, extraction pipelines, entity resolution, and how to merge an existing organizational ontology into your agent's vertical knowledge graph without losing your mind.
- Chapter 4 covers memory systems, including episodic, semantic, and procedural memory, along with the temporal patterns that let an agent reason about how the world looked before an incident rather than only how it looks now.

Part III (Chapters 5 and 6) brings the agent to life:

- Chapter 5 covers reasoning and planning. You'll build the horizontal workflow graph, implement graph traversal as a reasoning primitive, and watch strategic decomposition and tactical execution work together on a real latency investigation.
- Chapter 6 covers tool orchestration and structured output engineering, showing how the agent discovers and calls tools through a graph-based orchestrator and how structured generation makes the handoff between a probabilistic model and a deterministic API boring and reliable.

Part IV (Chapters 7 and 8) makes the system trustworthy and affordable:

- Chapter 7 covers self-evolution and evaluation. You'll generate an execution graph of what the agent actually did, build a multilayered evaluation framework, and use semantic backpropagation to send targeted feedback to the specific reasoning node that got something wrong.
- Chapter 8 covers optimization, including selective intelligence, the federation-of-specialists pattern that lets you use small, cheap models for routine work and reserve expensive ones for the decisions that matter. It also covers data governance, access control, and the kind of hardware acceleration that makes graph traversal fast enough for real-time monitoring.

If you're new to the space, read straight through. If you're already shipping graph-based systems, Chapters 2, 5, 7, and 8 are where we expect most of the new patterns will surface for you.

Every chapter ends with a summary that threads back to the eight pillars and forward to what's next. We use the autonomous DevOps agent example to make every concept concrete, and the agent grows up alongside you across the chapters.

## Conventions Used in This Book

The following typographical conventions are used in this book:

*Italic*
: Indicates new terms, URLs, email addresses, filenames, and file extensions.

`Constant width`
: Used for program listings, as well as within paragraphs to refer to program elements such as variable or function names, databases, data types, environment variables, statements, and keywords.

*`Constant width italic`*
: Shows text that should be replaced with user-supplied values or by values determined by context.

> This element signifies a tip or suggestion.

This element signifies a general note.

This element indicates a warning or caution.

## Using Code Examples

Supplemental material (code examples, exercises, etc.) is available for download at *https://github.com/AnthonyAlcaraz/agentic-graph-rag-skills*.

If you have a technical question or a problem using the code examples, please send email to *support@oreilly.com*.

This book is here to help you get your job done. In general, if example code is offered with this book, you may use it in your programs and documentation. You do not need to contact us for permission unless you're reproducing a significant portion of the code. For example, writing a program that uses several chunks of code from this book does not require permission. Selling or distributing examples from O'Reilly books does require permission. Answering a question by citing this book and quoting example code does not require permission. Incorporating a significant amount of example code from this book into your product's documentation does require permission.

We appreciate, but generally do not require, attribution. An attribution usually includes the title, author, publisher, and ISBN. For example: "*Agentic GraphRAG* by Anthony Alcaraz and Sam Julien (O'Reilly). Copyright 2026 Anthony Alcaraz and Sam Julien, 979-8-341-62317-0."

If you feel your use of code examples falls outside fair use or the permission given above, feel free to contact us at *permissions@oreilly.com*.

## O'Reilly Online Learning

For more than 40 years, O'Reilly Media has provided technology and business training, knowledge, and insight to help companies succeed.

Our unique network of experts and innovators share their knowledge and expertise through books, articles, and our online learning platform. O'Reilly's online learning platform gives you on-demand access to live training courses, in-depth learning paths, interactive coding environments, and a vast collection of text and video from O'Reilly and 200+ other publishers. For more information, visit *https://oreilly.com*.

## How to Contact Us

Please address comments and questions concerning this book to the publisher:


O'Reilly Media, Inc.
141 Stony Circle, Suite 195
Santa Rosa, CA 95401
800-889-8969 (in the United States or Canada)
707-827-7019 (international or local)
707-829-0104 (fax)
*support@oreilly.com*
*https://oreilly.com/about/contact.html*


We have a web page for this book, where we list errata and any additional information. You can access this page at *https://oreil.ly/agentic-graphrag*.

For news and information about our books and courses, visit *https://oreilly.com*.

Find us on LinkedIn: *https://linkedin.com/company/oreilly*.

Watch us on YouTube: *https://youtube.com/oreillymedia*.

## Acknowledgments


A book like this goes well beyond its authors. It's the accumulated work of a field, filtered through the patience of a lot of generous people.

Thank you to our technical reviewers—Ashok Singamaneni, Jorge Reyes, and Alison Cossette—who caught errors we would have shipped and pushed back on arguments that needed sharpening. Thank you to the engineers and architects who shared production war stories. Thank you to the teams at Neo4j, Microsoft Research, WRITER, the Latent Space LLM Paper Club, and the broader GraphRAG community for building in the open and publishing the foundational work this book rests on.

To the editorial and production team at O'Reilly: thank you for trusting us to take on a topic that was still moving while we wrote it, holding the bar high, and supporting us at every step along the way.

Finally, to our families, who supported us while we disappeared into chapter drafts, research tangents, and weekends full of revisions: thank you. None of this could happen without you.

# PART I
# Foundations of Graph-Based Agentic Systems

Part I establishes the foundational theory of the book and introduces the end-to-end example you will build for the rest of it. Before we can construct an agentic system, we have to be honest about why the current generation of agents keeps stalling out in production: stateless retrieval, flat embeddings, no temporal model, monolithic prompts, and ad hoc tool integration. Those five flaws are not separate bugs. They are symptoms of a single representational gap, and closing that gap is what this book is about.

From there, we introduce the structural answer: the move from strings to things, the dual-graph architecture of a *vertical knowledge graph* (what the agent knows) and a *horizontal workflow graph* (how the agent acts), and the eight pillars that turn that structure into a working system. By the end of Part I, you will have a complete mental model of where we are going and why, along with the autonomous DevOps agent as a concrete system to anchor every later chapter.

- Chapter 1 defines agentic AI along three dimensions of agency, places systems on the workflow-agent spectrum, diagnoses the five flaws of vector retrieval-augmented generation (RAG) for agents, and motivates GraphRAG as the evolution of contextual retrieval.
- Chapter 2 introduces the dual-graph architecture, lays out the eight pillars and how they map to the rest of the book, and introduces the autonomous DevOps agent in its initial reactive state.

CHAPTER 1

# The Crisis of Enterprise Agentic AI

Imagine a world where AI doesn't just wait for your questions but pursues your goals.

It doesn't simply respond to *What's our inventory?* It notices declining inventory, predicts stockouts, evaluates suppliers, and places orders. It doesn't just give you suggestions for product copy. It creates a plan, writes the copy, sends it to different retail platforms, and then reports back on sales.

Sounds great, right? Unfortunately, it's a lot more complicated than that, especially in the enterprise.

You fire up your favorite LLM, add it to your agentic framework of choice (no code, low code, or full code), and connect it to a vector-based RAG system. Should be easy, right? Wrong.

A naive approach using simple vector-based retrieval creates five fatal flaws:

*Context amnesia*
: LLMs are amnesia incarnate. Every conversation starts from scratch. There's no memory of past interactions, no ability to build expertise, and no capacity to learn from mistakes. It's like hiring a brilliant employee who forgets everything the moment they leave the room. Your agent can't connect today's supply chain issue with last week's vendor problem.

*Relationship blindness*
: Information sits in silos. Your agent sees the *customer* and the *purchase* but not how they connect through preferences, history, and behavior.

*Temporal ignorance*
: Static embeddings can't capture change. Your agent treats outdated configurations as the current truth.

*Reasoning paralysis*
: Vector search finds similar text rather than logical connections. There's little hope of the agent understanding the cascading effects of a system change.

*Tool chaos*
: Without understanding tool relationships, your agent guesses which API to call instead of orchestrating intelligently.

Unfortunately, these aren't bugs. They represent an architectural failure that prevents your enterprise AI system from becoming truly agentic. In the real world, agents need more than data. They need understanding.

Google learned this during a decade of running one of the world's largest knowledge graphs, powering Search, Maps, and YouTube. Its key insight was the shift from "strings to things" (Singhal, 2012, *https://oreil.ly/uxJaw*).

When you search *Jaguar*, Google doesn't just match letters. It understands that you might mean any of a few things:

- The luxury car manufacturer
- The large cat
- The NFL team

This understanding of entities, known as the *semantic layer*, separates keyword matching from genuine comprehension and allows your agents to move from answering *What happened?* to deciding *What should I do?*

Knowledge graphs transform your AI from a query engine into a cognitive operating system. Graph-based agents use the following:

*Entities, not keywords*
: They understand that *John Smith (ID:42)* is the same person across the customer relationship management (CRM) system, email, and payroll.

*Relationships, not isolation*
: They trace how a server failure impacts dependent services before taking action.

*Evolution, not snapshots*
: They track how configurations change over time, preventing dangerous rollbacks.

*Reasoning, not just retrieval*
: They navigate cause-and-effect chains to predict outcomes.

*Orchestration, not guessing*
: They understand tool dependencies to execute complex workflows.

The impact of knowledge graphs on AI systems isn't just theoretical. In a six-month production deployment, LinkedIn's knowledge graph–augmented RAG system reduced median per-issue resolution time (Xu et al., 2024, *https://oreil.ly/wDSwf*) by 28.6% while significantly improving retrieval quality.

While it's easy to tout the benefits of knowledge graphs, building one is like building city infrastructure. Constructing a knowledge graph can be challenging, and operating it in the real world necessitates iteration and improvements. Here are some of the things you need:

- Real-time updates as your business evolves
- Schema flexibility without breaking existing connections
- Performance at scale (billions of relationships)
- Governance that doesn't strangle innovation

This chapter lays the foundation for your journey into building graph-based agentic systems. We'll start with defining some terminology and reviewing the architecture of AI agents. Then we'll look at vector-based agents and where they fall short. Finally, we'll take a first look at graph-based architecture and why graph-based agents solve many of the problems enterprises face when building and deploying agents and scale.

# Defining Agentic AI

What exactly do we mean by *agentic AI*? Let's first back up and consider conventional AI systems: when interacting with these, you're essentially engaging with sophisticated pattern-matching engines. The typical interaction follows a linear path: you provide input, the system responds based on statistical patterns, and the interaction terminates. Agentic systems, on the other hand, fundamentally transform this paradigm by implementing continuous observe-think-act cycles that persist across multiple interactions.

Non-agentic AI applications or systems require you to define the solution, specifying exactly how to solve your problem. Agentic AI allows you to simply state your problem and let the system determine the solution path. This shift from solution definition to problem statement represents the most significant advancement in human-computer interaction since the graphical user interface.

So, how do we build such a system? Before we dive into architectural patterns, let's define *agency* and how to classify agentic systems.

## What Is an Agent, Anyway?

If you ask a random sampling of product managers, marketers, researchers, and engineers to define an *AI agent*, you're likely to get a dozen different answers, but most agent definitions jump straight into implementation—like Simon Willison's 2025 "An LLM agent runs tools in a loop to achieve a goal" (*https://oreil.ly/QL5-7*). Let's take a step back and first define what we mean by *agency* in a system. *Agentic* systems operate along three critical dimensions:

*Autonomy*
: The degree to which your system makes independent decisions without external direction. A thermostat has high autonomy within its narrow domain—it decides when to activate heating without asking permission.

*Action*
: The ability to execute decisions by taking actions that affect the environment. Without this capability to effect change, you have an assistant or advisor, not an agent.

*Authority*
: The scope and limitations of permitted actions. Your system's authority defines its operational boundaries, or what it can and cannot do within your organization.

These dimensions exist on sliding scales, not as binary attributes. Consider how a real estate agent may have high autonomy to create and distribute marketing material for properties or respond to informational queries but little or no authority on pricing decisions. Your AI agents will similarly require carefully calibrated configurations across these dimensions.

So, what do the three dimensions of agentic systems actually translate to in practice? When an agent operates across these three dimensions, four critical capabilities emerge:

*Autonomous decision making*
: Agents navigate complexity and context without requiring step-by-step human guidance. This mirrors how human professionals operate within defined authority boundaries.

*Contextual understanding*
: Agents maintain awareness of relationships among concepts, temporal dependencies, and organizational structures. Unlike traditional AI, which treats each query in isolation, agentic systems understand how current decisions relate to past actions and future implications.

*Strategic tool utilization*
: Agents don't just access tools; they understand when and why to use them. Like an experienced professional selecting the right instrument for each task, your agentic system orchestrates specialized capabilities based on situational requirements.

*Memory persistence*
: Agentic systems possess both short-term memory during a session and long-term memory across sessions. They develop institutional knowledge through experience. Each interaction strengthens successful patterns and adapts unsuccessful ones, creating a self-improving system that becomes more valuable over time.

Taking all this together, we can define *agentic AI* as follows:

> Systems that autonomously pursue goals through continuous observe-think-act cycles, make independent decisions, and take actions within defined boundaries rather than simply responding to individual queries

The fundamental shift is that while non-agentic systems require you to define the solution (specify how to solve your problem), agentic systems let you define the outcome or goal, and the agent determines the solution path itself.

As you'll learn throughout this book, graph-based agents go further: they understand the problem space through structured relationships, reason about solutions using multi-hop traversal, and learn from outcomes by evolving their knowledge structures, creating systems that don't just act autonomously but understand why and improve continuously.

At an implementation level, this is not too far off from how Lilian Weng defined agents (*https://oreil.ly/IAZFL*) in 2023. In LLM-powered agent systems, "the LLM functions as the agent's brain," with key components of planning, memory, and tool use.

Agentic capabilities directly address the three critical bottlenecks that plague enterprise AI implementations:

*Context fragmentation*
: Enterprise knowledge exists as an interconnected web rather than as isolated documents. Agentic systems should navigate these connections naturally.

*Execution discontinuity*
: Multistep processes require maintaining state across operations. Agentic architectures must provide the persistence mechanisms that traditional AI lacks.

*Organizational disconnection*

Enterprises operate through complex hierarchies and relationships. Agentic systems must model and leverage these structures rather than fighting against them.

> Agency transforms AI from a reactive query tool into a proactive business partner that understands context, learns from experience, and autonomously pursues objectives.

## Classifying Agentic Systems: The Workflow-Agent Spectrum

As previously mentioned, the three dimensions of agency are not necessarily binary. As Andrew Ng observes (*https://oreil.ly/38ub9*), systems can be "agent-like to different degrees." Many researchers and engineers, like those at Anthropic (*https://oreil.ly/E7CNs*), consider a distinction between workflows and true agents to be helpful. Rather than conceptualizing agents as either fully autonomous or deterministically scripted, we find it's more productive to position your AI systems along a continuous spectrum between workflows and agents, as shown in Figure 1-1.

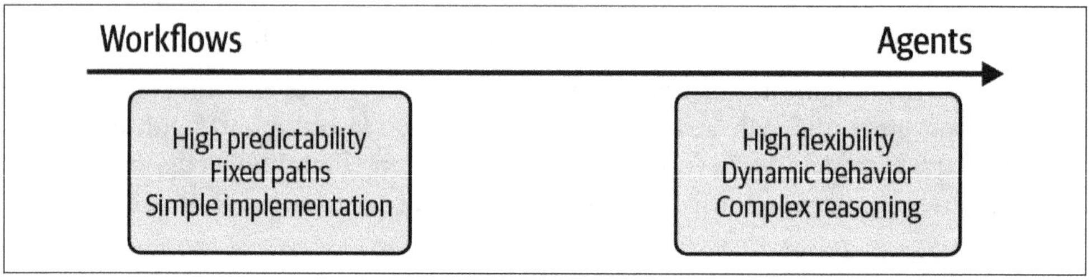


*Figure 1-1. Workflow-agent spectrum*

At the workflow end of this spectrum, you're implementing systems with predefined execution paths: orchestrated sequences that follow explicit instructions. These provide reliability and deterministic outcomes but offer limited adaptability to novel situations. Many of the standard AI applications that have emerged in recent years have followed this pattern—for example, an FAQ generator that receives support conversation text (e.g., chat logs) or a fund analysis application that receives performance data.

At the agent end, your systems determine processes dynamically, providing flexibility at the cost of predictability. The most common working examples of this end of the spectrum are coding agents and deep research agents. Simply give the agent a desired outcome and answer a few clarifying questions, and the agent will scamper off to complete the task at hand.

For enterprises, many of the most complex—and thus most expensive—business processes fall somewhere in between these ends of the spectrum. These processes blend deterministic workflows with nondeterministic LLMs inserted at key points of the process. Think of a complex market commentary report process at an investment firm, where multiple stakeholders must be involved to not only pull the data required and assemble the report but also to review the output for compliance and submit it to regulatory bodies. An LLM can fulfill some of those duties, such as retrieving information through tool calls (via APIs), analyzing data, and even submitting the report, but humans must remain in the loop and exercise judgment at specific points in the process.

This complex interplay among APIs, LLMs, and humans in agentic systems leads us to what we call the agent constraint triangle.

## The Agent Constraint Triangle

When developing AI agents, you'll encounter a fundamental challenge known as the agent constraint triangle. The *agent constraint triangle* represents three interconnected constraints that create an inherently difficult operational problem: complexity management, tool orchestration, and context utilization.

The *complexity management constraint* concerns your agent's ability to handle multi-step planning and reasoning across complex tasks. As tasks require more steps and deeper analysis, cognitive load increases exponentially. When not managed correctly, agents struggle to maintain coherence across lengthy reasoning chains, resulting in compounding errors as the step count increases.

The *tool orchestration constraint* involves translating between natural language instructions and precisely structured API calls. As Anthropic's Applied AI team notes in their 2025 article "Effective Context Engineering for AI Agents," (*https://oreil.ly/EFHbG*) one of the most common failure modes is bloated tool sets that cover too much functionality or lead to ambiguous decision points about which tool to use. The authors make the principle clear: "If a human engineer can't definitively say which tool should be used in a given situation, an AI agent can't be expected to do better." This translation challenge intensifies as the number and diversity of tools expand, creating additional potential failure points while consuming precious context space.

The *context utilization constraint* encompasses organizing and efficiently using limited information space. Your agents operate within fixed context windows that must contain all relevant information for the task. Think of the context window as the model's attention budget. As tasks grow more complex, these finite context resources become increasingly constrained. Research on needle-in-a-haystack benchmarking, such as that by Chroma's research team (Hong, Troynikov, and Huber, 2025, *https://oreil.ly/MdqMr*), has revealed the phenomenon of *context rot*: as the number of tokens in the context window increases, the model's ability to accurately recall information from that context decreases. This isn't a hard cliff but rather a performance gradient that emerges from architectural constraints.

These constraints don't exist in isolation, but form a system of competing trade-offs. When improving performance along one dimension, you typically create additional pressure on the others:

*Complexity → tools → context*
: As task complexity increases, more specialized tools become necessary to handle diverse operations. Each additional tool consumes context space for its definition, increases the cognitive load of tool selection, and adds more potential points of ambiguity in orchestration.

*Tools → context → complexity*
: Expanding your tool set to handle nuanced operations depletes available context for actual task reasoning. This forces either aggressive context management (risking information loss) or simplified task decomposition (limiting capability).

*Context → complexity → tools*
: Aggressive context optimization—through techniques like compaction or selective retrieval—can inadvertently discard subtle but critical context whose importance only becomes apparent later. This loss of nuance forces agents to either operate with incomplete information or require more tool calls to reconstruct missing context.

The challenge of context engineering is to find the smallest possible set of high-signal tokens that maximizes the likelihood of some desired outcome while navigating these fundamental tensions. This principle applies across all three constraints: minimal but sufficient complexity decomposition, minimal but complete tool coverage, and minimal but adequate context retention.

## Agent Architecture

Now that you understand what agency and agent capabilities are, as well as the typical constraints that agents face, let's walk through agent architecture, as we will use it throughout this book (as illustrated in Figure 1-2).

The *agent core* is the continuous observe-think-act cycle in which the LLM operates. It must observe and understand its environment, capabilities, and resources, then plan and act accordingly.

To initiate the cycle, a user must give the agent *capabilities*. These capabilities might be shared with the agent in the form of prompts, permissions to various systems, desired outcomes and goals, initial context provided, or prior knowledge.

To devise and execute on the plan, the agent will make use of an assortment of resources. *Resources* usually consist of other models (such as smaller models for simple tasks or domain-specific models for specialized tasks), tools made available directly or through protocols such as Model Context Protocol (MCP), and external knowledge such as RAG or memory systems.

Throughout the process, the agent will interact with its environment. The *environment* is where the agent performs its tasks and generates its output. It may include filesystems, terminal commands, a web browser, or even other hardware.

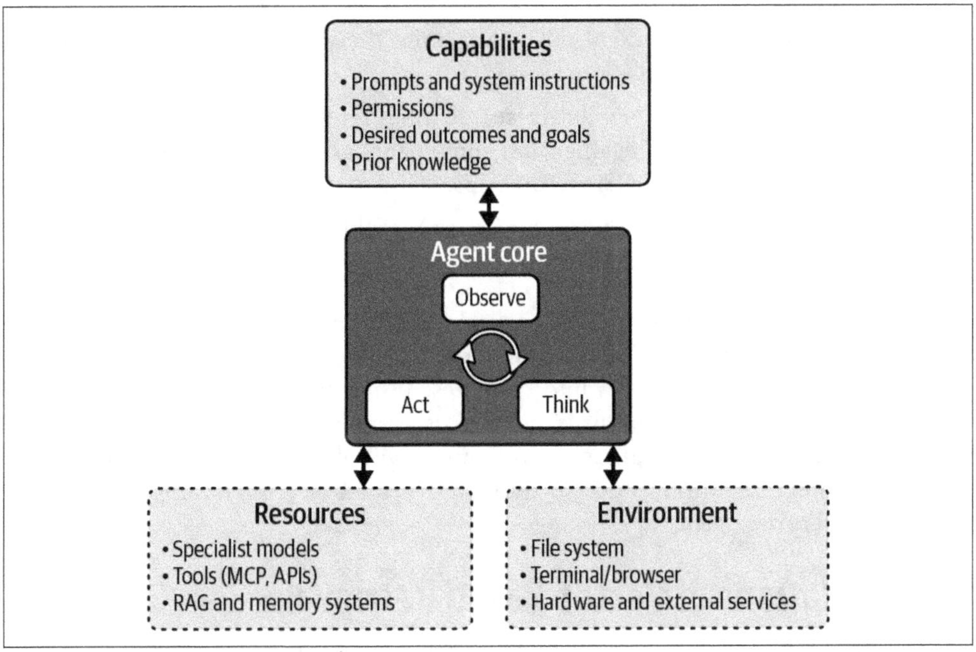


*Figure 1-2. AI agent architecture: a component-based framework for agent design*

Each part of the agentic system must work together smoothly in order for the agent to form a plan and achieve a successful outcome. Any part of this system can become a weak link as each forms a web of dependencies. For example, imagine you have an agent designed to purchase clothing based on next week's weather. The agent might do these things:

1. Check for prior knowledge of the user's location using memory or RAG, and if nothing is found, ask the user for a specific location.
2. Call a tool to access a weather API to retrieve information about next week's forecast.
3. Check available tools and knowledge related to retail clothing options and build a shopping cart.

4. Submit the shopping cart to the user for approval.
5. Upon receiving approval, use tool calls to submit the order and send the user an email.

There are many possible failure points along this path:

- Problems with the environment may prevent the user interaction and approval.
- Memory or retrieval problems could result in the model using no location or an incorrect location.
- Incorrect tool selection might mean searching the wrong retailer or submitting the order to the wrong location.
- Vector embeddings and similarity search might result in the wrong items of clothing being selected. Leggings and snow pants are technically both *pants*, but only one makes sense on a trip to the Alps.
- Permissions issues (a capabilities limitation) might derail the ordering or email process.

While each of these components of agent architecture can allow for failures, retrieval is a particular stumbling block in the enterprise, where terminology is dense and specialized, and data often scales into terabytes. When retrieval fails, the rest of the system fails. If, for example, an insurance claims agent retrieves the wrong policy, no amount of prompting, tool calling, or reasoning will allow the agent to accomplish its goal. The next section digs deeper into why vector-based retrieval is such a poor choice for enterprise agents.

## The Limitations of Vector-Based Retrieval

Despite recent advancements in LLM capabilities, traditional vector-based RAG approaches remain fundamentally constrained when applied to enterprise environments. Engineers cannot address these limitations simply by expanding context windows or refining embedding techniques, as they stem from architectural inadequacies that prevent your AI systems from fully comprehending the complexity of enterprise knowledge networks. In this section, we'll look at the strengths and limitations of vector-based retrieval and how they affect agent development.

### A Brief Overview of Vector Retrieval

While a nuanced look at vector-based retrieval techniques is beyond the scope of this chapter, let's review the basics. *Vector-based retrieval* finds relevant information by representing queries and documents as numerical vectors in a shared semantic space, usually stored in a vector database. Instead of relying on exact keyword matches (like traditional search), this approach uses machine learning models to encode the meaning of text into vector representations called embeddings. *Embeddings* capture semantic similarities (though not relationships), so documents about similar concepts will have vectors that are close together in the vector space, even if they use different words. For example, *cat* and *feline* would have similar vector embeddings.

When a user submits a query, it gets converted into the same vector format as the documents, and the system finds the most relevant documents by calculating similarity scores between the query vector and all document vectors in the database. This enables semantic search capabilities where a query about *cats* can successfully retrieve documents about *tigers* or *housecats*.

The retrieved text chunks are then converted back to text and combined with the original query to provide context to the language model. Typically, this is done by constructing a prompt that includes the question and the retrieved reference passages.

The LLM processes the query along with the injected relevant context and generates an answer. The generation is thus *augmented* (the *A* in RAG) by real-time retrieved information, grounding the LLM's output in the provided documents.

## Where Vector RAG Succeeds and Fails

This process of converting back and forth between embeddings and using similarity search does have its advantages. Vector RAG excels at indexing and searching through large volumes of unstructured text by semantic content. It does not require a predefined schema, so any text can be embedded. This makes it very flexible in domains where knowledge isn't neatly structured.

Vector search is also highly scalable for the right types of queries. Approximate nearest-neighbor (ANN) algorithms allow fast retrieval even from millions of documents. This makes vector search suitable for high-throughput applications. For instance, vector databases can quickly fetch relevant information from very large datasets based on similarity.

Lastly, because it uses dense embeddings, vector RAG can retrieve information that is semantically related to the query even if the exact terms aren't present. This can surface relevant content via either synonyms or conceptual similarity.

> Vector-based RAG is a great fit for things like customer support assistants and FAQs, where queries usually map to some existing text snippet and vector search can efficiently sift through thousands of documents for the answer. It also works well in recommendation systems. Imagine an ecommerce platform that uses vector RAG to recommend products using a user's browsing history and similar product descriptions. This unstructured similarity matching is a great fit for vector RAG.

While vector-based RAG works very well for simple lookups, it struggles with complex reasoning, particularly when data is dense or specialized (as is often the case in the enterprise). Microsoft's BenchmarkQED research (Edge, Trinh, Esquivel, and Larson, 2025, *https://oreil.ly/uNSH3*) quantifies this with vector RAG handling simple lookups with more than 90% accuracy but complex reasoning with just 20%–30% accuracy. BenchmarkQED is a new suite of tools that automates RAG benchmarking at scale and builds upon Microsoft's original GraphRAG paper, "From Local to Global: A GraphRAG Approach to Query-Focused Summarization," (Edge et al., 2025, *https://oreil.ly/6Y7u-*). In the paper, the authors identify a spectrum of queries that delineate exactly when and why vector systems fail in production (Figure 1-3).

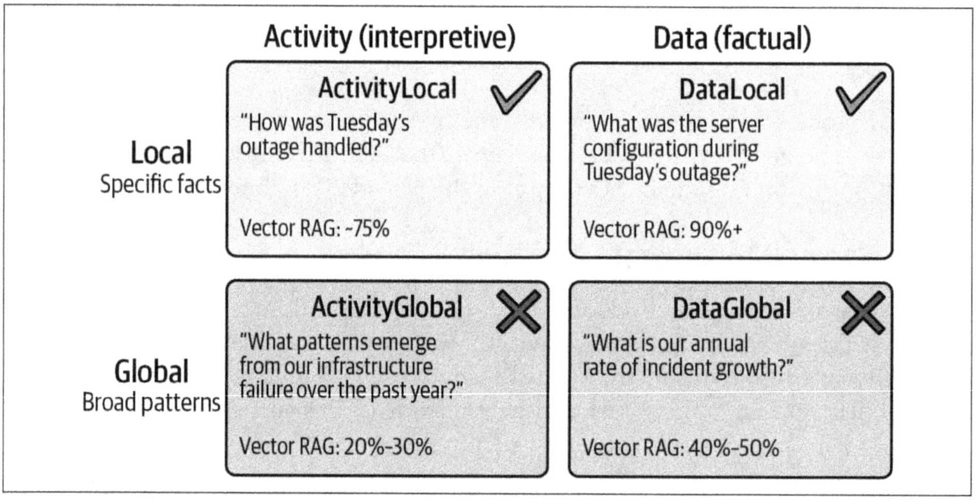


*Figure 1-3. Local and global query scopes and sources in BenchmarkQED*

*Local* queries—such as *What was the server configuration during Tuesday's outage?*—ask about specific facts in a small number of text regions and sometimes even a single region. *Global* queries—for example, *What patterns emerge from our infrastructure failures over the past year?*—require reasoning over large portions of the dataset or even the entire dataset. The paper also refers to these as *sensemaking* queries.

In BenchmarkQED, each query scope (local and global) also has two broad query types (activity and data):

*ActivityLocal queries*
: Are around local processes and are interpretive

*DataLocal queries*
: Call for direct retrieval of specific facts

*ActivityGlobal queries*
  Ask for holistic analysis and strategic insights

*DataGlobal queries*
  Request identification of data patterns and synthesis

Vector RAG excels at the local query scope, achieving greater than 90% performance on DataLocal queries, because the answer exists in a specific source that semantic similarity naturally finds. However, vector RAG catastrophically fails at the global query scope, achieving only 20%–30% performance on ActivityGlobal queries. The very mechanism that makes vector search efficient—comparing query embeddings to chunk embeddings—becomes its fundamental limitation.

This finding reveals why vector-based retrieval delivers such inconsistent results. When your DevOps team asks about a specific error message, vector RAG delivers. When they ask about systematic issues across your infrastructure, it returns random chunks that happen to contain similar words but miss the bigger picture entirely.

As you dig deeper into this trade-off, some major limitations with vector-based architecture emerge. The first issue is *semantic gaps*. A fundamental disconnect exists between query vectors and relevant content vectors. When you ask *What is the capital of France?* it may not closely match text stating *Paris is the most populous city in France*, even though the passage contains the correct answer.

Additionally, you may face *granularity trade-offs*. When constructing vector embeddings, you must choose between document-level representations that lack precision and sentence-level chunks that fragment context and increase computational overhead. This trade-off becomes critical in ActivityLocal queries, where understanding procedures requires maintaining coherent context across multiple steps.

We also see *reasoning limitations* in vector-based retrieval. Vector similarity scores struggle to support complex reasoning tasks that require synthesizing information across multiple documents or following intricate logical chains.

*Contextual amnesia* also plagues vector-based systems. They find it difficult to maintain a coherent understanding across multiple interactions and decision points, and they lack temporal awareness, treating all chunks as eternally present facts. When your infrastructure evolves—services get updated, configurations change, dependencies shift—vector embeddings remain frozen, making every chunk that mentions old configurations actively misleading.

Finally, there is the *associativity gap*. Vector-based retrieval systems lack the ability to form transitive relationships across multiple documents, failing to construct logical chains when information is distributed across separate entries. Consider this query: *Which services were affected by the database migration that followed the security patch we discussed in last month's architecture review?* This requires traversing relationships that simply don't exist in isolated embeddings.

As queries require more synthesis, more relationship understanding, or more temporal awareness, vector RAG's performance collapses.

### Won't a larger context window solve this?

It's natural to assume that larger context windows solve these problems. Surely if we simply pull more sources and give the model more information to choose from, results will improve, right?

BenchmarkQED tested this hypothesis directly, comparing LazyGraphRAG against vector RAG with a one-million token context window—essentially the entire dataset. Even with nearly all information in context, vector RAG still lost on every query type except the most basic factual questions.

Research by EyeLevel.ai (Warfield, 2024, *https://oreil.ly/V_roj*) further quantifies these challenges in practical deployments. The study demonstrates that as dataset sizes increase, the accuracy of vector-based RAG systems degrades significantly—losing up to 12% accuracy at 100,000 pages—while graph-based approaches maintain high accuracy levels, dropping only about 2% at the same scale.

Dumping more information into a context window doesn't create understanding of relationships, temporal evolution, or systematic patterns. Rather, larger context windows make retrieval slower and worsen the lost in the middle problem. Vector-based retrieval will still fail on critical questions about system-wide patterns. A model with a million tokens of unstructured context is like a human trying to manage a datacenter by reading every log file simultaneously. Without the ability to build mental models, track state changes, and understand relationships, more context just creates more confusion.

### Consequences for vector-based agents

The shift from simple Q&A to agentic AI fundamentally changes what we demand from retrieval systems. Agents don't just answer questions; they take actions, maintain state, reason about consequences, and operate autonomously over extended periods. When your DevOps agent needs to diagnose a production issue, it's not performing a single retrieval. It's building a mental model of your system, understanding dependencies, tracking what's changed, and reasoning about potential impacts. Agentic behavior also requires constantly moving between local and global understanding. For example, a DevOps agent must check specific configurations while maintaining awareness of system-wide implications.

Vector-based retrieval, designed for single-shot similarity matching, becomes a critical bottleneck that prevents true agentic behavior. As we've seen, vector embeddings create contextual amnesia, where each query exists in isolation, unable to build upon previous understanding. They also inevitably flatten complex relationships, losing the crucial connections between entities that drive human-like reasoning.

Context amnesia and a lack of relational understanding translate to the loss of intentionality that distinguishes true agents from simple retrieval systems. Agents need to understand not just what information exists, but why it matters, how it connects to their goals, and what actions it enables. They need to maintain persistent models of the world that evolve with new information, reason about hypotheticals and counterfactuals, and understand the temporal dynamics of the systems they operate within.

Each limitation of vector retrieval compounds into agent failure:

*Action blindness*
: Without understanding relationships between entities, agents can't predict the consequences of their actions. For example, they might restart a service without knowing it will cascade failures through dependent systems.

*Memory fragmentation*
: Agents need coherent, evolving memory across interactions, but vector retrieval gives them amnesia. Each query starts fresh, unable to build upon previous understanding or learn from past actions.

*Planning paralysis*
: Complex tasks require multistep reasoning with clear dependencies. When agents can't traverse relationships or understand temporal sequences, they can't decompose goals into executable plans.

*Context drift*
: As agents operate over time, the world changes around them. Vector embeddings remain static, causing agents to operate on outdated models of reality and make increasingly dangerous decisions as drift accumulates.

Each failure mode reinforces others, creating a cascade of agent incompetence:

- Miss the relationship between services, and your agent suggests fixes that break dependencies.
- Lack temporal awareness, and it recommends reverting to configurations that no longer exist.
- Fail at global pattern recognition, and it never identifies the systematic issues that cause repeated outages.
- Lack the ability to form transitive relationships, and it fails to predict second-order effects of its actions.

Vector retrieval forces your agents to be either myopic (focused on local details) or blind (unable to see the bigger picture). This means your agents become less reliable precisely when you need them most: when dealing with complex, large-scale systems where human oversight becomes impossible. The very scenarios that demand autonomous agents are where vector-based approaches fail most catastrophically.

The compounding failures of vector retrieval cannot be addressed by optimizing search or tweaking embedding models. Though excellent for local, fact-based queries, vector-based retrieval fundamentally cannot support the cognitive architecture required for agentic behavior. You need an architecture built for understanding, not just similarity. You need one that preserves the semantic richness, complex relationships, and temporal dynamics that enable agents to think, plan, and act autonomously in your enterprise environment. Enter GraphRAG.

## GraphRAG: The Evolution of Contextual Retrieval Systems

GraphRAG reimagines how your AI systems interact with knowledge. Unlike vector-based RAG approaches that treat information as isolated passages, GraphRAG represents knowledge as a richly interconnected web of concepts, entities, and relationships. This paradigm transformation elevates your retrieval systems from passive data fetchers into active, context-aware reasoning agents. In the last section of this chapter, we'll look at the advantages of GraphRAG and its implications for agents.

> *GraphRAG* as we use it does not necessarily mean pure graph database implementation. We are using this term as a shorthand for graph-based retrieval that encompasses a number of different techniques.

### A Brief Overview of GraphRAG Architecture

*GraphRAG systems* use a knowledge graph to store facts as nodes and edges, and they retrieve information by traversing this graph structure. Instead of relying on semantic similarity in a vector space, a graph-based approach explicitly leverages relationships between entities to fetch relevant knowledge. The architecture consists of a knowledge graph (often, though not always, managed in a graph database) and mechanisms to query and extract a subgraph relevant to the query.

As you'll see, this book devotes Chapter 2 to digging into agentic GraphRAG architecture and Chapter 3 to exploring graph construction, but here we'll briefly define GraphRAG and give an example architecture.

The first step in the general methodology is *knowledge graph construction*. Domain knowledge is structured into a graph format, with nodes representing entities or concepts and edges representing relationships between those entities. Each node can also have properties or textual descriptions. Building the graph may involve parsing structured data or extracting entities and relations from text. For example, in a medical knowledge graph, nodes could be diseases, symptoms, and treatments, with edges like *treats* or *causes* connecting them.

Next is *graph data storage*. The graph is typically (though not always) stored in a graph database, such as Neo4j or Amazon Neptune, that is optimized for storing nodes and edges and executing graph queries. Such databases support query languages like Cypher (Neo4j) or SPARQL for retrieving subgraphs and querying relationships. Note that it is becoming increasingly common to store graph structures in familiar databases like PostgreSQL. The enterprise AI company WRITER, for example, switched from using a graph database to storing graph structures in PostgreSQL (see "Fireside Chat with Harrison Chase & Waseem AlShikh", *https://oreil.ly/b1YLO*). This trend is driven by the desire to consolidate data infrastructure: by using PostgreSQL with extensions like Apache AGE for graph capabilities, alongside pgvector for embeddings, teams can avoid the operational overhead of managing multiple specialized databases. This approach keeps source documents, their embeddings, and their graph relationships in a single system with native transaction support, eliminating the synchronization challenges that arise when spanning multiple databases. For many applications, the performance trade-offs are acceptable given the significant reduction in architectural complexity and the ability to maintain data consistency through standard database mechanisms rather than custom ETL pipelines.

After the graph is constructed and stored, the next step is during user interaction, with query interpretation and graph traversal (Figure 1-4). The user's question is mapped to a graph query. This could be done by identifying relevant entities in the query or by using predefined query templates. The system then performs a graph traversal or search: it finds the node(s) matching the query subject and explores connected nodes and edges to gather relevant facts. For example, a Cypher query can find a path of relationships between an entity and others (for example, retrieving all nodes connected within *N* hops) that pertain to the question. The result of this retrieval is a *subgraph* (a set of related entities and their relations represented as triples) relevant to the query.

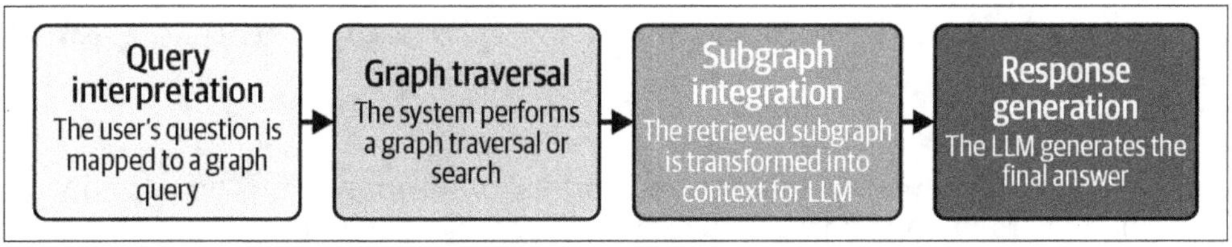


*Figure 1-4. Standard graph traversal*

After the subgraph is retrieved, it is then transformed into a form the LLM can understand in a process known as *context integration*. This often means converting the graph data into textual statements or a structured context. For instance, if the query is *What is the capital of France?*, the system might query the graph for the `(:Country {name:"France"})-[:HAS_CAPITAL]->(c)` relation and obtain the node `c = Paris`. It would then provide the fact that *France's capital is Paris* as context to the LLM.

Finally, as with vector-based retrieval, there comes *response generation*. With the query-focused subgraph results available as text, the LLM generates the final answer. The answer is informed by the explicit facts and relationships retrieved from the knowledge graph, combined with the LLM's own reasoning. The LLM might chain together the facts to produce a coherent explanation or answer.

Since we've been referencing Microsoft's GraphRAG and BenchmarkQED, let's look at researchers' methodology for GraphRAG as an example. This involves a two-stage LLM-based pipeline for indexing and querying.

The first stage is *indexing*, using an LLM to build the graph index in two main parts:

1. *Derive an entity knowledge graph.*
   The LLM extracts instances of important entities and relationships from the source documents to construct a knowledge graph, where nodes represent key entities and edges represent relationships.

2. *Pregenerate community summaries.*
   The system partitions the resulting knowledge graph into a hierarchy of closely related entities called *communities* (essentially, strongly connected nodes within the knowledge graph). Then, in a bottom-up, recursive manner, the LLM generates community summaries for these groups, which collectively provide global descriptions and insights over the corpus.

The second stage is the *query*, where GraphRAG answers user queries using a map-reduce process applied to the pregenerated community summaries:

1. *Map*
   Given a question, each community summary is used to generate a partial response.

2. *Reduce*
   All partial responses are summarized in a final round of query-focused summarization to produce the final global answer returned to the user.

GraphRAG explicitly preserves structured relationships in its knowledge source. This structured approach can reduce open-ended ambiguity and helps the model ground its answers in known relationships, thereby reducing hallucinations and increasing factual accuracy.

## Where GraphRAG Succeeds and Struggles

The preservation of relationships in GraphRAG leads to numerous advantages. In this section, we'll take a look at a handful of the benefits that are especially useful in building enterprise agents, as well as some of the challenges.

### Context control

The key architectural advantage that graphs provide is *context control*—the ability to precisely manage what information reaches your model at each decision point.

When vector embeddings alone are used, relationships between concepts get flattened into statistical similarities. When working with graphs, you explicitly model these connections, ensuring that your language models receive not just relevant information but also the crucial relationships between information elements.

Consider how this impacts an enterprise scenario: when a user inquires about the financial implications of a product launch, your graph-based system navigates relationships between specifications, manufacturing costs, pricing strategies, and revenue projections—delivering coherent, multistep reasoning that isolated vector lookups simply cannot achieve.

### Flexibility

Earlier, we walked through the workflow-agent spectrum. When you're building production-grade systems, you need an architecture that effectively handles both predictable processes and flexible reasoning. Graph-based architectures enable you to model this spectrum using nodes and edges, allowing you to calibrate the precise balance required for specific applications:

- For workflow-like scenarios, you can design explicit, deterministic paths with fixed transitions, providing the reliability that mission-critical applications demand.
- For agent-like behavior, you can implement conditional edges that adapt based on context, enabling dynamic reasoning without sacrificing structural clarity.

By structuring your knowledge domain as a formal graph, you establish a foundation where relationship patterns remain explicit while traversal paths maintain flexibility. This enables precise control over which system components exhibit workflow-like predictability and which leverage agent-like adaptability.

### Better reasoning

Graphs enable better reasoning. In BenchmarkQED, LazyGraphRAG outperforms vector RAG by 50%–60% on queries requiring multi-hop reasoning, not through marginal improvements but through fundamental architectural advantages. By representing tasks as directed acyclic graphs (DAGs), your systems decompose complex problems into manageable components with explicit dependencies. Independent subtasks can execute in parallel, dramatically improving efficiency. For particularly complex problems, you can implement recursive decomposition, creating nested subgraphs that encapsulate complexity where needed while maintaining simpler structures elsewhere.

> When enhanced with declarative grammars, your systems can simultaneously maintain deterministic guarantees for critical operations—such as structured API interactions—while preserving dynamic reasoning capabilities for contextual interpretation. The grammar formally defines execution semantics, while the graph structure provides the navigational framework.

### Explainability and traceability

GraphRAG offers greater transparency, an especially important advantage in the enterprise. The retrieved subgraph or path can effectively serve as an explanation chain for the answer. Users or developers can trace which nodes and relations led the model to an answer. For instance, if asked *How are Person A and Company B connected?*, the system might return a path like A → (works at) → C (subsidiary of) → B. This trace is human readable and lends credibility, as one can inspect the sources of each fact. In sensitive domains (e.g., medical, financial, legal), this auditability is a major advantage.

### Self-evolution data flywheel

What truly differentiates this approach is the *self-evolution data flywheel* it enables. As your graph-based system operates, it continuously enriches its own knowledge structures through experience. Each interaction generates valuable data that feeds back into the system, improving entity relationships, refining reasoning pathways, and enhancing tool selection. This creates a virtuous cycle where usage leads to improvement, which drives further adoption, creating an ever-strengthening competitive advantage that static systems cannot match.

> Taken together, these benefits make GraphRAG an exceptionally good fit in enterprises, particularly those with specialized domain knowledge like health care and finance. Large organizations often have siloed data. A knowledge graph can unify these by representing key entities and their interrelations.

### Where GraphRAG struggles

Even though GraphRAG has significant advantages, especially in the enterprise, it's important to be aware of some challenges you may encounter.

First, building and maintaining a knowledge graph requires *significant up-front effort*. The data must either exist in structured form or be extracted and curated into a graph. This often makes GraphRAG most feasible in specific domains (where schema and relationships are known). If your knowledge is broad or constantly changing, creating a comprehensive graph can be impractical. GraphRAG shines with domain-specific, structured knowledge, but it is less straightforward for open-domain or highly unstructured data sources. In scenarios where data doesn't naturally fit a relational structure, forcing it into a graph may be complex and limiting.

Second, graph queries, especially those involving many hops or searching large subgraphs, can be computationally expensive. Traversing a large knowledge graph may introduce latency that grows with graph size and complexity. While graph databases are optimized, they generally don't match the raw speed of a vector similarity lookup for simple retrieval. As a result, high-query-rate applications or extremely large-scale graphs might face performance bottlenecks. Careful indexing (such as by adding indexes on node properties) and limiting traversal depth are needed to keep response times reasonable. In short, pure graph traversal can be slower and more resource intensive than vector search for very large or complex queries.

Additionally, by condensing information into discrete triples or nodes, some contextual nuance can be lost. A graph might tell you that fact A relates to B, but not the full narrative or qualifier around that fact that was present in the source text. For example, a graph edge might state *Drug X treats Condition Y*, but the context that this is true only in certain patient populations might be omitted unless modeled. The LLM might therefore get facts without caveats or surrounding explanation, potentially leading to answers that lack detail. In contrast, vector RAG would retrieve the original text, which includes the nuance (though it might also include irrelevant information). Designing the graph schema to include important qualifiers or context is a nontrivial challenge.

Finally, although graphs excel at maintaining consistent relationships, updating a knowledge graph can be complex if the schema needs to evolve. Each update might need reconciliation with existing ontology. If a new relationship type emerges or a concept changes, developers must adjust the graph structure. In rapidly evolving knowledge domains, this can slow down the ability to incorporate the latest information. By comparison, vector stores can ingest new documents on the fly by embedding them, without needing up-front schema alignment. Thus, GraphRAG systems might lag behind if the knowledge graph is not continuously and carefully maintained.

> These trade-offs can be mitigated, and the effort is worthwhile in specialized domains at scale, as we often see in the enterprise. We'll address all of these issues throughout this book, giving guidance and techniques along the way so you can effectively build, deploy, and optimize your graph-based agents.

## Hybrid GraphRAG

In practice, many of the challenges of GraphRAG can be solved through a hybrid architecture rather than relying only on a graph. Throughout the book, you'll see that we recommend a hybrid approach that maintains parallel vector and graph representations of knowledge. This dual representation enables your system to leverage both statistical similarity and structured relational reasoning simultaneously. The processing pipeline consists of three sequential stages that progressively enrich the context representation:

1. Your journey begins with vector search, employing traditional semantic similarity techniques to identify candidate nodes based on embedding proximity. This statistical foundation establishes initial relevance as the first step in the retrieval process.
2. From these candidate nodes, the system initiates graph traversal. Each relationship type receives specific traversal parameters, including weight coefficients that prioritize certain relationship types in particular contexts.
3. The final stage, context synthesis, integrates information gathered through both vector similarity and graph traversal. This harmonization of statistical and structural insights produces a coherent response that reflects the multidimensional nature of the query context.

This architecture provides you with several advantages over traditional vector-based approaches. You gain the ability to handle multi-hop reasoning, connecting information across documents through relationship paths. The graph structure naturally preserves context across interactions, addressing the contextual amnesia problem. Most importantly, you can represent and navigate the complex, interconnected nature of enterprise knowledge, understanding not just what information exists but how it connects across organizational boundaries.

Note how in Example 1-1 the `graph_traverse` method enables exploration of relationship networks that vector search alone cannot access.

*Example 1-1. Simplified implementation of the three-stage GraphRAG architecture*

```
class GraphAgent:
    def __init__(self, vector_index, graph_db):
        self.vector_index = vector_index  # For initial semantic search
        self.graph_db = graph_db  # For relationship traversal
        self.relationship_config = {
            "depends_on": {"weight": 0.8, "max_depth": 2},
            "precedes": {"weight": 0.6, "max_depth": 3},
            "influences": {"weight": 0.7, "max_depth": 2},
            "contains": {"weight": 0.9, "max_depth": 1},
        }

    def process_query(self, query):
        # Stage 1: Vector Search
        initial_candidates = self.vector_search(query)

        # Stage 2: Graph Traversal
        expanded_context = self.graph_traverse(
            starting_nodes=initial_candidates,
            relationship_types=self.relationship_config.keys(),
            max_depth=3,
        )

        # Stage 3: Context Synthesis
        return self.synthesize_response(expanded_context)
```

When implementing the graph portion of the architecture, you'll still need to carefully consider the knowledge representation, index construction, and retrieval mechanisms to ensure optimal performance for your specific use cases. Don't worry: we will cover all of that in subsequent chapters.

## Learned Graph Reasoning Models

While the approaches described above rely on search algorithms or LLM-based community summarization, another emerging direction involves training dedicated neural models to reason over graph structures. These *graph foundation models* (GFMs) learn to traverse knowledge graphs and identify relevant information through training on large-scale graph datasets rather than using heuristic search or multiple LLM calls.

G-reasoner (*https://oreil.ly/QMDOt*) exemplifies this approach. The system trains a 34-million parameter graph neural network (GNN) on hundreds of knowledge graphs containing millions of nodes and edges. Rather than querying the graph through search algorithms, the trained GFM directly predicts which nodes and documents are most relevant to a query by propagating information through the graph structure. The model learns patterns of multi-hop reasoning during training, enabling it to efficiently identify relevant subgraphs in a single forward pass. This learned approach offers distinct advantages: it can perform multi-hop reasoning in one step rather than multiple retrieval rounds, generalizes across different graph structures without task-specific tuning, and runs significantly faster than methods requiring multiple LLM invocations. The trade-off is the up-front cost of training the GFM and the requirement for training data that covers the types of reasoning patterns you expect to encounter.

A parallel approach involves *reinforcement learning (RL)–optimized agentic methods* like KG-R1 (*https://oreil.ly/KceGL*), which train general-purpose LLM agents through reinforcement learning to iteratively reason and retrieve from knowledge graphs. Unlike specialized GNNs that embed graph traversal in neural weights, agentic methods learn policies for interacting with any graph through schema-agnostic action interfaces. KG-R1 trains a 3B parameter LLM agent that alternates between reasoning and retrieval over multiple turns, optimized end to end with RL. This enables plug-and-play transferability; the trained agent works across diverse knowledge graphs without modification or retraining. The trade-off is multiturn interaction latency versus single-pass inference, balanced against superior cross–knowledge graph generalization.

> The choice among search-based methods (like traditional graph traversal), summarization-based approaches (like Microsoft's GraphRAG), learned models (like G-reasoner), and RL-optimized agents (like KG-R1) depends on the specific constraints around latency, training resources, cross-domain transferability, and the complexity of reasoning required for your application.

## Summary

By implementing agentic systems with graph-based architectures, you create AI that doesn't merely retrieve information but comprehends interconnections. Your systems build on each interaction, continuously improving through the self-evolution data flywheel. There, operational usage generates insights that enhance knowledge structures, creating a sustainable competitive advantage that static systems cannot match.

The next chapter explores the core components that make this architecture possible. We'll first examine the foundational concepts of knowledge representation in graphs, then explore specialized memory structures, planning mechanisms, tool orchestration patterns, and reasoning engines. Finally, we'll cover optimization techniques that make these systems practical for production deployment.

CHAPTER 2

# Agentic Graph Architecture Foundations

Your AI system sees the world as floating text fragments. It can tell you that two paragraphs are semantically similar. But ask it whether Service A depends on Service B, whether that dependency was introduced last Tuesday, or whether removing it will cascade through four downstream services, and it draws a blank.

That is the gap that Chapter 1 diagnosed as a representation problem rather than a model bottleneck. Vector RAG treats everything as points in embedding space. It knows that things are *near* each other but not *how they're connected.* The five flaws (context amnesia, relationship blindness, temporal ignorance, reasoning paralysis, and tool chaos) are all symptoms of this underlying representation problem. You cannot reason about relationships that don't exist in your data. You cannot plan across dependencies that are invisible to your retrieval system. You cannot learn from experience when every query starts from scratch.

This chapter introduces the architecture that closes the gap. We will start with the conceptual shift that makes it possible: moving from strings to things, from flat text embeddings to structured entities with explicit relationships. From there, we will introduce the dual-graph architecture, the central framework of this book, which pairs a vertical knowledge graph with a horizontal workflow graph. We will preview the eight pillars of implementation that turn this architecture into a working system, mapping each pillar to its chapter so you have a clear roadmap for everything ahead. Finally, we will introduce the autonomous DevOps agent, the running example that threads through every chapter, and trace how the architecture transforms it from a collection of disconnected monitoring tools into a proactive, self-healing system.

By the end of this chapter, you will have the architectural mental model that every subsequent chapter builds on. When Chapter 5 talks about the horizontal workflow graph, you will know what it is and why it exists. When Chapter 7 talks about sending targeted feedback through the graph, you will understand the structure that makes targeted feedback possible.

## From Strings to Things

When Google launched its knowledge graph in 2012, Amit Singhal described the shift as moving to "things, not strings" (*https://oreil.ly/0bo7p*): understanding entities and their relationships rather than matching keywords. That phrase captures the most important conceptual shift in this book. It is the difference between treating information as text to be matched and treating information as entities to be reasoned about.

In a vector store, everything is a string (or more precisely, a numerical projection of a string). A sentence about your payment service, a paragraph from a runbook, a JSON snippet from a config file, a line from a Terraform definition...they all become floating-point vectors in the same high-dimensional space. Their identities are gone. Their relationships to other pieces of information are gone. All that remains is their position in embedding space, measured by cosine similarity to whatever query comes next.

Consider what happens when you index your infrastructure documentation into a vector store. A paragraph about the payment service becomes a 1536-dimensional vector. A paragraph about the database it depends on becomes another vector. A configuration file specifying the connection pool settings becomes a third. These vectors float in embedding space, close together if the language is similar, far apart if it isn't.

Now ask: *What services depend on the payments database, and which of them were deployed in the last 24 hours?* The vector store cannot answer this question. It can find paragraphs that mention the payments database. It can rank them by semantic similarity to your query. But it cannot traverse a dependency chain because no dependency chain exists in its data model. The relationships among services, databases, and deployments are at best implicit and at worst invisible. You are searching through *strings*—fragments of text stripped of their structural context.

The same question against a knowledge graph is a direct traversal, as in Example 2-1.

*Example 2-1. Vector retrieval versus graph query*

```
# Vector retrieval: find similar text
results = vector_store.similarity_search(
    "services that depend on payments database",
    k=5
)
# Returns: 5 text chunks ranked by cosine similarity.
# No guarantee they mention actual dependencies.
```

```
# No way to filter by deployment date.

# Graph query: traverse explicit relationships
results = graph.query("""
    MATCH (db:Database {name: 'payments-db'})<-[:DEPENDS_ON]-(s:Service)
    WHERE s.last_deployed > datetime() - duration('P1D')
    RETURN s.name, s.status, s.last_deployed
""")
# Returns: every service that depends on payments-db
# and was deployed in the last 24 hours,
# with current status and deployment timestamps.
```

The graph query is answering a different kind of question entirely. The vector search asks, *What text is similar to my query?* The graph query asks, *What is true about the relationships in my system?*

This distinction matters for agentic systems. An agent that only retrieves similar text is limited to pattern matching: find relevant chunks, pass them to the model, and hope the model infers the right answer. An agent that can traverse a graph of explicit relationships can *reason* about dependencies, *trace* causation, *query* temporal sequences, and *verify* that a planned action is structurally valid before executing it.

The "strings to things" shift does not mean abandoning vector search. Vectors are excellent at doing fuzzy matching, discerning semantic similarity, and handling unstructured text. The point is that vectors alone cannot represent the structured knowledge that agents need to act reliably. You need *entities* with identity. You need *relationships* with types and properties. You need a data model where the connection between Service A and Database B is an explicit, queryable fact, not a statistical inference from embedding proximity. That is what a knowledge graph gives you and what the rest of this book is built on.

The shift can apply in many fields. In healthcare, "strings to things" means moving from text about drug interactions to a graph where `Drug A` has an `INTERACTS_WITH` edge to `Drug B`, with properties specifying the interaction severity and the evidence level. In financial compliance, it means moving from regulatory text passages to a graph where `Transaction` nodes connect to `Account` nodes via `ORIGINATED_FROM` edges, with temporal metadata that supports audit queries. In any domain where the relationships between entities matter as much as the entities themselves (and for agents, they almost always do), the shift from strings to things is the shift from retrieval to reasoning.

This shift also changes what failure looks like. When a vector-based system fails, the failure mode is invisible. It retrieves the wrong paragraphs, or it retrieves the right paragraphs but the model infers the wrong relationships, and you cannot tell where things went wrong because there is no reasoning structure to inspect. When a graph-based system fails, the failure is traceable. You can see which traversal path the agent took, which relationship it followed, and where the chain of evidence broke down. That traceability is the prerequisite for self-improvement, which we will build in Chapter 7.

## The Dual-Graph Architecture

With the "strings to things" shift in mind, we can introduce the central architectural concept of this book: the *dual-graph architecture*.

Most attempts to build agentic systems stop at one graph or, more commonly, at no graph at all. The typical agent framework gives you a model, a prompt template, and a set of tools, then asks you to express the entire workflow in natural language. Some teams add a knowledge graph for better retrieval, which is a clear improvement over vector-only approaches. Microsoft's GraphRAG implementation (*https://oreil.ly/TuBAk*) demonstrated that graph-based retrieval enables whole-dataset reasoning that vector search cannot match—a significant advance. But a knowledge graph alone does not tell the agent how to use that knowledge. The model still has to figure out the sequence of operations, manage dependencies between steps, and recover from failures—all within a single context window.

Other teams reach for multi-agent frameworks, hoping that distributing work across specialized agents will solve the complexity problem. But without an explicit workflow structure, multi-agent systems introduce coordination overhead without guaranteeing coherence. Each agent acts on its own understanding, and there is no shared process model to keep them aligned.

The insight behind the dual-graph architecture is that an agentic system needs two complementary kinds of structure: a representation of *what it knows* (the entities, relationships, and constraints in its domain) and a representation of *how it acts* (the steps, decisions, and dependencies in its reasoning process). These are different concerns, and they work best as separate graph structures:

*Vertical knowledge graph*
: This is the agent's understanding of its world. It is a semantic network of entities and relationships that encodes domain knowledge with the precision that vector stores cannot provide.

*Horizontal workflow graph*
: This is the agent's plan of action. It is a DAG of reasoning and execution nodes that structures decision making into inspectable, enforceable steps.

The vertical graph is the map. The horizontal graph is the route. Together, they address all five architectural flaws identified in Chapter 1. Figure 2-1 illustrates this.

The vertical knowledge graph (left) encodes what the agent knows: entities, relationships, and temporal metadata. The horizontal workflow graph (right) encodes how the agent acts: reasoning nodes, execution nodes, and the dependencies between them. The two graphs interact at every step: workflow nodes query the knowledge graph for context, and their results update it.

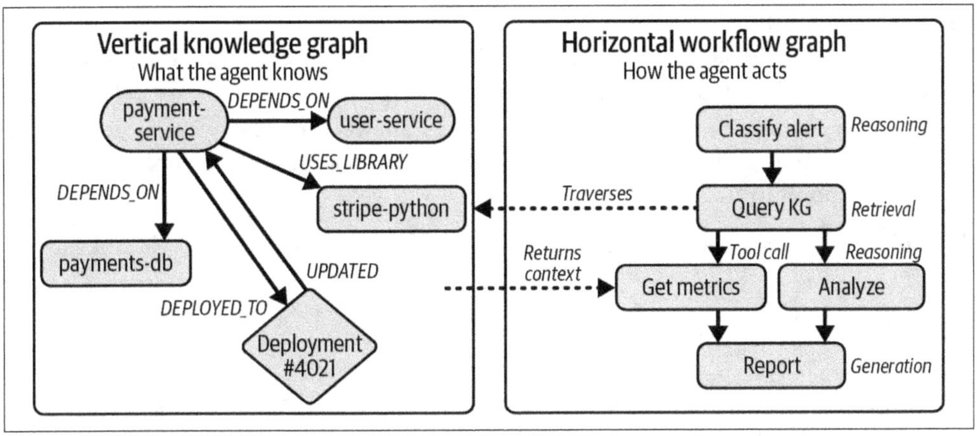


*Figure 2-1. The dual-graph architecture in which workflow nodes query the knowledge graph for context and results update it*

## The Vertical Knowledge Graph

The *vertical knowledge graph* is a structured representation of everything the agent knows about its domain. Unlike a vector store, where information exists as isolated embedding points, the knowledge graph encodes entities, their properties, and the relationships between them as first-class data structures. The building blocks are straightforward:

*Nodes represent entities.*
: Such as services, databases, configurations, incidents, users, and deployments. Each node has a type and a set of properties (name, version, status, timestamp).

*Edges represent relationships.*
: Such as `DEPENDS_ON`, `DEPLOYED_TO`, `CAUSED_BY`, and `USES_LIBRARY`. Each edge has a type, a direction, and optional properties (weight, confidence, timestamp).

*Properties carry metadata.*
: Metadata may include when a relationship was created, how confident the system is about it, and which source it came from.

This structure directly addresses two of the five flaws from Chapter 1:

*Relationship blindness*
: Relationship blindness disappears because relationships are explicit. The fact that the payment service depends on the user service is not something the model

must infer from similar paragraphs. It is a DEPENDS_ON edge in the graph, queryable and traversable.

*Temporal ignorance*
: Temporal ignorance becomes addressable because temporal metadata is a property of nodes and edges. Every entity can carry timestamps. Every relationship can carry a since property. The graph can answer not just what is connected but when the connection was established and what the system looked like at a specific point in time.

Example 2-2 shows what a fragment of an infrastructure knowledge graph looks like.

*Example 2-2. A fragment of an infrastructure vertical knowledge graph*

```
// Entities: services, databases, libraries
CREATE (:Service {name: 'checkout-service', version: '3.2.1', status: 'healthy'})
CREATE (:Service {name: 'user-service', version: '2.1.0', status: 'healthy'})
CREATE (:Database {name: 'payments-db', engine: 'PostgreSQL', version: '15.2'})
CREATE (:Library {name: 'stripe-python', version: '5.4.0'})

// Relationships: typed, directed, with temporal metadata
CREATE (checkout)-[:DEPENDS_ON {since: '2024-01-15'}]->(payments_db)
CREATE (checkout)-[:DEPENDS_ON {since: '2024-03-01'}]->(user_service)
CREATE (checkout)-[:USES_LIBRARY {version: '5.4.0'}]->(stripe)
```

This is a simplified example, but notice what it makes possible. A single graph traversal starting from checkout-service can reach every service, database, and library it depends on. Two hops out reveals the transitive dependencies: everything that *those* services depend on. The entire dependency tree is navigable, not because someone wrote a function to calculate it but because the structure of the data makes it queryable by default.

The choice of graph model matters, and the right choice depends on your reasoning requirements. *Property graphs* (the format shown in Example 2-2, used by Neo4j and other graph databases) store nodes with properties connected by labeled edges. They are fast, intuitive, and well-suited to traversal-heavy workloads like dependency analysis. The Resource Description Framework (RDF) takes a different approach, representing everything as subject-predicate-object triples with formal logical semantics. RDF enables native reasoning: if you tell the system that Disease1 causes Symptom1 and Patient exhibits Symptom1, it can infer Disease1 as a potential diagnosis without you writing that logic. The trade-off is complexity and speed. For most agentic systems, property graphs provide the right balance of expressiveness and performance, with RDF reserved for domains where formal inference is a hard requirement.

Beyond the graph model itself, the schema design—which entity types exist, which relationship types connect them, and which properties they carry—shapes what the agent can reason about. Get the schema wrong, and your agent will be structurally incapable of answering the questions it needs to answer, no matter how powerful the model behind it is. This is why Chapter 3 spends significant time on schema patterns specifically designed for agent interaction: event-centric patterns for modeling deployments and incidents as temporal sequences, contextual boundary patterns for preventing the agent from accidentally mixing information across domains or time periods, and capability models that let the agent understand its own limitations.

Chapter 3 covers knowledge graph construction in depth: the vertical knowledge graph as described here is a single conceptual layer, but Chapter 3 unpacks it into a more granular internal structure and walks through the full construction pipeline from raw data to queryable graph.

## The Horizontal Workflow Graph

The *horizontal workflow graph* structures how the agent acts. It represents the agent's reasoning and execution process as a DAG: nodes are discrete operations, and edges encode the dependencies between them. Each node in the workflow graph has a focused responsibility:

*Reasoning nodes*
: These perform analysis such as interpreting alerts, evaluating evidence, and identifying patterns. They query the vertical knowledge graph for context and produce structured conclusions.

*Execution nodes*
: These take actions; they may call APIs, query metrics databases, or run diagnostic commands. They interact with the outside world through tools.

*Decision nodes*
: These choose paths: based on the output of a reasoning node, the workflow branches to different next steps.

*Validation nodes*
: These check work, verifying that an output conforms to a schema, that a conclusion is supported by evidence, or that an action is permitted.

The edges between nodes encode which operations must complete before others can begin. This is not a linear sequence. It is a DAG, which means that independent operations can run in parallel while dependent operations wait for their inputs. For example, a node that queries the knowledge graph for service dependencies and a node that queries live metrics for CPU usage can run simultaneously if neither depends on the other's output.

This structure addresses two more of the five flaws:

*Reasoning paralysis*
: Replaced by structured decomposition. Instead of stuffing an entire complex problem into a single prompt and hoping the model figures it out, you decompose the problem into focused nodes, each responsible for one piece of the reasoning. Multistep reliability goes from single digits (for monolithic prompts) to production-viable levels (for decomposed workflows).

*Tool chaos*
: Replaced by orchestrated execution. Tools are invoked through explicit nodes in the workflow graph, with typed inputs and outputs, and clear dependency relationships. The agent does not improvise a sequence of tool calls. It follows a plan.

### Defining the harness

The horizontal workflow graph describes what the agent should do, but it does not execute itself. Execution is the job of the agent's harness, and defining the harness precisely matters because harness design, rather than model capability, sets the upper bound on agent behavior. The *harness* is a runtime with six surfaces, each with its own responsibility:

- It holds the workflow graph as an inspectable state.
- It advances the graph under a *named policy* that chooses which nodes fire next, in what order, under sequential, parallel, or dynamic-replanning execution.
- It exposes a *typed tool registry* through which nodes invoke side-effectful operations, from API calls to graph writes to model invocations.
- It mediates a *typed memory interface* through which nodes read from and write to the vertical knowledge graph and any temporal or episodic memory layers.
- It enforces a *schema validator* that constrains the output of each node to match the input contract of its downstream neighbors.
- It maintains an *append-only observation record* of every node invocation, every tool call, every input and output, and every timing annotation.

Claude Code, LangChain, DSPy, and bespoke loops written in a hundred lines of Python are all instantiations of this structure. They differ in which of the six surfaces they expose to the developer and which they hide. Each surface has chapter dedicated to it in this book:

- Chapter 3 formalizes the knowledge interface and the structure of the vertical knowledge graph it reads from.
- Chapter 4 extends that interface with temporal and episodic memory.

- Chapter 5 develops the advancement policy under the heading of planning and reasoning, treating the workflow graph and its execution rule as the substrate for multi-hop inference.
- Chapter 6 specifies the tool registry, including information-flow control and the ontological structure of tools, and treats the schema validator through the lens of Pydantic enforcement at tool boundaries.
- Chapter 7 shows that the observation record is the execution graph: the harness's log of what actually happened is the data on which self-evolution runs.
- Chapter 8 covers what happens when the advancement policy becomes cost aware, routing different nodes to different model tiers.

Each pillar in "The Eight Pillars of Agentic Graph Architecture" on page 42 is a design decision about one or more of these six surfaces.

A semantic reading of the structure follows from Mark Burgess's promise theory (*https://oreil.ly/ELp3_*). Each node in the workflow graph promises an output that satisfies the schema validator. The harness observes the output through the observation record and enforces the advancement policy accordingly. Coordination quality is a function of observation bandwidth, which is the fidelity and depth of the record, not a function of instruction specificity. A harness with a rich observation record can detect and recover from broken promises in a way that a harness with a thin record cannot.

The structure admits a testable asymmetry that the rest of this book leans on. For a fixed harness and a fixed vertical knowledge graph, swapping the language model used inside individual nodes produces bounded variation in agent behavior. The advancement policy, the schema validator, and the tool registry constrain what any model can do. For a fixed model and a fixed vertical knowledge graph, swapping the harness produces unbounded variation. A workflow graph executed under a harness with permissive validation and shallow observation behaves qualitatively differently from the same graph executed under a harness with strict validation and full-trace observation. The argument developed across Chapters 5 through 8 is that investments in harness design yield compounding returns, while investments in model capability alone do not.

The sixth surface, the observation record, deserves a second look because it is what makes self-evolution possible. Chapter 7 treats the execution graph as the dynamic counterpart to the horizontal workflow graph: whereas the workflow graph is the plan, the execution graph is the immutable trace of what the harness actually did for a specific query. Every Chapter 7 mechanism reads from or writes to this trace. The multi-layered evaluation framework classifies failures by reading the observation record node by node. Then semantic backpropagation sends corrective feedback to the specific node that made the error. This is possible only because the record preserves per-node input-output pairs to which the framework can attribute blame. The graduated validation protocol adjusts schema constraints and advancement policy thresholds based on trends in the record.

A system that self-evolves is a harness with a high-fidelity observation record and a feedback loop closed over it. A system without that record cannot self-improve because there is nothing to diagnose, nothing to attribute, and nothing to validate an improvement against. The harness is not only the executor of the present workflow. It is the substrate on which future workflows are trained. Example 2-3 illustrates what a simple workflow graph looks like for a latency investigation.

*Example 2-3. A horizontal workflow graph for latency investigation*

```
# A simplified horizontal workflow graph as a DAG.
# Each node is an operation; each edge is a dependency.
investigation = {
    "nodes": [
        {
            "id": "classify",
            "type": "reasoning",
            "task": "Classify alert severity and type",
        },
        {
            "id": "query_kg",
            "type": "retrieval",
            "task": "Find affected services and dependencies",
        },
        {
            "id": "get_metrics",
            "type": "tool_call",
            "task": "Query live metrics API for affected services",
        },
        {
            "id": "analyze",
            "type": "reasoning",
            "task": "Correlate evidence and identify root cause",
        },
        {
            "id": "report",
            "type": "generation",
            "task": "Generate structured incident report",
        },
    ],
    "edges": [
        # Severity determines scope of graph traversal
        ("classify", "query_kg"),
        # Dependencies determine which metrics to check
        ("query_kg", "get_metrics"),
        # Graph context feeds into root cause analysis
        ("query_kg", "analyze"),
```

```
        # Live metrics feed into root cause analysis
        ("get_metrics", "analyze"),
        # Analysis becomes the incident report
        ("analyze", "report"),
    ]
}
```

Notice that `query_kg` feeds into both `get_metrics` and `analyze`. The analysis node waits for both the graph context and the live metrics before it runs. This is the DAG in action: dependencies are explicit, parallelism is automatic where the structure allows it, and every node's inputs and outputs are traceable.

A DAG is not just a flowchart. It has three properties that make it particularly well-suited to agentic workflows:

*Parallel execution*
: Independent branches run simultaneously. In Example 2-3, if we added a node that checked recent deployment history (which depends only on `query_kg`, not on `get_metrics`), it would run in parallel with the metrics query. This reduces end-to-end latency for complex investigations.

*Failure isolation*
: When a node fails (a tool call times out, a reasoning step produces low-confidence output), the failure stays local. Other branches continue. The workflow can retry the failed node, route around it, or flag it for human review without restarting the entire investigation from scratch.

*Modularity*
: Nodes are self-contained. A reasoning node that analyzes service dependencies can be reused in different workflow graphs: the same node might appear in a latency investigation, a capacity-planning workflow, and a security audit. The node does not need to know which workflow it is part of. It only needs its inputs and its task definition.

These properties are not unique to agentic systems. Business process engineers have been building DAG-based workflows for decades. The twist is that in an agentic system, a language model sits inside many of the nodes as the execution engine. That combination—a deterministic workflow structure situated around probabilistic model execution—is what makes complex agent behavior tractable.

Chapter 5 covers the construction and execution of horizontal workflow graphs in depth: how to decompose problems into node structures, how to implement reasoning nodes that query the knowledge graph for multi-hop inference, and how to build planning systems that generate these DAGs dynamically rather than relying on hardcoded workflows.

### Splitting a workflow into nodes

Splitting a workflow into nodes is a design decision you pay for in every subsequent chapter. The rule that cuts through the design space is that nodes differ by tool surface, not by prompt.

The sharpest public example comes from security tooling. Kyle Polley's RedAI (*https://oreil.ly/GSVmL*), made open source in April 2026, splits vulnerability discovery across two node roles whose distinction is entirely tool level:

*Scanner node*
: Holds a filesystem and an LLM. It threat-models source code and emits candidate findings, optimized for recall.

*Validator node*
: Holds a browser driver, an iOS simulator, a network stack, and a scripting runtime. It drives each candidate into a live environment and reports one of three verdicts: *confirmed*, *unable-to-test*, or *disproved*.

Swap the scanner's prompt into the validator's runtime, and nothing changes. The validator can still drive the browser because it holds the tool. Swap the validator's prompt into the scanner's runtime, and you have a scanner with a misleading name. The role lives in the tool surface, not in the instructions.

Your horizontal workflow graph should follow the same rule. When two nodes need different tool surfaces, split them. When they need the same tool surface, merge them and vary the prompt. Skipping this check produces the common failure mode where a single retrieval-and-reasoning node both queries the graph and does causal analysis, with neither pass achieving the quality that a specialist node would deliver.

> Before you add a node to the workflow graph, list the tools it will call. If the list overlaps more than 80% with that of an existing node, you have a prompt variation of that node rather than a new role. Merge them and vary the prompt at the input. If the tool lists differ substantially, on the other hand, split the nodes.

## Where the Two Graphs Meet

The dual-graph architecture's value emerges at the intersection of the two graphs. As mentioned, the horizontal workflow graph provides the reasoning skeleton, while the vertical knowledge graph supplies the domain knowledge that each operation needs to do its job.

Consider the latency investigation from Example 2-3. The `query_kg` node does not search for paragraphs about dependencies. Instead, it traverses the vertical knowledge graph, following `DEPENDS_ON` edges outward from the affected service. The results (a concrete list of services, databases, and libraries with their properties and relationships) flow into the `get_metrics` node (which knows exactly which services to check) and the `analyze` node (which has the structural context to distinguish a root cause from a symptom).

The interaction goes both ways. When the investigation concludes and identifies a root cause, the result can update the vertical knowledge graph, either adding a new `CAUSED_BY` edge between the incident and its root cause or updating a service node's status. The workflow graph drives the process; the knowledge graph supplies and receives the facts. Each graph makes the other more useful than it could be alone.

This bidirectional interaction is where the architecture earns its keep. Consider what happens when the agent encounters an ambiguous situation during the investigation. The `analyze` node receives metrics showing that the payment service's response time spiked at 2:47 a.m. Was it the recent deployment? A database issue? Increased traffic? A monolithic agent would guess based on whatever text chunks it retrieved. A dual-graph agent traverses the knowledge graph to check the following:

- What deployments occurred in the hour before the spike? (Temporal traversal)
- Which services share the same database connection pool? (Dependency traversal)
- Has this pattern occurred before, and if so, what was the root cause? (Historical traversal, using the memory systems from Chapter 4)

Each traversal narrows the hypothesis space based on structural evidence, not embedding similarity. The workflow graph coordinates the inquiry. The knowledge graph provides the evidence. The result is a diagnosis grounded in verified relationships rather than statistical inference.

This interaction pattern (workflow graph as the process skeleton, knowledge graph as the information substrate) is the foundation upon which every subsequent chapter in this book will build. Chapter 3 builds the knowledge graph. Chapter 4 adds temporal depth to it. Chapter 5 builds the workflow graph and teaches the agent to reason. Chapter 6 connects it to external tools. Chapter 7 uses the structure to enable self-improvement. And finally Chapter 8 makes all of it fast, secure, and affordable.

The two graphs are complementary by design. You need both. A knowledge graph without a workflow graph is a database that nobody queries intelligently. A workflow graph without a knowledge graph is a process with no grounding, prone to hallucination and drift. Together, they form a complete architecture for agentic intelligence: grounded knowledge and structured action.

## A Note on Context Graphs

If you have spent any time in the agent-infrastructure conversation, you have probably seen the term *context graph*. It is the label the field is converging on for knowledge graphs built specifically to support agent memory and reasoning, and the work behind it is substantive. On the research side, Rasmussen and colleagues (2025) published "Zep: A Temporal Knowledge Graph Architecture for Agent Memory" (*https://oreil.ly/QlvPj*), which describes a bitemporal knowledge graph engine for LLM agents and benchmarks it against the previous state of the art for long-horizon memory. On the investment side, Foundation Capital's widely circulated 2025 essay, "AI's Trillion-Dollar Opportunity: Context Graphs" (*https://oreil.ly/ufFUj*), by Jaya Gupta and Ashu Garg, argued that the defining property of a context graph is not the data model but the capture point: "agents don't just need rules. They need access to decision traces that show how rules were applied." Those traces can be captured only by systems sitting in the execution path at decision time; they can't be retrofitted from data warehouses after the fact. Before we go further, it is worth describing exactly what a context graph is and how it relates to the architecture we have just defined.

A *context graph* is a knowledge graph optimized for agent use. The underlying data structure is the same one this chapter has already described, with nodes, edges, and properties. What changes is what the graph is built to do. A context graph treats important relationships as first-class objects that carry their own history and provenance, attaches bitemporal metadata to every fact, and captures not just *what* the system knows but *why* it believes it, *when* the belief became true, and *which* source produced it.

Three ideas distinguish a context graph from a plain knowledge graph:

*Reification as a first-class practice*
: Instead of treating a relationship as a bare edge between two nodes, you promote important relationships into nodes of their own so that metadata, provenance, and temporal bounds can hang off them. Reification is a long-standing technique in the semantic web literature. The W3C Working Group Note, "Defining N-ary Relations on the Semantic Web," (Noy and Rector, 2006, *https://oreil.ly/Bjw1n*) is the canonical reference, and modern variants like RDF-star (*https://oreil.ly/I2Sxv*) (based on Hartig's "Foundations of an Alternative Approach to Reification in RDF", *https://oreil.ly/QnpEy*, rev. 2021) reduce the overhead. Reification is a property of context graphs, introduced in Chapter 3, and several of the

schema patterns in that chapter (event-centric, multiperspective) are reification in practice.

*Bitemporal metadata*
: Every node and edge carry both *valid time* (when the fact was true in the world) and *transaction time* (when the system recorded it). This distinction comes from Snodgrass's work on temporal databases (see *Developing Time-Oriented Database Applications in SQL*, [Morgan Kaufmann, 2000 (*https://oreil.ly/By2pO*)], for the canonical treatment) and is the basis of the SQL:2011 temporal standard. "Bitemporal Property Graphs" (Anselma et al., 2026, *https://oreil.ly/PPcbx*) extends the model to labeled property graphs, and Rasmussen's Zep paper applies it directly to agent memory. This is what makes point-in-time queries like *What did the infrastructure look like right before the outage?* answerable from the graph itself rather than needing a reply reconstructed from logs.

*Governed memory and decision traces*
: Entities, events, decisions, policies, and evidence all live in the same structure, queryable together. Foundation Capital's "Context Graphs" essay frames this as the core asset: a context graph captures not just the rules but the *decision traces*, or what inputs were gathered, which policies were applied, what exceptions were granted, and the rationale behind each choice. An agent does not just retrieve facts about the payment service but what we knew about the payment service at 02:47 a.m. last Tuesday, where that knowledge came from, which policy governed how we acted on it, and why the on-call engineer chose to override the default response.

Given all that, why does this book use the term *vertical knowledge graph* instead of *context graph*? First, *context graph* describes a set of capabilities one graph can have, whereas the *dual-graph architecture* describes a relationship between two complementary graphs. The industry term collapses the distinction between what the agent knows and how the agent acts, and that distinction is the load-bearing idea of this book. Second, *context* is the single most overloaded word in agentic AI. *Context window, context engineering, in-context learning, contextual boundary*...the word is already carrying more weight than it can hold.

For most practical purposes, you can read the rest of this book with a simple mental translation. When you build the vertical knowledge graph using the schema patterns in Chapter 3, layer in the temporal memory of Chapter 4, and add the execution-graph reification of Chapter 7, you have built what the industry calls a "context graph." The dual-graph architecture goes one step further by separating that graph from the workflow structure that drives it. Everything the context-graph literature recommends, you will build. You will just build it alongside a horizontal workflow graph that tells the agent what to do with it.

## The Eight Pillars of Agentic Graph Architecture

The dual-graph architecture is the structural framework. The *eight pillars* are the implementation roadmap: the specific capabilities you need to build to turn that framework into a working system.

Why eight pillars, and why these eight? Each emerged from a recurring failure pattern in production agent deployments. Knowledge representation exists because agents given unstructured data make ungrounded claims. Memory systems exist because stateless agents repeat mistakes. Reasoning and planning exist because monolithic prompts collapse under multistep complexity. Tool orchestration exists because ad hoc tool integration becomes unmanageable past a handful of tools. Structured output exists because probabilistic models and deterministic APIs do not naturally speak the same language. Self-evolution exists because agents without learning loops degrade silently. Finally, optimization exists because an agent that works brilliantly in a notebook may be too expensive, too slow, or too insecure for production.

The pillars are not independent modules you can implement in any order. They are layered. Knowledge representation (Chapter 3) must come first because every other pillar depends on the knowledge graph. Memory systems (Chapter 4) are built on top of it. Reasoning and planning (Chapter 5) require both knowledge and memory. Tool orchestration (Chapter 6) requires all of these. Each pillar amplifies the ones before it, and the final two, self-evolution and optimization, depend on the complete architecture being in place.

Each pillar also addresses one or more of the five flaws from Chapter 1. Table 2-1 maps the connection explicitly.

*Table 2-1. Mapping the five flaws to the eight pillars*

| Flaw (Chapter 1) | Root cause | Pillar(s) that address it | Chapter(s) |
|---|---|---|---|
| Context amnesia | Stateless retrieval with no memory | Memory systems | 4 |
| Relationship blindness | Flat embeddings with no structure | Knowledge representation | 3 |
| Temporal ignorance | No time dimension in data model | Knowledge representation, memory systems | 3, 4 |
| Reasoning paralysis | Monolithic prompts, no decomposition | Reasoning with graphs, planning systems | 5 |
| Tool chaos | Uncoordinated, ad hoc tool integration | Tool orchestration, structured output | 5, 6 |

The remaining pillars, self-evolution and optimization, do not map to specific flaws. They map to a different problem: making the system viable in production. An agent that reasons well but never improves, or one that works brilliantly at a cost no organization can sustain, is not a solution. These pillars close the gap between a prototype and a system you can actually deploy.

The rest of this book is organized around these pillars in three parts, each building on the previous one, as illustrated in Figure 2-2.

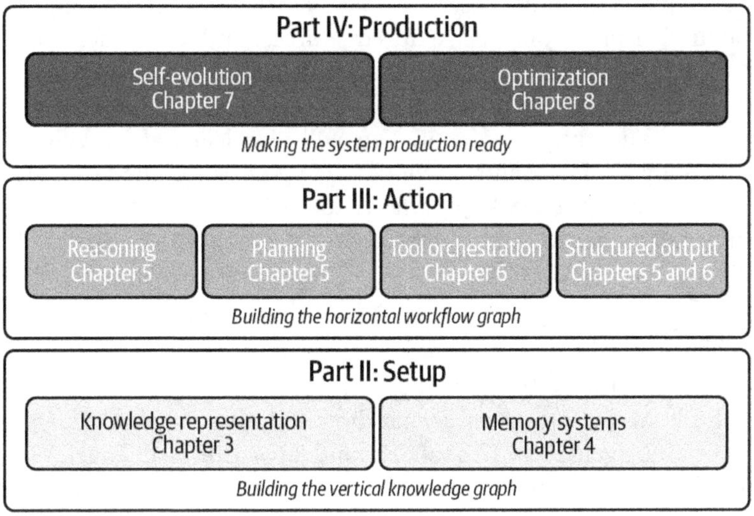


*Figure 2-2. The eight pillars of agentic graph architecture mapped to the parts of the book*

## Setup: Building the Digital Twin of a Tech Stack (Part II)

Part II constructs the agent's "brain": the vertical knowledge graph and the memory systems that give it temporal depth. By the end of Chapter 4, the agent possesses a queryable, historically aware digital twin of its domain.

### Knowledge representation (Chapter 3)

*Knowledge representation* is the process of transforming raw, messy data into the structured entities and relationships of the vertical knowledge graph. It is the first pillar because everything else depends on it. Without a well-constructed knowledge graph, the agent has nothing to reason about, nothing to remember, and no grounding for its actions.

Real-world data does not arrive in graph form. Your infrastructure knowledge lives in server logs, JSON configuration files, database schemas, Terraform definitions, wiki pages, and the heads of engineers who built the systems. Getting from that raw material to a structured graph of entities and relationships requires a pipeline: extracting entities from unstructured text, resolving duplicates across data sources, validating quality, and choosing the right graph model for your reasoning requirements.

Chapter 3 covers all this. You will learn when to choose property graphs versus RDF and how Chapter 3's three-graph architecture (separating trusted domain knowledge, raw textual evidence, and extracted interpretations) extends the vertical knowledge graph into something an agent can query without contaminating ground truth.

You will build extraction pipelines that use LLMs with strict schema enforcement to pull structured triples from unstructured sources, and you'll tackle *entity resolution*, the problem of recognizing that the same Amazon Elastic Compute Cloud (EC2) instance referenced by instance ID, IP address, DNS name, and Terraform resource name is one entity, not four. You will also learn about schema patterns that matter specifically for agents: *event-centric patterns* for modeling deployments and incidents, *contextual boundary patterns* for preventing the agent from mixing information across domains, and *capability models* that let the agent understand its own limitations.

#### Memory systems (Chapter 4)

*Memory systems* give the vertical knowledge graph a temporal dimension. A knowledge graph built in Chapter 3 is a snapshot: it captures what the system looks like *right now*. But agents need to understand how things change. What did the infrastructure look like *before* the outage? When was this dependency added? What was the last configuration change before performance degraded?

The need to store historical data is only part of the problem. The harder part is organizing memory so the agent can recall the right information at the right time, consolidate patterns from past experiences, and prune information that is no longer relevant without losing the context that might matter later.

Chapter 4 covers *graph memory systems*: specialized graph structures that go well beyond adding timestamps to the knowledge graph. You will learn about using *episodic memory* for capturing complete events, *semantic memory* for entity-relationship networks, and *procedural memory* for executable task knowledge. You will learn *bitemporal modeling* (tracking both when events actually occurred and when the system learned about them); consolidation patterns that compress raw experience into reusable knowledge; and retrieval strategies that combine semantic, temporal, and relational signals. The chapter also surveys the production memory platforms (Cognee, mem0, Zep) that are already serving these patterns at scale, and it covers a newer approach where agents learn their own memory strategies through reinforcement learning rather than following hand-coded rules.

## Action: From Firefighting to Foresight (Part III)

Part III brings the agent to life. With a knowledge graph and memory in place, the agent has a brain—but a brain without a nervous system is inert. Part III builds the horizontal workflow graph and connects the agent to the outside world through tools.

### Reasoning with graphs (Chapter 5)

*Reasoning with graphs* is the inference engine that sits at the intersection of the two graphs. It is the mechanism by which the agent uses the vertical knowledge graph to answer questions, follow chains of evidence, and draw conclusions that span multiple relationships and data sources.

Chapter 5 starts from a premise that reframes the argument elaborated through the rest of the book: agentic AI looks like artificial intelligence, but it behaves like process engineering. The agent's job is to execute a workflow, and graph-based reasoning is the mechanism that makes each step in that workflow grounded and verifiable. Real reasoning is rarely a single lookup. When a site reliability engineer (SRE) reports high latency in a service, finding the root cause might require traversing dependency chains (multi-hop reasoning), correlating temporal patterns (what changed recently?), and integrating information from different parts of the graph (service topology, deployment history, resource metrics). The agent needs to do all this without hallucinating connections that don't exist or losing track of the evidence trail.

Chapter 5 introduces graph traversal strategies for multi-hop reasoning, structural approaches like PathRAG (Chen et al., 2025, *https://oreil.ly/iDbY6*) that protect against hallucination by requiring verified relational paths rather than retrieved text passages and adaptive retrieval techniques that teach the agent when and how to query the knowledge graph at each step. You will see how graph-based reasoning transforms retrieval from finding similar text to tracing verified relationships and why that distinction is the difference between an agent that guesses and one that reasons.

### Planning systems (Chapter 5)

*Planning systems* give the agent the ability to decompose complex problems into the horizontal workflow graphs described earlier in this chapter. While reasoning handles the *thinking*, planning handles the *organizing*: breaking a vague objective into concrete steps, ordering those steps by dependency, and adapting the plan when something unexpected happens.

LLMs are next-token predictors at heart. They excel at local coherence but struggle with long-horizon planning, keeping track of constraints, dependencies, and intermediate results across dozens of steps. Encoding an entire complex workflow into a single prompt is like running a factory off verbal instructions alone with no diagrams, no checkpoints, and no verification.

Chapter 5 covers DAG-based planning architectures that decompose objectives into interconnected nodes with explicit dependencies. You will learn about parallel execution (independent subtasks running simultaneously), resilient failure management (failures isolated to specific branches so they don't crash the entire plan), causal knowledge integration (using the knowledge graph to initialize plans with domain-specific cause-effect understanding), and dynamic replanning when the environment changes midexecution.

### Tool orchestration (Chapter 6)

*Tool orchestration* connects the agent to the outside world. An agent that can reason and plan but cannot query a metrics API, read a log file, or send an alert is confined to the knowledge graph. Tools are the bridge between the agent's intelligence and the systems it needs to influence.

Calling APIs is the easy part. The real work is discovering which tools exist, selecting the right ones for a given task, managing dependencies between tool calls (where the output of one becomes the input to the next), and doing all this securely at enterprise scale. When an organization exposes hundreds of tools through a protocol like the Model Context Protocol (MCP) (*https://oreil.ly/pyFrw*), naive approaches hit a wall: stuffing all tool descriptions into the context window degrades model performance measurably.

Chapter 6 works through the challenges layer by layer. It starts with MCP as the protocol foundation, then addresses the prompt bloat crisis through RAG-based tool discovery. From there, it moves tools into the knowledge graph itself, making them graph nodes with typed dependencies and data flow relationships rather than standalone API definitions. Security is woven throughout: MCP authentication, information flow control (taint tracking to prevent data from untrusted sources from propagating through tool chains), and verification-based trust for tools that may game the system. The chapter also covers how tool ecosystems evolve, describing ontology-driven tools that define themselves; meta-tooling where the system generates new tools from usage patterns; and orchestration patterns at enterprise scale, including hierarchical routing and functional clustering for resilience.

### Structured output engineering (Chapters 5 and 6)

*Structured output engineering* bridges the gap between probabilistic language model outputs and deterministic software interfaces. Every tool call the agent makes requires correctly formatted input. Every node in the workflow graph needs to pass structured data to the next node. A single misplaced bracket or unexpected field type cascades through the entire pipeline.

The problem is an *impedance mismatch*. Traditional software components communicate through strictly formatted data structures, but language models generate text by sampling from probability distributions, a process that introduces structural variability. Grammar-constrained generation with tools like Outlines (*https://oreil.ly/SrqlJ*) solves this at the token level: instead of hoping the model produces valid output and retrying when it doesn't, you make invalid output impossible by construction.

This pillar spans two chapters. Chapter 5 covers the theory: how Outlines enforces internode contracts across the workflow graph so that reasoning, planning, and action nodes communicate through guaranteed structures rather than fragile text parsing. Chapter 6 applies it to tool orchestration, using Pydantic schema enforcement and constrained generation to ensure that every API call the agent makes is syntactically valid.

## Production: Creating a Self-Healing System (Part IV)

Part IV addresses the gap between a working prototype and a system you can deploy. An agent that reasons well in a notebook is not the same as an agent that runs 24/7 at acceptable cost, under governance constraints, with improvement over time. Part IV makes the architecture production-ready.

### Self-evolution and evaluation (Chapter 7)

*Self-evolution* is the agent's ability to learn from its own mistakes without human intervention. Without it, the agent can execute but never reflect. It cannot identify patterns in its successes, adapt its strategies as conditions change, or even notice that its performance is degrading. The result is silent drift—and a team of human experts in a state of constant reactive vigilance.

In a monolithic system, diagnosing a failure means searching through an undifferentiated mass of model outputs. In a graph-based architecture, failures are localized. When a specific reasoning node produces a bad conclusion, you know which node failed, what inputs it received, and which part of the knowledge graph it traversed. The graph structure makes targeted learning possible.

Chapter 7 covers the full arc of self-evolution. It starts with the *execution graph*, the dynamic counterpart to the horizontal workflow graph. While the workflow graph is the plan for what the agent should do, the execution graph is an immutable record of what it actually did for a specific query. That record feeds into a multi-layered evaluation framework, a diagnostic engine that classifies failures by type and location, and then into semantic backpropagation (*https://oreil.ly/6hSHF*), which sends targeted feedback to the specific node that made the error without breaking nodes that worked correctly. The graduated validation protocol makes it safe to deploy these improvements in production.

### Optimization (Chapter 8)

*Optimization*, the final pillar, addresses the three forces that derail agent projects in production: cost, governance, and performance:

- Cost is the most immediate. If every node in your horizontal workflow graph runs on a frontier model, the economics don't work at scale.
- Governance comes next. An agent with unrestricted access to the knowledge graph can traverse from a public service catalog to internal cost data to employee records in a single query.
- Performance is the third. Graph traversals that complete in milliseconds on a development dataset take seconds at production scale, and a federation of specialist models that reasons beautifully offline becomes a latency bottleneck under real traffic.

Chapter 8 covers selective intelligence (deploying the right model for the right node, from fine-tuned 3B models for classification to frontier models for complex reasoning), subgraph-level access control and handling of personally identifiable information (PII), schema evolution and lifecycle management for production knowledge graphs, deployment patterns, and GPU-accelerated graph operations using tools like NVIDIA's cuGraph (*https://oreil.ly/KEAih*) that turn multi-minute traversals into subsecond queries.

## The Autonomous DevOps Agent

Throughout this book, we build one system from start to finish. Every architectural concept, every implementation pattern, and every production technique is applied to the same example: the *autonomous DevOps agent.*

The choice of DevOps is deliberate. Cloud infrastructure is a domain where all five of the architectural flaws from Chapter 1 show up constantly. Services depend on each other in complex, often undocumented ways that no single person fully understands. Configurations change daily. Deployments happen dozens of times per day. When something breaks, the response depends on understanding relationships, temporal sequences, and cascading dependencies—exactly the kind of reasoning that vector-based systems cannot support.

The DevOps agent's mission is to transform a reactive cloud-monitoring system (one that pages humans at 3:00 a.m. and waits for someone to diagnose the problem) into a proactive, self-healing one that detects issues before they become incidents, diagnoses root causes autonomously, and learns from every interaction.

Companies like AnyShift (*https://oreil.ly/DEdk8*) are already building production graph-based DevOps agents using this architecture. Their system creates a digital twin of cloud infrastructure by combining deterministic knowledge graphs with probabilistic AI reasoning, the same dual-graph architecture we will implement across the next six chapters. We will return to AnyShift's production patterns later in this section.

## The Initial State

Imagine your enterprise runs hundreds of microservices across multiple cloud providers. When something breaks at 3:47 a.m., the following is what happens.

PagerDuty fires an alert: *High latency on checkout-service*. An SRE is woken up. They open Grafana and see the latency spike, but Grafana does not tell them *why* it's happening. They switch to Datadog for metrics—CPU, memory, request rates—and notice the database connection pool is saturated. But is the database the root cause, or is it a symptom of something upstream? They switch to Splunk and search the logs, filtering by timestamp. They see errors from `stripe-python`, a library that was updated two hours ago. They check the deployment history in their CI/CD tool. They mentally trace the dependency chain: `checkout-service` uses `stripe-python`, which connects to the Stripe API, which...is that the issue, or is it the database?

Forty-five minutes later, the SRE has the answer: the new version of `stripe-python` changed its connection-pooling behavior, and the new behavior exhausted the database's available connections. The fix takes 5 minutes. The diagnosis took 45. And the SRE needed tribal knowledge of the dependency chain, the ability to manually query across four different tools, and the kind of correlative reasoning that cannot be scripted.

This is the state the agent begins in. The tools exist. The data exists. But they are disconnected:

*Fragmented monitoring*
: Datadog for metrics, PagerDuty for alerts, Splunk for logs, Grafana for dashboards. Each captures one slice of the picture. None of them represents how the slices connect.

*Manual diagnosis*
: The SRE is the reasoning engine. They hold the dependency map in their head, correlate timestamps manually, and test hypotheses by running queries across multiple systems. This process is skilled, expensive, slow, and dependent on institutional knowledge that walks out the door when people leave.

*Reactive response*
: Problems are noticed only after users are affected. By the time the alert fires, the damage is already propagating through the dependency chain. There is no prediction, no early warning, no proactive intervention.

The initial state is a representation problem, not a technology problem. The information needed to diagnose incidents already exists in logs, metrics, configs, and deployment records. But it is fragmented across tools and formats, with no structural representation of the relationships that connect them. There is no graph. There are only strings.

## The Transformation Arc

With the architecture and pillars laid out, we can trace how each part of the book transforms this starting point (Figure 2-3).

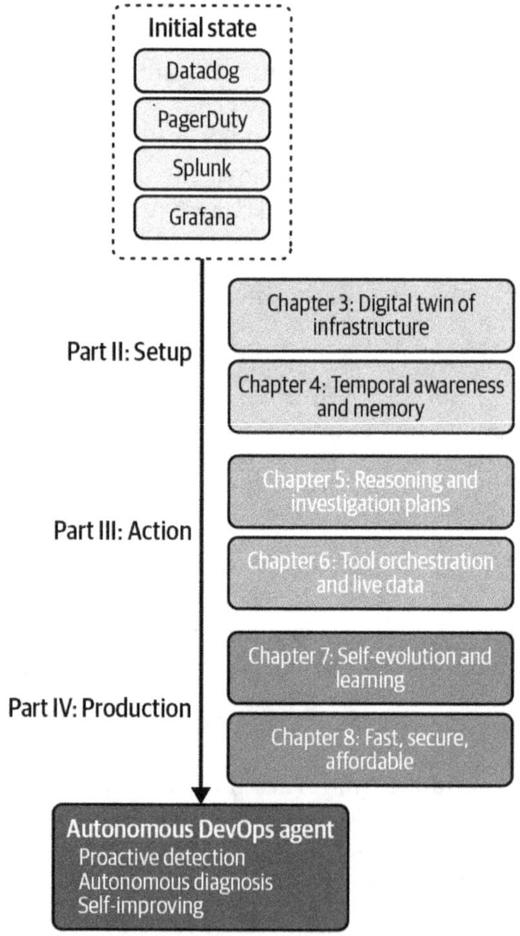


*Figure 2-3. The DevOps agent's progression from disconnected tools to autonomous, self-healing system*

Each part of this book adds a new layer of capability to the agent. By the end, the collection of disconnected tools becomes a system that sees the infrastructure as a coherent whole, reasons about it, acts on it, and learns from the results.

### Part II: Building the digital twin

In Chapter 3, we take the raw material of the tech stack (server logs, JSON configs, database metrics, Terraform definitions) and construct the initial vertical knowledge graph. We model services as nodes, dependencies as edges, and deployments as events. We apply entity resolution to deduplicate across data sources and quality validation to catch extraction errors. By the end of Chapter 3, the agent has a detailed digital twin of the infrastructure: every service, every database, and every dependency are queryable and traversable.

In Chapter 4, we give the digital twin a memory. The knowledge graph from Chapter 3 is a snapshot; Chapter 4 makes it temporal. We implement bitemporal modeling so the agent can distinguish between when an event occurred and when the system learned about it. We add memory consolidation and archival patterns so the graph stays manageable as history accumulates. By the end of Chapter 4, the agent can ask, *What did our infrastructure look like right before the outage last Tuesday?*

### Part III: From firefighting to foresight

In Chapter 5, we present the agent with its first real challenge: an SRE reports vague high latency in a critical service. The agent constructs a horizontal workflow graph, a multistep investigation plan with reasoning nodes to analyze dependencies from the knowledge graph and execution nodes to query live metrics. It decomposes the problem, follows the evidence, and identifies the root cause. It becomes a diagnostician.

In Chapter 6, we connect the agent to the outside world. The investigation from Chapter 5 requires live metrics data that the knowledge graph does not contain. We implement tool orchestration through MCP, register the `QueryMetricsAPI` as a graph node, and use structured output engineering to ensure that every API call is syntactically valid. The agent is no longer confined to its own graph; it can interact with external systems.

### Part IV: Creating a self-healing system

In Chapter 7, a routine dependency update arrives: `stripe-python 3.2.1 → 3.3.0` in the `checkout-service`. The agent predicts a future outage, but the prediction is only partially correct: it identifies the right risk pathway but attributes the wrong mechanism (predicting an API contract violation when the actual failure is connection timeout exhaustion). The system performs a cognitive autopsy, localizes the error to a specific reasoning node, and sends targeted feedback through semantic backpropagation. Then the next prediction is more accurate.

In Chapter 8, we make all this practical. Selective intelligence assigns the cheapest model that meets each node's quality threshold: a fine-tuned 3B model for alert classification and a frontier model for causal reasoning. GPU-accelerated graph operations bring dependency analysis within production latency budgets. Governance controls ensure the agent never traverses into unauthorized data. The complete system processes a deployment event end to end in under 2 seconds, at a fraction of a cent per event.

## A Real-World Parallel

This is not purely theoretical. AnyShift has built a production system using the same architectural principles:

*Structured relationship modeling*
: AnyShift handcrafted approximately a hundred relationship types between infrastructure entities (like *subnet is in a VPC* or *lambda executes in a VPC*), then used AI to discover additional valid relationships automatically. This hybrid human-AI ontology development is the kind of pattern Chapter 3 covers.

*Temporal awareness*
: Each node in the Neo4j graph maintains both current state and a historical queue of changes, enabling queries like *What did my infrastructure look like right before the outage at 23:00 yesterday?* This temporal dimension, which static vector embeddings cannot provide, is what Chapter 4 builds.

*Multisource knowledge integration*
: It scans AWS APIs for runtime state, parses Terraform code for infrastructure-as-code (IaC) definitions, and creates relationships between actual resources and their code representations. This knowledge acquisition pipeline mirrors the patterns in Chapter 3.

*Event-driven updates*
: Rather than performing periodic full scans, the system updates incrementally when changes occur: pull requests, deployments, configuration changes. This incremental approach is an optimization strategy covered in Chapter 8.

AnyShift's experience validates a key architectural decision: combining deterministic knowledge (the graph) with probabilistic AI capabilities (the language models) creates a system that understands complex infrastructure relationships in ways that language models alone cannot.

## What the Completed Agent Looks Like

By Chapter 8, the DevOps agent handles the same 3:47 a.m. scenario from the initial state, but the outcome is different. A deployment pipeline pushes `stripe-python 3.2.1 → 3.3.0` to `checkout-service`. The agent's knowledge graph updates incrementally (event-driven, not a full scan). A few minutes later, the agent detects a subtle shift in connection pool metrics. It does not wait for a latency spike. It does not page anyone.

Instead, the agent constructs a horizontal workflow graph to investigate. An alert classification node (running on a fine-tuned 3B model, cost: fractions of a cent) categorizes the pattern. A knowledge graph traversal identifies every service that depends on `checkout-service` and the `stripe-python` library. A tool orchestration node queries live metrics via the `QueryMetricsAPI`. A reasoning node (running on a frontier model because causal reasoning is genuinely hard) correlates the library update, the connection pool behavior change, and the dependency chain. A synthesis node generates a structured incident report.

Total elapsed time: under 2 seconds. Total cost: approximately $0.002. The SRE sleeps through the night and reviews the report in the morning. If the prediction was partially wrong (the agent identified the right risk pathway but attributed the wrong mechanism), the self-evolution system from Chapter 7 performs a cognitive autopsy, localizes the error, and sends targeted feedback to improve the next prediction.

That is the system we will build, one pillar at a time, starting in Chapter 3.

# Summary

This chapter laid out the architectural blueprint. You now have the mental model that every subsequent chapter builds on: the *strings to things* shift that motivates graph-based representation, the *dual-graph architecture* that pairs a vertical knowledge graph with a horizontal workflow graph, the *eight pillars* that turn the architecture into a working system, and the *DevOps agent* that gives you a concrete system to follow from initial state to production deployment.

The architecture addresses all five of the flaws identified in Chapter 1. Explicit graph relationships solve relationship blindness. Memory systems solve context amnesia. Temporal modeling in the knowledge graph solves temporal ignorance. Decomposed workflow graphs solve reasoning paralysis. Structured orchestration solves tool chaos. This is a different way to build agent systems than incrementally upgrading to vector RAG.

The architecture described here, though, has no knowledge until you populate the graph; no memory until you implement temporal structures; and no production viability until you solve for cost, governance, and performance.

Chapter 3 is where we start building. We will take the vertical knowledge graph from concept to implementation as we choose graph models, design schemas for agent interaction, build extraction pipelines that transform enterprise data into structured entities and relationships, and validate quality at every step. By the end of Chapter 3, the DevOps agent will have its first real capability: a queryable digital twin of the tech stack.

# PART II

# Setup: Building the Digital Twin of a Tech Stack

In Part II, we'll construct the agent's "brain": the vertical knowledge graph and the memory systems that give it temporal depth. Real-world data does not arrive in graph form. Infrastructure knowledge lives in server logs, JSON configs, database schemas, Terraform definitions, wiki pages, and the heads of the engineers who built the systems. Part II is the pipeline that turns that raw material into a structured, queryable, historically aware model of the agent's domain.

By the end of Part II, the DevOps agent will have a high-fidelity *digital twin* of its tech stack, a model that can be asked what the infrastructure looked like right before last Tuesday's outage. It will have a map of its world and understand how that map changes over time. It will not yet know how to reason or act on that map—that comes in Part III.

- Chapter 3 covers knowledge graph foundations and design patterns for agents, knowledge acquisition pipelines (extraction, entity resolution, validation), integration with existing organizational graphs and ontologies, and agent-friendly knowledge structures. Each of these is applied to build the DevOps agent's initial vertical knowledge graph.
- Chapter 4 covers episodic, semantic, and procedural memory; bitemporal modeling; retrieval strategies; and consolidation and pruning. These give the digital twin a temporal dimension so the agent can reason about change over time.

CHAPTER 3

# Graph-Based Knowledge Modeling for Agentic Systems

When you are building sophisticated AI systems, the way you represent, organize, and access knowledge serves as the engine for your entire system. Relational databases, document stores, or vector embeddings fall short when your systems must reason about complex relationships, maintain contextual awareness, and adapt their understanding over time. This chapter explains how graph-based knowledge modeling creates the foundation you need for truly agentic systems.

Forward-thinking organizations are discovering that meaningful AI impact requires a fundamental shift: the flow of intelligence must be reversed. Instead of just extracting insights from data, companies must learn to use AI to restructure and connect fragmented organizational knowledge, transforming siloed information into machine-comprehensible structures that enable sophisticated reasoning.

By the end of this chapter, you'll understand how to design, implement, and maintain knowledge graphs that enable sophisticated agent reasoning. You'll discover how to give your data stable, connectable identities, capture domain knowledge through ontologies, and leverage AI to build these structures automatically. Instead of just theoretical principles, you'll learn practical techniques to integrate these knowledge structures with your existing organizational data frameworks, turning tribal knowledge and disconnected systems into a unified semantic foundation.

This foundation will empower your agents to understand relationships between entities, maintain memory across interactions, and develop more intelligent reasoning capabilities. Most importantly, you'll learn how to build AI systems that truly understand your business by creating data structures that reflect how your organization actually thinks.

# Knowledge Graph Foundations

Although a comprehensive look at knowledge graphs and data modeling is beyond the scope of this book, there are some key concepts that engineers should become familiar with when building a graph-based RAG system for agents. This section will introduce you to the components of GraphRAG systems, provide some guidance on when to build your own graph system and when to buy an off-the-shelf solution, and review some graph data models and structures relevant to building agents.

## Components of GraphRAG Systems

As you prepare to implement a GraphRAG system for agents (illustrated in Figure 3-1), it's helpful to orient on some of their key components in order to understand, compare, and improve them. In their 2026 paper "In-Depth Analysis of Graph-Based RAG in a Unified Framework" (*https://oreil.ly/fWpUD*), Zhou and colleagues introduce a four-stage framework:

1. *Graph building*
   Transforms a corpus of knowledge into an appropriate graph structure, laying the foundation for all subsequent processing. This stage determines what information is captured and how it's organized, with significant implications for downstream retrieval capabilities.

2. *Index construction*
   Creates efficient lookup mechanisms that enable real-time query performance. This stage bridges the semantic richness of the graph with the practical requirements of production systems, balancing expressiveness against computational efficiency.

3. *Operator configuration*
   Selects and arranges retrieval operators to implement specific retrieval strategies. This stage determines how the system navigates the graph, combining different operators to extract relevant information based on the query characteristics.

4. *Retrieval and generation*
   Connects the graph traversal with language model integration, retrieving context and generating coherent responses. This stage synthesizes the structured information from the graph with the generative capabilities of the language model.

Understanding this framework helps you systematically approach the implementation of graph-based RAG systems, focusing on the key components and their interrelationships.

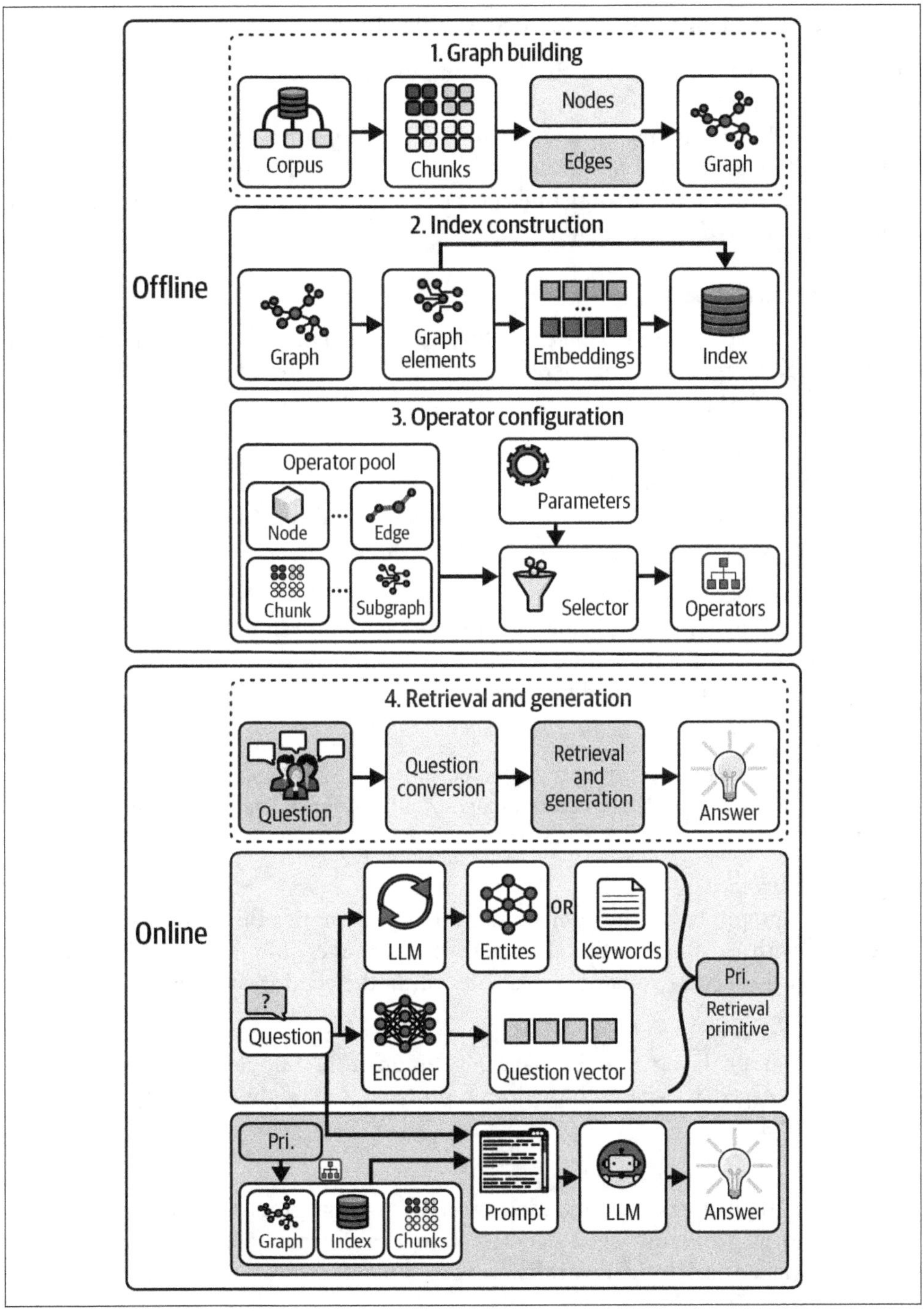


*Figure 3-1. Graph-based RAG systems (adapted from Zhou et al., 2026)*

## Building Versus Buying a GraphRAG System

Once you begin to understand the key components of a GraphRAG system, your immediate question might be: *When should I adopt an existing graph database, and when should I build graph capabilities in my own infrastructure?* It's important to understand the advantages and disadvantages of both building and buying, and the trade-offs made when you choose one approach or the other, as well as what tasks will remain, regardless of your decision.

### Factors to consider

You can use six criteria to evaluate whether to use a managed graph database (such as Neo4j, TigerGraph, Amazon Neptune, or FalkorDB) or build a custom implementation (such as PostgreSQL with Apache AGE, MongoDB, or another custom layer):

*Control and flexibility*
: Building a custom graph layer gives you full control over the design of your schema semantics, inference logic, and hybrid pipelines. A managed graph database will be constrained by vendor APIs and model types.

*Performance and scale*
: A custom build will be tunable to your workload but require engineering investment (sometimes significant). A managed solution will be highly optimized out of the box for traversals and reasoning.

*Operational complexity*
: Custom builds have high operational complexity, since you manage the indexes, storage, and scaling. Managed databases naturally have managed operations and support.

*Integration flexibility*
: Custom graph layers have maximum integration flexibility, allowing you to embed with existing relational systems or data lakes. Managed graph databases may constrain you to adapters available within the vendor ecosystem.

*Cost*
: Custom graph layers usually have higher up-front but lower recurring costs, while managed databases have lower up-front but higher ongoing license or usage costs.

*Use case*
: Custom graph layers are often ideal when knowledge graphs are part of a custom AI platform, while managed databases are ideal for analytics, recommendation, or knowledge enrichment workloads.

In practice, most enterprise teams begin with a managed graph database to validate data modeling and reasoning needs. They then may switch to custom graph implementations when they need deeper control over schema evolution, hybrid vector reasoning, or integration with proprietary AI systems.

#### What remains

As you read this chapter, you might wonder whether you actually need to understand the modeling and schema theory if you buy a solution like Neo4j or Neptune. This is a common point of confusion. Buying a graph database doesn't remove the need for modeling or structure design. It just means you're outsourcing the storage and query engine; you are still responsible for the semantic design or integration logic.

When you use a managed database, you get a graph storage and traversal engine that controls how nodes and edges are stored, queried, and indexed. You also get a query language runtime (such as Cypher, GSQL, or SPARQL) and tooling like dashboards, connectors, and APIs. However, a managed graph database does not provide you with your domain schema. For example, it will not provide the actual model of *Customer → Order → Product → Support ticket*. It also will not give you reasoning patterns such as the ones covered later in this chapter or integration logic around how the graph interacts with your data lake, CRM, or LLM pipelines. Finally, it will not provide ontology or vocabulary mapping, the layer of meaning that turns data into knowledge.

In other words, managed graph systems give you where and how to store relationships, but you still decide what those relationships mean and how to represent them. Even if you choose a managed graph database, you will design the schema, define the reasoning paths, structure the integration, and decide the ontology scope.

## Graph Data Models

Regardless of whether you adopt a managed solution or build a custom implementation, having a grasp on several relevant graph data models will help. After all, AI agents are only as intelligent as the knowledge structures you give them. When you build production-grade agentic systems, your first foundational challenge is to effectively represent knowledge. If your knowledge graph can't represent temporal sequences, your agent can't understand cause and effect. If it can't handle contradictory perspectives from different sources, it will either make arbitrary choices or break altogether. If it can't model its own capabilities and limitations, your agent will attempt unauthorized actions.

Graph-based knowledge representation fundamentally differs from the conventional storage paradigms you may currently use. Relational databases, document stores, and vector indexes excel at their specialized functions, but they all share a common limitation: they fragment knowledge into isolated records or embeddings that lack native relationship awareness.

Graph models overcome this limitation by directly encoding relationships as first-class elements within your data architecture. This approach creates a semantic foundation optimized specifically for the sophisticated reasoning processes that agentic systems require.

Consider how a typical enterprise knowledge domain contains complex, interconnected entities. A product connects to specifications, which link to manufacturing processes, which relate to supply chain dependencies, which impact financial projections. In conventional storage systems, these connections exist only implicitly (through foreign key relationships, for example), if at all. In graph structures, you explicitly model and leverage these relationships.

This section examines how graph-based knowledge structures transform static information into dynamic, semantically rich networks that mirror the complex relationships of your enterprise domains.

## Types of Graph Data Models

Knowledge graph modeling is about building a cognitive architecture for artificial intelligence, not just organizing data. Every decision—from representation choice to schema patterns to optimization strategies—should be evaluated based on whether it enables or constrains the reasoning capabilities your agents need.

Start with your reasoning requirements, not your data. First ask: *What kind of reasoning do my agents need to perform?* Formal *logical inference* (as in medical diagnosis systems) will require a different approach than network analysis and traversals, where speed matters more than inference, or complex events involving many entities (e.g., prescriptions, transactions, meetings). The representation you choose directly constrains what your agents can understand, so this decision shapes everything downstream.

Once you have determined your reasoning requirements, you can pick a graph model. The simplest approach is *labeled property graphs* (LPGs), which store nodes with properties connected by labeled edges. They're fast and intuitive, but they can only tell you what you've explicitly programmed. They work well for queries like *Find all customers who bought product X*, but they can't infer new knowledge on their own.

*Resource Description Framework* (RDF) takes a different approach, representing everything as subject-predicate-object triples with formal logical semantics. This enables native reasoning. For example, if you tell an RDF system *Disease1 causes Symptom1* and *Patient exhibits Symptom1*, it can automatically infer *Disease1 is a potential diagnosis* without you writing that logic. Unfortunately, this means that RDF is slower and more complex to work with.

*Hypergraphs* let you connect multiple entities in a single relationship (like a prescription linking doctor, patient, medication, dosage, date, and condition all at once), avoiding the artificial complexity of forcing everything into binary relationships.

## Evaluating Graph Models

Every knowledge representation decision you make must take into account the reasoning-representation trade-off (*https://oreil.ly/rfdFi*). Property graphs offer flexibility and performance advantages but lack the formal logical semantics required for sophisticated reasoning. RDF, on the other hand, provides formal logical semantics that enable native reasoning capabilities.

Consider an agent that is tasked with medical diagnosis encountering this simple knowledge:

> *Disease1 causes Symptom1*
> *Patient exhibits Symptom1*

A graph with proper reasoning capabilities would infer that *Disease1* is a potential diagnosis to consider. Using LPGs, you would need to explicitly code such inference patterns, whereas RDF-based systems would handle this natively through their built-in reasoning capabilities.

This distinction becomes crucial as your agent systems scale. The representation you choose directly affects your system's ability to make connections, discover insights, and reason accurately without explicitly programmed rules. To make this process easier, it's helpful to evaluate graph-modeling approaches across five critical implementation features. Let's look at each one.

### Formal reasoning

The first dimension to consider is *formal reasoning capabilities*. RDF excels in formal reasoning capabilities due to its strong semantic foundation. It supports complex ontological structures, enabling robust inference, consistency checking, and logical deduction. This makes it ideal for applications requiring high precision and explainability in their reasoning processes, such as semantic web applications and expert systems.

Property graphs, though excellent for capturing relationships, typically offer limited intrinsic support for formal reasoning. Reasoning often relies on application-level logic or external engines rather than the graph model itself. This can lead to less standardized and more ad hoc reasoning capabilities, which are suitable for use cases where explicit logical inference is not a primary requirement.

Hypergraphs offer better support for representing complex relationships as they can implicitly facilitate reasoning through the structure of hyperedges. Although not as formally rigorous as RDF, their ability to model multiway relationships can simplify certain types of inference, especially those involving more than two entities.

### N-ary relations

Knowledge graphs based on binary relations (*subject-predicate-object* triples) sometimes struggle to represent complex real-world relationships involving multiple entities. Consider this statement: *Dr. Smith prescribed 50 mg of medication X to patient Jones on Tuesday for condition Y*. This involves at least five entities in a single relationship. Forcing this into binary relations creates artificial complexity and loses the holistic nature of the event.

RDF inherently models binary relations through triples. To represent n-*ary relations* involving more than two entities requires a technique called *reification*, where the relation itself is treated as an entity with its own properties. While effective, reification adds complexity and can make querying less straightforward.

Property graphs can represent *n*-ary relations by introducing intermediate nodes that act as the relations themselves, with edges connecting a *relation node* to all participating entities. This approach is similar to reification and adds extra nodes and edges, potentially complicating the graph structure for certain queries.

Hypergraphs, in contrast, naturally support *n*-ary relations through hyperedges (Cagle, 2024, *https://oreil.ly/MaJjF*). A single *hyperedge* can connect any number of nodes, directly representing relationships involving multiple entities without auxiliary nodes or complex reification patterns. This makes hypergraphs highly intuitive and efficient for modeling complex, multiway interactions. Example 3-1 shows how you might represent complex interactions using a hypergraph model.

*Example 3-1. Hypergraph implementation*

```
# Representation of a prescription event as a hyperedge
prescription = HyperEdge(
    type="Prescription",
    nodes={
        "doctor": dr_smith,
        "patient": patient_jones,
        "medication": med_x,
        "dosage": "50mg",
        "date": tuesday,
        "condition": condition_y
    },
    attributes={
        "status": "active"
    }
)
```

This approach maintains semantic unity by connecting all entities in one structure. For your agentic systems, this dramatically simplifies reasoning about complex events and scenarios, since an agent can query all entities involved in a single relationship without traversing multiple edges, preserving contextual integrity.

### Performance

You'll next want to understand the impact of graph model choice on *performance*. RDF systems can experience performance challenges, especially with very large datasets and complex queries. The overhead associated with semantic reasoning, schema validation, and the triple-store architecture can lead to slower query execution than with other graph models. Optimization often requires specialized indexing and query planning.

Property graphs are generally recognized for their high performance, particularly in traversal-intensive operations. Their native graph storage and indexing, coupled with optimized algorithms for pathfinding and neighborhood exploration, make them very efficient for querying connected data. This makes them ideal for applications requiring rapid graph traversals and real-time analytics.

Hypergraphs offer moderate performance. While their ability to represent *n*-ary relations directly can simplify the graph structure and improve certain types of queries, the more complex data structures for hyperedges can sometimes introduce more overhead than with simple binary relations. Performance depends heavily on the specific hypergraph database implementation and query patterns.

### Tool ecosystem

Next, consider the wider tool ecosystem. The RDF ecosystem is mature but somewhat fragmented. It boasts a variety of tools for ontology editing, reasoning, and querying. However, the complexity of the standards can make the learning curve steep, and integration with other systems often requires custom development.

Property graphs benefit from a robust and rapidly growing tool ecosystem. Databases like Neo4j, Amazon Neptune, and ArangoDB offer comprehensive development environments, visualization tools, and integration capabilities. Their widespread adoption and active communities contribute to a rich set of libraries and frameworks, making development and deployment relatively straightforward.

The tool ecosystem for hypergraphs is considerably less mature than for property graphs or even RDF, and there are fewer commercial and open source database implementations, visualization tools, and community resources. This can pose challenges for development, which often requires more custom tooling and expertise.

### Constraint expressiveness

Finally, you'll want to consider the *constraint expressiveness* of each model. While RDF is strong in formal reasoning, it has limited direct support for expressing complex constraints beyond what can be inferred from the ontology itself. Web Ontology Language (OWL) can define classes, properties, and restrictions, but expressing procedural or intricate data integrity constraints often requires additional rule languages or application-level logic.

Property graphs generally provide limited constraint expressiveness natively. Although unique constraints on properties and relationships can be defined, expressing complex business rules, integrity checks, or conditional constraints typically requires application-level code or external validation frameworks.

Hypergraphs share similar limitations, focusing primarily on the structural representation of multiway relationships. Defining and enforcing complex data validation or business logic constraints usually falls to the application layer.

### Putting it all together

The choice of a knowledge graph model for an agentic system depends heavily on the application's requirements. RDF is best suited for scenarios that demand strong formal reasoning, semantic interoperability, and robust ontological representations, though it may suffer from performance trade-offs and complexity in handling *n*-ary relations. Property graphs are ideal for applications requiring high performance in graph traversals, flexible data modeling, and a rich tool ecosystem, though they lack strong native support for formal reasoning and complex constraints.

Hypergraphs shine when *n*-ary relations are central to the knowledge representation, offering a natural and efficient way to model complex interactions, though their ecosystem remains underdeveloped.

Ultimately, a hybrid approach combining elements from different models, or leveraging specialized tools for specific aspects (for example, a property graph for high-performance traversals combined with an RDF/OWL layer for formal reasoning), might offer the most robust solution for complex agentic system architectures.

For practical implementations today, consider these approaches:

*RDF-based with SHACL*
: Use standard RDF with Shapes Constraint Language (SHACL), a language for validating RDF graphs against a set of conditions, for formal reasoning with adequate constraint validation.

*Hybrid LPG-RDF*
: Maintain an LPG for performance-critical operations while keeping an RDF mapping for reasoning tasks.

*Enhanced property graph*
: Use a property graph with custom inference rules and validation logic.

*Knowledge graph database with hyperedge support*
: Use products like Stardog or specialized hypergraph databases that natively support *n*-ary relationships.

Organizations have also found success in implementing graph-like structures directly within PostgreSQL (*https://oreil.ly/L8EJQ*), eliminating the need for separate graph databases.

Example 3-2 is a simple PostgreSQL schema that lets you implement a knowledge graph without specialized graph databases. Each row represents a semantic relationship (subject-predicate-object) with a confidence score, striking a balance between conceptual structure and operational simplicity.

*Example 3-2. Graph model in PostgreSQL*

```
CREATE TABLE triples (
    subject_id TEXT,
    predicate TEXT,
    object_id TEXT,
    confidence FLOAT
);
```

For retrieval-focused systems where query patterns are relatively predictable, this PostgreSQL-based approach can significantly simplify infrastructure management. However, for agentic systems requiring sophisticated temporal reasoning, contradiction management, and incremental processing, dedicated graph architectures remain advantageous due to their native support for these capabilities.

### Open world, closed world, and agent safety

The comparison so far has weighed graph models on formal reasoning, performance, tool ecosystem, and constraint expressiveness. One more axis matters more for agentic systems than it has for any previous consumer of graph data: what the graph assumes about information that is not present in it.

RDF was designed around the *open-world assumption* (OWA), where a fact that is not in the graph is treated as unknown rather than false. Relational databases, most property graph stores, and anything built around schema-on-write follow the *closed-world assumption* (CWA), where absence means negation. Agents are the first large-scale consumer of graph data that routinely reason *from* absence (checking whether a deployment has an outstanding security exception or whether a patient has a contraindication to a drug), turning the distinction from a philosophical one into a safety concern. Under OWA, the answer to *Is there a contraindication?* is *unknown*, which is not a decision an agent can act on. Under CWA, the answer is *no*, which is such a decision.

The practical problem is that the two assumptions coexist inside a single graph system and switch between each other silently. The canonical example is a SPARQL (*https://oreil.ly/3xsEN*) query that opens an `OPTIONAL` block to bind a variable and then adds a `FILTER` that compares that variable to some value: solutions where the variable is unbound cause the filter expression to error, the engine drops them without warning, and the query has applied CWA semantics to an OWA dataset while advertising the opposite. Cagle (2026) (*https://oreil.ly/2qbWB*) identifies this collapse as one of several places the assumption shifts underneath production code. Named graphs act as implicit CWA scopes, property-path optimization drops the entailment that OWA reasoning depends on, and `OPTIONAL` + `FILTER` compositions silently narrow the result set. The takeaway is not that RDF is broken; it is that responsible design for agents means knowing which assumption governs each layer of the stack rather than trusting that the model advertised in the standards document is the one running at query time.

SHACL (*https://oreil.ly/vidsn*) is the W3C standard that makes the problem tractable. A SHACL *shape* specifies what a node of a given type must look like (which properties it must carry, how many values each property may take, what datatypes and values are permitted) and rejects nodes that do not match. Unlike OWL, which infers new facts, SHACL validates against a contract. The reason it matters for agents is a scope trick: SHACL 1.2 enforces CWA-style validation at the scope of a named graph while the underlying ontology continues to operate under OWA. Queries against the domain-level ontology preserve OWA semantics, and queries against a SHACL-validated named graph context can rely on CWA semantics safely because the shape registry guarantees the context is complete.

Three SHACL usage patterns address the three points at which an agent interacts with the graph:

*Pre-retrieval shapes*
: These validate that the entities a query targets carry the required structure before the agent trusts a result built from them. A shape on a `Service` node might require `:owningTeam`, `:deploymentTarget`, and a recent `:dependencyStatusTimestamp`, so a query that looks up a service runs only after the node has cleared validation.

*Pre-action shapes*
: These validate the preconditions that a tool requires before the agent invokes it. A `RollbackDeployment` tool might require its target to carry a `:rollbackApproved true` triple and a `:lastKnownGoodVersion` property; SHACL runs the check in milliseconds, and the tool call proceeds only if the shape matches.

*Post-write shapes*
: These validate anything the agent writes back to the graph before the transaction commits, so writer-agents become constrained writers rather than free-form updaters. A post-write shape on a new `CAUSED_BY` edge might require both endpoints to exist and the edge itself to carry provenance metadata.

Layered against the three-graph architecture introduced earlier in the chapter, the assumption map falls out cleanly. The *domain graph* runs under OWA because entities are incomplete by design and new relationships can always be added. The *lexical graph* runs under CWA per document because a document either contains a chunk or it does not. The *subject graph* is mixed: semantic relationships inherit OWA from the domain graph, and node-level constraints enforced by SHACL operate under CWA. Agents querying across the three layers need to know which layer they are in, and the shape registry is where that metadata belongs.

> If your agents both read from and write to the same graph, SHACL shapes are mandatory infrastructure, not optional quality tooling. Never use `OPTIONAL + FILTER` as a decision gate for an agent; use `ASK` with a SHACL prevalidation pass instead and record in your schema registry which named graphs run under OWA versus CWA.

### Graph structures

Graph rdata models reflect how information is represented, structured, and reasoned about inside the graph. They are schema-level or knowledge-representation frameworks defining how nodes, edges, and relationships behave and what kinds of queries and reasoning the system can support. Graph *structures* refer to the source and purpose of the content being represented as unstructured text is transformed into structured graph formats that you can efficiently traverse and query. Several graph structures have emerged, each offering different trade-offs between simplicity and expressiveness:

*Passage graphs*
: These are perhaps the simplest approach, where document chunks become nodes connected when they share common entities. This lightweight representation requires minimal processing but captures basic document-to-document relationships.

*Trees*
: Trees introduce hierarchical organization, creating multiresolution representations where higher-level nodes summarize their children. This structure allows your system to match queries at varying levels of detail, retrieving general concepts or specific facts as needed.

*Knowledge graphs*
: Knowledge graphs capture explicit semantic relationships between entities, following the subject-predicate-object pattern common in knowledge representation. These structures excel at supporting reasoning tasks but require more sophisticated extraction techniques.

*Textual knowledge graphs*
: These enhance standard knowledge graphs by attaching descriptive text to entities and relationships. This addition preserves contextual information that might otherwise be lost during the transformation from text to graph.

*Rich knowledge graphs*
: These graphs further extend this approach with additional metadata like entity types, relationship keywords, and edge weights. This rich representation supports nuanced reasoning but increases the complexity of both construction and querying.

Your choice of graph representation will significantly impact the capabilities and performance of your system. Simpler representations like passage graphs are easier to implement but provide less sophisticated reasoning capabilities. Richer representations like knowledge graphs enable more complex reasoning but require more sophisticated extraction and management. Most agentic systems will use some form of knowledge graph.

This section, though dense, laid important groundwork for understanding graph-based knowledge modeling in agentic systems that will help you as you move through this book. Understanding the four key components of GraphRAG systems (graph building, index construction, operator configuration, and retrieval and generation) will help you evaluate whether to build your own GraphRAG system or adopt an existing solution as you look at factors like control, performance, operational complexity, integration flexibility, cost, and use case.

Whether you build or buy, data modeling and schema design remain fundamental tasks regardless of your choice. Understanding graph data models like LPGs, RDF, and hypergraphs is important. Each model balances formal reasoning, *n*-ary relation handling, performance, tool ecosystem maturity, and constraint expressiveness. With this foundation, you'll then know how to use practical graph structures like passage graphs, trees, and rich knowledge graphs.

## Graph Design Principles for Agentic Systems

Building agentic systems requires giving agents a knowledge substrate that reflects how real-world information actually behaves: it is uncertain, contextual, temporal, multiperspectival, and continually evolving. This section traces the full stack of design principles and structures needed to support that kind of reasoning.

It begins with the three-graph architecture, which separates trusted domain knowledge, raw textual evidence, and extracted interpretations. This separation preserves provenance, prevents contamination of ground truth, and allows agents to maintain explicit awareness of uncertainty as they traverse from canonical entities to LLM-extracted facts and back to original source passages.

Once you have the right layers of knowledge, you must shape that knowledge using schema design patterns that reflect how agents reason. These patterns give structure to the cognitive operations agents must perform.

Finally, the section expands beyond data modeling to homoiconic knowledge representation, where schemas, rules, and operational logic live in the same graph as the data itself.

Together, these architectural, structural, and metastructural techniques form the cognitive foundation required for sophisticated, adaptive agent intelligence.

### The Three-Graph Architecture for Agent Knowledge

Graph design patterns begin with a foundational architecture pattern: *the three-graph model*. This architecture separates knowledge based on origin, certainty level, and semantic role, creating a robust foundation for agent reasoning under uncertainty.

Real-world agentic systems must integrate radically different data sources, such as structured, trusted data from CSV files and databases alongside unstructured, extracted data from documents and reviews. Attempting to merge these directly into a single graph creates serious problems. Unverified information pollutes trusted data, provenance to source documents is lost, extraction errors cascade through the entire graph, and validation of agent reasoning becomes impossible.

As you can see in Figure 3-2, the three-graph model solves these problems through architectural separation into domain, lexical, and subject graphs.

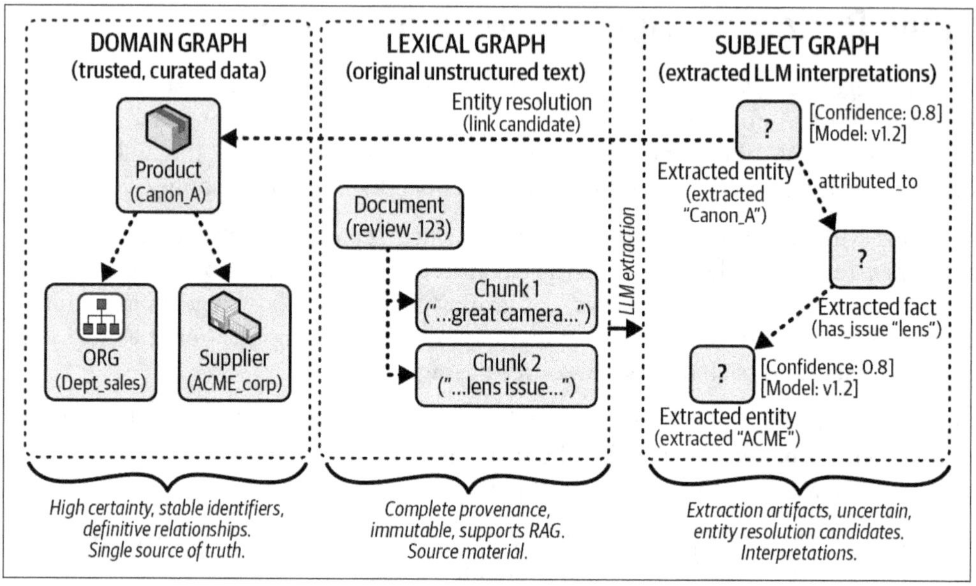


*Figure 3-2. The three-graph architecture for agent knowledge*

### Domain graph

The *domain graph* contains your trusted, curated, validated data as a single source of truth. It's typically built from structured sources that have undergone entity resolution. This is where your official entities live, such as the canonical list of products, the definitive organizational hierarchy, and the authoritative supplier relationships.

Key characteristics include high certainty (data validated through multiple sources), stable identifiers from entity resolution that persist over time, definitive relationships you can rely on for agent reasoning, and protection from contamination by unverified extractions.

### Lexical graph

The *lexical graph* holds your original unstructured text in structured format. When processing customer reviews, internal documents, or investigative reports, this graph preserves source material exactly as received.

Key characteristics include complete provenance (every text chunk links back to source document), immutability (the original text is never modified), enabling RAG (providing the "retrieval" in retrieval-augmented generation), and supporting verification (agents can cite specific passages to support claims).

The structure is straightforward. Document nodes contain metadata (such as file path, author, and date), chunk nodes contain text segments with embeddings for vector search, and relationships preserve document order and hierarchy.

### Subject graph

Finally, the *subject graph* is where the architecture's sophistication becomes clear. This graph contains entities and facts as extracted by LLMs from the lexical graph but, critically, keeps them separate from the domain graph until entity resolution establishes confident links.

Key characteristics include acknowledgment that these are extraction artifacts representing what the LLM interpreted. The uncertainty is acknowledged explicitly (these are interpretations, not ground truth), enabling entity resolution by providing candidates for linking to domain entities and maintaining extraction metadata like confidence scores, model versions, and timestamps.

### Why this architecture works

The critical operation making this architecture work is entity resolution that connects the subject graph to the domain graph. Consider a customer review mentioning *the Stockholm chair*. The system extracts a `Subject_Product` entity with this mention, finds potential matches in the domain graph using similarity search, calculates similarity between the extracted name and domain names, and creates `CORRESPONDS_TO` relationships for matches exceeding the confidence threshold.

This linkage enables powerful cross-graph queries: a query starts from a domain product, finds all customer-reported issues via subject entities, traces back to original review text in lexical chunks, and returns aggregated evidence with full provenance.

Your choice of graph data model affects how effectively you implement the three-graph architecture. LPGs naturally support the model through node labels and relationship types. The label system (`:Product:Domain` versus `:Product:Subject`) provides clear separation while allowing flexible queries. RDF models the architecture using separate named graphs for domain, subject, and lexical data with explicit cross-graph relationships in a mapping graph. This approach provides strong separation guarantees but makes cross-graph queries more complex. Hypergraphs can represent complex extraction relationships elegantly. A single hyperedge connects the extracted fact (subject graph), source chunk (lexical graph), resolved domain entities (domain graph), and metadata about the extraction, capturing the entire extraction context without artificial intermediate nodes.

> The three-graph architecture is a well-tested pattern used in production implementations where it handles billions of entities across structured and unstructured data sources. By maintaining clear boundaries while enabling precise linkage, it gives agents the foundation they need to reason reliably about uncertain, evolving knowledge.

#### Why this architecture matters for agents

The three-graph architecture enables sophisticated agent reasoning patterns that would be impossible with a single graph. For example, when querying, *What issues do customers report with our products?* agents can start from the domain graph (the official product list), traverse `CORRESPONDS_TO` links to the subject graph (extracted issues), and follow `EXTRACTED_FROM` links to the lexical graph (original review text). This traversal path maintains uncertainty levels, as agents know which information comes from trusted sources versus extraction.

The architecture also allows for better provenance and explainability. When presenting findings, agents can cite evidence with full traceability: the claim, confidence level based on mention count, specific review excerpts, and links to actual source chunks. Analysts can then audit agent reasoning by checking whether domain entities are correctly identified (entity resolution quality), verifying that extracted facts match source text (extraction quality), and reviewing which chunks the agent retrieved (retrieval quality).

As extraction models improve, you can re-extract the subject graph from the lexical graph, compare new extractions with old ones, and preserve the domain graph completely. Your trusted data remains unaffected.

> Implementation options range from physical separation (three separate graph databases) to logical separation (single database with node labels like `:Product` versus `:Subject_Product`) to schema namespacing (label prefixes like `:Domain_Product`). Start with logical separation for development, then migrate to schema namespacing for production to prevent accidental cross-contamination.

#### Multimodal knowledge graphs

The three-graph architecture scales to multimodal knowledge by assigning each graph a modality-specific role: the domain graph stores canonical multimodal entities, the lexical graph stores raw media chunks with per-modality embeddings, and the subject graph stores extracted cross-modal relationships. Cross-modal edges are first-class graph citizens, not ETL artifacts.

However, enterprise graphs have a modality problem. A product entity in a domain graph has a canonical text description, a CAD image, a spec table, and a sales call recording, but these are not separate systems. They are the same entity, just viewed through four modality lenses. A text-only graph loses three lenses.

A unified embedding space can help here as an enabling technology. Gemini Embedding 2 (*https://oreil.ly/Nlmhu*)'s unified embedding space places image, table, and text embeddings in the same high-dimensional space without per-modality fusion pipelines. This eliminates the architectural seam that made multimodal RAG expensive. Cross-modal retrieval becomes a single ANN query, not a pipeline with modality routers.

This can extend to all of the three graphs:

*Domain graph*
: The entity nodes carry modality metadata (such as `modality: image|table|audio|text`), and the canonical entity has cross-modal edges to all representations.

*Lexical graph*
: Per-chunk embeddings use modality-appropriate encoders but land in the unified space.

*Subject graph*
: The cross-modal relationships (e.g., `image_depicts -> entity`, `table_specifies -> property`) become typed edge classes.

Multimodal graph traversal requires modality-aware scoring. A text query may match an image node through shared embedding proximity, but the agent must know which modality it retrieved to generate a grounded response. Edge metadata carries modality provenance.

> When extending the three-graph architecture to multimodal, the domain graph entity nodes should carry a `modality` property. The lexical graph lands all modality embeddings in the unified space. The subject graph uses typed edge classes for cross-modal relationships. This keeps the architecture consistent while supporting image, table, audio, and text retrieval from a single ANN query.

## Schema Design Patterns

Effective agent reasoning begins with schema patterns explicitly designed to support machine cognition across temporal, contextual, and perspectival dimensions. This section examines several key schema patterns helpful in designing agentic systems.

### Event-centric pattern

Temporal reasoning forms a cornerstone of agent intelligence. The *event-centric pattern* structures knowledge around occurrences rather than static entities. Consider Example 3-3.

*Example 3-3. Event-centric pattern*

```
Event [type: Meeting]
|-- hasParticipant --> Person [id: Alice]
|-- hasParticipant --> Person [id: Bob]
|-- hasStartTime --> Timestamp [value: 2026-04-01T15:00:00Z]
|-- hasEndTime --> Timestamp [value: 2026-04-01T16:00:00Z]
|-- hasLocation --> Room [id: Conference-A]
|-- hasPrecedingEvent --> Event [id: Team-Standup]
|-- hasFollowingEvent --> Event [id: Project-Review]
```

The event-centric pattern shown in this code represents knowledge as interconnected temporal occurrences. Here, a `Meeting` event is modeled with multiple relationship types that capture temporal and contextual dimensions.

The example defines a `Meeting` event with two participants (`Alice` and `Bob`), precise start and end timestamps (April 1, 2023, 3:00–4:00 p.m.), a physical location (`Conference-A`), and temporal relationships to other events (preceded by a `Team-Standup` and followed by a `Project-Review`).

This structured approach enables agents to reason about temporal sequences, participation patterns, and cause-effect relationships. By modeling events as first-class entities with explicit temporal connections, agents can answer complex queries like *What meetings did Alice attend before the project review?* or *Which events occurred in conference room A during April 2023?* These capabilities would be difficult to achieve with entity-centric modeling alone.

This pattern enables temporal reasoning and causal analysis, which are critical capabilities for agent planning and explanation generation. By explicitly modeling event sequences, your agents can infer cause-effect relationships, identify temporal patterns, and reason about process dynamics.

### Contextual boundary pattern

Knowledge validity frequently depends on specific contextual parameters. The *contextual boundary pattern* explicitly encapsulates information within defined scopes, as shown in Example 3-4.

*Example 3-4. Contextual boundary pattern*

```
Context [type: Project-X]
|-- contains --> Task [id: Task-1]
|-- contains --> Task [id: Task-2]
|-- validDuring --> TimeRange [start: 2023-01-01, end: 2023-06-30]
|-- appliesTo --> Team [id: Engineering]
```

This example illustrates how contextual boundaries are represented. The code defines a `Context` entity (`Project-X`) that explicitly establishes boundaries around related information. The pattern shows the following:

- Containment relationships that group related tasks (`Task-1` and `Task-2`) within the project context
- Temporal boundaries through the `validDuring` relationship, indicating this context only applies during a specific time frame (January–June 2023)
- Organizational boundaries via the `appliesTo` relationship, limiting relevance to a particular team (`Engineering`)

This pattern is essential for preventing *context mixing*, a common source of reasoning errors in AI systems. By explicitly modeling contextual boundaries, agents can determine when certain facts or rules apply and when they don't. For instance, an agent could recognize that `Task-1` is relevant to the engineering team during the first half of 2023, but it wouldn't inappropriately apply that knowledge when reasoning about other teams or time periods. This compartmentalization enables more coherent and accurate reasoning within properly bounded knowledge domains.

#### Multiperspective pattern

Real-world knowledge often incorporates multiple, sometimes contradictory perspectives. The *multiperspective pattern* explicitly models these viewpoints, as shown in Example 3-5.

*Example 3-5. Multiperspective pattern*

```
Statement [id: Revenue-Forecast]
|-- hasValue --> Value [amount: 10M, currency: USD]
|-- according-to --> Perspective [source: Finance-Dept, confidence: 0.8]
|-- according-to --> Perspective [source: Sales-Dept,
|                                  value: 12M, confidence: 0.7]
```

This example demonstrates sophisticated handling of divergent information. The code models a `Revenue-Forecast` statement with differing perspectives from two departments. Rather than forcing a single "correct" value, the pattern explicitly represents:

- The base statement (`Revenue-Forecast`) and its primary value (`10M USD`)
- The finance department's (`Finance-Dept`) perspective with high confidence (`0.8`)
- The sales department's (`Sales-Dept`) differing perspective (`12M USD`) with slightly lower confidence (`0.7`)

This pattern transforms what would traditionally be a reasoning challenge into a structural advantage. By explicitly modeling contradictory information with attribution and confidence levels, agents can perform sophisticated reasoning about conflicting data. The agent can consider source authority, confidence scores, and contextual relevance when determining which perspective to prioritize in different scenarios.

This approach enables agents to handle real-world information complexity, where multiple valid perspectives might exist simultaneously. Rather than forcing artificial consistency, the pattern allows agents to reason about the nature of disagreements, consider multiple viewpoints, and make nuanced judgments based on relative confidence and authority of different sources.

### Capability model pattern

Self-aware agents must understand their own capabilities and limitations. The *capability model pattern* explicitly represents operational parameters, such as in Example 3-6.

*Example 3-6. The capability model pattern*

```
Agent [id: Customer-Support-Agent]
|-- hasCapability --> Capability [
    type: Answer-Product-Question,
    requires: Product-Knowledge,
    authorization-level: Public
]
|-- hasCapability --> Capability [
    type: Process-Refund,
    requires: Financial-System-Access,
    authorization-level: Supervisor,
    limit: 500-USD
]
```

This example shows how self-awareness can be structured. The code models a `Customer-Support-Agent` with explicitly defined capabilities and limitations. The `Answer-Product-Question` capability specifies the required knowledge domain (`Product-Knowledge`) and authorization level (`Public`), indicating that any agent instance can perform this action.

The `Process-Refund` capability defines more restrictive parameters: a specific system access requirement (`Financial-System-Access`), higher authorization level (`Supervisor`), and a quantitative limit (`500 USD`) capping the agent's authority.

Given explicitly modeled capabilities with their requirements and boundaries, agents can make informed decisions about what they can handle independently and when escalation is necessary. During planning, an agent can determine if it has the necessary access, authorization, and operational limits to fulfill a request before attempting it.

This transforms vague operational guidelines into concrete, queryable knowledge structures. For instance, when receiving a refund request for $600, the agent can immediately recognize this exceeds its authority limit and route the request appropriately instead of attempting a prohibited action—creating more reliable, trustworthy automation with appropriate human oversight.

> When implementing these schema patterns, consider using a hybrid approach that combines them as needed. For example, event-centric patterns can incorporate multiperspective elements to track different interpretations of the same event, while capability models can be bounded by contextual constraints.

Events, contextual boundaries, multiperspective statements, and capability models all make the same structural move: they take something that would naively be modeled as an edge or a property and promote it to a first-class node so that metadata, provenance, and temporal bounds can hang off it. That move has a name in the semantic web literature, *reification*, and it is the single feature that distinguishes a plain knowledge graph from what the industry has started calling a *context graph* (see "A Note on Context Graphs" on page 40 and the Zep architecture described by Rasmussen et al., 2025, *https://oreil.ly/JqsPE*). The patterns in this section are how reification shows up in day-to-day agent modeling. Chapter 4 picks up the temporal side of the same idea when it formalizes bitemporal memory.

## Homoiconic Knowledge Representation

Beyond schema patterns, agent-friendly knowledge graphs require *homoiconicity*, where code and data share the same representation. Homoiconicity enables agents to modify their own operational logic. This section examines two approaches to maintain homoiconicity: metaknowledge structures and executable knowledge patterns.

### Metaknowledge structures

In *metaknowledge structures*, you store knowledge about knowledge using the same graph structures as for the knowledge itself, as seen in Example 3-7.

*Example 3-7. Metaknowledge structure*

```
# Define a metaschema that describes the schema itself
metaschema = {
    "entities": [
        {
            "type": "EntityType",
            "properties": [
                {"name": "name", "type": "string", "required": true},
                {"name": "description", "type": "string"},
                {"name": "properties", "type": "list", "items": "PropertyDefinition"}
            ]
        }
    ]
}

# Now the schema and data use the same representation
knowledge_graph.add_entity("EntityType", {
    "name": "Person",
    "description": "A human individual",
    "properties": [
        {"name": "name", "type": "string", "required": true},
        {"name": "birth_date", "type": "date"},
        {"name": "occupation", "type": "string"}
    ]
})
```

This code illustrates metaknowledge structures that allow agents to reason about and modify their own knowledge representations using two key components. First, there is a metaschema definition that describes the schema itself:

- It defines what an `EntityType` is.
- It specifies that entity types have properties like `name` (required), `description`, and `properties`.
- The schema itself is represented as a data structure within the knowledge graph.

Then, the agent uses an application of this metaschema to create actual domain knowledge, using the same representation format to define a `Person` entity type, specifying its properties (`name`, `birth_date`, `occupation`). Note that the syntax and structure for both schema and data are identical.

This homoiconic approach is powerful for agent systems because it enables agents to inspect and modify their own knowledge structures using the same mechanisms they use for regular data. This means agents can reason about their own knowledge representation, dynamically update schemas as they learn new information, perform metareasoning about knowledge completeness and quality, and self-evolve their knowledge structures without external reprogramming.

Unlike traditional systems where schema and data are fundamentally different entities, this unified representation creates truly adaptable, self-aware agent architectures that can modify their own operational logic as circumstances change.

#### Executable knowledge patterns

To support procedural knowledge, Example 3-8 encodes operational rules within the graph structure itself as *executable knowledge patterns*.

*Example 3-8. Executable knowledge patterns*

```
# Define a rule directly in the knowledge graph
rule = knowledge_graph.add_entity("Rule", {
    "name": "DetermineCustomerSegment",
    "description": "Assigns customer segment based on purchase history",
    "condition": """
        MATCH (c:Customer)-[:PURCHASED]->(p:Product)
        WITH c, COUNT(p) as purchase_count
        RETURN c, purchase_count
    """,
    "action": """
        WHEN purchase_count > 20 THEN
            SET c.segment = 'Premium'
        WHEN purchase_count > 10 THEN
            SET c.segment = 'Regular'
        ELSE
            SET c.segment = 'Basic'
    """
})
```

This code showcases how business rules become first-class citizens in the knowledge graph using procedural knowledge and operational logic encoded directly within the knowledge graph structure. The example defines a customer segmentation rule with both declarative and executable components. The rule is created as an entity of type `Rule` with descriptive metadata (`name` and `description`). The `condition` component contains graph pattern–matching syntax that identifies customer-product purchase relationships in the graph, uses a graph query pattern to count purchases per customer, and returns the customer and their `purchase_count` for evaluation. Finally, the action component contains executable logic that implements a tiered segmentation strategy based on purchase history, assigning `Premium` status to customers with over 20 purchases, `Regular` status to customers with 10–20 purchases, and `Basic` status to all others.

This approach transforms traditionally implicit procedural knowledge (usually hidden in application code) into explicit, queryable knowledge structures. By representing rules within the same graph as domain data, agents gain remarkable capabilities. They can reason about the rules themselves, not just follow them. They can discover, modify, and create new rules dynamically. They can explain their decision-making process by referencing specific rules. They can adapt rule sets based on changing business requirements.

This pattern is fundamental for truly autonomous systems that need to understand not just what to do but why and how rules should be applied in different contexts.

Knowledge structures for agentic systems must facilitate sophisticated reasoning, contextual awareness, and self-modification. The three-graph architecture lets your agents maintain clear boundaries while enabling precise linkage to reason reliably about uncertain and evolving knowledge. Schema design patterns like the event-centric pattern, contextual boundary pattern, multiperspective pattern, and capability model pattern empower agents with temporal reasoning and the abilities to encapsulate information within defined scopes and handle conflicting viewpoints. Homoiconic knowledge representation through metaknowledge structures and executable knowledge patterns enables agents to reason about and modify their own knowledge and operational logic. Ultimately, these structures provide the cognitive foundation for sophisticated and adaptable agent intelligence.

# Integrating with Existing Systems

Few organizations build knowledge graphs from scratch. Most need to integrate existing taxonomies, ontologies, and data structures. When building your graph-based RAG system, you'll need to understand how to bring in these existing knowledge structures. This section digs into entity resolution and ontologies, cornerstones of data management crucial to understand in graph-based system construction.

Ontologies and entity resolution have traditionally been specialized disciplines, handled by knowledge engineers, information architects, and master data management teams. However, as organizations adopt AI platforms, graph-based RAG systems, and semantic layers that depend on accurate entities and well-structured relationships, ontologies and entity resolution have become central to how AI features actually work. These functions have shifted from back-office concerns to core platform capabilities that AI engineers must understand and configure directly. Modern knowledge engineers collaborate closely with AI and data engineering teams, while entity resolution is increasingly delivered as a platform capability that ML/AI engineers and domain teams configure rather than hand-build. The net effect is a shift from practicing niche disciplines to sharing responsibilities across the AI, data, and platform organizations. Thus, more engineers must understand the basics, even as specialists still guide deeper modeling and governance.

## Knowledge Organization and Ontology Fundamentals

An *ontology* is a form of knowledge organization. Nearly all enterprises must form some sort of *organizational vocabulary* in order to standardize terminology and understanding around institutional knowledge. Organizational vocabularies provide essential semantic foundations for agent knowledge graphs for several fundamental reasons:

*Semantic consistency*
: Without standardized vocabularies, the same concept might be represented with different terms across systems (e.g., *customer* versus *client* versus *patron*).

*Institutional knowledge preservation*
: Vocabularies encode organizational wisdom about entity relationships, domain hierarchies, and contextual meaning that has evolved over time.

*Governance and compliance*
: In regulated industries, specific terminology carries legal implications. Organizational vocabularies standardize terminology to ensure compliance.

All of these benefits to organizations also benefit agents. Semantic consistency ensures that agents recognize when references point to the same entity type, institutional knowledge is crucial for agent understanding, and standardized vocabularies ensure agents use terms correctly within their proper regulatory context. Organizational vocabularies also help with *cross-system integration*. Agents often need to reason across multiple systems, departments, and external data sources, and standardized vocabularies provide the translation layer that enables coherent cross-domain reasoning.

All of these capabilities add up to enhanced *reasoning reliability*. Agents perform logical inference based on relationship patterns. Inconsistent terminology creates false negative paths where relationships aren't recognized and false positive paths where unrelated concepts appear connected.

How do you actually organize and represent this organizational vocabulary? Let's look at knowledge organization systems to find out.

### The knowledge organization spectrum

Knowledge organization systems exist on a spectrum from simple to complex:

*Pick lists*
: These represent the simplest form—controlled value lists without hierarchical structure. Examples include country lists or currency codes.

*Taxonomies*
: These introduce parent-child hierarchical relationships with predefined terms and synonyms. For instance, *transportation* (parent) encompasses *bike*, *bus*, *car*, *truck*, *boat*, and *scooter* (children).

*Thesauruses*
: These extend taxonomies with richer structures, including parent-child hierarchies, predefined terms with synonyms, and generic associated relationships to other structural elements.

*Ontologies*
: The most sophisticated systems, these are graph or network structures describing combinations of classes with robust relationship descriptors, predefined classes and properties, expanded relationship types, scope notes for context, and inference capabilities.

The main advantage of ontologies is flexibility. Pick lists, taxonomies, and thesauruses require reorganizing entire hierarchies when introducing new instances. Ontologies, structured as networks of nodes and relationships, expand easily without structural disruption. This flexibility becomes essential as organizational knowledge systems scale and evolve.

### Ontology core components

Every ontology consists of five fundamental components:

*Classes*
: Collections of related objects, individuals, or instances that serve as the organizing metadata framework. In healthcare, classes might include `Person`, `Disease`, and `Test`. Classes can inherit attributes from parent classes, establishing hierarchical structure.

*Subclasses*
: Represent more specific categories within classes, inheriting parent properties. `Person` subdivides into `Patient` and `Oncologist`; `Disease` into `Cancer`, `Glioblastoma`, and `Medulloblastoma`; `Test` into `MRI` and `CT Scan`.

*Individuals (instances)*
: Specific examples of classes or subclasses as actual data records. `John Doe` represents an instance of `Patient`. From a machine perspective, inference becomes possible: `John Doe` is a `Patient` *and* a `Person`. If `Jane Smith` is an `Oncologist`, metadata automatically applies the title `Doctor`.

*Axioms*
: These codify domain truths, expressible in class attributes or relationships. They define rules and constraints. For example, `Cancer` is a subclass of `Disease`, since many diseases exist; different types of cancer are subclasses of `Cancer`. A patient can have at most one primary physician, medications have specific dosage information, and treatments have eligibility criteria.

*Relationships (object properties)*
: These convey meaning by connecting entities, defining how things interact. In healthcare, `personUtilizesFacility` (*patient → hospital*), `employsDoctor` (*hospital → primary care physician*), `testUsedForDisease` (*MRI → glioblastoma*), `diseaseHasSymptom` (*glioblastoma → headaches*), `doctorSpecializesIn` (*oncologist →* disease types).

These components work together to create semantic networks; connections without context provide no meaning, but relationships transform isolated data into actionable knowledge.

#### From access to context

Understanding why organizational ontologies matter requires recognizing a fundamental shift in enterprise challenges. Search engines and chatbots gave organizations instant access to information. However, the bottleneck is no longer in finding data but in providing context. Systems often contain accurate, high-quality data that remains unusable because the individual pieces aren't connected to reflect operational reality.

Context starts simply: *this click belonged to this person; this purchase closed that research journey; this entitlement applies to that product in this region*. When context exists, AI agents don't rely on averages or guesses. Instead, they act based on specifics about individual customers, products, and situations. This shift from access to context represents the fundamental value proposition of organizational ontologies: transforming accurate data into actionable intelligence.

Consider how marketing systems might capture a father and daughter's shared car research as independent events, then market to both individuals separately, wasting budget on duplicate efforts. The data was accurate, but the context was missing. An ontology mapping *household → person → research journey → purchase* enables systems to recognize these as connected events within a single conversion.

## Creating a Unified Semantic Foundation

Transforming disconnected terminologies into a unified semantic foundation prevents agents from operating with fragmented, contradictory understanding. This addresses what practitioners call "the machinery behind 360 views": the ontology makes customer views consistent across teams and systems, eliminating endless reconciliation efforts.

Consider this five-step process to build such a foundation:

1. *Inventory existing resources*
   Catalog all taxonomies, terminologies, and controlled vocabularies.
2. *Assess quality*
   Evaluate completeness, consistency, and currency.
3. *Normalize formats*
   Convert to standard formats like OWL and others.
4. *Align concepts*
   Establish mappings between overlapping terminologies.
5. *Enrich semantics*
   Add missing relationships and constraints.
6. *Publish as services*
   Make vocabularies accessible via APIs.

Example 3-9 uses the *Simple Knowledge Organization System* (SKOS) to map between different terminologies.

*Example 3-9. SKOS mapping*

```
# SKOS mapping between different terminology systems
:CompanyProduct skos:exactMatch orgVocab:Product .
:CompanyProduct skos:broader industryVocab:Offering .
:CompanyProduct skos:related financeVocab:Revenue_Source .
```

The code snippet demonstrates SKOS mappings that establish precise semantic relationships between terms across different vocabularies. The mapping `:CompanyProduct skos:exactMatch orgVocab:Product` establishes an equivalence relationship that allows agents to understand that different organizations are referring to the same concept, even when using different terminology. The `skos:broader` relationship identifies that a `CompanyProduct` is a more specific concept than an `industryVocab:Offering`, enabling agents to perform reasoning that respects taxonomic hierarchies. Finally, the `skos:related` mapping to `financeVocab:Revenue_Source` creates cross-domain connections, allowing agents to traverse between product information and financial concepts.

Without these controlled vocabulary mappings, your agent would treat identical concepts with different names as entirely separate entities, leading to knowledge fragmentation. Terms like *automobile*, *car*, and *vehicle* would exist as disconnected concepts rather than related entities in a semantic hierarchy.

These mappings transform isolated terminology islands into an interconnected semantic network, enabling agents to reason across organizational boundaries, integrate information from diverse sources, and maintain conceptual coherence despite terminology differences. This foundation is essential for agents that need to operate across multiple domains or integrate information from various enterprise systems.

### Enterprise ontology challenges and practical solutions

Consider clinical trial eligibility determination. Assessors manually navigate 80+ pages of eligibility criteria, taking hours per assessment. An ontology mapping *patient → encounters → vitals → lab results → insurance* enables agents to walk decision trees instantly, shifting response time from hours to seconds. The challenge isn't in enhancing LLM capability but in ensuring the consistent meaning of inputs.

This pattern applies across enterprise contexts. When organizations spin up 30 AI agents in a day, they face the question: Now what? When hiring 30 people, organizations provide playbooks, processes, clear definitions, escalation paths, and domain knowledge. Agents need this structure as well, but one that is more explicitly defined, because they don't bring domain intuition or expertise. The ontology becomes the playbook: Which entities exist in the business? How do entities connect? Where does authority live for each entity? What actions achieve outcome targets? What are the business rules and constraints? With this foundation, organizations can safely scale agents across marketing, sales, and service without reteaching each agent what a "customer" is or what qualifies a "lead."

### Merging multiple ontologies

Ontologies serve as the semantic backbone for sophisticated agent reasoning, but you may need to integrate multiple ontologies when building a graph-based agentic system. Real-world agents must reason across domains that no single ontology completely covers, requiring integration of specialized knowledge structures. In addition, different systems and data sources often use distinct ontologies. These independently developed ontologies often contain conflicting axioms or contradictory class definitions that must be harmonized to prevent reasoning errors. Without proper integration, agents cannot make connections between related concepts across boundaries.

Several techniques can be helpful when merging multiple ontologies. For example, *class hierarchy alignment* maps class hierarchies using semantic similarity. *Property alignment* establishes equivalence between properties with similar semantics, and *instance matching* links instances that represent the same real-world entities. Finally, *axiom harmonization* is used to resolve conflicts between logical axioms. Figure 3-3 illustrates these techniques.

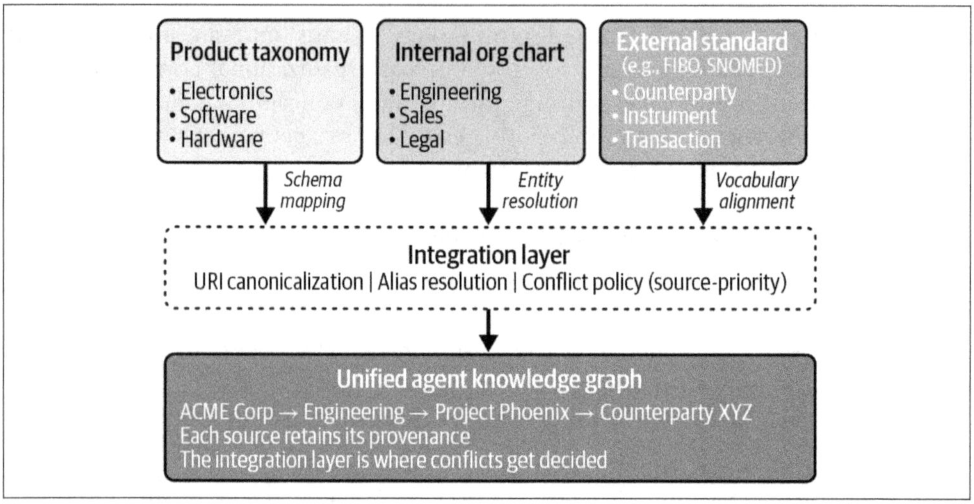


*Figure 3-3. Merging multiple ontologies into a unified agent knowledge graph*

Properly integrated ontologies enable richer cross-domain reasoning that would be impossible with isolated knowledge structures. Using integration approaches allows your system to incorporate new domain ontologies without a rebuild of the entire knowledge structure.

#### Annotating ontologies to control agent behavior

Traditional ontologies describe what exists in a domain—the entity types, their properties, and their relationships. But sophisticated agent systems require ontologies that go further: they must also encode how agents should interact with the knowledge graph. This transforms ontologies from passive schema descriptions into active control structures that can guide agent behavior without hard-coded logic.

The key insight is that behavioral annotations can be used within the ontology itself. Beyond stating that the `Artist` class has an `artist_name` property, you annotate that property as `identifying`—marking it as the unique key agents should use when looking up artists. Rather than just defining a `CREATED` relationship from `Artist` to `Artwork`, you annotate it as contextualizing, signaling that agents should traverse this relationship when gathering relevant context.

Consider an art gallery recommendation agent. When a user expresses interest in *Andy Warhol*, vector similarity search might match either an `Artist` node or a `Subject` node (works about Warhol). Without behavioral annotations, you'd have to write entity-specific code for each type. With annotated ontologies, the agent queries the ontology itself: *What property identifies this entity?* and *Which relationships provide context?* Finding an `Artist` node, the ontology responds with `artist_name` and `CREATED` relationships. The agent executes these instructions dynamically, adapting to whatever entity type appears. The same tools work across healthcare (`Patient` identified by `patient_id`, contextualized through `DIAGNOSED_WITH`) or supply chain (`Product` identified by `sku`, contextualized through `SUPPLIED_BY`) without code changes.

This approach also enables selective traversal. Some relationships carry immediate contextual value for agent reasoning, while others serve different purposes. In a museum catalog, the `CREATED` relationship from `Artist` to `Artwork` provides essential context for recommendations. But the `BROADER` relationship between `Subject` nodes, which organizes topics into taxonomies, typically shouldn't be traversed automatically during contextualization—it serves navigational purposes rather than contextual enrichment.

By marking relationships as contextualizing or noncontextualizing, you give agents precise guidance about graph traversal without writing traversal algorithms. The ontology becomes a declarative specification of agent behavior. Want to change how agents contextualize information? Update the ontology annotations, not the agent code.

The implications for organizational knowledge graphs are profound. Rather than building separate agents for each domain with custom logic for each schema, you build generic agent capabilities that consult domain-specific ontologies. The ontology tells agents what entities exist, how to identify them, and how to gather context. This architectural approach enables rapid deployment of agents across multiple business domains while maintaining consistent, predictable behavior.

This approach enables modifiability (update annotations, not code), reusability (use the same tools across domains), explainability (decisions trace to explicit definitions), and domain adaptation (deploy to new graphs by providing ontologies).

The practice transforms agents from brittle, domain-specific implementations into flexible, adaptable systems. The ontology becomes not just a data model but an agent instruction manual, encoding both what the domain contains and how agents should navigate it.

### Upper ontologies

While integrating existing organizational knowledge structures, you'll inevitably encounter ontologies built using traditional languages like OWL. Understanding their capabilities and limitations is crucial for developing truly effective agentic systems.

OWL-based ontologies offer formal logic foundations but present limitations for agentic systems: an atomic subject-predicate-object structure complicates *n*-ary relationships (prescriptions involving doctor, patient, medication, dosage, condition), first-order logic limits higher-order reasoning (sets of sets, metarelationships), and blending data modeling with logic reasoning creates conceptual tensions. Example 3-10 is a simple OWL representation of a medical prescription event.

*Example 3-10. OWL representation*

```
:prescription123 a :Prescription ;
    :hasPrescriber :drSmith ;
    :hasPatient :patientJones ;
    :hasMedication :medicationX ;
    :hasDosage "50mg" ;
    :hasDate :tuesday ;
    :hasCondition :conditionY .
```

While this approach works for basic scenarios, it faces challenges when addressing more complex semantic relationships or higher-order structures needed for sophisticated agent reasoning.

As knowledge graphs evolve, it becomes necessary to manage two change types: data change (structure remains stable while sources refresh) and ontology change (entities and relationships are added as metadata).

Using upper ontologies like *Basic Formal Ontology* (BFO) or DOLCE (*https://oreil.ly/9ynct*) as integration points can provide a more stable semantic foundation, as Example 3-11 shows.

*Example 3-11. BFO example*

```
# Using BFO as an upper ontology integration point
:Person rdfs:subClassOf bfo:Object .
:Event rdfs:subClassOf bfo:Process .
:Location rdfs:subClassOf bfo:SpatialRegion .
```

This code demonstrates the *foundational anchoring* approach to ontology integration using BFO as a semantic bridge. The snippet shows three critical alignments:

- It maps the domain-specific concept `:Person` as a subclass of BFO's `Object` category, establishing that entities in the local ontology are continuants that maintain identity over time.
- It classifies `:Event` as a subclass of BFO's `Process` category, indicating that events are occurrences that unfold over time with temporal parts.
- It defines `:Location` as a subclass of BFO's `SpatialRegion` category, specifying that locations represent spatial dimensions rather than material entities.

By anchoring domain-specific concepts to these foundational categories, the system creates a consistent ontological framework where concepts from different domains with similar BFO mappings can be related, even if they were developed independently. This upper ontology approach provides standard integration points that preserve meaning across domain boundaries while enabling sophisticated cross-domain reasoning.

#### Iterative ontology creation with AI assistance

Modern workflows leverage AI agents to accelerate ontology development while maintaining quality through human oversight. Agents perform initial entity identification from sample data, validate structural requirements (relationships reference existing nodes, property names are unique, entities have identifying properties), and generate visualizations for expert review. Domain experts provide conceptual refinement while agents handle mechanical validation and format conversion, producing higher-quality ontologies in days rather than months.

## Entity Resolution: The Foundation of Agent Knowledge

Where ontologies create the structure of the knowledge, *entity resolution* determines when different data records refer to the same real-world entity. While this might sound like a technical data-cleaning task, it's actually the cornerstone that enables agents to maintain coherent understanding across fragmented organizational knowledge. In fact, Forrester's 2025 "Total Economic Impact study of Senzing" (*https://oreil.ly/8s5L1*), an entity resolution software developer kit (SDK), found that entity resolution begins delivering payback in less than six months, a 226% return on investment over three years, and a 95% reduction in time to add new data sources. For agentic systems, this translates to faster agent deployment, higher agent reliability, and better human trust through explainable reasoning.

Consider the scale of the problem that entity resolution is meant to solve. As an example, financial crimes cause trillions of dollars in loss annually, yet investigators struggle with a fundamental question: Is the *Bob Smith* in this transaction the same person as *Robert Smith Jr.* opening an account across town? For human analysts, making these connections requires weeks of manual investigation. For AI agents reasoning about organizational knowledge, these identity questions become existential. If the agent cannot determine when two references point to the same entity, its entire reasoning framework collapses.

### Why traditional approaches fail

Identity information fragments naturally across enterprise systems. As demonstrated in the Connected Data London 2025 Masterclass framework (*https://oreil.ly/AA4pV*), your CRM has customer contact information, your billing system has payment details, and your support platform contains interaction history. Each system uses different identifiers, formats dates differently, and handles name variations inconsistently. This fragmentation creates real consequences: mortgage loans denied, insurance claims rejected, ballots voided, tax filings miscredited. When mistakes happen, people are harmed, and organizations end up in court.

For agentic systems, the stakes are equally high. An agent making procurement recommendations needs to know that *Acme Corp*, *Acme Corporation*, and *ACME Co., Ltd* all refer to the same supplier. Without this capability, agents cannot maintain the coherent worldview that sophisticated reasoning requires.

The challenge intensifies when adversaries actively work to defeat entity resolution. In antifraud domains, *channel separation* is a primary tradecraft of bad actors. Consider the following realistic scenario from financial crime investigations.

A known money launderer appears as *Bob Smith* at 123 Main Street. The same individual opens an account as *Bob R. Smith II* at the same address with slightly different phone formatting. They apply for employment as *Robert Smith Jr.* at a different address but with overlapping contact information. Each appearance uses strategic variations such as name formats, address representations, date formats, and phone number conventions designed to pass simple filters while appearing distinct.

Simple string matching fails catastrophically here. Fuzzy matching on individual attributes often fails because variations are intentionally designed to evade detection. What's needed is *channel consolidation*, connecting fragmented identities based on evidence from multiple overlapping features. That's the advantage of evidence-based resolution, the subject of the next section.

### Evidence-based resolution versus generalization-based AI

Understanding entity resolution's role requires examining a fundamental distinction in how AI systems reason. This distinction matters profoundly for applications involving identity, compliance, and high-stakes decisions.

In *generalization-based reasoning* (typical of LLMs), the system learns patterns from training data and generalizes to new situations. When asked *Are these two records the same person?*, an LLM considers statistical patterns learned from examples. It might respond *These seem like the same person because the names are similar and they share an address.* The confidence comes from statistical regularities, not specific evidence.

This approach has serious limitations for entity resolution: decisions are nondeterministic, explanations are post hoc rationalizations, cultural variations break down on non-Western names, and confidence scores don't reflect actual accuracy.

With *evidence-based reasoning* (entity resolution), the system examines specific features from data records, applies domain-specific matching rules, and builds a case based on concrete evidence. The system can explain its conclusions like this: *These records match with 89% confidence because NAME matched at 87%, ADDRESS matched at 100%, and PHONE matched at 95%.*

This type of reasoning makes agentic systems more deterministic (the same input produces the same output), explainable (every match includes specific evidence), culturally robust (explicit rules handle Arabic, Chinese, Russian, etc. naming conventions), and confident (scores reflect actual match accuracy).

When determining whether two records represent the same person for fraud investigation purposes, what matters is evidence, not whether an LLM's statistical patterns suggest similarity.

#### Entity resolution as graph building blocks

Entity resolution generates the fundamental components of agent knowledge graphs:

*Entities (nodes)*
: Each resolved entity becomes a node with a stable identifier that persists even as new records are added or corrected. This stability is critical for agent memory so that agents maintain consistent references to entities over time.

*Relations (edges)*
: Entity resolution systems identify several relationship types: `RESOLVED` (strong matches indicating records refer to the same entity), `POSSIBLY_RELATED` (weaker evidence of connection), and `DISCLOSED` (known relationships from data). These relationship types support different reasoning patterns. An agent investigating fraud might traverse `RESOLVED` edges to find all aliases, then follow `POSSIBLY_RELATED` edges to discover associates.

*Properties*
: The resolved entity aggregates properties from all contributing records, giving agents access to all known information even when it was originally fragmented across systems.

*Evidence metadata*
: Critically, entity resolution systems preserve evidence for each match decision, such as which features drove the match, their individual scores, and confidence

levels. This metadata enables explainable AI. When an agent makes a decision based on entity connections, it can cite the specific evidence that established those connections.

#### Edge cases

Production entity resolution systems must handle nuanced cases that simple approaches miss.

For example, you may have very different texts referring to the same entity. The names *al-Hajj Abdullah Qardash* and *Abu Abdullah Qardash bin Amir* appear dramatically different as strings. Yet sophisticated systems recognize common patterns—honorifics, shared name components, and Arabic naming conventions—to correctly identify these as the same person with 89% confidence.

You may also encounter nearly identical text referring to different entities. *John R Smith* and *John E Smith* differ by only a single letter. Yet this difference is significant—they are potentially father and son or simply unrelated individuals. Without additional evidence, a system should be cautious about merging them.

Finally, you may see very different addresses referring to the same location. The addresses *#03-28, 400 Orchard Road, 238875 SNG* and *400 Orchard Tower #03-28 Orchard Rd, Singapore 238875 Singapore* look completely different as strings but reference the same location. Systems must parse address components and normalize variations while understanding cultural formatting conventions.

These edge cases illustrate why entity resolution requires domain expertise, cultural knowledge, and sophisticated algorithms. They also reveal why this capability is foundational for agent knowledge graphs. Without it, the graph will either conflate distinct entities or fragment single entities, with either error undermining agent reasoning.

> Modern entity resolution platforms like Senzing follow a "JSON in, JSON out" architecture, making integration straightforward. The system maintains a persistent entity graph internally, automatically resolving new records against existing entities. Your agent's knowledge graph references resolved entities with stable identifiers, gaining unified, disambiguated identities without implementing complex matching logic.

You now possess the essential theoretical and practical knowledge for building a robust, intelligent foundation for graph-based agentic systems. Let's now explore how to build your knowledge graph.

## Building the Knowledge Graph

A knowledge graph is only as valuable as the information it contains. For agentic systems, the knowledge acquisition pipeline must be designed to continuously ingest, validate, and integrate new information while maintaining quality and coherence. This section reviews techniques for three stages of the knowledge acquisition pipeline: extraction, entity resolution, and validation.

### Extraction Approaches for Heterogeneous Sources

Agents require knowledge from diverse sources: structured databases, semistructured documents, unstructured text, and even multimodal content. Each source requires specific extraction strategies. This section examines structured and unstructured data ingestion, as well as two frameworks for LLM-based knowledge graph construction.

#### Structured database integration

When incorporating existing relational or NoSQL databases, consider these approaches:

*Graph materialization*
: Transform database content into actual graph nodes and edges, either through batch processes or change data capture (CDC) streams.

*Virtual graph views*
: Create mapping layers that expose relational data as virtual graph structures without physical duplication.

*Hybrid materialization*
: Materialize frequently used information while dynamically mapping less common patterns.

Example 3-12 uses Neo4j's APOC library (*https://oreil.ly/enevI*) to import from a relational database.

*Example 3-12. Neo4j APOC library*

```
# Using Neo4j's APOC library to import from a relational database
CALL apoc.load.jdbc("jdbc:mysql://localhost:3306/customer_db",
    "SELECT * FROM customers")
YIELD row
CREATE (c:Customer {id: row.customer_id, name: row.name, email: row.email})
```

### LLM-based extraction from unstructured text

LLMs excel at extracting structured information from unstructured text. For agentic systems, you can implement a pattern like Example 3-13.

*Example 3-13. Extraction of unstructured text*

```
def extract_knowledge_triples(text, domain_ontology):
    """Extract subject-predicate-object triples from text using LLM."""
    prompt = f"""
    Extract knowledge triples from the following text.
    Use only predicates from the domain ontology: {domain_ontology.predicates}
    Format: [(subject, predicate, object), ...]
    Text: {text}
    """

    llm_response = call_llm_with_structured_output(prompt,
                                                   output_format='json',
                                                   schema=TRIPLE_SCHEMA)

    validation_results = validate_against_ontology(llm_response.triples,
                                                   domain_ontology)

    return validation_results.valid_triples
```

The `extract_knowledge_triples` function constrains LLM extraction to predicates defined in the domain ontology, ensuring consistency with the knowledge graph's semantic structure. The function constructs a formatted prompt, applies structured output validation, and filters results against ontological constraints. Production enhancements include extraction templates, multistage pipelines, confidence scoring, and human-in-the-loop (HITL) verification for low-confidence extractions.

### LLM-based knowledge graph construction frameworks

Building upon the extraction techniques we've explored, recent innovations have introduced end-to-end frameworks specifically designed for constructing knowledge graphs using LLMs. These frameworks address several challenges, particularly around entity disambiguation, schema flexibility, and cross-document knowledge integration.

**The incremental approach: iText2KG.** The iText2KG framework (*https://oreil.ly/BiCBs*) (now enhanced as ATOM, discussed in "Temporal dynamics: ATOM" on page 98) represents an innovative method for incremental, topic-independent knowledge graph construction without the need for postprocessing. Unlike batch-oriented approaches, iText2KG enables continuous updating and expansion of knowledge graphs as new information becomes available. The system also operates without domain-specific schemas, making it adaptable across various subject areas. Finally, advanced disambiguation techniques ensure that each entity and relation maintains semantic distinctiveness. Example 3-14 uses an iText2KG modular pipeline for entity extraction and disambiguation.

*Example 3-14. iText2KG implementation*

```
def extract_entities_for_all_sections(self, sections: List[str], ent_threshold=0.8):
    all_entities = []
    for section in sections:
        # Extract entities from the current section
        section_entities = self.ientities_extractor.extract_entities(context=section)

        # Perform entity disambiguation
        if all_entities:
            # Compare with previously extracted entities
            all_entities = self.matcher.process_lists(
                all_entities, section_entities, "entity", ent_threshold
            )
        else:
            all_entities = section_entities

    return all_entities
```

This function incrementally builds a consistent entity set across document sections. By comparing new entities with previously extracted ones using a similarity threshold, it maintains semantic uniqueness while avoiding duplication.

**Document-level extraction: RAKG.** Whereas iText2KG focuses on incremental construction, the Document-level Retrieval Augmented Knowledge Graph Construction (RAKG) framework (*https://oreil.ly/KbNNA*) takes a different approach, addressing the limitations of traditional sentence-level extraction. RAKG introduces several novel concepts. It uses intermediate representation units that simplify entity disambiguation and address LLM context limitations, and it gathers all text segments where an entity appears, providing comprehensive contextual information. It also maintains consistency with existing knowledge by retrieving relevant subgraphs and assessing the quality of LLM-generated relationships, filtering out hallucinations.

Example 3-15 uses the RAKG retrieval augmentation process for relationship extraction.

*Example 3-15. RAKG implementation*

```
def extract_relations(self, entity, retrieverVT, retrieverVkg):
    # Retrieve all text segments mentioning the entity
    text_segments = retrieverVT(entity)

    # Retrieve similar entities from existing knowledge graph
```

```
    related_subgraphs = retrieverVkg(entity)

    # Generate relationships using LLM with retrieved context
    return self.llm_rel(entity, text_segments, related_subgraphs)
```

This function gets comprehensive entity context by retrieving all relevant text mentions and existing graph relationships before generating new connections. This document-level approach reduces hallucination by providing broader context to the LLM.

Performance evaluations show that these approaches significantly outperform traditional methods. RAKG demonstrates superior performance (*https://oreil.ly/KiBPL*) with approximately 96% accuracy, 88% entity coverage, and 95% relationship fidelity, outperforming both traditional Knowledge Graph Conference (KGC) and iText2KG methods. Higher relationship fidelity scores are particularly significant for agentic systems that rely on connection patterns for reasoning. These benchmarks highlight how reasoning-enhanced extraction techniques can significantly improve knowledge graph quality for agent applications.

**Temporal dynamics: ATOM.** While iText2KG and RAKG excel at static knowledge extraction, the ATOM (AdapTive and OptiMized) dynamic temporal knowledge graph construction framework (Lairgi, 2026, *https://oreil.ly/0-ZZz*) addresses a critical limitation: the temporal dimension of knowledge. Many extraction approaches struggle with two fundamental challenges. First, LLMs exhibit a "forgetting effect" where relationship extraction deteriorates significantly as context length increases. This is particularly problematic for extracting temporal information from longer documents. Second, existing methods conflate observation time (when information was recorded) with validity periods (when facts actually occurred), preventing the accurate temporal reasoning that is essential for agent memory and historical analysis.

ATOM introduces atomic fact decomposition as its core innovation. Rather than processing entire documents or lengthy paragraphs, the system decomposes text into minimal, self-contained atomic facts—single statements that each convey exactly one piece of information. Empirical evaluation has determined that maintaining chunk sizes below 400 tokens preserves extraction exhaustivity above 0.8, addressing the forgetting effect while maintaining semantic coherence.

The framework employs a three-module parallel architecture optimized for scalability:

*Atomic fact decomposition*
: Documents are split into atomic facts through LLM-guided extraction with careful attention to preserving temporal expressions. Each atomic fact is designed to be understood independently, eliminating the ambiguity that causes extraction errors in longer contexts.

*Parallel 5-tuple extraction*
: Rather than separating entity and relation extraction (requiring multiple LLM calls), ATOM directly extracts complete temporal 5-tuples (`subject`, `predicate`, `object`, `t_start`, `t_end`) from each atomic fact in a single pass. Critically, the system performs temporal preprocessing during extraction, transforming end-validity statements into affirmative counterparts. For example, *John Doe is no longer CEO on 01-01-2026* becomes `(John_Doe, is_ceo, X, [.], [01-01-2026])`, enabling subsequent LLM-independent temporal resolution.

*LLM-independent merge*
: Atomic temporal knowledge graphs are merged using distance metric–based entity and relation resolution rather than expensive LLM calls. The parallel merge algorithm employs iterative pairwise merging in a binary tree structure, reducing merge complexity to $O(\log N)$ rounds. Temporal resolution extends validity period histories as new observations arrive, tracking how knowledge evolves over time.

ATOM's distinguishing feature is *dual-time modeling*, which allows it to maintain separate observation timestamps and validity periods for each fact. Consider a news article published January 23, 2020, stating that *The virus spread to 10 countries*. The observation time records when this information became known (January 23), while the validity period captures when the spread actually occurred (potentially days earlier). This distinction prevents the temporal misattribution that plagues single-timestamp approaches and enables agents to reason about the difference between "when we learned it" versus "when it happened."

Performance evaluations on the COVID-19 temporal dataset demonstrate ATOM's advantages. The framework achieves approximately 31% improvement in factual exhaustivity and 18% improvement in temporal exhaustivity compared to baseline methods processing full paragraphs. Stability across multiple runs improves by 17%, addressing the nondeterministic output problem common in LLM-based extraction. Perhaps most significantly for production deployment, ATOM reduces latency by over 93% compared to existing temporal knowledge graph construction methods through its parallel architecture and LLM-independent merging strategy.

For agentic systems requiring dynamic knowledge bases, such as those tracking evolving situations, maintaining agent memory over extended interactions, or reasoning about temporal causality, ATOM's combination of temporal precision, extraction reliability, and scalable architecture makes continuous knowledge graph updates practical. The framework's ability to track observation history alongside fact validity enables agents to distinguish between certain knowledge and evolving information, supporting more nuanced reasoning about uncertainty and change over time.

## Automating Knowledge Graph Construction with Multi-Agent Systems

Large-scale knowledge graph construction can leverage multi-agent pipelines following the proposer-approver pattern, where specialized agents analyze data, propose schemas, and execute construction with human oversight at critical checkpoints; this is documented in a DeepLearning.AI lecture (*https://oreil.ly/-aE3h*).

The pipeline architecture includes:

*Intent clarification*
: Transforming vague goals into structured objectives

*File discovery*
: Identifying and proposing relevant data sources

*Schema proposal*
: Inferring nodes, relationships, and properties from structured or unstructured data using proposer-critic validation

*Deterministic construction*
: Executing approved schemas through rule-based processes

Information flows through persistent session state, enabling agents to share context without re-asking users. Human approval gates ensure quality control before expensive execution while building trust and maintaining flexibility for course correction.

Current limitations include how it handles ambiguity (when similar terms require context-aware extraction), complex schema inferences (those requiring domain-specific models), and entity resolution accuracy (addressed through hybrid approaches combining embeddings with string similarity).

## Entity Resolution and Linking Across Graphs

*Entity linking* connects entities extracted from unstructured text (subject graph) to trusted entities in structured data (domain graph), creating `CORRESPONDS_TO` relationships that integrate the three-graph architecture.

### The entity linking challenge

Subject entities lack the identifiers and complete attributes of domain entities. For example, `Subject_Product(name="the Stockholm chair")` must link to `Product (product_id="PROD_12345", product_name="Stockholm Chair")` despite text differences, attribute mismatches, and extraction uncertainty.

#### Three-stage linking pipeline

Production-grade entity linking progressively narrows from candidates to confident matches:

*Property key correlation*
: Normalizes different property names to map concepts (removing prefixes, handling case variations: `"product_name"` → `"name"`).

*Value similarity matching*
: Compares actual values using Jaro-Winkler distance (0.0–1.0 scores handling typos and prefix matching). Threshold selection balances precision and recall: 0.95 for high-stakes applications, 0.85 as recommended default, 0.75 for exploratory analysis.

*Context-aware validation*
: Uses graph neighborhood patterns to validate matches through co-occurrence patterns (do both entities appear with the same related entities?), temporal consistency (do review dates align with product availability?), and cross-entity validation (do multiple links form coherent patterns?). Subject and domain neighborhoods naturally differ due to different graph layers, so focus validation on temporal alignment and structural coherence rather than exact neighborhood matching.

#### Quality metrics and edge cases

Measure linking rate (target >75%), average confidence (target >0.85), ambiguous subjects (target <5%), and coverage. Handle unmatched entities by reviewing high-mention unlinked subjects to identify catalog gaps, disambiguate vague mentions using context and temporal alignment, and add type validation to prevent false positives between similar entities.

## Knowledge Representation in Practice: DevOps Agent

To demonstrate how graph-based knowledge modeling enables sophisticated agent reasoning, let's examine a DevOps agent that must understand complex cloud infrastructure environments. This example will illustrate how the theoretical concepts explored throughout this chapter translate into a practical system. The remaining chapters will build upon this foundation and add memory systems, reasoning capabilities, and tool orchestration.

This example draws from real-world implementations, particularly the approach taken by AnyShift (*https://oreil.ly/DEdk8*), a startup building AI-powered site reliability engineering systems. AnyShift reconciles cloud APIs (AWS, GCP, Azure), Kubernetes, Terraform state, Git repositories, and observability platforms into a time-versioned knowledge graph where resources are nodes and relationships (dependencies, ownership, deployments) are edges. Although we'll simplify certain aspects for pedagogical clarity, the core principles and patterns reflect production requirements for DevOps automation.

## Context Engineering for DevOps Automation

*Context engineering*, or providing LLMs with accurate, structured data about operational environments, determines whether agents generate valid, executable infrastructure code or plausible-sounding nonsense. Without awareness of actual cloud state, LLMs generate Terraform code referencing `vpc-123abc`, a hardcoded identifier that doesn't exist. With graph-based context from Terraform state and live cloud data, the same LLM generates code referencing `data.terraform_remote_state.vpc.outputs.vpc_id`, pulling actual infrastructure identifiers.

The DevOps domain exemplifies why graph-based context engineering is essential. Infrastructure forms dependency chains where load balancers route to target groups, which connect to EC2 instances, which assume identify and access management (IAM) roles, which access databases. Graph-based context enables agents to trace dependencies across multiple hops, isolate configuration drift, and understand blast radius of proposed changes. Our goal is to build a queryable digital twin that provides the structured context necessary for sophisticated reasoning about every service, resource, and dependency.

## The DevOps Knowledge Representation Challenge

DevOps environments exemplify graph-based modeling requirements: production systems comprising hundreds of EC2 instances, microservices, databases, load balancers, security groups, and IAM policies form dependency chains where services rely on compute instances residing in subnets, protected by security groups, and accessing databases through IAM roles. Configuration spans Terraform modules, CI/CD pipelines, Jira tickets, and observability tools. Graph-based knowledge representation captures this web of relationships as it naturally exists—a network of typed entities with explicit, queryable relationships—rather than forcing interconnected reality into tables or documents.

## Designing the DevOps Ontology

The foundation of an effective DevOps agent begins with an ontology that captures infrastructure semantics while abstracting away provider-specific details. Following the graph data model principles discussed earlier, we need to define entity types (nodes), their properties, and the relationships (edges) that connect them.

### Multi-cloud abstraction through canonical types

The DevOps ontology implements multicloud abstraction by defining canonical resource types that map to provider-specific implementations. For example, a `Compute` entity type represents compute instances across Amazon EC2, Google Cloud Compute Engine, and Azure Virtual Machines (VMs). This abstraction enables your agent to reason about items like production compute instances with elevated IAM permissions without requiring provider-specific logic.

The ontology defines several core entity categories:

*Compute resources*
: Represent VMs and container instances across cloud providers.

*Networking resources*
: Include load balancers, virtual private clouds (VPCs), subnets, and security groups that control traffic flow.

*Storage resources*
: Encompass object storage buckets, block storage volumes, and databases.

*Access control resources*
: Model IAM roles, policies, and service accounts that govern permissions.

*Service abstractions*
: Represent logical groupings of infrastructure that typically map to application services or business capabilities.

*Operational entities*
: Capture work items (Jira tickets), code artifacts (Git commits), and organizational structures (teams, customers).

Relationship types in the ontology capture how resources connect and depend on each other. `DEPENDS_ON` relationships indicate functional dependencies where one resource requires another to operate. `ROUTES_TO` captures network traffic flows. `ASSUMES_ROLE` models identity and access relationships. `OWNED_BY` and `PART_OF` establish organizational structure and resource hierarchy. `DEPLOYED_BY` links infrastructure to the deployment events that created or modified it. `LINKS_TO` connects operational artifacts like Jira tickets to technical resources.

This ontological structure transforms provider-specific API responses into semantically rich, queryable knowledge. When your agent encounters an Amazon EC2 instance, it doesn't store raw JSON from the Amazon API. Instead, it creates a `Compute` node with standardized properties and establishes typed relationships to its VPC, security groups, and IAM role. This semantic layer is what enables sophisticated reasoning.

### Applying schema patterns to infrastructure

The schema design patterns introduced earlier in this chapter directly address DevOps reasoning requirements. Let's examine how each pattern manifests in infrastructure knowledge representation.

The *event-centric pattern* (see Example 3-16) structures deployment history and configuration changes as first-class entities. Rather than storing a deployment as a property update on a service node, you create a `DeploymentEvent` node with explicit timestamp, associated Git commit, affected services, and modified resources. This event becomes a queryable artifact in the knowledge graph, enabling questions like *What deployments affected the payment service in the past week?* or *Which Git commit deployed version 2.3.1 to production?*

*Example 3-16. Event-centric schema*

```
def create_deployment_event(graph, deployment_data):
    """Create event-centric deployment node with relationships."""
    event_node = graph.create_node("DeploymentEvent", properties={
        "event_id": deployment_data["id"],
        "timestamp": deployment_data["timestamp"],
        "git_sha": deployment_data["commit"]
    })

    # Link to affected services and modified resources
    for service_name in deployment_data["services"]:
    graph.create_edge(
        event_node,
        graph.find_node("Service", name=service_name),
        "DEPLOYS",
    )

    for resource_id in deployment_data["resources_changed"]:
    graph.create_edge(
        event_node,
        graph.find_node("Compute", instance_id=resource_id),
        "MODIFIES",
    )

    return event_node
```

This pattern establishes deployments as tangible entities in the knowledge graph rather than ephemeral actions. The agent can query deployment history, examine which resources each deployment touched, and understand the current state by following the chain of modifications.

The contextual boundary pattern prevents context mixing across environments through explicit `EnvironmentContext` nodes connected via `CONTAINS` relationships.

This enables filtering queries by environment, ensuring that *Show me all critical services* returns only production services with critical service level agreement (SLA) tiers, not staging resources.

Consider a security group configuration where Terraform defines two ingress rules but Amazon reports three. The graph-based representation creates a `Configuration Statement` node with two linked `Perspective` nodes, one from Terraform state (`confidence: 1.0, source: "terraform_state"`) and one from the Amazon API (`confidence: 1.0, source: "aws_api"`). The agent can now query configuration drift systematically: *Which resources have different configurations between Terraform and Amazon?* This becomes a graph traversal problem rather than requiring custom comparison logic.

The capability model pattern represents agent operational boundaries as queryable nodes (read metrics, query logs, describe infrastructure), each with authorization levels. This queryable authority model determines which actions agents can take during tool orchestration in Chapter 6.

## Populating the Knowledge Graph: Building the Digital Twin

With ontology and schema patterns defined, the next challenge is to acquire knowledge from diverse infrastructure sources. The DevOps domain requires integrating structured data from cloud APIs, semistructured IaC definitions, operational ticketing systems, and observability metadata. This section implements the knowledge acquisition pipeline discussed earlier in the chapter.

### Structured data integration from cloud providers

The foundation of your DevOps knowledge graph comes from cloud provider APIs. Following the extraction approaches for heterogeneous sources discussed earlier, you'll implement a hybrid materialization strategy: frequently accessed resources and critical relationships are materialized as graph nodes and edges, while less common patterns are computed on demand.

When ingesting Amazon infrastructure, you materialize EC2 instances as `Compute` nodes with their properties (`instance_id`, `type`, `region`, `status`). You create relationships with their VPCs (`PART_OF`), security groups (`PROTECTED_BY`), and IAM roles (`ASSUMES_ROLE`). This materialized structure enables rapid traversal during queries, allowing you to find all compute instances with a specific IAM role in milliseconds rather than making repeated API calls.

The ingestion process transforms raw API responses into semantically rich graph structures. An Amazon `DescribeInstances` API call returns nested JSON with instance metadata, network interfaces, block device mappings, and tags. Your knowledge acquisition pipeline extracts this information, maps it to your ontology's canonical types, and establishes typed relationships.

For load balancers, you materialize their target groups and backend instances. For Amazon Relational Database Service (RDS) databases, you capture their security groups, subnet groups, and parameter groups. Each resource type follows the same pattern: extract properties, create a typed node, and establish relationships with connected resources. The graph topology emerges naturally from how the infrastructure actually connects.

### Code and configuration integration

IaC repositories define desired state, while cloud APIs report actual state. Integrating both creates a complete picture that enables drift detection and impact analysis.

When ingesting Terraform state, you create `TerraformResource` nodes that link to their corresponding live infrastructure through `DEFINES` relationships. Each IaC definition node includes the filepath and Git repository information, establishing traceability from running infrastructure back to the code that created it.

This bidirectional mapping proves essential for understanding infrastructure provenance. A DevOps engineer asks: *Which Terraform module created this RDS database?* The agent traverses backward from the `Database` node through the `DEFINED_BY` relationship to the `TerraformResource` node, revealing the exact module, filepath, and Git commit responsible.

The integration captures not just resource definitions but also their module structure and dependencies. Terraform modules often reference other modules through `module` blocks, creating a hierarchical structure. Your knowledge graph represents this through `DEPENDS_ON` relationships between `TerraformResource` nodes, enabling queries like *If I modify the networking module, which downstream modules are affected?*

Git commits become nodes linked to Terraform resources through `DEFINED_IN` relationships. This establishes the complete lineage from code changes through infrastructure definitions to running resources, the foundation for impact analysis and change tracking.

### Observability platform integration

Following the just-in-time telemetry integration principle discussed earlier, you create durable links between infrastructure resources and their observability signals, establishing the connections without duplicating data.

For each service, you create `Monitor` nodes representing Datadog Monitors, Amazon CloudWatch alarms, or Grafana dashboards. These link to services through `MONITORS` relationships. You create `LogSource` nodes that capture the query patterns needed to retrieve relevant logs, for example, a Datadog log query like `service:payment-api status:error`.

This architecture keeps the graph as a structural skeleton, capturing what resources exist, how they relate, and where to find their telemetry, without attempting to replicate specialized observability platforms. The graph answers the *what* and *how* questions about infrastructure structure; external systems answer *how much* and *what happened* questions about runtime behavior.

#### Operational metadata for business context

Technical infrastructure relationships tell only part of the story. Integrating operational metadata, SLAs, team ownership, customer dependencies, and work tracking transforms technical knowledge into business-aware intelligence.

Services link to SLA nodes that define uptime targets, response time requirements, and error rate thresholds. Customer relationships through `SERVES` edges enable impact assessment. Team ownership through `OWNED_BY` relationships establishes organizational context and responsibilities.

Crucially, you integrate operational artifacts like Jira tickets. When bugs are reported or features requested, work items link to affected services through `RELATES_TO` relationships. When deployments occur, they link back to triggering Jira tickets through `IMPLEMENTS` relationships. This integration creates a complete operational picture. With integrated operational metadata, a single graph traversal from a Jira issue reveals the Git commit, deployment timestamp, affected resources, at-risk SLAs, and impacted customers, demonstrating how graph structure enables holistic reasoning from operational artifacts to business impact.

#### Integrating organizational ontologies and controlled vocabularies

Organizations typically maintain established taxonomies and controlled vocabularies. The DevOps agent integrates these existing semantic structures through SKOS mappings (e.g., `:Service skos:exactMatch orgVocab:ApplicationService`), ensuring that the agent uses organizational terminology rather than introducing conflicting vocabularies. Integration might include Information Technology Infrastructure Library (ITIL) ontologies for incident management, cloud provider taxonomies for resource types, security frameworks like National Institute of Standards and Technology (NIST), and organizational role hierarchies that define teams and escalation paths.

## Homoiconic Knowledge Representation for Agent Adaptability

Beyond capturing current infrastructure state, sophisticated agents benefit from homoiconic knowledge representation, representing the ontology itself as data within the knowledge graph. This enables agents to query their own schema structures and reason about schema evolution.

By representing entity type definitions as nodes with properties describing required relationships and attributes, the agent can query *What entity types are defined?* or *Which relationships are required for a compute resource?* As the agent observes infrastructure patterns, it can propose schema extensions. Operational rules can similarly be represented as executable patterns within the graph:

```
deployment_validation_rule = graph.create_node("OperationalRule", properties={
    "rule_name": "ValidateProductionDeployment",
    "condition": "MATCH (d:DeploymentEvent)-[:DEPLOYS]->(s:Service)...",
    "validation": "REQUIRE sla.uptime_target >= 99.9..."
})
```

This establishes the foundation for autonomous schema improvement explored in Chapter 7.

## Querying the Knowledge Graph: Making the Digital Twin Useful

With the knowledge graph populated, graph structure enables sophisticated queries that would be difficult or impossible with traditional storage systems. These queries illustrate how relationship-centric knowledge representation provides the contextual foundation for agent reasoning. Following patterns documented in production DevOps knowledge graph implementations, including AnyShift's approach to infrastructure modeling, three query categories demonstrate essential reasoning capabilities.

### Understanding service dependencies

Infrastructure dependencies form the foundation for change impact analysis and root cause investigation. Graph traversal makes dependency discovery straightforward:

```
// Find all infrastructure dependencies for a service
MATCH (service:Service {name: 'payment-api'})-[:DEPENDS_ON*1..4]->(resource)
RETURN service, resource, labels(resource) as resource_type
```

This query traverses up to four hops from the service node, following `DEPENDS_ON` relationships to discover compute instances, databases, load balancers, and caches. This dependency context enables LLMs to reason about infrastructure changes with complete awareness: rather than asking *Will this change break anything?* with no context, the agent receives the complete dependency graph to analyze whether proposed changes affect dependent resources.

### Configuration drift detection

The multiperspective pattern enables systematic identification of discrepancies between desired and actual infrastructure state:

```
// Find resources where Terraform state differs from cloud state
MATCH (config:ConfigurationStatement)-
[:ACCORDING_TO]->(tf:Perspective {source: 'terraform_state'}),
      (config)-[:ACCORDING_TO]-
>(cloud:Perspective {source: 'aws_api'})
WHERE tf.value <> cloud.value
RETURN config.resource_id,
      tf.value AS desired_state,
      cloud.value AS actual_state
```

This query compares perspectives from Terraform definitions against Amazon API responses, identifying configuration drift as a graph traversal problem rather than requiring custom comparison logic. The results reveal which resources have diverged from the defined state, providing the foundation for the drift remediation workflows implemented in Chapter 6.

### Impact analysis for infrastructure changes

Before executing infrastructure modifications, understanding downstream effects across services, SLAs, and team ownership becomes essential for risk assessment:

```
// Determine impact of changing a specific VPC
MATCH (vpc:VPC {vpc_id: 'vpc-abc123'})
  <-[:PART_OF*1..3]-(resource)
  <-[:DEPENDS_ON]-(service:Service)
MATCH (service)-[:BOUND_BY]->(sla:SLA)
MATCH (service)-[:OWNED_BY]->(team:Team)
RETURN DISTINCT
  service.name,
  sla.uptime_target,
  team.name,
  collect(resource.instance_id) AS affected_resources
ORDER BY sla.uptime_target DESC
```

This traversal moves from infrastructure components through contained resources to dependent services, then enriches the results with SLA commitments and team ownership. The output provides a complete impact assessment—which services depend on the VPC and their criticality based on SLA tiers, owning teams, and exact affected resources—enabling agents to reason about risk: *This VPC change affects three critical services with 99.99% SLAs, owned by the payments and fraud detection teams, requiring careful coordination and approval.*

These three query patterns demonstrate how graph structure transforms infrastructure knowledge into actionable context. Dependency traversal reveals technical relationships, multiperspective comparison identifies discrepancies systematically, and impact analysis connects technical changes to business consequences through integrated operational metadata.

## Entity Resolution for Infrastructure Identity

DevOps knowledge graphs face entity resolution challenges when the same resource appears across systems with different identifiers. An EC2 instance might be referenced by Amazon instance ID (`i-abc123`), private IP (`10.0.1.45`), DNS name (`api-server-01.internal`), Terraform resource name (`aws_instance.api_server`), or tag-based references.

Following the multistage entity resolution approach discussed earlier, the knowledge acquisition pipeline generates embeddings for candidate references, performs vector similarity search against existing graph entities, and applies context-aware resolution considering relationship patterns:

```
def resolve_compute_instance(graph, candidate_references):
    embeddings = {ref: generate_embedding(ref) for ref in candidate_references}
    potential_matches = []

    for ref, embedding in embeddings.items():
        matches = graph.vector_search("Compute", embedding,
                                      limit=5, threshold=0.85)
        potential_matches.extend(matches)

    for match in potential_matches:
        neighbors = graph.get_relationships(match['id'])
        if relationship_patterns_match(neighbors, candidate_references):
            return match

    return create_new_compute_entity(graph, candidate_references[0])
```

Rather than relying solely on attribute similarity, this context-aware approach considers whether candidates share the same VPC, security groups, and subnet and uses these relationship patterns to indicate whether resources reference the same entity.

## Measuring Context Quality: Ensuring the Digital Twin Stays Accurate

Implementing continuous measurement of knowledge graph quality across four dimensions—precision, exhaustiveness, freshness, and coverage—can ensure that the context your agent receives remains accurate enough for reliable reasoning:

*Precision*
: Measures whether graph relationships match actual infrastructure state. Sample random edges and verify them against live cloud APIs. Does the `ROUTES_TO` relationship between this load balancer and target group actually exist in Amazon? A precision score below 0.95 indicates drift between your graph and reality.

*Exhaustiveness*
: Ensures that all critical infrastructure is represented. Count resources in your cloud accounts and compare them to resource counts in the graph. Missing resources create blind spots where your agent cannot reason effectively. If your Amazon account contains 247 EC2 instances but your graph has only 198 `Compute` nodes, you're missing 20% of your infrastructure. Context gaps like these lead to incorrect reasoning.

*Freshness*
: Tracks how recently data was updated. Infrastructure changes frequently, and stale data leads to incorrect reasoning. Calculate the average age of the graph nodes and set alerts when data exceeds acceptable staleness thresholds, typically one hour for production infrastructure.

*Coverage*
: Verifies that all critical relationship types are captured. Your ontology might define 15 relationship types, but if only 8 appear in the graph, you're missing essential connections that enable reasoning. Low coverage often indicates incomplete data ingestion pipelines; perhaps you're materializing compute instances but not their security group relationships.

These metrics should be instrumented from day one. Without quality measurement, knowledge graphs inevitably drift from ground truth, gradually degrading agent reasoning capabilities. The quality framework becomes the foundation for the self-evolution mechanisms we'll implement in Chapter 7.

## Summary

When developing advanced agentic systems, the knowledge structures you build fundamentally determine what your agents can understand, reason about, and accomplish. Throughout this chapter, you've explored how graph-based knowledge modeling creates the essential cognitive foundation that enables sophisticated agent behavior.

The knowledge representation approaches you choose directly impact your agents' reasoning capabilities. Property graphs offer computational efficiency but require explicit programming for inference, while RDF-based systems provide formal semantics that enable native reasoning. For complex real-world relationships, hypergraph structures allow you to represent multi-entity connections that maintain contextual integrity, a crucial capability when modeling domains like healthcare or enterprise operations.

When building the DevOps agent, you began with context engineering, the discipline of feeding LLMs the right data, at the right time, and in the right format. This meant building a high-fidelity digital twin of the infrastructure where relationships matter as much as the resources themselves. You designed an ontology that abstracts multicloud complexity into canonical types, enabling provider-agnostic reasoning. You applied schema patterns that address specific agentic reasoning requirements. These were event-centric for temporal awareness, had a contextual boundary for environment separation, were multiperspective for configuration drift, and used capability model to represent operational boundaries.

The knowledge acquisition pipeline transformed diverse infrastructure sources into a coherent graph. Structured data integration from cloud APIs materialized resources and relationships. Code and configuration integration established traceability between IaC and running infrastructure. Observability platform integration created durable links to telemetry. Operational metadata integration brought in business context, that powerful traversal from Jira ticket through deployment to customer impact. Entity resolution ensured coherent identity across systems, while organizational ontology integration preserved institutional semantics. Homoiconic representation enables future adaptability through metaknowledge structures and executable patterns.

Continuous quality measurement across precision, exhaustiveness, freshness, and coverage ensures that your knowledge graph maintains the accuracy necessary for reliable reasoning. Through the DevOps example, you've seen these theoretical concepts translate into practical systems, with a digital twin capturing infrastructure resources, relationships, operational context, and business impact.

Yet this digital twin remains fundamentally limited: it represents a snapshot in time. The agent has a map but doesn't yet understand how that map changes. As you move forward through the book, you'll see how these knowledge foundations connect with reasoning frameworks to create complete agent cognitive systems. The graph structures you've learned to build will serve as the semantic substrate upon which more sophisticated agent behaviors can develop, enabling systems that understand context, maintain coherent memory over time, resolve contradictions, and adapt their understanding as new information emerges. The agent's brain is now built; the digital twin is in place. In the chapters ahead, we'll bring that brain to life.

CHAPTER 4

# Agentic Graph Memory Systems

You shipped your AI agent last month. For the first week, users were thrilled. Then the tickets started rolling in: *Why doesn't it remember me?* Suddenly, your agent forgets preferences, blanks on previous conversations, and keeps asking the same questions as if it has never spoken with you before.

If that feels uncomfortably familiar, your memory implementation may not just be a little off. It's likely fundamentally broken.

This chapter shows you how to build *graph memory systems* that turn your agents from goldfish into elephants. You will move from understanding why current approaches fail to implementing living memory architectures and training your agents to actually use those architectures. Along the way, we will look at production systems like Cognee (*https://cognee.ai*), mem0 (*https://mem0.ai*), and Zep (*https://getzep.com*) that are already solving these challenges at scale.

By the end of the chapter, you will understand how to design graph structures that capture relationships your vector database misses, introduce temporal awareness so your agent understands how information changes over time, and construct memory hierarchies that keep recent data hot while archiving the rest. You'll learn how to support active memory management, where agents optimize their own storage, and how to borrow production patterns already serving millions of users.

## Architecting Graph Memory Systems

An effective agent does not just "have" memory; it sits on top of a deliberately designed memory architecture. In this section, we will look at what it actually means to architect graph-based memory systems: how to move beyond ever-larger context windows, how to separate storage concerns from reasoning, and how to layer graphs alongside your existing databases and vector indexes. We'll start by unpacking why common approaches fail under real-world constraints, then work through the design choices you need to make—schemas, temporal models, hierarchies, and boundaries between individual and shared knowledge—that set your agents up for reliable, long-running work.

## The Problem: Why Your Current Memory Approach Fails

The Letta Leaderboard for benchmarking agentic memory (*https://oreil.ly/ILMc6*) describes eight distinct failure modes that tend to show up together.

### Sources of failure

Models fail to recognize when relevant information is already available and issue unnecessary searches. Memory hierarchies break down, so trivia sits in prime memory while critical facts get archived or dropped. During conversation, agents regularly miss key pieces of information even when they are present. As the volume of data grows, retrieval accuracy degrades and performance drops.

Conflicts make the situation even messier. New information often overwrites old facts instead of being layered as context, so the system cannot explain how or why things changed. Related pieces of information remain isolated in separate silos, preventing cross-reference and pattern recognition. Event timelines blur together, and agents lose temporal coherence altogether. Systems that work acceptably with hundreds of facts quietly collapse when exposed to thousands.

You might think that larger context windows solve everything. Unfortunately, they do not. Even a one million–token context window will fill faster than you think; a few months of user interactions will exhaust your budget. At that point, either you drop old information and your agent forgets, or you compress everything and lose critical details. Recent work on recursive language models (RLMs) (Zhang, 2025, *https://oreil.ly/852Ca*) demonstrates that even state-of-the-art systems suffer from *context rot*, where performance degrades as context length increases regardless of whether you hit the hard limit. The RLM research points toward externalizing knowledge to create an environment in which agents interact with information programmatically rather than cramming everything into the input, but externalization without version control creates failures that are harder to diagnose and impossible to audit.

Things get worse when you consider time. Information changes: users move, change jobs, and develop new preferences. Without temporal awareness, your agent either forgets the past or gets confused by contradictions. It cannot answer *What was the configuration when the outage occurred?* after you have updated everything, because the underlying system has no way to represent *what used to be true*. When multiple agents process information concurrently, the problem compounds. Without coordination, whichever writes last wins, and you have no record that a conflict existed. The agentic memory system must be treated like a Git repository: version every ontological commit, let agents branch when they begin processing and merge when they finish, and run continuous integration (CI) checks before accepting changes. With these safeguards, schema drift becomes visible and reversible rather than silent corruption.

Flat context windows also erase relationships. That server issue from three months ago may be tied to a specific network change, which in turn is similar to incidents in another region. In a simple window of text, those connections disappear. Your agent sees isolated statements instead of an evolving story.

Finally, as contexts grow, retrieval itself starts to fail. The *lost in the middle* problem means that critical facts buried inside huge prompts might as well not exist. The very mechanism you rely on to improve memory (larger context windows) ends up hiding the information you care about most.

Underneath all of this is a multidimensional design problem. On one axis, you need both storage and reasoning. Databases are excellent at storing and indexing information but do not reason. LLMs are excellent at reasoning but cannot reliably store or retrieve information. A serious memory architecture has to combine the two into a coherent system.

On another axis, you must balance persistence and adaptability. If your storage layer is too static, your agent slowly drifts out of sync with reality. If you constantly overwrite facts in place, you lose the historical trace that makes explanations and audits possible. The goal is to achieve a form of evolution with preservation: the system continues to learn while keeping track of how the world used to look.

Structure and flexibility introduce a third tension. Rigid schemas let you express powerful queries and invariants, but they struggle with messy, real-world text and edge cases. Purely unstructured storage makes it easy to ingest anything but hard to maintain reliability. Practical systems mix both: structured cores for trusted data surrounded by more flexible layers for exploratory or extracted knowledge. The deeper insight is that ontology can be learned rather than prescribed. Agent trajectories discover structure through problem-directed traversal. The relationships that are traversed are the relationships that are real. Structural equivalences reveal themselves when different agents solving different problems follow analogous paths. The schema is not the starting point; it is the output.

You also need to think about whose memory you are building. Agents require private, per-user histories as well as shared, global knowledge. Drawing and enforcing boundaries between those spaces—what is personal, what can be shared, what must never leak—adds another layer of complexity, especially in regulated environments.

### Cache sharing in multi-agent systems

The chapter has established that agents require private, per-user histories as well as shared, global knowledge. But stating that shared memory exists does not specify how it works in practice. When Agent A discovers a constraint and Agent B needs that constraint two steps later, the transfer mechanism matters. Without a cache-sharing protocol, Agent B must re-derive or re-retrieve what Agent A already found, wasting tokens and time, and sometimes producing a contradictory result.

Three cache-sharing patterns emerge from distributed systems practice, each with different trade-offs:

*Broadcast*
: This is the simplest pattern: every agent's cache updates are visible to every other agent. When a planning agent identifies a budget constraint, all execution agents see it immediately. Broadcast works for small agent teams (two to four agents) where coordination overhead is low and all agents operate in the same problem domain. It fails at scale because agents drown in irrelevant updates.

*Publish-subscribe*
: This adds selectivity. Agents declare which cache partitions they care about. A security review agent subscribes to cache updates tagged with "permissions" or "authentication" but ignores updates about UI layout. This is the pattern that multi-agent frameworks like Agora (*https://oreil.ly/JVos3*) implement: agents publish findings to named channels, and other agents consume from channels relevant to their role. Overhead is incurred in defining the channel taxonomy, but the payoff is that agents receive only what they need.

*Request-grant*
: This pattern gives the most control. Agent B explicitly requests a specific piece of cached knowledge from Agent A. No data moves until requested. This pattern suits workflows where agents have clear handoff points: a code generation agent finishes a module, and a test generation agent requests its interface signatures before writing tests. Request-grant produces the least cache pollution, but because it requires agents to know what to ask for, it assumes well-defined task boundaries.

Consider this scenario in a DevOps multi-agent system:

1. A diagnostics agent identifies that a deployment failure stems from a misconfigured environment variable.
2. A remediation agent needs that root cause to generate a fix.
3. A communication agent needs both the root cause and the fix to draft an incident report.

Broadcast would work here—there are only three agents, tightly coupled. But add a monitoring agent, a capacity-planning agent, and a post mortem agent, and broadcast just becomes noise. Pub-sub with channels like "root-cause," "remediation-action," and "incident-status" would scale correctly in this case.

Finally, performance and completeness are always in tension. Exhaustive systems that consider every possible fact tend to be too slow or too expensive. Highly optimized systems that look only at a small subset of data risk missing the very information that matters. The "right" balance varies by use case, which means your memory architecture must make trade-offs explicit rather than hiding them. Figure 4-1 illustrates these multidimensional tensions.

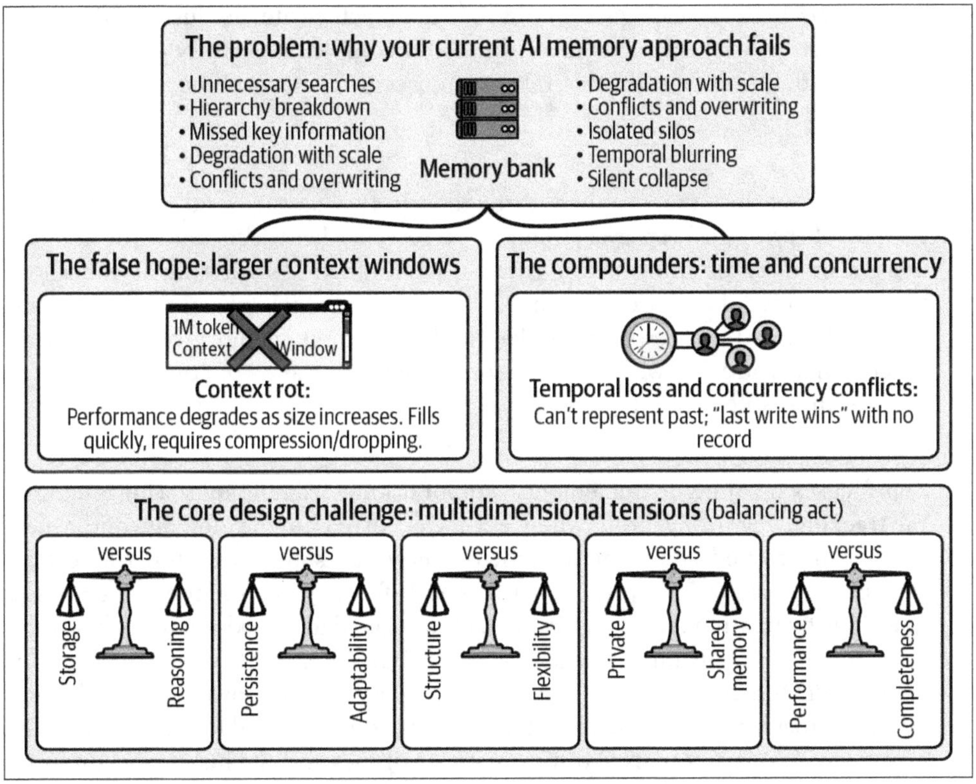


*Figure 4-1. The multidimensional tensions of agentic memory systems*

## The Solution: Graph Memory

*Graph memory* addresses these failures by enabling what Letta calls *agentic memory management*: agents that actively control their memory through deliberate operations instead of passively relying on whatever happens to be in the context window.

### Graph memory in production

Production systems like Cognee, mem0, and Zep have each developed strategies to address these specific failure modes. Throughout this chapter, we will use them as reference points, considering what they choose to prioritize, where they trade complexity for performance, and how those decisions play out in real workloads:

*Cognee*
: Cognee starts from a graph-first architecture, treating memory as interconnected knowledge networks rather than as rows, documents, or vectors. Its *extract-cognify-load (ECL) pipeline* focuses on building semantic relationships during ingestion, not as an afterthought. Benchmarks report high accuracy on memory tasks precisely because Cognee emphasizes how facts relate, not just whether they exist. When your agent needs to reason about complex regulatory documents or analyze code dependencies, this relationship-centric approach becomes a major advantage.

*Mem0*
: Mem0 approaches the problem through selective storage and consolidation. Instead of trying to keep everything, it preserves salient facts and continuously merges or discards information based on relevance. As a result, it can show higher accuracy than baseline "built-in" memories while substantially reducing latency. Its two-phase pipeline is designed to prevent memory bloat, which is exactly what you need when your agent handles thousands of conversations per day and must still respond quickly.

*Zep*
: Zep focuses on time. It implements temporal knowledge graphs with bitemporal tracking, recording both when events occurred in the domain and when the system learned about them. Built on the open source Graphiti framework (*https://oreil.ly/IX1i_*), Zep demonstrates significant gains on preference-based questions by treating temporal history as first-class data. For domains like healthcare, finance, or customer support—where *What did we know, and when did we know it?* is a core question—this design is particularly powerful. This bitemporal approach is the foundation for treating your knowledge graph like a Git repository. Just as Git tracks both the content of files and the history of commits, bitemporal graphs track both what was true in the world and when the system recorded that truth.

Together, these systems show that graph-based memory is not just a research idea. It is already being used in production to tame complex knowledge, maintain temporal history, and keep agents grounded in long-running interactions.

### What graph memory gives you

Graph memory changes how your agent manages context. Instead of stuffing more tokens into a window, you explicitly represent relationships among entities, events, and concepts. When server X's configuration issue connects to a network topology change and a series of similar incidents, those connections become edges in a graph that the system can traverse. In Cognee's case, RDF-style ontologies and rules layer formal semantics on top of these connections, enabling reasoning that goes beyond simple pattern matching.

The same structure supports dynamic reorganization. As new information arrives, the graph can be reshaped: nodes can be merged or split, edges can be strengthened or weakened, and new patterns can emerge over time. Mem0's self-improving memory makes this explicit by deciding, for each new piece of information, whether to add it as a fresh node, update an existing node, or just discard the information. The result is a memory that evolves rather than just accumulates.

This evolution needs governance. Therefore, treat each modification as a commit with metadata: what changed, why, and based on what evidence. When multiple agents process information concurrently, let them write to isolated branches. Merge conflicts will surface explicit contradictions—Document A says Maria won; Document B says Camille won—rather than allowing silent overwrites.

Graphs also make multi-hop reasoning tractable. Questions like *Who directed the movie that won the award mentioned in Tuesday's meeting?* become pathfinding problems instead of brittle prompt gymnastics. Variants like mem0$^g$, which is mentioned in Chhikara and colleagues' 2025 mem0 paper (*https://oreil.ly/9JMOU*), lean into this, using the graph structure to support more complex chains of inference across meetings, documents, and user interactions.

At scale, graph memory helps you keep performance under control. Systems like Zep precompute graph-based artifacts and avoid LLM calls at retrieval time, allowing them to maintain sub-second latency even as the number of nodes and edges grows into the millions. Temporal indices and hierarchical organization mean you can quickly retrieve "what was true last week" without wading through everything that has ever happened. The audit question becomes answerable: *Why did your system believe X when it made that recommendation on January 15?* With temporal versioning, you can reconstruct the exact graph state at decision time, trace which sources contributed to which facts, and explain how confidence evolved. Without it, the answer is a shrug.

The main lesson from the Letta Leaderboard is straightforward: the quality of memory management directly determines agent performance on long-running tasks. Systems that treat memory as passive storage eventually fail. Systems that treat memory as an actively managed resource—one that can be queried, reorganized, and optimized—are the ones that scale.

For your agents, this implies a shift in mindset. They must learn to optimize their own memory patterns through experience rather than relying on fixed heuristics. They need to track *when* facts were true, not just *what* was true, so they can answer temporally grounded questions. They have to build and maintain semantic relationships that support reasoning, not just recall. And when contradictions appear, they must handle them by maintaining versioned, time-aware knowledge instead of blindly overwriting the past. Run CI checks before accepting changes to the graph. Validate that new facts do not violate constraints, that sources still exist, and that extractions are reproducible. Schema drift becomes visible and reversible. Every ontological change is a commit you can inspect, blame, or revert. The failures described by the Letta Leaderboard—missed information, lost temporal coherence, silent corruption at scale—are symptoms of building without version control. The foundation that your memory architecture is missing is a Git for knowledge.

### Memory consistency models for agent coordination

The Git metaphor introduced earlier in this chapter handles versioning well, but it leaves open a question that distributed systems engineers will recognize immediately: when Agent A writes a fact to shared memory, when does Agent B see it? This is the memory consistency problem, and getting it wrong produces agents that contradict each other, overwrite each other's conclusions, or act on stale information.

Three consistency models, borrowed directly from distributed databases, apply to multi-agent memory:

*Eventual consistency*
: This is the guarantee that all agents will converge to the same state, but not when. Agent A adds a fact, but Agent B may not see it for several reasoning steps. This works for knowledge accumulation tasks: a team of research agents building a literature review can tolerate temporary disagreement because no single fact is safety critical and the final synthesis step reconciles everything.

*Strong consistency*
: This is the guarantee that all agents see the same memory state before any agent proceeds. This is expensive—it requires a synchronization barrier after every write—but it is necessary for safety-critical decisions. A medical diagnosis multi-agent system where one agent identifies a drug interaction must ensure that every other agent sees that interaction before recommending treatment.

*Causal consistency*
: Here is the practical middle ground. Agents see causally related updates in order, but unrelated updates may arrive out of sequence. If Agent A's conclusion depends on Agent B's finding, any agent reading A's conclusion is guaranteed to also see B's finding, while unrelated updates from Agent C may arrive later. This matches how most agentic workflows actually operate: tasks have causal dependencies, but not every piece of knowledge relates to every other piece.

Most production systems should default to causal consistency and escalate to strong consistency only for decision points that trigger irreversible actions. The Git metaphor maps here too: a pull request review (strong consistency—all reviewers must approve before merge) versus CI on feature branches (there is eventual consistency as tests converge over time) versus a merge queue that respects dependency order (causal consistency).

The rest of this chapter will show you how to design and implement these agentic graph memory systems in practice.

# Representing Memory as Graphs

By this point, you have already modeled the static world of your system: services, dependencies, configurations, and events. Memory adds a different dimension. Now you care about *when* things happened, *how* they relate across time, and *what* the agent should remember or forget. The most powerful way to capture this is to represent memory itself as a graph.

## Understanding the Architecture Evolution

Most teams start simple. They log conversations to a database table or drop chunks of text into a vector store for similarity search. That works for basic retrieval, but it collapses as soon as the agent needs to understand relationships, track changes, or reason across multiple pieces of information.

### The hierarchy of memory architecture

In practice, memory architectures tend to evolve through a common progression:

*Flat storage*
: Each interaction or fact is stored independently.

*Vector-enhanced storage*
: You add embeddings for semantic search.

*Structured relationships*
: You explicitly model how things connect.

*Temporal awareness*
: You track when facts and relationships change.

*Hierarchical organization*
: You introduce layers and abstractions.

Each step unlocks new behaviors. Flat storage lets you recall raw text. Vectors help the agent find conceptually similar information. Structured relationships allow graph traversal. Temporal awareness lets the agent reason about change. Hierarchies provide summaries and rollups instead of forcing the agent to wade through every raw event.

### The computer architecture of agent memory

The progression from flat key-value stores through vector, structured, temporal, and hierarchical memory mirrors a progression that hardware engineers solved decades ago. CPU architecture organizes memory into three layers: registers and I/O buffers for immediate data, cache for active working sets, and persistent storage (RAM, disk) for everything else. Agent memory benefits from the same decomposition.

The *I/O layer* handles raw inputs and tool outputs as they arrive. When an agent calls a web search API, parses a PDF, or receives a user message, that data lands in the I/O buffer. The data is unstructured, ephemeral, and high volume. Most of it will be discarded. A coding agent running a test suite generates hundreds of lines of standard output; the I/O layer holds all of it, but only the failure traceback matters for reasoning.

The *cache layer* holds the agent's active reasoning context—the subset of knowledge the agent is working with right now. This is not the full conversation history; it is the extracted facts, constraints, and intermediate conclusions that bear on the current task. When a research agent is synthesizing three papers, its cache contains the key claims from each paper, the contradictions it has identified, and its emerging thesis. The cache is structured, typically as a subgraph of the full knowledge graph; it is mutable, being updated as reasoning progresses; and it is bounded because an agent that caches everything has cached nothing).

The *persistent layer* stores the full history—every fact the agent has ever learned, every decision it has made, and every correction it has received—with temporal versioning. This is where the Git metaphor from earlier in this chapter applies most directly. Persistent memory supports branching (exploring alternative reasoning paths), tagging (marking significant state snapshots), and merging (reconciling divergent knowledge). The persistent layer is the only layer that survives across sessions.

The practical value of this decomposition is capacity planning. I/O buffers can be large and cheap because they are write-heavy and read-once. Cache must be fast and selective because it feeds directly into the LLM's context window—the scarcest resource in any agentic system. Persistent storage must be durable and queryable because it serves as the agent's long-term institutional knowledge. Systems like Cognee (*https://oreil.ly/khEhD*), mem0 (*https://oreil.ly/dIMAU*), Zep (*https://oreil.ly/Pm1qu*), and Letta (*https://oreil.ly/UDHpT*) each implement these three layers, though they draw the boundaries differently. Cognee emphasizes the persistent layer with its graph construction pipeline. Mem0 optimizes the cache layer with its memory extraction and retrieval. Zep balances both with its temporal knowledge graphs. Letta puts the cache-to-persistent boundary under the agent's own control, paging facts between a small working set and a larger archive. The architecture is the same; the tuning differs.

While Cognee, mem0, Zep, and Letta combine these ingredients in different ways, they all converge on the same idea: memory is not a log; it is a graph that evolves over time. To see how to get there, we will start with the building blocks.

## Essential Graph Components

A graph-based memory system is built from three core pieces: *nodes*, *edges*, and *subgraphs* (Figure 4-2). Nodes hold the things you care about. Edges describe how those things relate. Subgraphs bundle related pieces of memory into coherent contexts.

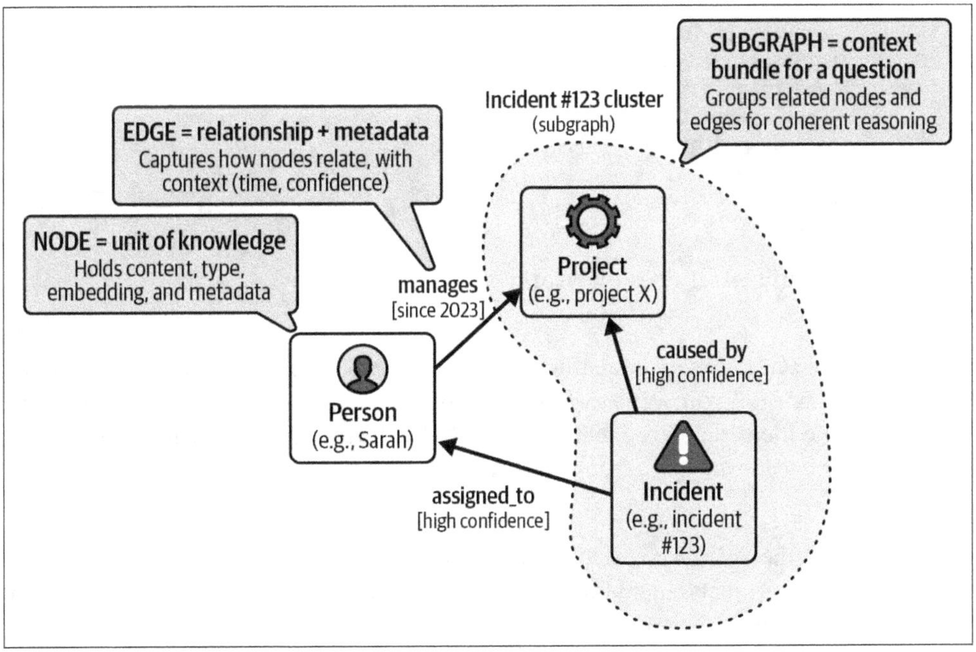


*Figure 4-2. Essential graph components for agentic memory*

### Nodes: Your knowledge units

A *node* represents a unit of knowledge: a person, project, incident, decision, or even a specific conversation turn. The key design challenge is determining how to balance structure and flexibility. You want enough structure for consistent processing but enough flexibility to handle new and messy information. A simple node model might look like Example 4-1.

*Example 4-1. Memory node*

```
class MemoryNode:
    def __init__(self, content, node_type):
        self.id = generate_uuid()
        self.content = content
        self.type = node_type
        self.created_at = datetime.now()
        self.embedding = generate_embedding(content)
        self.metadata = {}
        self.edges = []

    def add_edge(self, target_node, relationship_type, metadata=None):
        edge = Edge(
            source=self.id,
            target=target_node.id,
            type=relationship_type,
            created_at=datetime.now(),
            metadata=metadata or {},
        )
        self.edges.append(edge)
        return edge
```

Each field in Example 4-1 does real work:

`id`
: This is the stable identity for this node. When you later learn more about "John from marketing," you want to find and update the same node, not create a new one. Stable identifiers are what make consolidation and entity-centric reasoning possible.

`content`
: This holds the primary text or payload for the node, while `type` distinguishes people from projects, incidents from decisions, and so on. This lets you branch logic: a `person` node might trigger one extraction pipeline, while an `incident` node uses another.

`embedding`
: This is computed when the node is created. That vector representation powers semantic search so you can find relevant memories even when the question uses

different wording than the original content. Doing this once at creation time avoids recomputing embeddings on every query.

`metadata`
: This gives you extensibility without constant schema migrations. You can add importance scores, confidence levels, source URLs, or user IDs as your system matures without breaking earlier data.

`edges` *and* `add_edge`
: These make nodes more than isolated blobs of text. When you learn that *Sarah manages Project X*, you create an edge connecting Sarah's node to Project X's node. The relationship is now traversable from either side: *Which projects does Sarah manage?* and *Who manages Project X?* become the same operation in reverse.

Beyond basic node types like `person` or `incident`, production systems benefit from separating nodes by their *epistemic status*—distinguishing what the agent has observed from what it believes. In their 2025 paper "Hindsight is 20/20: Building Agent Memory That Retains, Recalls, and Reflects" (*https://oreil.ly/H-flJ*), Latimer and colleagues organize memory into four networks:

*World network*
: Objective facts about external reality

*Experience network*
: The agent's own actions (first-person)

*Opinion network*
: Subjective beliefs with confidence scores

*Observation network*
: Synthesized entity summaries

This separation enables traceability: when users ask, *How do you know that?* the agent can distinguish evidence (world/experience) from inference (opinion) from summary (observation). As the authors note, "Developers and users can see what the agent knows versus what it believes."

### Edges: Your relationships

An *edge* captures how two nodes relate. In a memory system, the edge is usually more interesting than either endpoint on its own.

At a minimum, edges should record the relationship type (for example, `manages`, `assigned_to`, `caused_by`) so the agent can interpret what the connection means. For production systems, you will typically also track when the relationship was valid, how confident you are in it, and any extra context that will help explain the link later.

In other words, an edge is not just *A connects to B*; it is *A connects to B in this way, during this time, for these reasons.* That extra structure is what enables reasoning about organizational charts, incident timelines, or changing user preferences.

### Subgraphs: Your contexts

A *subgraph* is a cluster of nodes and edges that work together to answer a particular kind of question. Instead of throwing all memories into a single undifferentiated graph, you group related information into contextual slices.

Zep's production architecture is a useful mental model. It separates memory into the following:

*Episode subgraphs*
: Store raw interactions—the literal conversations and events.

*Semantic entity subgraphs*
: Store extracted knowledge—what the system has learned about people, projects, and concepts.

*Community subgraphs*
: Represent higher-level clusters—how entities and ideas group together over time.

This separation lets you optimize each layer differently. Episodes can be append-only and heavily compressed. Entities can be carefully deduplicated and enriched. Communities can be rebuilt or reclustered as new information arrives. The edges between these subgraphs keep the whole system coherent: you can always trace a high-level belief back to the raw interactions that produced it.

## Temporal Awareness: Making Memory Evolve

So far, our graph is timeless. It tells you that Sarah has managed marketing but not whether she still does. In real systems, this quickly becomes a problem. Your agent needs to answer both *Who manages marketing now?* and *Who managed marketing in January?* and it needs to understand when it learned each fact.

Temporal awareness solves this by tracking three different notions of time:

- When a relationship was valid in the real world
- When your system ingested or updated that relationship
- When you want to query the state of the world

Graphiti has popularized a bitemporal model for this: each relationship has a *validity window* and an *ingestion timeline*. A simple implementation might look like Example 4-2.

*Example 4-2. A temporal edge*

```
class TemporalEdge:
    def __init__(self, source, target, relationship):
        self.source = source
        self.target = target
        self.relationship = relationship
        self.valid_from = datetime.now()
        self.valid_until = None  # None means currently valid
        self.ingested_at = datetime.now()
        self.invalidation_reason = None
 # Link type for weighted traversal (Latimer et al., 2025)
 self.link_type = "entity" # {temporal, semantic, entity, causal}
 self.weight = 1.0 # Traversal weight for graph search==

    def invalidate(self, reason = None):
        """Mark this relationship as no longer valid."""
        self.valid_until = datetime.now()
        self.invalidation_reason = reason

    def was_valid_at(self, timestamp):
        """Check if relationship was valid at a specific time."""
        return (
            self.valid_from <= timestamp
            and (self.valid_until is None or timestamp < self.valid_until)
        )
```

Here is how these fields change what your agent can do:

- `valid_from` and `valid_until` define when the relationship was considered true. When you first learn "Sarah manages the marketing team," you set `valid_from` to now and leave `valid_until` as `None`. When Sarah changes roles, you call `invalidate`, which closes the window without deleting history.
- `ingested_at` reflects when your system found out about the change, which might be days after it became true. This is crucial for debugging: if the agent made a decision on Wednesday based on stale data, `ingested_at` will tell you that the updated information was not yet available.
- `invalidation_reason` gives you an audit trail. Instead of a mysterious change in state, you see why the relationship ended: perhaps it was a role change, project completion, correction of bad data, or some other reason. This extra line of text can make the difference between a user trusting or distrusting the system.
- `was_valid_at` lets you reconstruct the world at any point in time. Now, questions like *What did our infrastructure look like right before the outage?* or *Who did the agent think owned this service when it made that prediction?* become first-class queries rather than forensic guesswork.

The "Hindsight" paper extends temporal edges with typed links that carry different traversal weights. During graph search, causal and entity edges receive multipliers $\mu > 1$, while weak semantic or long-range temporal edges receive $\mu \leq 1$. This ensures that spreading activation favors explanatory connections when traversing the graph, prioritizing paths through causally related facts over paths through merely similar facts.

Temporal edges turn your memory graph from a static snapshot into a movie you can pause, rewind, and inspect.

## Implementation: Building Your First Graph Memory System

With the building blocks in place, we can put them together into a minimal but realistic graph memory system. We will focus on the core loop: turning raw text into entities and relationships, storing them with temporal awareness, and then querying them effectively.

At a minimum, you need four capabilities:

- A place to store the graph (an in-memory structure is fine to start; a graph database like Neo4j comes later)
- An embedding model for semantic search over nodes and content
- An entity and relationship extractor to decide what to remember and how it connects
- A query layer that can combine vector search, keyword search, and graph traversal

#### Initial integration

The encouraging part is that the initial integration does not need to be complicated. Mem0 advertises four lines of integration code (*https://oreil.ly/n3Ghq*), and Cognee markets memory for AI agents in six lines of code (*https://oreil.ly/Pe0si*). The complexity shows up in optimization and scale, not in bootstrapping a basic memory loop. A simple orchestration class might look like Example 4-3.

*Example 4-3. Memory orchestration class*

```
class GraphMemory:
    def __init__(self, embedding_model):
        self.nodes = {}
        self.edges = []
        self.embedding_model = embedding_model

    def add_memory(self, content, context=None):
        # Extract entities and relationships
        entities = self.extract_entities(content)
```

```
        # Create or update nodes
        for entity in entities:
            node = self.find_or_create_node(entity)

        # Identify relationships
        relationships = self.extract_relationships(content, entities)

        # Create edges with temporal awareness
        for rel in relationships:
            self.create_temporal_edge(
                rel["source"],
                rel["target"],
                rel["type"],
                context,
            )

    def query(self, question, timestamp=None):
        # Generate query embedding
        query_embedding = self.embedding_model.embed(question)

        # Find relevant nodes through multiple methods
        semantic_matches = self.semantic_search(query_embedding)
        keyword_matches = self.keyword_search(question)

        # Traverse graph for connected information
        expanded_context = self.expand_search_context(
            semantic_matches + keyword_matches,
            timestamp,
        )

        return self.format_memories_for_llm(expanded_context)
```

The `add_memory` method is where unstructured input becomes structured graph data. The methods `extract_entities` and `extract_relationships` can be implemented using classic natural language processing (NLP), LLM-based extraction, or a mix of both. The important pattern is `find_or_create_node`: every time *Project Phoenix* or *John from marketing* appears, you either reuse the existing node or create a new one in a controlled way. That is how the system gradually builds rich, coherent entities instead of scattering facts across many disconnected nodes.

A critical design choice is extraction *granularity*. Sentence-level extraction produces fragmented facts that lose cross-turn context. The "Hindsight" paper instead extracts two to five comprehensive narrative facts per conversation, each intended to cover an entire exchange rather than a single utterance, be narrative and self-contained, include all relevant participants, and preserve the pragmatic flow.

For example, instead of storing five separate facts like *Bob suggested "Summer Vibes"* or *Alice wanted something unique*, a narrative approach produces:

> Alice and Bob discussed naming their summer party playlist. Bob suggested "Summer Vibes" because it is catchy and seasonal, but Alice wanted something more unique. They ultimately decided on "Beach Beats" for its playful tone.

This makes downstream retrieval and reasoning less sensitive to local segmentation decisions.

When `create_temporal_edge` is called, you attach time and context to each relationship. For a DevOps agent, that context might be the timestamp of a deployment, the incident ID, or the specific run of a pipeline. Later, when you query the graph, you can filter by `timestamp` to reconstruct the world as it was at a specific moment.

The `query` method shows a hybrid retrieval strategy. Semantic search finds conceptually related nodes (*team leads*, *managers*, *owners*), while keyword search catches exact identifiers (*service-api-gateway-prod*). The `expand_search_context` method then walks the graph outward from those starting points, following `owns`, `depends_on`, or `caused_by` edges to assemble the smallest subgraph that still gives the agent enough context to answer generatively.

This is the core loop of a graph memory system: extract, normalize, connect, timestamp, and then traverse.

#### Handling complex relationships

So far, every relationship has linked two nodes. Real life is rarely that simple. A single incident can involve many services, multiple people, and a series of decisions. Modeling this as pairwise edges quickly becomes unwieldy: for a meeting with 10 participants, you would need 45 edges just to represent "attended together."

As covered in Chapter 3, a *hypergraph* solves this by allowing edges that connect more than two nodes. In a memory system, this is especially useful for multiparty events: meetings, incident reviews, deployments, or customer escalations.

You can layer hypergraph behavior on top of your existing memory class, as in Example 4-4.

*Example 4-4. Hyperedge*

```
class HypergraphMemory(GraphMemory):
    def create_multi_entity_relationship(
        self,
        entities,
        relationship_type,
        metadata
    ):
```

```
    # Create a hyperedge connecting multiple nodes
    hyperedge = HyperEdge(
        id=generate_uuid(),
        type=relationship_type,
        participants=[e.id for e in entities],
        metadata=metadata,
        created_at=datetime.now(),
    )

    # Link all participants
    for entity in entities:
        entity.add_hyperedge(hyperedge)

    # Enable efficient queries
    self.index_hyperedge(hyperedge)

    return hyperedge
```

Here, the *hyperedge* is the first-class object. Its `participants` field lists all involved nodes. Its `metadata` holds the shared context: agenda, decisions made, action items, timestamps. Instead of smearing this information across dozens of pairwise edges, you keep it in one place.

The bidirectional links make querying natural. Starting from a person, you can traverse to every hyperedge they participate in and then to the other participants and topics. Starting from a hyperedge, you can ask *Who was in the room?* or *What other meetings involved this same group?* Indexing hyperedges by type, time, and participant IDs keeps these queries fast even as the number of events grows.

The result is a memory system that can represent not only what happened and when but also *who* was involved together and *how* those interactions unfolded. That level of structure is what enables agentic systems to move beyond recall into real, context-aware reasoning over time.

# Four Essential Memory Operations

You've now learned what to store and how to represent it. The next question is how your agent uses memory over time. In practice, robust memory systems come down to the four essential operations illustrated in Figure 4-2: consolidating noisy experiences into stable knowledge, indexing that knowledge for fast access, updating it as reality changes, and retrieving the right slice at the right moment.

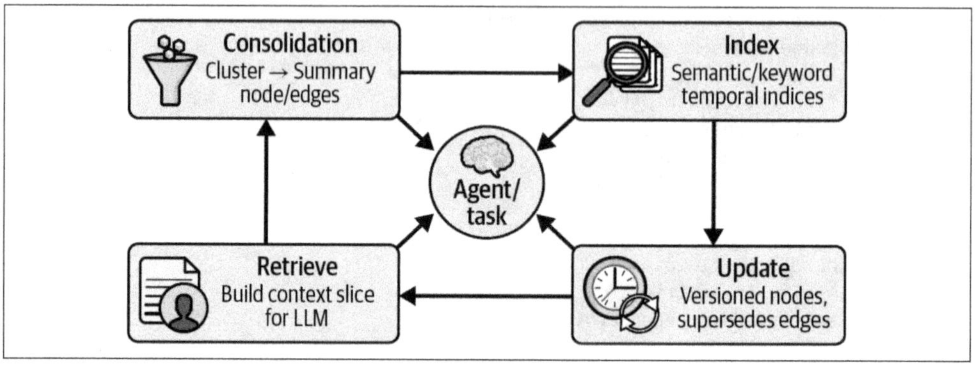


*Figure 4-3. Memory operations cycle*

## Consolidation: From Experience to Knowledge

Your agent accumulates many interactions, but most of them are redundant, overlapping, or partially inconsistent. *Consolidation* transforms these raw experiences into structured, durable knowledge. You can think of this as your agent's *sleep* phase, where short-term experiences are compressed into long-term understanding.

This is not just a metaphor. Research from Letta and University of California, Berkeley on sleep-time compute (Lin et al., 2025, *https://oreil.ly/rHCOt*) demonstrates that shifting heavy computation to idle periods—rather than performing it while users wait—can reduce active inference costs by five times while maintaining accuracy. When multiple queries share the same underlying context, the cost savings compound: precomputed enrichments amortize across every subsequent interaction. Your consolidation process should run during natural idle periods, not as a synchronous step in the response path.

At a high level, the consolidation process (Example 4-5) groups related memories, extracts key insights, turns them into graph structures, and keeps a clear provenance trail for trust and debugging.

*Example 4-5. Consolidation process*

```
def consolidate_memories(self, short_term_memories):
    # Group related memories
    clusters = self.cluster_by_topic(short_term_memories)

    for cluster in clusters:
        # Extract key facts and relationships
        summary = self.summarize_cluster(cluster)

        # Create permanent nodes and edges
        self.create_consolidated_memory(summary)
```

```
        # Link to source memories for provenance
        self.maintain_provenance_chain(summary, cluster)
```

The `cluster_by_topic` step groups related conversations. If a user has discussed the same project across multiple interactions, those exchanges end up in the same cluster. This typically uses *semantic similarity*—measuring how conceptually close memories are—to identify natural groupings, regardless of exact wording.

Then, `summarize_cluster` pulls out the essential information from each group. Instead of storing every repetition like *On Monday you said the deadline is Friday*, *on Tuesday you confirmed Friday*, and *on Wednesday you mentioned Friday again*, consolidation produces a single fact such as *Project deadline: Friday (confirmed multiple times)*. The meaning is preserved; the redundancy is not. This is also the moment to precompute inferences that anticipate likely queries. The sleep-time compute research shows that accuracy improvements of 13%–18% are achievable with the same computational budget when systems preprocess context during idle periods. If the consolidated knowledge includes a project deadline and a list of dependencies, sleep-time processing can derive which tasks are at risk before anyone asks. The enriched context then supports faster, more accurate responses when the question inevitably arrives.

Next, `create_consolidated_memory` turns these summaries into permanent graph structures. Key facts become nodes, relationships become edges, and the consolidated understanding becomes queryable knowledge that other components can rely on.

Finally, `maintain_provenance_chain` preserves the connection between consolidated knowledge and its sources. When a user asks *How do you know the deadline is Friday?*, your agent can trace that belief back to specific conversations. This transparency builds trust and gives you a clear path for debugging when something looks wrong: you can inspect exactly which interactions led to a mistaken conclusion.

## Indexing: Organizing for Speed

Once you have consolidated knowledge in the graph, the next challenge is getting to it quickly. Without indexing, your graph becomes a maze. Everything is technically there, but nothing is easy to reach. *Indexing* creates multiple access paths so queries can find relevant memories regardless of how users phrase their requests. In practice, you will often layer:

- Semantic indices for concept-level similarity (what is *about* the same thing)
- Keyword or lexical indices for exact terms and identifiers
- Temporal indices keyed by time ranges or event order
- Relational indices that make it cheap to traverse common patterns in the graph

For example, when your DevOps agent receives a vague alert about latency, semantic search might surface similar past incidents, temporal indices help narrow the search to the incidents from the last week, and relational indices make it trivial to walk from an affected service to its upstream dependencies. Indexing is the bridge between raw graph structure and responsive, production-grade queries.

## Updating: Handling Change Gracefully

Real systems do not stand still. Services move, owners change, feature flags flip, and yesterday's truth becomes today's misunderstanding. *Updating* is the operation that lets your agent absorb new information without corrupting its understanding of the past.

The key design principle is to preserve history while clearly marking current truth. When your agent learns something new that contradicts existing knowledge, it should:

- Attach the new information with a timestamp and provenance
- Mark previous facts as outdated, superseded, or deprecated rather than deleting them
- Maintain links between old and new states so it can explain how its understanding evolved

This is especially important for debugging and root cause analysis. If the agent misdiagnoses an outage, you want to see not just the final, corrected belief but the entire chain of updates that led it there. In a graph, this often means versioned nodes, timestamped edges, or explicit `supersedes` relationships that encode the evolution of knowledge over time.

## Retrieval: Finding What Matters

Finally, *retrieval* is where memory meets behavior. Retrieval is not just a database query; it is intelligent context assembly under uncertainty. No single retrieval strategy catches everything. Production systems typically combine:

- Semantic search to find conceptually related memories
- Keyword search for precise identifiers and error messages
- Graph traversal to uncover connected entities and events
- Temporal filters to bias toward recent or time-relevant information

The magic of merging these signals can be formalized. Hindsight (Latimer et al., 2025) runs all four retrieval channels in parallel, then combines them using reciprocal rank fusion (RRF). This approach has key advantages over score-based fusion. It's rank based, so scores don't need calibration across systems. It's also robust to missing items, since absent items simply contribute nothing. Finally, facts appearing high in multiple lists naturally surface. After RRF, a neural cross-encoder reranker refines precision on top candidates; then token budget filtering ensures that results fit the downstream LLM's context window.

The magic happens in how you merge these signals. Given an incident, your agent might start with a semantic query over past outages, filter to those involving the same service and region, expand along graph edges to include related deployments and configuration changes, and then rank results by recency and provenance quality.

What comes back from retrieval is not just a list of documents. It is a curated context window: a slice of the agent's entire memory that is most relevant to the current decision. Designing this slice carefully—what to include, what to exclude, and how to explain it—is what turns memory from a storage problem into a reasoning advantage.

# Production Patterns and Architectures

Now that you've learned the basic components and operations of graph-based memory systems, let's look at how some real systems structure that memory in production. These patterns recur in agent architectures, even when the names and implementations differ. We'll walk through three representative approaches:

- Hierarchical memory in Letta (MemGPT)
- Evolving knowledge networks in the A-Mem pattern
- Real-time incremental updates in Graphiti by Zep

Each solves for a different pain point: balancing fast access with long-term storage, updating a knowledge graph as beliefs change, and keeping latency low as the graph grows.

## The Letta (MemGPT) Approach: Hierarchical Memory

Letta popularized *hierarchical memory* (Packer et al., 2024, *https://oreil.ly/LonVK*), which mirrors human cognition. It's a small, fast working set backed by a much larger searchable archive. The core idea is to make forgetting and archiving explicit parts of the design instead of afterthoughts. A simplified version of the pattern looks like Example 4-6.

*Example 4-6. Hierarchical memory*

```
class HierarchicalMemory:
    def __init__(self, core_limit=2000):
        self.core_memory = CoreMemory(limit=core_limit)
        self.archival_memory = ArchivalMemory()
        self.recall_memory = RecallMemory()

    def process_interaction(self, user_input, agent_response):
        # Store in recall memory
        self.recall_memory.add(user_input, agent_response)

        # Extract important facts for core memory
        facts = self.extract_key_facts(user_input, agent_response)

        for fact in facts:
            if self.core_memory.is_full():
                # Move least-used items to archival
                archived = self.core_memory.evict_least_used()
                self.archival_memory.store(archived)

            self.core_memory.add(fact)
```

This three-tier architecture gives each memory layer a clear job:

`recall_memory`
: Keeps raw interaction history so you can answer questions like *What did we talk about yesterday?*

`core_memory`
: Holds the highest-value, most frequently accessed facts that should be instantly available.

`archival_memory`
: Provides effectively unlimited, slower storage for everything else.

The `extract_key_facts` method decides what deserves scarce core space. For example, it might promote *User is allergic to peanuts* as a durable fact and ignore *User is having coffee right now*. That distinction between long-lived attributes and short-lived states is crucial if you want agents that feel consistent over time.

The `core_limit=2000` parameter is not just a tuning knob but a forcing function. Once `core_memory` is full, `evict_least_used` must choose something to downgrade into `archival_memory`. A good implementation tracks usage patterns (access frequency, recency, or a combined score) rather than using naive first-in, first-out (FIFO) eviction. Facts you rely on often stay hot; everything else slowly drifts to the archive.

Importantly, *eviction is not deletion*. The archival layer keeps everything searchable. If a user asks about a detail from six months ago, the system can still find it via `archival_memory`, just with a slightly slower path than going to `core_memory`. You get fast responses for what matters most, without giving up full-history recall when you need it.

## The A-Mem Pattern: Evolving Knowledge Networks

While hierarchical memory focuses on *where* to store information, the A-Mem pattern (Xu et al., 2025, *https://oreil.ly/0uipl*) focuses on *how new information changes what you already know*. In practice, new facts rarely arrive in isolation. When your agent learns something like *Sarah now leads the product team*, that should ripple through existing beliefs about Sarah, the product team, and the org chart.

A minimal sketch of an A-Mem-style evolving knowledge network looks like Example 4-7.

*Example 4-7. Evolving memory*

```
class EvolvingMemory:
    def add_memory(self, content):
        # Create new memory node
        new_node = self.create_node(content)

        # Find related existing memories
        related = self.find_related_memories(new_node)

        # Form connections and trigger evolution
        for related_node in related:
            relationship = self.determine_relationship(new_node, related_node)
            self.create_edge(new_node, related_node, relationship)

        # Evolve the network
        self.evolve_connected_memories(new_node, related)
```

Each step is doing something more subtle than might appear at first glance:

`find_related_memories` *method*
: Uses semantic similarity (and sometimes structural hints) to locate memories that might be impacted. For *Sarah now leads the product team*, that includes prior nodes about Sarah, the previous leader, the product org, and related projects.

`determine_relationship` *method*
: Classifies how the new node relates to each existing one: is this an update, a refinement, a contradiction, or a new branch? Those relationship types drive how aggressively you propagate changes.

`create_edge` *method*
: Ties the new fact into the existing network, but the real work happens in `evolve_connected_memories`. That step revises the context of affected nodes: older memories about Sarah's previous role may be marked as historical, and nodes about the product team may be updated to reference the new leadership.

The result is a graph that doesn't just accumulate facts but maintains an evolving worldview. Each new memory can adjust confidence scores, invalidate outdated beliefs, or mark previous assertions as superseded. Importantly for agents operating in dynamic environments (org changes, product updates, evolving user preferences), this pattern prevents the knowledge graph from slowly drifting out of sync with reality.

## The Graphiti Pattern: Real-Time Performance

As your memory graph grows, performance becomes the next challenge. Graphiti by Zep illustrates a pattern for keeping query and update times low (Rasmussen et al., 2025, *https://oreil.ly/Qp75T*): *do everything incrementally*. Instead of recomputing embeddings, entities, or neighborhoods for the entire graph, touch only what the latest change requires. At a high level, adding a new interaction might look like Example 4-8.

*Example 4-8. Graphiti pattern*

```
def add_episode(self, episode_content):
    # Extract entities without reprocessing entire graph
    new_entities = self.extract_entities(episode_content)

    # Resolve against existing entities
    resolved_entities = self.entity_resolution(new_entities)

    # Update only affected portions
    self.incremental_update(resolved_entities)
```

Again, each step is designed to localize work:

`extract_entities` *method*
: Processes only the new episode content. There's no backfill over historical data and no full-graph re-embedding.

`entity_resolution` *method*
: Prevents graph bloat by matching new mentions to existing nodes. If the user refers to *the marketing director* and you already have `Sarah (Director of Marketing)` in the graph, this step ensures these references resolve to the same entity rather than creating duplicates.

`incremental_update` *method*
: Modifies only the impacted neighborhood: the few nodes and edges touched by the new entities and relationships. The rest of the graph stays untouched, which keeps write operations predictably fast.

Graphiti extends this incremental philosophy to retrieval as well. Instead of running one massive query over the entire graph, it uses parallel search strategies targeting different structures (for example, vector similarity over recent episodes, graph walks over entities, and keyword search over text) and then merges the results. This divide-and-conquer approach lets the system maintain sub-second response times even as the number of nodes and edges climbs into the millions.

Taken together, these patterns—hierarchical memory, evolving knowledge networks, and incremental graph updates—give you a practical toolkit. You can mix and match them depending on your constraints: latency, freshness, accuracy, and operational complexity. In the next sections, we'll look at how to adapt these ideas to your own stack and data.

# Comparing Production Systems

Most teams will not build graph memory systems entirely from scratch. You will either adopt an existing platform, integrate open source components, or borrow patterns from systems that are already running in production. Understanding how platforms like Cognee, mem0, and Zep implement graph memory shows you the trade-offs they make and the patterns you can reuse, even if you never adopt these particular tools.

In this section, we will use these systems less as product reviews and more as reference architectures. As you read, focus on the recurring ideas, such as graph-first modeling, selective storage, temporal reasoning, and lifecycle management, and think about how they might apply in your own environment.

## Cognee

Cognee takes a *graph-first* approach: it treats everything as relationships from the start. Its extract-cognify-load (ECL) pipeline creates semantic connections automatically during ingestion across more than 30 data sources and multiple backends, including LanceDB, Qdrant, Neo4j, and FalkorDB. The pipeline is deliberately modular:

*Extract*
: Parse documents, conversations, or structured data.

*Cognify*
: Build semantic relationships and apply ontologies.

*Load*
: Store data in the chosen backend with optimized indices.

This design pushes you to think in terms of graphs from the beginning. The trade-off is that developers need a solid grasp of graph concepts and ontology design to get the most out of the system. For applications where relationships matter more than isolated facts—such as regulatory compliance, safety analysis, or code understanding—that investment pays off in richer, more reliable reasoning.

Cognee is built to run at enterprise scale. It handles distributed processing across hundreds of containers and targets data sets ranging from gigabytes to terabytes. One gaming company, Dynamo.fyi, reported a 16% improvement in answer relevancy (*https://oreil.ly/Rzifs*) using Cognee's approach. The separation of extraction, cognification, and loading into distinct phases is not just a conceptual convenience; it is a scaling strategy. Each phase can be parallelized and tuned independently, from batch extraction jobs to specialized graph enrichment pipelines to backend-specific indexing strategies.

From an integration perspective, Cognee positions itself as an infrastructure building block inside broader agentic and RAG ecosystems. It provides an official `langchain-cognee` package with a `CogneeRetriever` class; deep LlamaIndex integration for graph-based retrieval; an MCP server for IDE integration in tools such as Cursor and Visual Studio (VS) Code; and support for model providers including OpenAI, Anyscale, Ollama, and Google Gemini. These integration points make Cognee feel less like a standalone application and more like a service you compose into existing workflows.

Cognee also has a strong story around memory lifecycle and enterprise operations. It relies on shared ontologies to enable multi-agent memory: common schemas allow agents to share a consistent understanding of entities and relationships. When one agent learns about a new regulation, other agents can immediately understand its implications through the shared semantic structures rather than through ad hoc string matching or prompt engineering. Its distributed architecture includes comprehensive logging and metrics, so you can track memory growth, query latency, and graph evolution patterns to identify issues before they affect users. For enterprises, this kind of observability becomes essential for debugging agent behavior and explaining why a particular answer was produced.

A recent API change consolidates these integration points around two calls, `cognee.remember()` and `cognee.recall()`, which fold in the older ingestion and retrieval functions and integrate skill management directly, so managing an agent's skills no longer requires a separate function. Cognee can also attach to agent harnesses such as Claude Code, Codex, and OpenClaw, switching between fast session memory for in-flight interactions and permanent, graph-structured memory for long-term knowledge.

## Mem0

Whereas Cognee starts with graphs, mem0 starts with *hybrid storage* and selective retention. It combines vector stores, graph databases, and key-value stores, choosing the right storage mechanism for each memory type. Its two-phase pipeline first extracts candidate memories and then decides whether to add, update, or discard them. Instead of treating storage as effectively infinite, mem0 assumes that long-term memory is scarce and must be curated.

This selective approach yields striking efficiency gains (Chhikara, 2025, *https://oreil.ly/qXnEs*):

- Roughly 90% token savings compared with full-context methods
- Around 91% latency reduction through intelligent filtering
- Basic integration in only a few lines of code

The trade-off is that mem0 focuses less on deep relationship modeling than would a pure graph system. For conversational AI and assistants where ease of integration and operational efficiency matter most, this pragmatic design is often exactly what you want.

On the performance side, mem0 leans heavily on the idea that most information does not deserve to become durable memory. On the LOCOMO benchmark, mem0 reports a 66.9% score from LLMs acting as judges, compared with 52.9% for OpenAI's native memory feature (Chhikara, 2025). Its selective storage strategy prevents the linear cost growth that plagues approaches that simply expand context windows over time. Rather than storing everything and hoping the model will pick the right tokens, mem0 tries to store only what is likely to matter later and aggressively avoids duplication. The result is a memory footprint that stays small and predictable as usage grows.

Mem0's integration story is about breadth and low friction. It provides native support for LangChain, LlamaIndex, LangGraph, CrewAI, and AutoGen; a browser extension that brings memory to tools such as ChatGPT, Perplexity, and Claude; SDKs in Python, JavaScript, and TypeScript; and multiple embedding providers, including OpenAI, BGE-m3, and Voyage AI. The project's popularity, reflected in its ecosystem and community activity, underscores how important easy integration is to teams experimenting with memory.

Under the hood, mem0's lifecycle model assumes that only a small fraction of information—often on the order of 10%—deserves permanent retention. The two-phase pipeline evaluates each potential memory and discards redundant or low-value items. This prevents memory bloat and the junk drawer problem where retrieval quality degrades over time, while also reducing costs by roughly 90% compared with naive store-everything approaches. Through its browser extension, what a user teaches one model, such as ChatGPT, can also become available to other models, like Claude or Perplexity. That makes memory feel attached to the user rather than to a single vendor or interface, which is an important pattern if you are designing cross-platform assistants.

## Zep

Zep, by contrast, centers its design on *temporal knowledge graphs* and explainability over time. It uses a three-tier architecture:

*Episode subgraphs*
: Raw interaction data

*Semantic entity subgraphs*
: Extracted entities and relationships

*Community subgraphs*
: Broader clusters that capture higher-level context

On top of that, Zep implements a bitemporal model: it tracks both the time of the event itself and the time at which the system learned about it. That lets you ask questions such as *What did we know about this customer when we made that recommendation?* rather than simply *What do we know now?* This temporal perspective is particularly important in enterprise settings where decisions need to be explained in terms of what information was available at the time.

Zep's production metrics (Rasmussen, 2025, *https://oreil.ly/GgPgB*) show where this design shines. On the Deep Memory Retrieval benchmark, it achieves around 94.8% retrieval accuracy. At the same time, it maintains a P95 latency of roughly 300 milliseconds even at scale by precomputing retrieval artifacts instead of calling LLMs during search. Zep spends compute at ingestion time to build optimized structures, then keeps runtime query paths simple and predictable.

Its integration patterns reflect an enterprise focus. Zep offers dedicated classes for LangChain, such as `ZepMemory` and `ZepChatMessageHistory`, a `ZepVectorStore` integration for LlamaIndex, native integration with LangGraph, and System and Organization Controls 2 (SOC 2) Type II certification for regulated environments. This combination of developer tooling and compliance posture is tailored to teams that need to convince both engineers and security reviewers of its trustworthiness.

Zep's scaling strategy emphasizes hierarchical clustering. The core idea is to organize memories into semantic clusters, then organize those clusters into higher-level superclusters, turning naive linear search into an effectively logarithmic process. Zep maintains near-constant retrieval times even with very large user populations by precomputing retrieval artifacts during ingestion. Rather than pushing each query through an expensive model invocation, it prepares searchable artifacts ahead of time and routes queries through them. When you implement similar clustering in your own system, focus on dynamic rebalancing: as a cluster grows too large, split it based on semantic similarity; as clusters become too small, merge them. This self-organizing behavior keeps performance stable as the overall graph size changes.

Zep also illustrates how to treat memory lifecycle and enterprise constraints together. Its temporal invalidation strategy treats facts as having expiration dates: when information becomes outdated, Zep marks it as invalid while still preserving the historical record. This keeps current answers accurate without sacrificing audit trails. Cost management follows the same philosophy. Full-context approaches incur roughly linear cost growth because every additional token costs money; mem0 shows that intelligent filtering can cut LLM costs by around 80% to 90%, while Zep's pricing focuses on message processing rather than raw storage, aligning cost more closely with perceived value.

## Choosing Your Approach

These production systems illustrate that successful graph memory is about matching the right architecture to your use case rather than following a single pattern.

You might use Cognee's patterns when:

- Relationships matter more than isolated facts.
- You need formal reasoning with ontologies.
- You must handle multimodal data such as text, images, and audio in a unified way.

You might apply mem0's approach when:

- Integration simplicity is paramount.
- Cost-efficient scaling is a constraint.
- Self-improving memory that refines itself over time adds value.

You might follow Zep's design when:

- Temporal reasoning is critical.
- Enterprise compliance and auditability are required.
- You need to integrate with existing business systems.

These are not mutually exclusive choices. In practice, you can combine graph-first relationship modeling from Cognee with selective storage from mem0 and temporal tracking from Zep and then tune the blend to match your domain, data, and risk profile. Taken together, these systems show that graph memory in production is less about picking the *right* vendor and more about understanding the underlying patterns, then composing them into an architecture that fits your constraints.

## Production-Ready Features and Operations

Production memory systems are not judged on how nicely they store data but on how well they reason, recommend, and stay healthy under real load. In this section, we'll look first at how graph memory changes your agent's reasoning and recommendations. Then we'll shift to the operational side to discuss debugging, maintenance, and use case–specific optimizations.

### Reasoning and Recommendations

We have focused so far on storing and retrieving information efficiently, but the whole point of memory is to support better reasoning. Graph memory changes what your agents can infer and recommend by letting them follow chains of evidence instead of treating each fact in isolation.

#### Multi-hop reasoning

With *multi-hop reasoning*, your memory moves from passive storage to active intelligence. Instead of answering questions with single lookups, your agent connects information across multiple nodes to build an argument.

The process works by decomposing complex queries into sub-questions, gathering evidence for each piece, then finding valid reasoning paths that connect those pieces. This mirrors how humans solve hard problems: we break them down, follow implications, and only then synthesize a conclusion.

For example, when asked *What technical decisions in Q1 led to the performance improvements mentioned in the July all-hands?*, your agent should:

1. Identify Q1 technical decisions
2. Find July all-hands performance mentions
3. Discover paths connecting decisions to outcomes
4. Validate that the connections are logically consistent
5. Synthesize a coherent answer that ties the chain together

In graph terms, the agent is not just retrieving nodes; it is traversing paths, ranking them by plausibility, and using those paths as the backbone of its explanation.

### Intelligent recommendations

Graph memory also upgrades recommendations from heuristic guesses to structured analogies. The key idea is that similar situations often share similar solutions, and a graph is a natural way to represent those similarities.

When generating recommendations, your agent can:

- Find analogous past situations in the graph
- Extract what made those past interventions successful
- Adapt those patterns to the current context, accounting for key differences
- Weight each recommendation by similarity, recency, and observed success rate

This approach turns your organization's history into a form of collective intelligence. When multiple users face similar challenges, their combined solutions form a library of graph-encoded precedents. Over time, those precedents often outperform any single expert's intuition.

### Debugging and maintenance

Powerful reasoning is useful only if the system remains stable, observable, and fixable. Production-grade graph memory needs guardrails: health monitoring, visualization, conflict handling, and ongoing performance tuning. Think of this as your operations playbook for living graph systems.

### Health monitoring

Start by making the health of your graph visible. A production graph is a living system: nodes and edges are constantly being added, updated, and pruned. Without explicit monitoring, you will not notice structural problems until they show up as user-visible failures or runaway infrastructure costs.

A practical way to begin is with a small dashboard of core metrics that describe how the graph is evolving, each of which tells you something different about how memory is behaving:

*Node growth rate*
: Tracks how quickly new entities and events are being added. A steady, domain-aligned growth curve usually signals healthy ingestion. Sudden spikes often mean a broken parser, a runaway source, or an ontology change that is exploding the number of nodes (for example, turning every log line into a separate entity). Watching this curve per source helps you catch ingestion problems before they flood the graph with junk.

*Edge density*
: Captures how interconnected your graph is. Too few edges, and your agent cannot perform multi-hop reasoning because everything looks isolated. Too many edges, and every traversal turns into a combinatorial explosion. In practice, you monitor average degree and the distribution of high-degree nodes (hubs). A growing tail of extremely high-degree nodes often indicates over-eager relationship extraction that needs tightening.

*Cluster balance*
: Tells you whether your graph is partitioned in a way that matches reality. Community detection or sharding schemes will naturally create clusters around services, teams, or domains. When a single cluster starts to dominate, it can signal modeling issues, such as overly generic entities that "glue" unrelated areas together, or misconfigured sharding that packs everything into one partition. Balanced clusters support more predictable query performance and easier reasoning about local neighborhoods.

*Query latency*
: Connects graph structure back to user experience. You care not only about the average but also P95 and P99 latencies for your key query types: retrieval, neighborhood expansion, multi-hop reasoning, and temporal lookups. Rising tail latencies often correlate with increasing edge density or poorly constrained queries. By tying latency metrics back to graph structure metrics, you can decide whether to tune the query layer, prune paths, or adjust schemas.

*Memory conflicts*
: Measures how often new facts contradict existing ones. This can be as simple as tracking how many updates flip a property's value, or as complex as logging explicit conflict markers when two sources disagree. A low, steady rate is expected in any dynamic environment. A sudden increase usually means an upstream data-quality issue or a new source with incompatible semantics. Monitoring conflicts gives you a quantitative signal that it is time to revisit extraction rules or source weighting.

*Temporal consistency*
: Focuses on whether your time-based data remains logically coherent. Here you look for impossible or overlapping sequences: resources that appear to be in two conflicting states at the same timestamp, events that reference future versions of entities, or validity windows that never close. Simple checks, such as verifying that start times precede end times or that version numbers increase monotonically, go a long way. More advanced systems track temporal invariants (for example, a deployment must precede the errors it causes) and alert when those invariants are violated.

These metrics only become useful when they are wired into action. When health checks cross thresholds, your system should trigger automated maintenance workflows: rebalancing clusters, rebuilding indices, tightening extraction rules, or throttling noisy sources. Over time, you can move from manual dashboards to self-healing mechanisms that keep the graph within safe operating bounds while escalating only the ambiguous cases to humans.

### Visualization and debugging tools

Even with good metrics, graphs can feel opaque in production. Mature systems lean on visualization and debugging tools to make memory behavior inspectable:

- Zep's Graph Explorer lets you visualize memory structures and relationships.
- Cognee's local UI helps you debug extraction pipelines and relationship formation.
- The browser extension of mem0 shows memory formation in real time, right alongside the user's activity.

These tools become essential when you are trying to explain why a particular memory did not show up in a response, why an edge exists between two entities, or how a specific reasoning path was chosen. They turn an opaque memory into something you can interrogate and refine.

### Conflict resolution

Contradictory information is inevitable as your system ingests more sources and as reality itself changes. A production system needs a consistent approach to conflict resolution. Instead of using ad hoc patches, handle conflicts by assessing credibility, temporal precedence, and source authority. In practice:

- When new information is more recent and more credible, you can treat it as the active truth while preserving the older version for history.
- When sources have different authority levels, you can maintain both facts but assign them different confidence weights.
- When uncertainty remains high, keep both versions, mark the conflict explicitly, and let downstream reasoning components decide how to use them.

Effective conflict resolution avoids premature convergence on a single answer while giving the agent a structured way to reason under uncertainty.

### Performance optimization

As your graph grows, performance tuning shifts from a nice-to-have to a survival skill. Three strategies tend to matter most in production:

*Path pruning*
: Remove redundant or low-value connections that slow traversal without improving answers. The goal is to keep enough edges for connectivity and reasoning while trimming those that only add noise.

*Node compression*
: Collapse highly similar nodes into summary or canonical representations, with links back to the original details when full fidelity is needed. This keeps the active graph compact while preserving provenance for debugging and compliance.

*Cold storage*
: Move rarely accessed memories to cheaper, slower storage tiers. They remain searchable via background processes or batched queries but do not burden your hot query path or primary infrastructure.

Together, these strategies help you sustain low-latency reasoning over a graph that continues to grow in both scale and complexity.

## Use Case Optimizations

Finally, production systems do not all optimize in the same way. The right operational and modeling choices depend heavily on your primary use case and the style of interaction you are supporting.

For conversational AI in the spirit of mem0's approach, you typically prioritize recent context and simplicity of integration. Recency weighting (for example, exponential decay) keeps the latest interactions front and center. A *one-day integration* story matters so that product teams can experiment quickly. The memory design focuses on user preferences and implicit signals, and it emphasizes cross-session continuity so conversations feel persistent rather than reset on every visit.

For complex reasoning in the spirit of Cognee's approach, you invest more in structure and depth. You build rich ontologies that capture domain knowledge explicitly, optimize for multi-hop traversal instead of just local neighborhoods, and, where appropriate, integrate formal logic. Explanation generation becomes a first-class requirement so that agents can show their work and justify decisions to humans.

For temporal applications in the spirit of Zep's approach, time becomes your organizing principle. You implement bitemporal tracking consistently, not just in a handful of tables. You optimize for time-range and point-in-time queries, maintain complete audit trails that link decisions to the knowledge available at the time, and support reconstructing past states for debugging and compliance reviews.

These are all variations on the same foundation: graph-based memory. By tuning the same core architecture for conversation, deep reasoning, or temporal analysis, you can align your system's behavior with the realities of your production use case.

# Training Your Agents to Use Memory

You have built an impressive memory system, complete with graph structures, temporal tracking, and hierarchical storage. You plug it into your LLM and expect magic. Instead, it fails spectacularly. Why? Because you are asking a concert pianist to pick up a guitar mid-performance. LLMs are trained to generate text from whatever context you hand them. They are not trained to decide what to remember, what to forget, or how to maintain a coherent internal state over time.

Out of the box, LLMs have no idea how to:

- Decide what is worth remembering (*coffee preference* versus *drinking coffee right now*)
- Choose between creating new memories and updating existing ones
- Balance retrieval benefits against context pollution

The result is predictable: your carefully designed graph turns into a digital hoarder's attic. Everything is saved, but you have almost nothing truly useful.

This is where recent work on learned memory, such as MEM1 (Zhou et al., 2025, *https://oreil.ly/p2_RZ*), becomes important. MEM1 is a research framework that treats memory not as a static database feature but as a behavior that agents learn through reinforcement learning. Instead of hardcoding memory policies, it trains agents end to end so they discover when to write, retrieve, and consolidate information in service of their tasks.

## The MEM1 Revelation: Let Them Learn, Not Follow Rules

The key insight from MEM1 is simple but profound: agents can *learn* effective memory strategies through experience instead of following handcrafted rules. Rather than encoding detailed policies about what to store and when to retrieve, you train the agent and memory system together and let memory behavior emerge.

The reported outcomes are striking:

- Agents learned to distinguish important information from trivia without explicit heuristics.
- Memory consolidation strategies emerged from the demands of the task, not from schema diagrams.

- Smaller 7B models with learned memory behavior outperformed 70B models with manually engineered memory policies.

The lesson is clear: stop trying to script memory usage in advance. Instead, create training conditions where good memory behavior is the shortest path to success.

## From Static Rules to Learned Strategies

Most production systems start with rule lists:

> *Store user preferences but not current activities.*
> *Update existing nodes when information changes.*
> *Retrieve only highly relevant memories.*

These rules work until they do not. They clash, produce edge cases, and become harder to maintain as your system grows. Every new behavior requires another exception and another round of debugging.

The MEM1 approach turns this upside down. Rather than micromanaging behavior, you define what *success* looks like and let the agent discover memory strategies that achieve it. You still design the environment, the reward structure, and the tools the agent can use, but you stop pretending you can enumerate every memory rule up front.

## The Three Phases of Training

MEM1 offers a concrete training pattern you can adapt in three phases (Figure 4-4): start from real tasks, enforce constraints, and then scale up complexity. Let's look at each of these in turn.

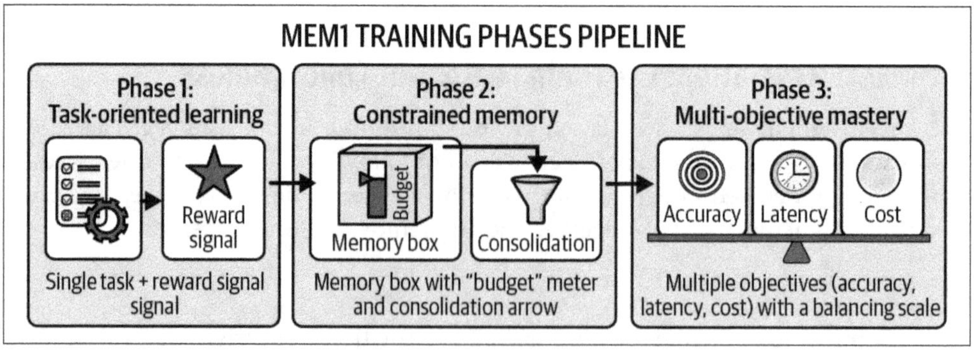


*Figure 4-4. MEM1 training phases*

### Phase 1: Task-oriented learning

Do not train memory in the abstract. Train on the tasks your agent actually needs to perform. Instead of generic memory training like *Learn to store and retrieve information effectively*, train with real task rewards. Determine if the agent completed the user's request.

In MEM1, agents trained on question-answering tasks. They did not learn generic storage habits; they learned whatever memory behavior improved answer accuracy. Your ecommerce agent should train on shopping flows. Your coding assistant should train on debugging and refactoring sessions. Memory becomes a tool in service of task success, not an isolated objective.

### Phase 2: Consolidation through constraints

The next step is to force trade-offs. MEM1's real breakthrough was not just training but training under a memory budget. When agents cannot store everything, they must learn what actually matters. Consider Example 4-9, which shows a simple implementation of constrained memory training.

*Example 4-9. Constrained memory training*

```
class ConstrainedMemoryTraining:
    def __init__(self, memory_budget=1000):
        self.budget = memory_budget

    def train_step(self, experience):
        # Agent must work within budget
        if self.memory_usage > self.budget:
            # Forces consolidation decisions
            self.agent.consolidate_or_fail()
```

This changes the default behavior from *Store everything that might be useful* to *Maintain the minimal state that sustains task performance*. The constraint is not an implementation detail; it is part of the training signal.

### Phase 3: Multi-objective mastery

Finally, MEM1 shows that agents trained on relatively simple, two-objective tasks can generalize to more complex, multi-objective scenarios. They do this by learning general consolidation strategies rather than brittle, task-specific tricks.

You can mirror this by gradually increasing task complexity:

1. *Single objectives*
   Answer one type of question or complete one kind of action.

2. *Dual objectives*
   Balance two goals, such as accuracy and latency.

3. *Realistic multi-goal interactions*
   Juggle user satisfaction, cost, latency, and safety.

Over time, agents learn compositional strategies that they can reuse as you introduce new tasks.

## Dynamic Memory Without Dynamic Schemas

Earlier in this chapter, we spent time on runtime schema evolution. MEM1 suggests a more radical possibility: maybe you do not need explicit schemas for every aspect of memory behavior. A traditional approach looks like this:

```
# Complex schema management
builder.add_schema({...})
builder.add_object({...})
# Hope the schema captures what matters
```

A learned approach instead treats the internal state as a trainable representation:

```
# Learned representation
internal_state = agent.consolidate(history, new_info)
# Trust the agent learned what matters for the task
```

Here, the consolidated state effectively becomes a learned schema, one that is tightly tailored to what your tasks require and unconcerned with modeling every possible detail of the world. You still need explicit graphs and schemas for many parts of your system, but learned representations can handle a surprising amount of the work.

## Practical Training Strategies

So how do you bring these ideas into your own system without reproducing the entire MEM1 stack? Start with a few pragmatic patterns.

### Reward task success, not memory perfection

If you reward agents for recalling or storing everything, they will happily overfit to hoarding. Instead, tie rewards to task outcomes and let memory be a means, not an end:

```
# Bad: reward for storing everything
reward = memories_stored / total_information

# Good: reward for task completion
reward = tasks_completed_successfully
```

When rewarded for outcomes, the agent learns to keep information that improves performance and drop the rest.

### Use masked training for specialized behaviors

MEM1 uses masked trajectories to keep training signals clear. You can apply the same idea by separating out learning signals for different memory components:

- Retrieval modules train only on retrieval decisions and their downstream impact.
- Storage modules train only on what gets written and how it affects success.
- Consolidation modules train on how state compression impacts future performance.

By isolating signals, you avoid cross-contamination where, for example, retrieval mistakes get incorrectly attributed to storage policies.

### Implement curriculum learning

Do not throw your agent into the deep end on day one. Build a curriculum that layers complexity:

*Week 1*
: Single facts about single entities

*Week 2*
: Relationships between entities

*Week 3*
: Temporal changes and before/after states

*Week 4*
: Conflicting information that must be reconciled

*Week 5*
: Multi-entity, multistep scenarios closer to production reality

Each stage reuses and stress-tests what the agent learned before, making memory behavior more robust.

## Evolving Your Memory System

A good memory system cannot be frozen in place. It has to evolve as your tasks, data, and users change—but that evolution does not need to be driven by ever more complex engineering. It can be driven by learning. Over time, well-trained agents develop several important behaviors.

### Learned contextual updates

When the agent encounters a statement like *Sarah now leads marketing*, it learns to:

- Find existing memories about Sarah
- Update relevant relationships and roles
- Propagate changes where they matter for downstream tasks

You do not hardcode these steps; the agent learns them because failing to update leads to worse task performance.

### Discovered relationship patterns

Agents also discover which relationships are predictive in your domain. A support agent learns that purchase history and ticket history jointly predict what to suggest. A coding assistant learns which error patterns correlate with specific function calls or dependency versions.

### Emergent consolidation

Perhaps the most surprising outcome is the emergence of compact summary representations. MEM1 agents learned to maintain task performance while discarding the vast majority of raw information, effectively compressing experience into dense, actionable state.

## Moving Beyond Traditional Training

If you are used to designing memory systems primarily through schemas and rules, this may feel like a big shift. However, the future of memory in agentic systems is not about inventing ever-smarter policies in configuration files. It is about building environments where agents *must* learn what to remember, what to forget, and how to evolve their internal understanding to succeed.

Here is a practical progression to start with:

1. Define clear task success metrics that matter for your application.
2. Introduce explicit memory constraints that force trade-offs.
3. Grow task complexity gradually with a curriculum.

4. Use masked training so each memory component gets proper feedback.
5. Allow strategies to emerge from experience rather than encoding them all up front.

Your agents do not need you to micromanage memory. Rather, they need you to shape the game so that good memory management is the winning strategy. MEM1 teaches us that we get farther by learning better consolidation than by building ever more elaborate memory machinery by hand.

# Adding Memory to the DevOps Agent

In Chapter 3, you built a knowledge graph that captures your infrastructure's current state: services, dependencies, configurations, and events. That graph is a snapshot—a digital twin of what exists right now. But DevOps is not a static discipline. Incidents unfold over hours. Configuration changes ripple through systems over days. Your agent needs memory that spans these timescales.

This section shows you how to extend the DevOps agent with graph-based memory that tracks change, learns what matters, and improves its own retention strategies through reinforcement learning.

## Designing the DevOps Memory Schema

The knowledge graph from Chapter 3 already models entities and relationships. Memory adds three new dimensions: episodes that capture raw operational events, temporal edges that track when facts were true, and consolidated knowledge that distills patterns from accumulated experience. Example 4-10 extends the schema to separate these concerns.

*Example 4-10. DevOps memory schema extensions*

```
# Episode types: raw operational events
EPISODE_TYPES = ["Incident", "Deployment", "ConfigChange", "Alert",
    "Conversation"]

# Temporal relationship types
TEMPORAL_EDGES = ["PRECEDED_BY", "CAUSED_BY", "CORRELATED_WITH", "SUPERSEDES"]

# Consolidated knowledge types
KNOWLEDGE_TYPES = ["Pattern", "Preference", "Runbook", "RiskFactor"]
```

Each category serves a distinct purpose. Episodes are append-only records of what happened. Temporal edges let you reconstruct sequences and trace causality. Consolidated knowledge represents what your agent has learned such as the patterns that predict outages and the runbooks that resolve specific error classes.

## Implementing Memory for Operational Context

The core abstraction is a `DevOpsMemory` class that handles ingestion, temporal tracking, and retrieval. The `ingest_episode` method on this class is shown in Example 4-11.

*Example 4-11. DevOps memory ingestion*

```
def ingest_episode(self, episode_type, content, metadata):
    """Record a new operational event."""
    episode = self.kg.create_node(
        node_type=episode_type,
        properties={
            "content": content,
            "embedding": self.embedder.embed(content),
            "ingested_at": datetime.now(),
            "valid_from": metadata.get("event_time", datetime.now()),
            **metadata
        }
    )

    # Link to affected infrastructure and preceding episodes
    self.link_to_affected_entities(episode, metadata)
    self.link_to_preceding_episodes(episode, window_hours=24)

    return episode
```

The method creates a richly attributed node with both semantic content (the embedding) and temporal metadata (when the event happened versus when the system learned about it). It links the episode to affected infrastructure entities and connects to preceding episodes, building the causal chains your agent will follow during incident investigation.

## Temporal Queries for Root Cause Analysis

The bitemporal model pays off when your agent needs to answer the question *What changed recently that might explain this failure?* Example 4-12 shows the query pattern.

*Example 4-12. Temporal query for root cause analysis*

```
def find_changes_before_incident(self, incident_id, lookback_hours=4):
    """Find configuration and deployment changes preceding an incident."""
    changes = self.kg.query("""
        MATCH (change)-[:AFFECTS]->(entity)<-[:AFFECTS]-(incident)
        WHERE incident.id = $incident_id
          AND change.valid_from >= $lookback_start
          AND change.type IN ['Deployment', 'ConfigChange']
```

```
        RETURN change, entity
        ORDER BY change.valid_from DESC
    """, params)

    return self.score_by_proximity_and_relationship(changes, incident)
```

This query combines temporal filtering with graph traversal, then scores results by both time proximity and relationship strength. Changes closer in time are more suspect, but changes with stronger causal connections matter more.

## Consolidation: Learning Patterns from Incidents

Raw episodes are too noisy for direct reasoning. Consolidation extracts durable patterns that generalize across incidents, as shown in Example 4-13.

*Example 4-13. Pattern consolidation*

```
def consolidate(self):
    """Extract patterns from buffered episodes."""
    clusters = self.cluster_episodes(self.episode_buffer)

    for cluster in clusters:
        if len(cluster) < 3:
            continue  # Need enough examples to generalize

        precursors = self.find_common_precursors(cluster)
        pattern = self.create_or_update_pattern(precursors, cluster)

        # Link to source episodes for provenance
        for episode in cluster:
            self.kg.create_edge(pattern, episode, "DERIVED_FROM")

    self.episode_buffer = []
```

Patterns are derived from clusters of similar episodes, not individual events. Each pattern maintains provenance links back to its source episodes, so you can always explain why the agent believes a particular risk factor matters.

## Training Memory Behavior with Reinforcement Learning

Handcrafted heuristics work, but they do not adapt to your specific environment. The MEM1 approach suggests letting the agent learn memory behavior through reinforcement learning. Amazon Nova Forge provides the infrastructure to implement this through its *bring your own orchestration* (BYOO) capability.

### Defining the memory training environment

Frame memory management as an RL problem where the agent takes actions (store, retrieve, consolidate, forget) and receives rewards based on incident resolution performance, as shown in Example 4-14.

*Example 4-14. DevOps memory RL environment*

```
class DevOpsMemoryEnvironment:
    """RL environment for training DevOps agent memory behavior."""

    def __init__(self, knowledge_graph, incident_dataset):
        self.memory = DevOpsMemory(knowledge_graph)
        self.incidents = incident_dataset
        self.memory_budget = 1000  # Maximum nodes in working memory

    def step(self, action):
        """Execute memory action and return reward."""
        self.execute_action(action)

        if self.memory.working_memory_size() > self.memory_budget:
            return {"reward": -1.0, "done": False, "info": "budget_exceeded"}

        # Reward based on incident resolution, not memory operations
        reward = self.evaluate_incident_resolution()
        return {"reward": reward, "done": False}
```

The memory budget constraint forces trade-offs. When working memory is full, the agent must consolidate or forget something before storing new information. Through training, the agent learns which information is worth keeping.

### Configuring Nova Forge for memory training

Nova Forge's BYOO mode connects your custom environment to the RL training loop, as shown in Example 4-15.

*Example 4-15. Nova Forge configuration*

```
run:
  name: devops-memory-training
  model_type: amazon.nova-2-lite-v1:0:256k
  data_s3_path: s3://your-bucket/devops-incidents.jsonl

training_config:
  max_seq_length: 16384  # Long context for multiturn memory interactions
  reasoning_effort: high

rollout:
  delegate: true  # Enable BYOO mode
  timeout: 900    # 15 minutes for complex incident sequences
```

The `max_seq_length` is set high because memory training involves multiturn conversations where context accumulates. The `rollout timeout` is generous because incident resolution can involve multiple retrieval and reasoning steps.

### What the agent learns

After training on hundreds of incident sequences, several behaviors consistently emerge:

- Selective storage becomes context dependent. Deployment metadata is high value immediately after release but can be consolidated once stable. Isolated alerts get lower retention priority.
- Retrieval strategies become multistage. Instead of performing a single similarity query, trained agents learn to first retrieve broad context, then narrow the query based on findings, and finally expand along causal edges.
- Consolidation timing adapts to workload. During quiet periods, the agent consolidates aggressively. During incident storms, it defers consolidation to preserve raw context.
- Forgetting becomes strategic. Successfully resolved incidents are forgotten faster than unresolved ones. High-severity service information is retained longer.

These behaviors emerge from the reward signal, not from rules you wrote. The agent discovers them because they improve incident resolution performance.

## Production Considerations

When taking this example to production, you'll need to consider three important factors to make it more robust:

*Continuous learning versus stability*
: Either freeze policies and periodically retrain for safety, or implement continuous learning with safeguards against catastrophic forgetting and distribution shift.

*Explaining learned behavior*
: Log the agent's reasoning at each memory decision. Track which memories contributed to successful resolutions. Build explanation capability into deployment.

*Monitoring memory health*
: Track action distribution, reward trajectory on held-out incidents, memory composition by type, and retrieval hit rate. These metrics catch policy degradation before it affects incident response.

The DevOps agent now has memory that spans from raw operational events to learned patterns, with behavior that adapts through RL rather than static rules.

In Chapter 5, you will add reasoning and planning capabilities that leverage this memory foundation.

## Future-Proofing Your Implementation

By now, you have the tools to design and operate a robust graph memory system with today's requirements in mind. Future-proofing is about making sure those decisions do not trap you tomorrow. The point is not to predict every trend but to choose patterns that adapt well as models improve, data grows, and expectations change. Three themes in particular will shape how your memory architecture evolves: neurosymbolic reasoning, distributed scaling, and continual learning.

### Neurosymbolic Integration

The next wave of memory systems blends neural networks with symbolic reasoning. *Neurosymbolic systems* (Garcez and Lamb, 2020, *https://oreil.ly/4TIQJ*) use neural models for pattern recognition and natural language, while symbolic components provide explicit, inspectable logic. Together, they handle queries that neither approach can reliably solve alone.

This hybrid design also changes how users trust your system. Neural components are effectively opaque, but symbolic reasoners can emit traceable steps: which nodes were traversed, which rules fired, and how a conclusion followed from prior facts. Users can see not just what the system decided but why it chose that path through the graph.

### Distributed Scaling

As your knowledge graphs grow beyond a single machine, you will eventually distribute them across multiple nodes. At that point, sharding decisions become architectural, not operational. You want to keep related subgraphs together while still balancing load, which means partitioning along natural boundaries like tenants, domains, or high-level entity types.

Once you distribute, query coordination becomes its own problem. Smart routing should send each request only to the shards that might have relevant information, rather than broadcasting everything everywhere. For large, exploratory queries, asynchronous processing helps: return partial results quickly, then stream or update more complete answers as the system finishes deeper traversals. The user experience stays responsive even as the graph and query workload grow.

### Continual Learning

A good memory system does not just store more data over time; it learns how to use that data more effectively. Track query patterns to discover common paths worth precomputing or materializing. Monitor which memories users actually click, reuse, or expand to refine your ranking algorithms. Adjust indices and cache strategies based on real access patterns as they emerge rather than sticking with your initial design assumptions.

This kind of empirical tuning turns your graph memory into a living system. It gradually reshapes itself around how people really query it, not how you imagined they would. Over time, your implementation becomes better at serving your specific users and workloads, even if the underlying hardware and models stay the same.

## Summary

Graph memory systems live or die by how well they are structured. When you model entities and relationships explicitly, you unlock capabilities that flat storage can never match. Time becomes a first-class dimension rather than an afterthought: your agents can distinguish current truths from stale ones, track how beliefs have changed, and explain what happened in between. Relationships move from being a convenience to being the core of your design. Facts are cheap; the connections between them are where the intelligence emerges.

These systems also need to evolve alongside your product. The most successful architectures favor steady evolution over dramatic rewrites. You introduce graph structures, then layer in temporal awareness, and finally add hierarchy and advanced reasoning as the demands on your system grow. At every step, performance remains a feature, not a nice-to-have. Users will not wait for slow retrieval, no matter how clever your reasoning paths look on a whiteboard.

You do not have to take this journey alone. Platforms like Cognee, mem0, and Zep show that these ideas work at scale, serving millions of users with sub-second latency while maintaining accuracy and temporal context. You might use Cognee when you need deep, relationship-heavy reasoning across many sources, mem0 when you want tight integration with conversational AI and quick setup, or Zep when enterprise-grade temporal awareness and governance are primary concerns. The specific choice matters less than your willingness to align the tool with your users' needs instead of chasing features for their own sake.

Whether you build from scratch, adapt an existing system, or land somewhere in between, the principles stay consistent. Agentic systems can only go so far, even with the best models. Give your agents memory that can grow, that understands change over time, and that treats relationships as first-class citizens. The graph-based memory techniques and production systems you have seen in this chapter prove that is not only possible but practical. In the next chapter, you'll put all of the material you learned in the first few chapters to work in order to build reasoning and planning systems into your agents.

# PART III
# Action: From Firefighting to Foresight

Part III brings the agent to life. A knowledge graph and memory give the agent a brain, but a brain without a nervous system is inert. Part III builds the horizontal workflow graph and connects the agent to the outside world through tools, transforming it from a queryable knowledge base into a system that thinks, plans, and acts.

By the end of Part III, the DevOps agent has faced its first real challenge—a vague high-latency alert from an SRE—and worked through it end to end. It decomposes the problem into a multistep plan, traverses dependencies in the knowledge graph, queries live metrics through an orchestrated tool, and identifies the root cause. It has gone from being a passive map to a competent diagnostician.

- Chapter 5 covers graph-based reasoning (multi-hop traversal, PathRAG-style verified paths, adaptive retrieval) and DAG-based planning (decomposition, parallel execution, resilient failure management, dynamic replanning) and applies these concepts to constructing the agent's first horizontal workflow graph.
- Chapter 6 covers MCP-based tool integration, graph-based tool representation and discovery, security and information flow control, and grammar-constrained structured output, enabling the agent to reliably interact with external systems and live data.

CHAPTER 5

# Reasoning and Planning

As agent architecture has evolved, one of the ongoing debates has been about the relative advantages of multi-agent and single-agent systems (reminiscent of the debates around monorepos in the development community). On one side, teams are shipping multi-agent systems—with lead agents delegating to specialist subagents, running branches in parallel, and then reconciling results—because they can dramatically improve breadth-first work like open-ended research. An example is Anthropic's multi-agent research system (*https://oreil.ly/xS-Fo*).

On the other side, people building real products keep running into the same ugly truth: every new agent you add is also a new coordination surface. If context isn't shared correctly, if handoffs are lossy, or if agents make implicit decisions that never get written down, the whole system becomes fragile in ways that look "mysterious" from the outside. (Cognition's article "Don't Build Multi-Agents" [Yan, 2025, *https://oreil.ly/KM5pH*] is one of the best examples of this argument.) Meanwhile, vendors are racing to bottle the chaos into something shippable, such as explicit handoffs and routines (as in the OpenAI cookbook for orchestration via routines and handoffs; Bigio, 2024, *https://oreil.ly/j_wBA*) and enterprise workflows plus state management (such as the Microsoft Agent Framework overview, *https://oreil.ly/vRm9x*).

That disagreement is real, but it's also a distraction from what actually determines whether your system works: reasoning and planning. Multi-agent orchestration is planning. A single "do-it-all" agent is still planning—just internally, implicitly, and often invisibly. When production agents fail, they usually don't fail because you picked the wrong number of agents; they fail because the system can't reliably do the following:

1. Decide what to do next
2. Represent state and constraints

3. Verify intermediate steps
4. Recover when reality disagrees

This chapter focuses on those mechanics: the concrete planning patterns that make agents dependable, the representations that keep them honest, and the control flow you need to turn "clever demos" into systems you can operate. Frameworks like LangGraph (*https://oreil.ly/rOcs4*) are a good tell here: they're less about "agents" and more about *controllable execution graphs* (whether single-agent or multi-agent) because control flow is the real product.

As it turns out, building agentic systems is about engineering better processes around models. When an agent books a flight, analyzes financial data, or synthesizes a stack of research papers, the difference isn't hidden in model capabilities but in the sequence of steps you designed: the decision points, the handoffs between components, and the information that's allowed to move forward at each stage. Agentic AI looks like artificial intelligence, but it behaves like process engineering.

Once you see that, a lot of common agent advice starts to look backwards. Many teams still treat agents as monoliths: a strong model wrapped in a prompt that's expected to power through a workflow by sheer capability. When it collapses, research such as "Why Do Multi-Agent LLM Systems Fail?" (Cemri et al., 2025, *https://oreil.ly/wF5fk*) shows that multi-step reliability often drops into single digits, underscoring the importance of explicit workflow structure. The usual response is to reach for a larger model, a longer prompt, or a more elaborate multi-agent choreography. Those moves can help at the margins, but they rarely fix the core issue: the workflow itself is underspecified.

What's actually happening when an agent completes a task? It has to break an objective into subtasks, choose an order that respects dependencies, carry state forward without losing key constraints, recover from tool failures, and validate outputs before they become inputs to the next step. Those are workflow design responsibilities. Business process engineers have been solving them for decades; the twist here is that a language model sits inside the loop as a probabilistic execution engine.

Most agent frameworks don't make that twist explicit. They hand you a powerful model and ask you to express an entire process in natural language, as if a prompt were a reasonable substitute for a flowchart, a state machine, and a set of guardrails. Picture running a factory off verbal instructions alone with no diagrams, no checkpoints, and no verification. The results would be chaotic. Agent workflows fail for the same reason.

This chapter introduces *graph-based reasoning and planning*: an architectural approach that turns process design into something you can represent, inspect, and enforce. Instead of hoping that the agent maintains context, you implement formal state management. Instead of relying on the model to "do the steps," you define *workflow graphs* with explicit transitions. Instead of trusting it to avoid invalid actions, you apply semantic validation against a knowledge graph that encodes what's allowed in your domain.

From there, we'll go deeper than "retrieve some chunks and ask the model." You'll build reasoning engines that use graph traversal for context-aware inference so your system can perform multi-hop reasoning across relationships and constraints. You'll see planning architectures that separate strategic decomposition (what to do) from tactical execution (how to do it), enabling agents that adapt their approach while still respecting the boundaries of the system they operate in.

Keep one perspective in mind throughout this chapter: you're not building artificial general intelligence. You're engineering processes that use language models as remarkably capable, but bounded, components inside a larger system. When you treat the workflow as the product, graph-based reasoning and planning stops feeling like a research curiosity and starts looking like the missing layer between toy demos and production systems that hold up under load.

We'll start with foundational concepts: why graphs matter, the two types you'll work with, and how ontologies keep your agent grounded in reality. From there, we'll explore retrieval mechanisms that avoid the "distracting effect" that derails most RAG systems. Then, we'll examine how individual nodes reason and generate structured outputs, before zooming out to pipeline architectures that connect those nodes. Planning comes next as the strategic layer that coordinates everything.

To make these patterns concrete, we'll follow an insurance claims processing agent throughout this chapter. When a claim arrives for an emergency appendectomy at an out-of-network hospital, the agent must traverse policy rules, verify provider credentials, check for fraud indicators, and produce a compliant decision—all while navigating the distracting effect of similar-sounding policies that don't actually apply. Finally, we'll see these patterns work together in production: first, we'll take a look at Kakao's ecommerce agent, and then we'll do a full walkthrough of a DevOps diagnostic agent that ties every concept together.

Let's start with the foundations.

## Foundations: Why Graph-Based Reasoning Matters for Agent Development

If you've built a few agents beyond toy demos, you've probably encountered the ceiling on prompt-only reasoning. Prompts are great for *expressing intent* and *shaping behavior*, but they're a brittle medium for representing long, conditional processes. Once your agent needs to reason across multiple sources, carry constraints across steps, and prove that an action is actually allowed, "just put it in the prompt" stops scaling.

*Graph-based reasoning* is a different way to think about the problem. Instead of treating reasoning as a single forward pass through text, you give the agent a structured space to move through: nodes that represent concepts, state, and decisions plus edges that represent relationships and legal transitions. The payoff is straightforward: reasoning becomes more inspectable, more verifiable, and easier to keep coherent over long horizons.

When an agent graduates from answering one question to steering a multistep workflow, three constraints show up immediately—constraints any process engineer would recognize:

*State*
: The agent has to remember enough of the past to act coherently, without dragging irrelevant history into every step. In system terms, this is *workflow state management.*

*Structure*
: It needs explicit links among facts, rules, and admissible actions so it can't hallucinate a step that reality (or your APIs) will reject. This is *control flow with validation gates.*

*Scale*
: It has to execute plans that span dozens of steps and heterogeneous data sources without collapsing under its own complexity. This is *orchestration with resource management.*

These are engineering problems, but they also expose a deeper design tension that shows up in every serious agent system. You're tuning two axes that you can't collapse into a single "more autonomous" dial.

*Axis 1—Context control*
: How precisely can the system feed the right information to the model at the right moment? This is *information flow design.*

*Axis 2—Workflow autonomy*
: How much latitude does the model have to choose and order its next actions? This is *control flow flexibility.*

If you treat agents as occupying a point on a spectrum from scripted to autonomous, you'll keep fighting the same failure mode. Maybe you crank up autonomy to reduce handwritten logic, but then you lose control of context and the agent drifts. Or you clamp down on context to prevent drift, but then the agent can't adapt. The systems that work in production live in the two-dimensional space where context richness and decision freedom are tuned independently, illustrated in Figure 5-1.

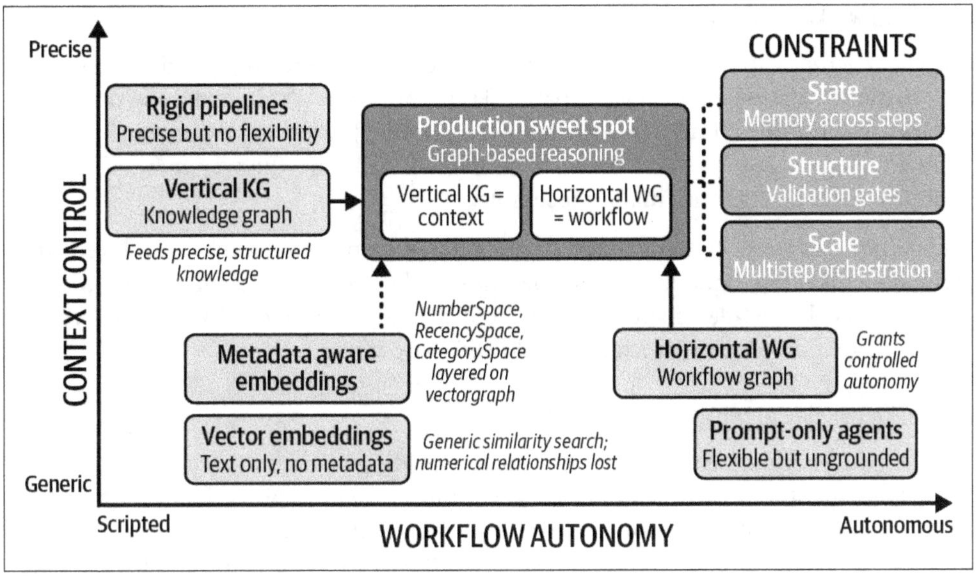


*Figure 5-1. Dual-graph architecture with two independent axes, not a single autonomy spectrum*

Consider what happens when Jane Smith's emergency appendectomy claim arrives. The agent must simultaneously check her policy coverage limits, verify whether St. Mary's Hospital participates in her provider network, apply the correct deductible based on her plan tier, confirm no preexisting condition exclusions apply, and ensure that the decision complies with state insurance regulations. These constraints don't exist in isolation but form an interconnected web where policy terms reference provider network definitions, which reference geographic regions, which determine applicable regulations. A prompt-only approach might retrieve Jane's policy document and the hospital's profile, but without explicit relationships connecting them, the agent can't reliably determine whether the "emergency out-of-network exception" in section 4.2.3 of her policy applies to this hospital in this situation. The graph makes these relationships traversable rather than inferable.

This is why the shift from building smart agents to engineering reliable processes matters. You stop asking *How do I make the model smart enough to do this?* and start asking *What process makes this task safe, decomposable, and checkable?* You stop debugging prompts and start debugging workflow design.

## The Two Graph Types: Horizontal and Vertical

Graph-centric architectures give you the control dials you're missing by making the process model explicit. This agent architecture employs two fundamental graph dimensions that transform knowledge processing and utilization capabilities.

### Horizontal workflow graphs

*Horizontal graphs* manage your agent's execution flow, replacing rigid if-then logic with dynamic, state-aware decision paths. Think of this as a state machine of reasoning and action nodes. Edges encode legal transitions, preserving a compact memory of how the agent got here and preventing illegal detours on the way forward. This is your process flow diagram, made executable.

When implementing stateful workflows, you create persistent memory layers that maintain reasoning context across operations, allowing your agent to build upon previous insights while ensuring logical consistency. The workflow graph records what the agent has done and what it is allowed to do next.

### Vertical knowledge graphs

*Vertical graphs* organize domain knowledge, providing structured access to expertise. This is a semantic network of entities, relations, and constraints. Unlike traditional vector databases that flood context windows with entire documents, vertical graphs enable your agent to follow semantic pathways that lead directly to relevant information while respecting domain relationships and hierarchies.

Traversing a knowledge graph supplies what is true about the world with surgical precision, reducing the context amnesia you get from pure vector search. This is your data model and business rules engine.

### The imaginary space

Together, these graphs create what Konrad Lorenz famously described as an *imaginary space*: a structured representation where thinking looks like movement. In an agent system, that movement is literal. A graph traversal is a mental action. A path exploration is a simulated decision. A transition from one workflow node to the next is the agent committing to a particular interpretation of the situation and a particular next step.

There's nothing mystical about that imaginary space. It's a formal process model.

When your agent walks a path through a knowledge graph, it's executing a grounded lookup and a set of constraints. When it evaluates alternatives at a decision node in the workflow graph, it's running control logic and validation checks. When it carries state across transitions, it's using patterns enterprise architects have relied on for decades—just with a language model embedded inside the loop.

Your reasoning engine sits at the intersection of these two graphs: the knowledge graph grounds what the agent knows, while the workflow graph records what the agent has done and what it is allowed to do next. Each step becomes traceable: which facts were used, which constraints were applied, which decisions were considered, and why a particular transition was taken.

Returning to our claims processing agent, the *horizontal workflow graph* captures the processing pipeline itself: claim intake → document verification → coverage determination → fraud screening → decision rendering → payment processing. Each node represents a discrete processing stage with clear inputs, outputs, and transition conditions. A claim moves through this pipeline, and the graph structure ensures that no step is skipped; you can't render a decision before determining coverage, and you can't process payment before rendering a decision.

The *vertical knowledge graph* captures the domain expertise the agent needs at each workflow stage. This graph contains policy hierarchies (Gold Plan → hospital coverage → emergency services → out-of-network exceptions), medical coding relationships (ICD-10 codes linked to procedure categories linked to coverage rules), provider network topologies (hospitals → physician groups → individual practitioners → credentialing status), and historical claim patterns (this claimant's previous claims, similar claims from other policyholders, known fraud patterns). When the workflow reaches "coverage determination," the agent queries this knowledge graph to traverse from Jane's policy through the relevant coverage rules to reach a determination.

The integration of horizontal and vertical graphs creates what we call the *agentic balance*, where workflow graphs handle the *how to think* dimension, knowledge graphs manage the *what to know* dimension, and structured outputs bridge the *how to communicate* dimension. This separation enables independent optimization while maintaining tight coupling at execution time.

#### The pattern in the wild: Coding agents as dual-graph systems

Before diving into the formal architecture, consider where you've likely already encountered it. Every production coding agent implements the dual-graph pattern, whether its designers name it or not.

Claude Code (*https://oreil.ly/1_kZD*) operates through a sense-act loop: bash gathers ground truth (Git status shows actual repository state, `npm test` produces real results), a persistent knowledge structure (*CLAUDE.md*) encodes project conventions and domain constraints, and the agent executes actions informed by that structured knowledge. The loop repeats—run, observe, fix, run again—until tests pass or the agent recognizes it needs a different approach.

Map this to the architecture we're building:

*CLAUDE.md*
: Functions as a vertical knowledge graph, a structured representation of what's true about this project, including dependency rules, naming conventions, API contracts, and architectural decisions. It's not a flat document that the agent reads once; it's a persistent reference that the agent consults at each decision

point, the same way our claims agent will traverse policy hierarchies and provider networks.

*Bash execution*
: Functions as a horizontal workflow graph: a sequence of states (write code, run tests, observe output, decide next action) with transitions governed by results. The agent can't skip from "write code" to "deploy" without passing through verification—the test results gate the transition, just as our claims workflow will gate coverage determination before payment processing.

Boris Cherny (2026) (*https://oreil.ly/3uiFb*) reports a 200% to 300% quality improvement when agents verify their own work through shell commands: "Claude tests every single change I land using the Chrome extension. It opens a browser, tests the UI, and iterates until the code works and the UX feels good." The verification loop—generate the candidate, execute tests via bash, observe results, iterate on failure—is the loop pipeline pattern from "Pipeline Architectures" on page 186, applied to a single developer's workflow.

Subagents provide the tree pattern. When a coding agent needs to research an API, refactor a module, and update tests, it spawns parallel subagents that access different parts of the codebase independently. Each subagent is a stateless consumer with a single capability, mirroring the single-responsibility principle that makes the pipeline architectures composable. Context engineering layers the state management: permanent knowledge (*CLAUDE.md*), session memory (conversation context), and ephemeral working state (current file edits) map directly to the state schema patterns we'll discuss for production pipelines.

The Unix philosophy (*https://oreil.ly/IDWWZ*) articulated by Doug McIlroy in 1978—write programs that do one thing well, write programs to work together, write programs that handle text streams—applies without modification. Agents execute focused tasks via bash primitives. Agents compose capabilities through pipes and graph structures. Agents communicate through structured data rather than graphical interfaces.

This matters because it means the architecture in this chapter isn't speculative. It's a formalization of patterns that are already working at scale. The insurance claims agent we'll build applies the same principles to a different domain: bash-equivalent execution (API calls, database queries, document processing), knowledge graph–equivalent structure (policy hierarchies, provider networks, regulatory constraints), and the same sense-act loop (retrieve information, reason about it, take action, verify the result).

## Ontological Grounding: Keeping Your Agent in Reality

As you build graph-based systems, you face a critical challenge: ensuring that your agent's outputs remain semantically valid within your domain. While graph structures provide the framework for reasoning, they don't guarantee that the content flowing through them makes semantic sense. This is where ontological grounding becomes essential.

Without semantic constraints, agents risk three fundamental failures that cascade through complex reasoning chains:

*Semantic drift*
: This occurs when your agent generates syntactically valid but semantically meaningless statements. A planning agent might propose "The restaurant manages the chef" when domain logic dictates that chefs manage restaurants, not the reverse. In multistep reasoning, such errors compound exponentially.

*Hallucination propagation*
: This transforms small inaccuracies into system-wide failures. When your agent operates autonomously across dozens of reasoning steps, a single semantically invalid statement cascades through the entire chain, making recovery impossible without semantic validation.

*Domain violations*
: These emerge when outputs conflict with fundamental business rules. Your agent might suggest impossible actions or create plans that violate core constraints, rendering the entire system unreliable for production use.

Research conducted to develop OntoMetric (Yu et al., 2026, *https://oreil.ly/XcL9h*), an ontology-guided framework for automated environmental, social, and governance (ESG) knowledge graph construction, found that ontology-based query checking demonstrates the severity of this problem: error rates of 83.3% in unconstrained systems drop to 19.44% when ontological validation is applied.

Without semantic constraints, our claims agent might approve a dental procedure under vision coverage. This action is syntactically valid (both are policy types with coverage amounts) but semantically meaningless. Ontological grounding prevents these category errors through explicit domain and range definitions. A `CoverageRule` can apply only to claims whose `procedureCategory` matches the rule's `coveredCategory`. An `InNetworkRate` can be applied only when the `providerNetworkStatus` equals `participating`. A `Deductible` has a `policyType` property that must match the claim's `policyType`. These constraints concern domain expertise, not just data validation. When the agent attempts to apply an auto insurance deductible to a health claim (perhaps because both policies belong to the same claimant and the embedding similarity is high), the ontology rejects the operation before it can corrupt the decision. The graph becomes self-correcting, refusing to represent relationships that domain experts would recognize as nonsensical.

Ontologies transform your knowledge graphs from simple node-and-edge structures into semantically rich, validated representations. They provide three critical capabilities:

*Domain and range validation*
: Prevents nonsensical connections by defining which types of entities can participate in specific relationships. When your agent attempts to create a relationship, the ontology verifies that both the subject and object are valid for that predicate.

*Inference rules*
: These enable your agent to derive implicit knowledge from explicit facts. Transitive properties, inverse relationships, and class hierarchies enrich your agent's understanding without requiring explicit encoding of every possible relationship.

*Consistency checking*
: Detects when proposed actions or reasoning steps would create logical contradictions. Before your agent commits to a plan, ontological validation ensures that it doesn't violate fundamental domain constraints.

This grounding becomes the foundation everything else builds upon. We'll return to the practical implementation—specifically, how structured generation with Outlines enforces these constraints at the token level—after exploring how information flows into your graphs in the first place.

## Retrieval Mechanisms

With the foundational concepts established, let's examine how information enters your graph-based systems. Retrieval might seem straightforward—find relevant information and pass it to the model—but naive approaches introduce a subtle danger that undermines everything else you build. The *distracting effect* occurs when irrelevant but similar-sounding content misleads your agent into confident wrong answers.

The examples in this section demonstrate three increasingly sophisticated approaches. PathRAG replaces passage retrieval with structural path traversal through your knowledge graph, ensuring that retrieved information has genuine connections to the query rather than mere surface similarity. R3-RAG adds a learned component that decides when retrieval helps versus when it would distract. Combined, these techniques create retrieval systems that not only resist distractions but also learn to avoid them proactively. Beyond these core techniques, the GraphRAG pattern taxonomy provides a framework for selecting the right retrieval complexity for your needs—from basic vector search at the foundation level, through structured

Cypher queries at the integration level, to sophisticated graph traversal combined with community detection at the advanced level.

## The Distracting Effect: Why Your Agents Get Misled

When you build RAG systems for your autonomous agents, you face a hidden danger known as the distracting effect. This occurs when irrelevant passages mislead your LLM into generating incorrect answers rather than abstaining. This phenomenon is documented in research on the distracting effect (Amiraz et al., 2025, *https://oreil.ly/BCrfN*) in retrieval-augmented systems.

Counterintuitively, as you make your retrieval systems more sophisticated, you might actually worsen this problem. The research reveals that even reranking amplifies this problem rather than solving it because sophisticated retrievers return passages that are semantically related to the query, even when they don't contain the answer. These passages create more convincing distractions for your LLM.

For agentic systems that operate autonomously, this presents critical dangers:

*Error amplification*
: Multistep reasoning compounds initial mistakes.

*Action irreversibility*
: Your agent might take consequential actions based on misleading information.

*Context pollution*
: Extended operations accumulate irrelevant information.

*Self-correction failure*
: Without structural guardrails, your agent can't recognize when it's been misled.

The distracting effect becomes concrete when processing Jane's emergency appendectomy claim. Her employer offers three health plan tiers: Bronze, Silver, and Gold. Jane has the Silver Plan. When the agent queries for "emergency hospital coverage rules," vector similarity might return the Gold Plan's emergency provisions—the plan document uses nearly identical language about "emergency room visits," "inpatient stays," and "surgical procedures." The Gold Plan's generous 90% coverage rate appears in the retrieved context, and the agent confidently calculates Jane's payment at the wrong rate based on these wrong rules, potentially overpaying by thousands of dollars. The semantic similarity between policy documents that *mention* similar concepts masks the structural fact that these are *different policies* covering *different people* with *different terms*. The agent retrieved highly relevant-seeming content that was completely wrong for this claim.

The next section examines three techniques to mitigate the distracting effect: PathRAG, R3-RAG, and GraphRAG pattern taxonomies.

## PathRAG: Structural Protection Against Distractions

PathRAG (*https://oreil.ly/EdNHO*) (Chen et al., 2025; its implementation code (*https://oreil.ly/WC-7W*)) addresses these challenges by fundamentally changing how you retrieve information. Instead of retrieving entire passages or document chunks, you extract and evaluate relational paths between entities. This structural approach provides natural immunity against the distracting effect.

When you implement PathRAG, you gain three key protections:

*Structural verification*
: Unlike semantic similarity alone, relational paths must exist in your knowledge graph. This prevents your agent from being misled by superficially related but structurally disconnected information.

*Flow-based pruning*
: PathRAG's algorithm assigns resources based on graph distance with decay. This ensures that distant, weakly connected information has minimal influence on your agent's decisions.

*Reliability scoring*
: Each path receives a reliability score based on average resource values. Your agent prioritizes high-reliability paths, naturally filtering out distracting information.

To integrate PathRAG into your graph-based agent system, you'll modify your retrieval layer as shown in Example 5-1.

*Example 5-1. PathRAG retriever implementation*

```
class PathRAGRetriever:
    def retrieve(self, query, graph, alpha=0.8, threshold=0.05, top_k=15):
    # Find paths between nodes with flow-based pruning
    paths = []
    for start, end in combinations(nodes, 2):
        path_candidates = self.flow_based_pruning(
            graph, start, end, alpha, threshold
        )
        paths.extend(path_candidates)

    # Score and rank paths
    scored_paths = [(path, self.calculate_reliability(path))
                    for path in paths]

    # Return top-k paths in reliability-ascending order
    return sorted(scored_paths, key=lambda x: x[1])[-top_k:]
```

This class implements graph-based retrieval for RAG systems. Given a query, it identifies relevant nodes in a knowledge graph, then discovers paths connecting pairs of those nodes using flow-based pruning controlled by `alpha` (decay factor) and `threshold` parameters. Each path receives a reliability score, and the method returns the top-k most reliable paths. By working with structural paths rather than text passages, this approach naturally filters out information that lacks genuine connections to your query.

Returning to our insurance claims agent, instead of keyword-matching policy documents and hoping the right one surfaces, PathRAG enforces structural traversal. For Jane's claim, the agent traces an explicit path:

```
Jane Smith → enrolled_in → Policy #POL-456789 → has_coverage →
    Emergency Services Coverage → includes_provision →
    Out-of-Network Exception → applies_when → "prudent layperson standard met"
```

Each hop is a verified relationship in the knowledge graph. The agent cannot accidentally jump to the Gold Plan's provisions because there is no edge connecting Jane to that policy. When the agent needs to determine the applicable coinsurance rate, it traverses:

```
Policy #POL-456789 → plan_tier → Silver → coinsurance_rate → 0.70
```

This is not a similarity search across all coinsurance rates in the corpus but a direct structural lookup that cannot return the wrong policy's terms. Path-based retrieval transforms "find relevant information" into "traverse verified relationships," eliminating the class of errors where similar-but-wrong content corrupts the reasoning.

## R3-RAG: Teaching Your Agents When and How to Retrieve

PathRAG provides structural protection, but it still follows fixed retrieval patterns. R3-RAG (*https://oreil.ly/iy30c*) (Li, 2025; reinforcement learning for reasoning and retrieval) takes a different approach: using RL to teach LLMs when and how to retrieve. Rather than following fixed rules, the agent learns optimal exploration of the retrieval environment through experience.

R3-RAG transforms your static retrieval system into an adaptive one that learns the following:

*When to retrieve*
: Not every reasoning step needs external information.

*What to retrieve*
: Different query types benefit from different retrieval strategies.

*How to decompose*
: Complex queries might need strategic decomposition.

R3-RAG transforms retrieval from a static operation into a learned behavior through a dual-reward system, as shown in Example 5-2.

*Example 5-2. Dual-reward system for retrieval learning*

```
# Outcome reward: Was the final answer correct?
outcome_reward = 1.0 if answer_correct else -1.0

# Process reward: Was each retrieval step helpful?
process_reward = sum([
    relevance_score(doc, query) * format_correct(doc)
    for doc in retrieved_docs
])

total_reward = outcome_reward + process_weight * process_reward
```

This example implements a hybrid reward function for training RAG systems using RL. The outcome reward provides a binary signal based on final answer correctness. The process reward offers denser feedback by scoring each retrieved document on both relevance and format compliance. The `process_weight` parameter controls how much step-by-step retrieval quality matters relative to final answer correctness, helping the model learn not just to answer correctly but to retrieve useful documents along the way.

In the research, R3-RAG achieves 52.6% average accuracy on multi-hop QA tasks—a 15% improvement over strong baselines. By using RL, the system learns step-by-step reasoning patterns: when to retrieve, what to retrieve, and how to integrate retrieval into reasoning chains.

When you combine PathRAG's structural approach with R3-RAG's learned strategies, you create a retrieval system that adapts its behavior to each query's characteristics, as shown in Example 5-3.

*Example 5-3. Adaptive retrieval combining PathRAG with R3-RAG*

```
class R3PathRAG:
    def __init__(self, path_retriever, policy_model):
        self.path_retriever = PathRAGRetriever()
        self.policy_model = R3RAGPolicy()  # Trained with RL

    def retrieve_adaptive(self, query, state):
        # Policy decides retrieval strategy
        action = self.policy_model.select_action(query, state)

        if action.type == 'retrieve_paths':
            paths = self.path_retriever.retrieve(
                query=action.query,
                alpha=action.learned_alpha,
```

```
            threshold=action.learned_threshold,
            top_k=action.learned_k
        )
        return self.format_paths_for_llm(paths)

    elif action.type == 'decompose_then_retrieve':
        subqueries = action.decompose(query)
        results = []
        for subquery in subqueries:
            paths = self.path_retriever.retrieve(subquery)
            results.extend(paths)
        return self.merge_and_rank(results)

    elif action.type == 'skip_retrieval':
        # R3-RAG learned retrieval would be distracting here
        return None
```

This class combines path-based graph retrieval with an RL-trained policy model. Instead of following fixed retrieval patterns, the policy dynamically chooses how to handle each query: retrieve paths directly using learned hyperparameters, decompose complex queries into subqueries and merge results, or skip retrieval entirely when external context would hurt more than help. This adaptive approach creates what functions as a cognitive immune system that not only filters distractions but also learns to avoid them proactively.

PathRAG guarantees that the agent traverses the right relationships, but it doesn't tell the agent how far to traverse. Not every aspect of claims processing demands the same retrieval depth. When the agent calculates Jane's copay for a routine office visit, a single foundational lookup suffices: fetch the specialist copay field from her Silver Plan record and apply it. When processing her emergency appendectomy, though, the agent recognizes that this requires deeper traversal. Out-of-network exceptions, emergency care provisions, and prudent layperson standards demand multi-hop paths across policy, provider, and regulatory nodes, and the stakes are high.

R3-RAG enables this adaptive behavior. The agent learns to recognize claim characteristics that signal retrieval depth such as unusual procedure codes, out-of-network providers, amounts exceeding typical ranges, and coordination of benefits situations. It also learns to decompose complex questions into targeted subqueries. *Is this emergency room visit covered?* becomes three parallel retrievals: (1) query network status for St. Mary's Hospital, (2) query emergency care authorization requirements for Silver Plan, and (3) query benefit limits for emergency inpatient stays. Each subquery is more focused than the original question, reducing the attack surface for distracting retrievals and enabling parallel execution.

## GraphRAG Pattern Taxonomy

PathRAG and R3-RAG address how to retrieve safely and when to retrieve at all. But as you implement graph-enhanced retrieval, you'll also need to decide *how much* graph sophistication each query demands. For some questions, a simple vector lookup will suffice, while other queries need the full power of graph traversal combined with community analysis. Microsoft's GraphRAG framework prescribes patterns at three tiers of complexity, demonstrating significant improvements in global reasoning capabilities:

*Foundation level*
: At the foundation level, patterns establish core retrieval capabilities using graph structures where nodes represent knowledge chunks and edges encode relationships. The Basic Retriever performs vector similarity search on text chunks. The Parent-Child Retriever automatically captures document context whenever your agent retrieves relevant chunks. The Hypothetical Question Retriever matches user queries against pregenerated questions, proving effective when your agent needs to understand implicit user intent.

*Integration level*
: As requirements evolve, you'll integrate structured data through domain-specific graph queries. Cypher Templates provide predefined, parameterized queries for reliable structured data access. Dynamic Cypher Generation enables your agent to construct queries by combining snippets based on user input. Text2Cypher translates natural language directly into graph queries, providing maximum adaptability.

*Advanced level*
: The most sophisticated patterns combine graph traversal with vector search. Graph-Enhanced Vector Search integrates semantic similarity with relationship traversal. Global Community Summary Retriever employs community detection algorithms to group related entities, enabling holistic answers by summarizing interconnected knowledge clusters.

The claims agent employs all three levels of the GraphRAG taxonomy, selecting the appropriate level based on query complexity. For simple questions like *What is Jane's policy number*?, foundational retrieval suffices: retrieve the policy document and extract the identifier.

For questions like *What is Jane's out-of-pocket maximum for in-network emergency care?*, integration-level retrieval uses structured queries:

```
MATCH (p:Policy {id: 'POL-456789'})
    -[:HAS_BENEFIT]->(b:Benefit {category: 'Emergency'})
    -[:HAS_LIMIT]->(l:Limit {type: 'OutOfPocketMax', network: 'InNetwork'})
RETURN l.amount
```

The graph query guarantees we retrieve the limit for the right policy, the right benefit category, and the right network status.

For questions like *Should this claim be flagged for fraud review?*, advanced retrieval traverses multiple relationship types: historical claims from this claimant (frequency patterns), claims from this provider (billing patterns), claims for this procedure code at this amount (regional benchmarks), and similar claims that were later identified as fraudulent (pattern matching). The agent synthesizes across these traversals to assess fraud risk, combining structural queries with pattern analysis.

These patterns enable bidirectional enhancement between retrieval and reasoning. Your agent actively uses logical analysis to enhance retrieval precision, while retrieved knowledge grounds reasoning in factual knowledge. This creates a powerful loop where each capability reinforces the other.

# Reasoning and Generation

With reliable retrieval in place, how do individual nodes reason and communicate? This section examines what happens inside the nodes of your graph architecture, looking at how individual nodes reason through problems and communicate their results. Two capabilities prove essential here. Interleaved thinking enables nodes to adapt their reasoning strategy mid-execution. When a node discovers information that fundamentally changes the problem, it can pivot rather than forcing a flawed analysis to completion. Structured generation addresses the communication side: even with perfect reasoning, your system fails if nodes can't reliably parse each other's outputs. Together, these capabilities ensure that nodes can think flexibly while communicating predictably.

## Interleaved Thinking: Real-Time Adaptive Reasoning

While R3-RAG teaches your agents when to retrieve through RL, production deployments reveal another critical limitation: agents cannot adapt their reasoning strategy mid-execution when they discover unexpected patterns.

Consider a recommendation node that is analyzing competitors. Traditional architectures force it to complete its analysis even after it discovers that margin pressure affects the entire industry, not individual companies. The node continues with the wrong analytical framework, producing flawed recommendations.

*Interleaved thinking*—alternating between explicit reasoning and tool use while carrying that reasoning forward—enables the node to recognize this pattern and pivot its entire approach midstream. This is essential for agent reliability. Research on MiniMax-M2 (*https://oreil.ly/KY0xD*) demonstrates that preserving prior-round thinking state significantly improves performance: SWE-bench Verified 69.4 versus

67.2 (+3.3%), Tau$^2$ 87 versus 64 (+35.9%), and BrowseComp 44.0 versus 31.4 (+40.1%).

This creates a three-tier cognitive architecture within your graph nodes:

- PathRAG provides structurally validated information paths.
- R3-RAG determines optimal retrieval timing.
- Interleaved thinking enables real-time strategy adaptation based on discovered information.

Each layer addresses different failure modes while reinforcing the others.

### Where interleaved thinking helps and hurts

Not every node benefits from this cognitive flexibility. Interleaved thinking proves most valuable for nodes that face inherent uncertainty in their problem space:

*Analysis nodes*
: Must interpret market signals

*Diagnostic nodes*
: Troubleshoot complex system failures

*Research nodes*
: Explore unfamiliar domains

*Planning nodes*
: Plans must account for discovered constraints

These nodes encounter information that fundamentally changes the nature of the problem during execution. A diagnostic node might start investigating a performance issue as a database problem, discover network anomalies during investigation, and need to pivot to distributed systems analysis.

Conversely, nodes with well-defined inputs and deterministic operations gain little from interleaved thinking:

- Transaction-processing nodes
- Format conversion nodes
- Simple routing nodes
- Compliance nodes where regulatory requirements demand predictable, auditable behavior

Adding adaptive reasoning to a node that validates payment information introduces unnecessary complexity without meaningful benefit.

### Implementation of interleaved thinking

Example 5-4 shows how to extend specific nodes with adaptive capabilities.

*Example 5-4. Interleaved reasoning node with adaptive execution*

```
class InterleavedReasoningNode(GraphReasoningNode):
    def execute_with_adaptation(self, context, structured_input):
        # PathRAG retrieval with R3-learned strategy
        initial_paths = self.retrieve_knowledge_paths(
            context.query,
            strategy=self.r3_policy.select_strategy(context)
        )

        # Execute with interleaved thinking enabled
        result = self.agent(
            prompt=self.format_contextual_prompt(structured_input, initial_paths),
            enable_adaptation=True
        )

        # Capture both response and reasoning trace
        return self.structure_adaptive_output(result)
```

This node class integrates the three-tier cognitive architecture: PathRAG provides structurally validated information paths, R3-RAG determines the optimal retrieval strategy, and interleaved thinking enables real-time strategy adaptation based on discovered information. The node retrieves initial context using a learned policy, then executes with adaptation enabled so it can pivot its approach midstream if it discovers information that fundamentally changes the problem. The method captures both the response and the reasoning trace for debugging and audit purposes.

Applying this paradigm to the insurance claims agent, it begins assessing Jane's claim with a clear plan: verify Silver Plan coverage for emergency appendectomy, check St. Mary's network status, apply the out-of-network exception if the prudent layperson standard is met, and calculate the patient's responsibility. Straightforward enough.

But while traversing Jane's coverage history, the agent discovers something unexpected: Jane changed employers six weeks ago. She had coverage under the old employer's plan through March 15, enrolled in the new employer's plan starting March 1 (with an overlap period for COBRA election), and the appendectomy occurred on March 10. This fundamentally changes the analysis. The claim is much more than a simple single-policy determination, as it really involves coordination of benefits between two policies. There are questions about which policy is primary, how to apply both deductibles, and whether the old policy's continuation of care provisions affect the new policy's out-of-network rules.

Interleaved thinking allows the agent to pivot mid-reasoning. Rather than forcing the original plan to completion and producing a wrong answer, the agent recognizes the discovery's significance, revises its approach, and constructs a new reasoning path for the more complex multi-policy scenario. The extended thinking process captures this pivot explicitly: the original plan, the disrupting discovery, the revised understanding, and the new approach. This is the much more natural way complex claims actually unfold, since investigation often reveals complications that reshape the entire analysis.

Most critically, interleaved thinking doesn't break your modular architecture. Each node maintains clear responsibilities and interfaces. The adaptation happens within node boundaries, not across them.

## Structured Generation: The Keystone of Reliable Communication

After implementing your graph architecture, a critical problem emerges: even with perfect reasoning paths and validated knowledge retrieval, your agents will still fail catastrophically if nodes can't parse each other's outputs.

The brutal truth from production deployments reveals that the majority of agent failures in graph-based systems stem not from bad reasoning but from internode communication breakdowns. Studies of 1,600+ annotated traces (Cemri, 2025, *https://oreil.ly/EwG6U*) identify 14 unique failure modes, with interagent misalignment being a primary category of failure. Your carefully designed workflow graph becomes useless when output formats vary unpredictably.

### Why structured output changes everything

Structured output generation fundamentally transforms this chaos into guaranteed reliability. Instead of hoping your model produces parseable formats, you ensure that generating anything else becomes mathematically impossible.

The Outlines library represents a paradigm shift in how you think about language model outputs. When you define a structure using Outlines—whether a Pydantic model, JSON schema, or regular expression—the library constructs a finite state machine that represents all valid token sequences. During generation, it examines the model's predicted token probabilities and zeros out any tokens that would lead to invalid states.

This delivers several transformative benefits:

*True zero-shot structured generation*
: The model doesn't need to "learn" your format—the structure is enforced mechanistically.

*No retry loops*
: Since invalid outputs are impossible, every generation succeeds on the first attempt.

*Complex nested structures*
: You can guarantee field validations and type constraints that would be impossible through prompting alone.

### The compound power of structure and graphs

When you combine Outlines' structured generation with graph architectures, three effects emerge:

*Internode contracts become unbreakable*
: Your recommendation node doesn't just aim to produce a specific format—it becomes incapable of producing anything else. This eliminates entire categories of integration failures.

*Consistency metrics become meaningful*
: Instead of measuring whether outputs are "similar enough" across runs, you can measure exact structural consistency.

*Complex reasoning becomes truly composable*
: Each node can rely absolutely on its inputs' structure, focusing its capacity on actual reasoning rather than defensive parsing.

### How Outlines transforms each component

Outlines brings structure and reliability to the various node types in your LLM-based application, ensuring predictable and reliable outputs. By enforcing specific schemas for each node's output, Outlines transforms the unpredictable nature of LLMs into structured, actionable data:

*For reasoning nodes*
: Outlines ensures that extracted knowledge, inference chains, and conclusions follow precise structures with explicit fields for premises, inference steps, and confidence scores.

*For planning nodes*
: Outlines guarantees that generated plans conform to executable specifications with explicit preconditions, parameters, expected outcomes, and rollback procedures.

*For action nodes*
: Outlines ensures that API calls, database queries, and system commands are always syntactically valid.

*For validation nodes*
: Outlines provides structured reports with specific violation types, severity levels, and remediation suggestions.

#### Real-world impact

Let's revisit our insurance claims agent to see the real impact of structured output in reasoning and planning. Every claim decision must include specific fields: determination (approve, deny, or pend), approved amount, patient responsibility amount, explanation of benefits code, regulatory basis for the decision, and appeal rights notice. Missing any field violates state insurance regulations and exposes the company to compliance penalties.

Structured generation through constrained decoding makes it impossible to issue an incomplete decision. The output schema defines each required field with its type constraints: `determination` must be one of three enumerated values, `approved_amount` must be a non-negative number, `explanation_code` must match a pattern from the standard explanation codes registry, and `appeal_rights` must include the mandatory regulatory language. The generation process cannot produce a decision that omits the appeal rights notice, as the grammar physically prevents that output sequence.

This matters beyond mere formatting convenience. When processing thousands of claims, even a 0.1% rate of malformed decisions creates significant compliance exposure. Structured generation reduces that rate to zero. The agent's claims decisions are valid by construction, not by post hoc validation that might be bypassed or might fail silently.

This transformation from probabilistic to deterministic behavior is why structured output serves as the keystone of production graph architectures.

## Pipeline Architectures

Individual nodes can now reason adaptively and communicate reliably. How do you connect them? Graph reasoning systems employ various architectural patterns, each suited to different complexity requirements.

### Sequential Pipeline: Linear Execution

*Sequential pipelines* offer simplicity through a fixed execution order, which is ideal for tasks with strict dependencies between steps. Example 5-5 demonstrates this pattern.

*Example 5-5. Sequential pipeline with linear execution*

```
builder = StateGraph(AgentState)
builder.add_edge("retrieve_context", "analyze_facts")
builder.add_edge("analyze_facts", "generate_hypothesis")
builder.add_edge("generate_hypothesis", "validate_reasoning")
```

A sequential workflow is defined where each node's output feeds directly into the next node's input. The agent moves through retrieve → analyze → hypothesize → validate in strict order. This architecture provides straightforward debugging since you can trace execution linearly through each node, and resource consumption remains predictable since only one node executes at a time.

> Choose a sequential pipeline when dependencies between steps are strict and well defined, each step's output directly feeds the next step's input, and debugging simplicity outweighs performance gains.

## Loop Pipeline: Iterative Refinement

*Loop pipelines* introduce feedback capabilities for self-correction when perfect first-attempt reasoning is unrealistic. Example 5-6 shows the routing logic that enables iterative refinement.

*Example 5-6. Loop pipeline with iterative refinement*

```
def check_plan_validity(state: AgentState) -> str:
    if state["validation_results"]["is_valid"]:
        return "execute_plan"
    elif state["retry_count"] < 3:
        return "refine_plan"
    else:
        return "fallback_planner"

builder.add_conditional_edges("validate_plan", check_plan_validity)
graph = builder.compile(recursion_limit=10)
```

This routing function determines whether to proceed with execution, retry with refinement, or fall back to an alternative planner. The conditional edges create a feedback loop: if validation fails but retries remain, the workflow returns to the refinement node. The `recursion_limit` parameter prevents infinite loops. This pattern provides error recovery mechanisms that prevent single failures from derailing entire workflows.

Choose a loop when perfect first-attempt solutions are unrealistic, validation can identify correctable errors, and you need resilience against transient failures.

## Tree Pipeline: Parallel Exploration

*Tree pipelines* enable parallel exploration of multiple hypotheses simultaneously, as shown in Example 5-7.

*Example 5-7. Tree pipeline with parallel hypothesis exploration*

```
def explore_reasoning_paths(state: AgentState):
    hypotheses = state["generated_hypotheses"]
    return [
        Send("verify_hypothesis", {"hypothesis": h, "context": state["context"]})
        for h in hypotheses
    ]

builder.add_node("explore_hypotheses", explore_reasoning_paths)
```

This function spawns parallel verification tasks for each hypothesis using LangGraph's `Send` API. All hypotheses are tested concurrently, and results merge back into the workflow. Parallel processing slashes latency for I/O-bound operations and prevents your agent from committing to the first plausible answer when better alternatives exist.

## Production Implementation Patterns

Moving from conceptual pipeline types to production deployment requires attention to three critical concerns: state management, error handling, and observability. Each pipeline architecture introduces distinct challenges in these areas.

### State management across pipelines

Your state schema becomes the contract between pipeline stages, defining what information flows forward and how concurrent updates resolve. Example 5-8 demonstrates typed state with reducer annotations.

*Example 5-8. State schema with reducer annotations*

```
class AgentState(TypedDict):
    messages: Annotated[list, add_messages]
    plan_steps: list
    completed_steps: Annotated[list, operator.add]
    validation_results: dict
```

The `Annotated` type with reducer functions like `add_messages` and `operator.add` handles the complexity of merging state from parallel branches. When tree pipelines spawn concurrent paths that each append to shared lists, the reducer pattern ensures deterministic merging regardless of execution order. Without proper reducers, you'd face race conditions or lost updates. The reducer pattern ensures deterministic merging regardless of execution order.

State schema design also affects debugging and recovery. You need to include enough context to reconstruct the agent's reasoning path but at the same time avoid bloating state with intermediate artifacts that balloon memory usage. A common pattern separates ephemeral working state from persistent audit state—the former gets cleared between major phases, while the latter accumulates for post hoc analysis.

### Error-handling strategies

Each pipeline type demands a different error-handling philosophy. Sequential pipelines benefit from simple retry policies because failures have clear causation—if step three fails, you know exactly what preceded it and can retry with confidence. Implement exponential backoff for transient failures like rate limits and circuit breakers for persistent failures that indicate systemic problems.

Loop pipelines require sophisticated error routing to distinguish between correctable errors and fundamental failures. Example 5-9 shows this routing logic.

*Example 5-9. Error routing for loop pipelines*

```
def route_after_validation(state: AgentState) -> str:
    error = state.get("validation_error")
    if error is None:
        return "proceed"
    elif error.severity == "correctable" and state["retry_count"] < 3:
        return "refine"
    elif error.severity == "correctable":
        return "fallback_strategy"
    else:
        return "terminate_with_partial"
```

This routing function examines validation errors and determines the appropriate response. Correctable errors with remaining retries trigger refinement; correctable errors without retries fall back to an alternative strategy; fundamental errors terminate with partial results. This nuanced error handling prevents both premature termination and infinite retry loops.

Tree pipelines need careful error aggregation. One branch's failure shouldn't cascade to others or corrupt shared state. Implement error isolation by catching exceptions within each branch and recording them in branch-specific state fields. The merge node then decides how to handle partial results. For example, sometimes three successful branches out of four could provide sufficient coverage, while other tasks may require all-or-nothing completion.

### Observability and debugging

Production pipelines demand visibility into execution flow. Instrument each node to emit structured logs capturing inputs, outputs, timing, and resource consumption. For tree pipelines, include branch identifiers so you can reconstruct the parallel execution timeline.

State snapshots at node boundaries enable replay debugging—when something goes wrong, you can restart from the last known good state rather than from scratch. This proves especially valuable for long-running pipelines where failures late in execution would otherwise waste significant computation.

## Hybrid Architectures

Production systems rarely use pure pipeline types. Real-world tasks exhibit variable complexity that demands adaptive architecture selection. A research query about a well-documented topic might need simple sequential processing, while an ambiguous query exploring cutting-edge developments could require parallel hypothesis exploration with iterative refinement. This section examines three hybrid architecture approaches to pipeline design.

### Dynamic architecture selection

One approach is to treat pipeline selection as a routing decision within a meta-pipeline. Example 5-10 demonstrates dynamic architecture selection.

*Example 5-10. Dynamic architecture selection based on task characteristics*

```
def analyze_and_route(state: AgentState) -> str:
    complexity = assess_task_complexity(state["query"])
    uncertainty = estimate_answer_uncertainty(state["query"])

    if complexity < SIMPLE_THRESHOLD and uncertainty < LOW_UNCERTAINTY:
        return "sequential_path"
    elif uncertainty > HIGH_UNCERTAINTY:
        return "exploratory_tree"
    else:
        return "iterative_refinement"

builder.add_conditional_edges(
    "analyze_complexity",
    analyze_and_route,
    {
        "sequential_path": "sequential_reasoning",
        "exploratory_tree": "tree_exploration",
        "iterative_refinement": "loop_refinement"
    }
)
```

This meta-routing function examines incoming tasks and directs them to the appropriate execution strategy. Simple, certain queries get fast sequential processing, highly uncertain queries get parallel hypothesis exploration, and everything else gets iterative refinement. The complexity analysis typically completes in a single LLM call, adding minimal latency while dramatically improving resource efficiency.

### Nested pipeline composition

More sophisticated hybrid architectures nest pipeline types within each other. A top-level sequential pipeline might contain a tree stage for parallel evidence gathering, followed by a loop stage for iterative synthesis refinement. Each *nested* pipeline maintains its own state management and error handling while contributing to the parent pipeline's flow.

Consider a due diligence agent analyzing a potential acquisition. The outer sequential pipeline moves through phases: initial screening, deep dive analysis, risk assessment, and recommendation synthesis. Within the deep dive phase, a tree pipeline parallelizes across financial analysis, legal review, market position assessment, and technology evaluation. Each of these branches might itself contain loop pipelines for iterative refinement as new information surfaces.

This compositional approach lets you match architectural patterns to the natural structure of complex tasks. The key is to maintain clear boundaries—each nested pipeline should have well-defined inputs and outputs that integrate cleanly with its parent context.

### Graceful degradation

Hybrid architectures should degrade gracefully when resource constraints bite. If parallel execution hits memory limits, fall back to sequential processing of the same subtasks. If iterative refinement exceeds time budgets, return the best result so far with confidence annotations. Build these fallback paths explicitly rather than relying on exception handling—graceful degradation is a feature, not an error case.

The routing logic can incorporate runtime constraints alongside task characteristics, as shown in Example 5-11.

*Example 5-11. Graceful degradation with resource-aware routing*

```
def route_with_constraints(state: AgentState) -> str:
    ideal_path = analyze_and_route(state)
    available_memory = get_available_memory()
    remaining_budget = state.get("time_budget", float("inf"))

    if (
        ideal_path == "exploratory_tree"
        and available_memory < TREE_MEMORY_THRESHOLD
    ):
        return "sequential_fallback"

    if (
        ideal_path == "iterative_refinement"
        and remaining_budget < ITERATION_TIME_MINIMUM
    ):
```

```
        return "single_pass_best_effort"

    return ideal_path
```

This function wraps the ideal architecture selection with runtime constraint checks. If parallel execution would exceed memory limits, it falls back to sequential processing. If iterative refinement would exceed time budgets, it returns a single-pass best effort. Building these fallback paths explicitly—rather than relying on exception handling—ensures that your agent delivers results within constraints rather than failing or timing out when the ideal execution path proves infeasible.

The claims-processing system demonstrates why production pipelines rarely commit to a single architecture. When a claim arrives, a routing node examines its characteristics—procedure codes, provider network status, billed amount, claimant history—and directs it to the appropriate processing path.

Jane's routine office visit takes the sequential path:

- Eligibility verification confirms that her policy is active.
- Coverage determination identifies the specialist copay.
- Benefit accumulator updates her year-to-date totals.
- Payment calculation determines the reimbursement.
- Decision rendering produces the explanation of benefits.

Each stage depends on its predecessor, but for straightforward claims, this linear flow completes in seconds with no human involvement. The predictability is a feature: every routine claim follows the same auditable path.

Her emergency appendectomy triggers tree expansion. The routing node observes: emergency procedure, out-of-network provider, amount exceeding typical range, flagged for manual review. This claim needs parallel verification:

- A fraud-scoring branch analyzes billing patterns and provider history.
- A provider verification branch confirms St. Mary's licensing and network exception eligibility.
- A medical necessity branch reviews procedure appropriateness.
- A pricing validation branch compares the numbers against regional benchmarks.

These branches read different data sources and execute simultaneously; the tree structure slashes latency while ensuring comprehensive review. The merge node combines findings: any red flag from any branch affects the routing, whether that's escalation to special investigations, peer review for medical necessity questions, or provider negotiation for pricing outliers.

But partway through processing, the document verification stage returns *incomplete*—the operative report lacks anesthesia time records. Here the pipeline shifts to a loop: request additional documentation, wait for provider response, and reverify. The loop has explicit bounds (three request cycles, 15-day timeout) before escalating to manual review rather than iterating indefinitely. The loop maintains state across iterations, tracking what documentation has arrived and what gaps remain, so each request is targeted rather than generic.

Some claims resist automated resolution entirely. When the parallel branches return conflicting signals—say an elevated fraud score but legitimate-looking medical necessity, or a pricing anomaly but verified provider credentials—the claim enters iterative refinement with human review. A claims examiner receives the agent's preliminary analysis, the specific uncertainties, and recommended next steps. The examiner can accept the recommendation, override it with a different decision, or request additional automated analysis on specific aspects. This HITL iteration continues until resolution, with the agent learning from examiner decisions to improve future routing.

The routing decision adds minimal latency—a single analysis pass over claim characteristics—while dramatically improving resource efficiency. Simple claims get fast sequential processing. Complex claims get thorough parallel verification. Incomplete claims get bounded iteration. Uncertain claims get human expertise applied precisely where it's needed. The same underlying capability (coverage determination, fraud detection, pricing validation) executes within whichever architectural pattern the specific claim demands.

## Event-Driven Orchestration: The Production Scaling Layer

The pipeline architectures discussed share an assumption: nodes execute in the same process, and state passes through shared memory. For systems processing fewer than 50 tasks per day, this holds. Beyond that threshold, a different failure mode emerges that no amount of in-process optimization resolves.

Ali Pourshahid (2025) (*https://oreil.ly/vPEi7*), chief technology officer at Solace, identifies the pattern precisely: agentic AI systems today repeat the architectural mistakes of early microservices circa 2015. Agents calling agents synchronously, whether through function calls, conversation threads, or HTTP requests, create what he calls a "distributed monolith."

There are technically separate components that are functionally inseparable. One slow LLM response can block the entire pipeline. One crashed node can lose all intermediate state. Alan Nichol (2025) (*https://oreil.ly/7raM_*) at Rasa comes at the same problem from the opposite direction: when agents communicate through natural language, you can't enforce contracts at runtime the way you can with typed API schemas.

*Event-driven orchestration* addresses this by making agents subscribers to event streams rather than callers of other agents. The event broker (Kafka, Redis Streams, or SQS) becomes the only shared interface. Agents consume messages from input topics, process them, and publish results to output topics. No agent knows about any other agent's existence.

This introduces a fourth pipeline architecture alongside sequential, loop, and tree:

*Layer 0—State*
: External stores (database, knowledge graph)

*Layer 1—Event backbone*
: Kafka/Redis Streams (durable, ordered, replayable)

*Layer 2—Agents*
: Stateless consumers with one capability each

*Layer 3—Meta-orchestrator*
: Reads *all* topics, monitors health, and intervenes

Figure 5-2 illustrates how event-driven orchestration works.

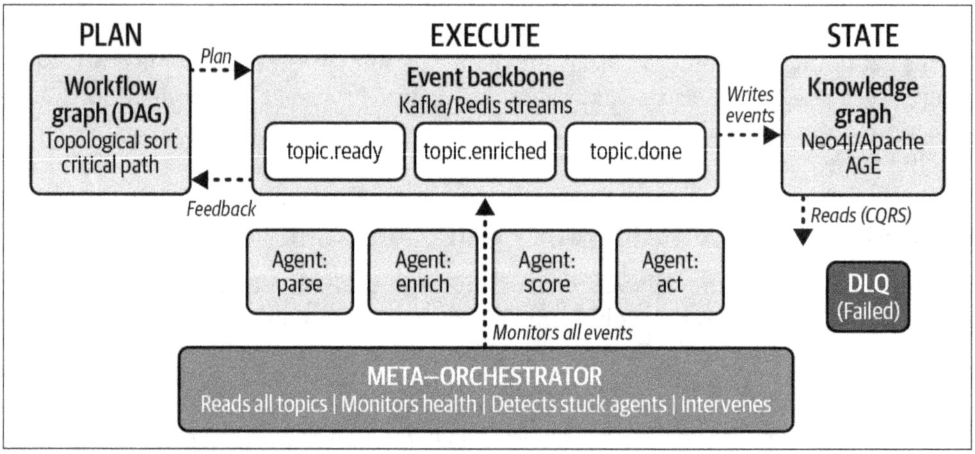


*Figure 5-2. Event-driven agent orchestration where the workflow graph plans, the event backbone executes, and results reshape the plan*

The meta-orchestrator reads all event streams and detects stuck agents (consumer lag growing on a topic), poison pills (same message retried five times), and throughput drops (processing rate fell 80%). It scales consumer instances, reroutes failures to dead letter queues, and publishes health metrics. Every event is a timestamped, typed log entry flowing through the broker. Observability becomes a free property of the architecture rather than instrumentation you bolt on afterward.

Three capabilities distinguish event-driven orchestration from in-process pipelines:

*Fault isolation*
When an agent crashes, its partition rebalances to another instance. The queue retains unprocessed events. Other agents continue working. Compare this to a LangGraph state machine where a node failure halts the entire graph execution and loses intermediate state.

*Replay and recovery*
Kafka retains events by default. Found a bug in your scoring agent? Fix the code, reset the consumer offset to yesterday, and replay all events through the corrected logic. Every other pipeline pattern loses intermediate state, meaning that you'd need to rerun the entire workflow from scratch.

*Framework interoperability*
Different teams build agents in different frameworks. One team uses LangGraph, another builds custom Python agents, and a third wraps a specialized ML model. Event-driven communication via Kafka topics means these agents share nothing but message schemas. The queue doesn't care what produced the message or what consumes it.

The trade-off is real: operational complexity increases. Kafka clusters require configuration, partition management, and retention policies. Debugging shifts from stepping through a call stack to correlating events across distributed topics. For solo developers processing 20 events per day, this infrastructure overhead doesn't justify the benefits. The cost-benefit flips at scale, however, where there are thousands of events per day or multiple teams, or when reliability matters more than simplicity.

Confluent (*https://oreil.ly/0gN_-*) documents four event-driven patterns for agent systems: orchestrator-worker for structured pipelines, hierarchical for multi-domain enterprises, Blackboard for collaborative problem solving, and market-based for dynamic workload distribution. Kai Waehner (*https://oreil.ly/6HEXL*) pairs Kafka with Apache Flink for stateful stream processing, routing MCP and A2A protocol messages through the event broker rather than through point-to-point connections.

Critically, event-driven orchestration doesn't replace graph-based planning. It complements it. The workflow graph computes execution order—topological sort, critical path, parallelization windows. The event backbone handles runtime execution—fault isolation, replay, adaptive scaling. Command Query Responsibility Segregation (CQRS) maps naturally: writes flow through the event backbone for durability and ordering, while reads go directly to the knowledge graph for low-latency traversal. The graph plans, events execute, and results reshape the graph.

This separation means you can tune the two layers independently. Improve your planning DAG without touching the event infrastructure. Scale your consumers without modifying the workflow logic. Replace a LangGraph-based agent with a custom implementation, and the rest of the system never notices; the message schema is the only contract.

## Planning and Coordination

Pipelines define flow, but who decides what to flow? The most sophisticated architectures share a common pattern: they separate thinking about what to do from actually doing it. Representing this strategic layer is the *planning node*, a dedicated component that reasons about approach before committing to execution.

Consider what happens when you ask your agent to analyze transformer architectures across multiple domains. Without a planning node, your agent immediately begins retrieving papers, potentially exploring irrelevant tangents. With a planning node, your agent first develops a strategy: identify key domains, determine temporal boundaries, plan parallel searches, and establish synthesis criteria.

This section examines that strategic layer that coordinates everything. You'll learn why planning deserves architectural separation, understand some techniques for planning, and take a deep dive into parallel execution.

### Why Planning Deserves Architectural Separation

When you combine planning and execution in a single component, you create competing optimization pressures that degrade both capabilities. An execution node optimized for tool usage struggles with abstract strategic reasoning, while a planning component burdened with execution details loses sight of the bigger picture.

Example 5-12 shows a basic planning node using the base language model without tool bindings.

*Example 5-12. Basic planning node implementation*

```
def planning_node(state: AgentState):
    system_prompt = SystemMessage(
        content=planning_prompt.format(
            tools=format_tools_description(tools)
        )
    )
    response = base_llm.invoke([system_prompt] + state["messages"])
    return {"messages": [response]}
```

Keeping the execution and planning nodes separate lets each excel at its specific function. The planning node receives descriptions of available tools but doesn't invoke them directly, thereby enabling pure strategic reasoning. By separating planning from execution, you avoid competing optimization pressures that degrade both capabilities.

In our insurance claims agent, when Jane's emergency appendectomy claim arrives flagged for manual review, the planning node doesn't immediately begin processing. Instead, it analyzes the claim to construct an efficient execution strategy. The planning node observes: this is an emergency claim (affects which coverage rules apply) at an out-of-network provider (requires network exception evaluation) with a flagged amount (needs pricing validation) for a policyholder with recent coverage changes (potential coordination of benefits).

From this analysis, the planning node determines that four verification branches are needed. Three can run in parallel (fraud scoring, provider verification, pricing validation), but coverage determination must wait for the coordination of benefits evaluation to complete. The regulatory timeline in this state is 30 days for emergency claims, and given the complexity of this case, a preliminary human review should occur before a final decision is rendered.

This planning happens before any substantive processing, ensuring that the agent doesn't waste effort on approaches that won't work or miss dependencies that would require reprocessing. The plan becomes an explicit artifact that guides execution and provides auditability. Reviewers can examine not just what the agent decided but how it planned to reach that decision.

## Hierarchical Planning

As requirements become more sophisticated, linear planning hits limitations. Complex queries involve multiple independent research tracks that could execute in parallel. Hypertree decomposition addresses this. Instead of flat sequences, your planning node identifies parallel subtasks and organizes them into tree structures, as shown in Example 5-13.

*Example 5-13. Hierarchical planning with hypertree decomposition*

```
class HierarchicalPlanningNode:
    def planning_node(self, state: AgentState):
        query_complexity = self._assess_complexity(state["messages"])

        if query_complexity > COMPLEXITY_THRESHOLD:
            hypertree_plan = self._construct_hypertree(state)
            plan_prompt = f"""
            Create a hierarchical plan with these parallel tracks:
            {self._format_parallel_tracks(hypertree_plan)}
            """
            response = self.base_llm.invoke(
                [SystemMessage(plan_prompt)] + state["messages"]
```

```
    )
    return {"messages": [response], "plan_structure": "hypertree"}
```

This planning node assesses query complexity and, when it exceeds a threshold, constructs a hierarchical plan with parallel tracks. Research that requires 60 sequential steps might decompose into four parallel tracks of 15 steps each. The `plan_structure` field in the return value signals downstream nodes how to execute the plan.

For the insurance claims agent, a multivehicle accident generates claims from four different policyholders. The hierarchical planner decomposes this into a coordinated structure: first process each claimant's claim independently; then synthesize for subrogation analysis (to determine which insurance company bears ultimate responsibility).

Each claimant's track becomes its own subplan: verify policy status, determine coverage for their specific injuries and treatments, and assess liability allocation. These four tracks can execute in parallel, since they're examining different policyholders with different policies and different claims. But the subrogation synthesis must wait for all four tracks to complete because determining who pays whom requires knowing the full picture of covered amounts across all parties.

The hierarchical structure allows the planning node to reason about parallelism at multiple levels:

- The four claimant tracks are independent and can be parallelized.
- Within each track, the standard claim processing parallelism applies (fraud, verification, pricing branches).

This multilevel parallelism significantly reduces total processing time for complex multiparty situations while maintaining the dependencies that ensure correct outcomes.

## Constraint-Guided Planning

In regulated environments, your planning node must ensure that plans respect domain constraints and business rules. Example 5-14 demonstrates constraint-guided planning.

*Example 5-14. Constraint-guided planning with validation*

```
class ConstraintAwarePlanningNode:
    def __init__(self):
        self.constraint_extractor = ConstraintExtractor()
        self.plan_validator = PlanValidator()
```

```
    def planning_node(self, state: AgentState):
        constraints = self.constraint_extractor.extract(state["messages"][0])
        initial_plan = self._generate_plan(state)
        validation_result = self.plan_validator.verify(initial_plan, constraints)

        if validation_result.score < THRESHOLD:
            refined_plan = self._refine_with_constraints(
                initial_plan, validation_result.feedback, constraints
            )
            return {"messages": [refined_plan]}
```

This planning node extracts constraints from the user's request, generates an initial plan, and validates that plan against the constraints. If validation fails, it refines the plan using the validator's feedback. This ensures that your agent won't attempt searches outside specified date ranges, exceed computational budgets, or violate other domain-specific rules.

## Dynamic DAG Construction

The most sophisticated evolution involves dynamic construction of directed acyclic graphs that represent optimal execution strategies. Example 5-15 shows this pattern.

*Example 5-15. Dynamic DAG construction for execution planning*

```
class GraphConstructingPlanningNode:
    def planning_node(self, state: AgentState):
        task_graph = self._extract_task_dependencies(state["messages"][0])
        parallel_groups = self._identify_parallel_opportunities(task_graph)

        execution_dag = self._construct_optimal_dag(
            task_graph, parallel_groups, state.get("resource_constraints", {})
        )

        return {
            "messages": [self._serialize_dag(execution_dag)],
            "execution_graph": execution_dag,
            "parallelism_factor": len(parallel_groups)
        }
```

This planning node analyzes task dependencies, identifies which tasks can run in parallel, and constructs an optimal execution DAG that respects resource constraints. The `parallelism_factor` indicates how many parallel tracks the plan contains. This DAG-based planning enables dramatic performance improvements while preventing the coordination failures that plague unstructured multi-agent systems.

## Empirical Evidence: Graph Planning at Repository Scale

The planning patterns in the previous section, such as hierarchical decomposition, constraint validation, and dynamic DAG construction, have theoretical appeal. Microsoft Research (Luo et al., 2025, *https://oreil.ly/HE2xy*) provides quantitative evidence that they work.

The Repository Planning Graph (RPG) and its companion, RPG-Encoder (Luo et al., 2026, *https://oreil.ly/_pCFS*) address the two directions of graph-based planning for software repositories. RPG solves the generation problem: given a specification, construct an entire repository through graph-guided planning. RPG-Encoder solves the comprehension problem: given an existing repository, encode it into the same graph structure so agents can navigate, localize bugs, and reason about code at scale.

The core data structure is a multilevel node hierarchy consisting of module nodes (architectural directories), component nodes (functional groupings), and feature nodes (concrete functions). These are connected by two edge types: functional edges that encode hierarchical decomposition and dependency edges that encode data flows and import relationships. This dual-view representation unifies what code means with how code connects, applying the by now familiar vertical knowledge graph principle to source code.

According to Luo and colleagues, the generation results quantify why graph planning outperforms text planning. ZeroRepo, built on RPG, generates repositories averaging 36,000 lines of code; these are 3.9 times larger than Claude Code repos and 64 times larger than other baselines. Functional coverage reaches 81.5%, matching gold-standard human projects, with a 69.7% test pass rate; these metrics exceed those of Claude Code by 27.3 and 35.8 percentage points respectively. The scaling behavior is the key finding: ZeroRepo exhibits near linear growth beyond 1,100 leaf features and 30,000 lines of code within 30 iterations, while baselines plateau. Natural language planning "rapidly accumulates inconsistencies across iterations" as the Microsoft team documents, with specification drift compounding at each step. The persistent graph structure maintains coherence because dependencies are explicit edges, not implicit assumptions in prose.

RPG-Encoder demonstrates the same principle in reverse. Given an existing codebase, it constructs the RPG automatically through semantic lifting (extracting functional intent), structure reorganization (recovering latent hierarchies), and artifact grounding (anchoring back to physical files). Agents navigate the resulting graph through three tools: `SearchNode` for global semantic retrieval, `FetchNode` for node-level source code extraction, and `ExploreRPG` for cross-view traversal along functional and dependency edges. On SWE-bench Verified, RPG-Encoder achieves 93.7% function-level localization accuracy—14.4 percentage points above the best baseline. Agents maintain a "high tool/action ratio for ExploreRPG," confirming that when structured graph traversal is available, agents prefer it over brute-force search.

Two findings connect directly to this chapter's architecture. First, incremental graph maintenance reduces overhead by 95.7% compared to full reconstruction. Three atomic protocols handle deletions, modifications, and additions without rebuilding the entire graph. This makes graph-based planning viable for production systems where the world changes between planning sessions—the same challenge the investigation DAG faces when new evidence surfaces during a DevOps diagnostic.

Second, the bidirectional loop matters. The same graph representation that guides generation also supports comprehension. When you build a repository, evolve it, and hand it to a new agent, the graph transfers knowledge without lossy summarization. This is the "imaginary space" discussed in "The Two Graph Types: Horizontal and Vertical" on page 169, but realized for code: it's a structured representation where an agent's movement through nodes and edges constitutes genuine reasoning about software architecture, not just pattern matching over flattened tokens.

The planning node patterns—hierarchical decomposition, constraint validation, DAG construction—gain empirical backing from RPG's results. Graph-structured plans don't just feel more principled than text plans. They produce measurably better outcomes at the scales where text planning collapses.

## From Architecture to Daily Practice: Task Graphs at Developer Scale

Dynamic DAG construction—and RPG's empirical validation of it—might suggest that graph-based planning requires significant infrastructure. It doesn't. The same architectural principles apply at the scale of a single developer managing their own work.

Beads (*https://oreil.ly/DvPMv*) is a Git-backed task graph where tasks are nodes and dependencies are edges. The command `bd ready` computes the topological sort, identifying tasks whose predecessors are all complete and are therefore unblocked. The command `bd update --status in_progress` is a state transition in the workflow graph. The command `bd close` triggers dependency resolution: the system checks which successor tasks just had their last blocker removed and promotes them to ready status. This is the feedback phase from the investigation DAG in which completing one node reshapes the readiness of downstream nodes.

The parallel is structural, not metaphorical. When the DevOps diagnostic agent constructs an investigation DAG with parallel phases, it's solving the same problem that Beads solves: given a set of tasks with dependency constraints, compute which ones can execute concurrently and in what order. When the claims processing agent's planning node determines that fraud scoring, provider verification, and pricing validation can run in parallel but coverage determination must wait for coordination of benefits, it's performing the same topological analysis.

The difference is in infrastructure weight. Beads stores its graph in a local database alongside your Git repository. Kafka stores its event streams in a distributed cluster. The planning logic is identical, but the execution substrate changes based on scale requirements. For teams building agent systems, starting with lightweight task graphs and graduating to event-driven infrastructure as volume grows follows the same maturity curve the chapter's decision framework recommends: sequential for simple workflows, tree for parallel opportunities, and event driven when fault tolerance and replay become nonnegotiable.

This progression also serves as a design validation tool. If you can model your agent's workflow as a task graph with explicit dependencies, you've confirmed that the process is decomposable and its constraints are explicit—two prerequisites for reliable agent execution. If you can't model the workflow as a task graph, that's a signal the workflow design needs more thought before you write a single line of agent code.

## The Multi-Agent Debate: Reconciling Parallel Execution

Once you've built your graph-based architecture, you'll face the question that divides the industry: Should you implement parallel agents? The heated debate between Cognition's warnings and Anthropic's successes, noted at the beginning of this chapter, might seem irreconcilable.

### The real problem: Uncoordinated parallelism

Parallelism itself isn't the enemy—uncoordinated parallelism is. When Cognition documents catastrophic failures, it's describing parallel agents operating without architectural constraints. When Anthropic reports 90.2% performance improvements, it is showcasing carefully orchestrated parallel execution.

Your graph architecture must provide the coordination framework that makes safe parallelism possible. Parallel agents work well when they are tools within your orchestrated system, not autonomous entities making independent decisions.

### When parallel execution makes sense

Parallel agents work well when they explore different information spaces without shared decision making. Example 5-16 shows an orchestrator coordinating parallel research tasks.

*Example 5-16. Parallel execution with safeguards*

```
class ResearchOrchestrator(GraphNode):
    def analyze_board_diversity(self, company_list):
        parallel_tasks = [
            self.gather_board_composition,
```

```
            self.research_diversity_metrics,
            self.compile_industry_benchmarks,
            self.analyze_regulations
        ]

        results = self.execute_parallel_with_safeguards(
            tasks=parallel_tasks,
            context=self.filtered_context,
            output_schema=self.research_schema
        )

        return self.synthesis_node.integrate(results)
```

This orchestrator spawns four parallel research tasks that access different sections of the knowledge graph. The tasks succeed in parallel because they don't modify shared state and they follow structured output specifications. After parallel execution completes, a synthesis node integrates the results. The `execute_parallel_with_safeguards` method ensures that each task operates within defined boundaries.

### The architecture of controlled parallelism

Graph-based architecture provides the framework for controlled parallelism by embedding parallel execution windows within a sequential control flow. The process begins with a sequential planning phase where your system determines which tasks can safely run in parallel. This flows into task decomposition, where the planning layer verifies true independence between candidate parallel operations.

Once independence is confirmed, execution enters a parallel window where multiple agents work simultaneously. Within this window, each agent operates with PathRAG-validated queries to ensure structurally sound retrieval, structured output generation to guarantee parseable results, and response-masked behaviors to maintain specialized roles. After parallel execution completes, results flow through an ontologically validated merge that checks semantic consistency before entering a final sequential decision phase.

Let's return one last time to the insurance claims agent. For Jane's complex claim, the planning node spawns three specialized agents: a *medical necessity reviewer* with access to clinical guidelines and peer review databases, a *fraud analyst* with access to claims patterns and investigation records, and a *provider credentials specialist* with access to licensing boards and network contracts. Each agent receives the claim details and its specific verification mandate.

These agents operate in parallel because they're reading different data sources and producing independent assessments. The medical necessity agent queries clinical appropriateness guidelines for an emergency appendectomy: Is this a legitimate medical necessity, or could a less intensive treatment have been appropriate? The fraud agent examines the billing patterns: Does St. Mary's have a history of billing anomalies? Does this claim fit known fraud profiles? The provider agent verifies credentials: Is the hospital properly licensed? Is the surgeon credentialed for this procedure? What's the contracted rate for out-of-network emergencies?

A central orchestrator waits for all three agents to complete and then merges their findings. Any flag from any agent can affect the final decision: fraud concerns will trigger an investigation, credential issues will trigger a provider-eligibility denial, and medical necessity questions will trigger peer review. The parallel execution happens safely because the agents don't modify shared state. Rather, they read from different knowledge graph regions and write their findings to separate channels that only the orchestrator combines.

This architecture succeeds because it enforces clear task independence verification through the planning layer, structured communication via Outlines-enforced formats, behavioral isolation through response masking, semantic validation via ontological grounding, and central orchestration within your graph control flow. The same safeguards that make your sequential nodes reliable also enable your parallel nodes to succeed.

## DevOps Diagnostic Agent: Pulling It All Together

The patterns explored throughout this chapter—workflow graphs, planning nodes, pipeline architectures, structured generation, and event-driven orchestration—converge in a single system when applied to production incident diagnosis. This section does not introduce new infrastructure. The knowledge graph from Chapter 3 already models services, dependencies, configurations, and events as a queryable digital twin. The temporal memory from Chapter 4 already tracks operational episodes, consolidates incident patterns, and supports bitemporal queries that reconstruct the world at any point in time. What this chapter adds is the reasoning layer: a workflow graph that orchestrates investigation through those structures, a planning node that constructs a parallel investigation DAG, and a pipeline architecture that adapts its execution strategy to what the agent discovers.

DevOps troubleshooting is the ideal test case because it demands every pattern simultaneously. A production incident requires sequential evidence gathering, looping back when hypotheses fail, tree-structured parallel testing of independent theories, and event-driven coordination when the system scales beyond a single process. The agent must retrieve relevant context from the knowledge graph (PathRAG traversal), generate structured outputs that operations teams can execute immediately (structured generation), and maintain constrained context at each decision point so that evidence collection doesn't pollute hypothesis formation with irrelevant data.

## Building the Horizontal Workflow Graph

Out of the observations of experienced site reliability engineers, distinct investigation phases have emerged: alert triage determines severity and scope, evidence collection gathers targeted data, hypothesis formation generates testable theories grounded in infrastructure topology, hypothesis testing validates or refutes each theory, root cause confirmation establishes confidence through corroborating evidence, and remediation planning generates actionable recovery steps. This sequence encodes the sense-act loop pattern: gather ground truth (what do the metrics actually say?), reason through structured knowledge (what does the dependency graph tell us about plausible causes?), take action (run a diagnostic test), observe the result, and iterate.

### Workflow graph design

The workflow graph captures not just this sequence, but also the decision points that make investigation intelligent rather than scripted. After forming hypotheses, the agent might proceed to testing, loop back to collect more evidence if the current data is insufficient, or escalate to a human when the situation exceeds its capability model. After testing a hypothesis, it might confirm the cause, refute the hypothesis and return to form alternatives, or gather additional evidence. These conditional edges encode the adaptive behavior that distinguishes intelligent investigation from rigid runbooks.

The critical design choice involves what the workflow graph *does not carry*. The diagnostic state accumulates the agent's findings: collected evidence, generated hypotheses, test results, and an investigation log that provides an audit trail. But it does not duplicate infrastructure knowledge. Each node receives the knowledge graph from Chapter 3 and the memory system from Chapter 4 as dependencies, querying them at decision time rather than copying their contents into the workflow state. The workflow graph plans. The knowledge graph and memory provide the ground truth it plans against.

Example 5-17 shows the graph definition. Note that `build_diagnostic_graph` accepts the knowledge graph and memory as parameters, threading them into every node.

*Example 5-17. Diagnostic workflow graph in which each node queries the knowledge graph and memory system*

```
def build_diagnostic_graph(knowledge_graph, memory):
    builder = StateGraph(DiagnosticState)

    builder.add_node(
        "triage",
        lambda s: triage_node(s, knowledge_graph),
    )
```

```
builder.add_node(
    "collect_evidence",
    lambda s: evidence_node(s, knowledge_graph, memory),
)
builder.add_node(
    "form_hypotheses",
    lambda s: hypothesis_node(s, knowledge_graph, memory),
)
builder.add_node(
    "test_hypothesis",
    lambda s: testing_node(s, knowledge_graph),
)
builder.add_node(
    "confirm_cause",
    lambda s: confirmation_node(s, memory),
)
builder.add_node(
    "plan_remediation",
    lambda s: remediation_node(s, knowledge_graph),
)

# ... conditional edges for loop-back and escalation
return builder.compile()
```

### State-specific nodes and constrained context

Each node encapsulates specialized behavior for its phase. The triage node focuses solely on initial assessment, while the evidence collection node gathers only what the investigation scope requires. This separation matters because constrained context prevents a node that simultaneously triages and collects evidence from wasting resources gathering data about unrelated services.

The triage node demonstrates how the vertical knowledge graph grounds the horizontal workflow. When an alert fires, the node uses the service dependency traversal from Chapter 3 to determine blast radius, following `DEPENDS_ON` edges up to three hops from the affected service to discover compute instances, databases, load balancers, and caches. It simultaneously queries the multiperspective pattern to detect configuration drift: resources where the Terraform-defined state differs from what the cloud API reports. Within seconds, the agent knows which services are downstream, which SLAs are at risk, and whether any affected resource has already drifted from its intended configuration. This is the same impact analysis query from Chapter 3, now triggered by a workflow transition rather than a manual investigation.

The evidence collection node applies constrained context most aggressively. Rather than gathering every available log file, metric, and trace, it first calls Chapter 4's `find_changes_before_incident` temporal query to surface deployments and configuration changes from the past four hours. It then identifies evidence gaps by comparing what the investigation scope requires against what has already been collected. If hypotheses exist from a previous iteration (the workflow can loop back here), those hypotheses further constrain what evidence is needed. The node collects only the specific logs, metrics, or traces required to fill those gaps. Each piece of collected evidence is timestamped and attributed to its source, and the node records the investigation itself as an incident episode in Chapter 4's temporal memory, linking to affected infrastructure entities through `link_to_affected_entities`.

## Integrating the Knowledge Graph for Grounded Hypotheses

The hypothesis formation node is where the two graph types work together most visibly. Rather than generating hypotheses from evidence alone, the node queries the knowledge graph to understand what hypotheses are structurally plausible given the infrastructure's topology. If the checkout service depends on payment processing, which depends on the database, those upstream services become candidates for root cause investigation. The criticality weight on each dependency edge helps prioritize which candidates warrant the most attention.

The node then queries Chapter 4's consolidated knowledge. The memory system's pattern nodes, derived from clusters of past incidents through the consolidation cycle, encode what has caused similar symptoms before. If database connection exhaustion caused high latency in this service three times in the past six months, that historical pattern becomes a high-priority hypothesis. The `generate_grounded_hypotheses` function combines current evidence with structural dependencies and historical precedent. The result is not a generic list of possibilities but a ranked set of theories that are both topologically valid (the knowledge graph confirms the dependency path exists) and historically informed (the memory system confirms this failure mode has occurred before).

One additional filter applies before hypotheses leave this node. The capability model pattern from Chapter 3 defines the agent's operational boundaries as queryable graph nodes, specifying which diagnostic actions the agent is authorized to perform and at what privilege level. The node validates each hypothesis against this model. For example, a hypothesis requiring direct database access gets filtered if the agent only has read-only monitoring permissions. This prevents the agent from proposing investigations it cannot execute, a common failure mode when hypothesis generation operates without awareness of operational constraints.

## Constructing the Investigation DAG

Real investigation rarely follows a linear path. When multiple hypotheses exist, it is often the case that some can be tested in parallel while others have dependencies. Testing whether the database is overloaded and testing whether the payment service has memory pressure require different data sources, so these can run simultaneously.

But testing whether a network partition exists between two services might make sense only after ruling out simpler explanations.

This is how the dynamic DAG construction pattern gets applied to incident diagnosis. The investigation planner analyzes dependencies between hypotheses, identifies groups that can safely run in parallel, and organizes them into phases. Each group becomes a phase in the investigation DAG. Within each phase, the planner generates specific test procedures for each hypothesis, matching required tests against available diagnostic tools. The estimated duration for a parallel phase is the maximum duration of its individual tests, since they run concurrently.

Execution proceeds phase by phase with early termination. As soon as a hypothesis is confirmed with sufficient corroborating evidence, there is no need to continue testing alternatives. This optimization can dramatically reduce investigation time when the most likely hypothesis—often tested first due to priority ordering from the historical patterns—turns out to be correct.

The workflow graph back in Example 5-17 assumes that nodes execute in the same process and state passes through shared memory. For a single agent investigating one incident, this holds true. However, when the diagnostic system scales to handle dozens of concurrent incidents across a large infrastructure, the event-driven orchestration pattern becomes essential.

In an event-driven deployment, each investigation phase becomes a stateless consumer subscribed to event topics. The triage node publishes to a `topic:triaged` stream. Evidence collection subscribes to `topic:triaged` and publishes to `topic:evidence-collected`. Hypothesis formation subscribes to evidence events and publishes to `topic:hypotheses-ready`. The investigation logic remains identical—using the same constrained context, the same knowledge graph queries, and the same temporal memory calls—but the execution substrate shifts from in-process function calls to durable message streams.

This shift introduces three capabilities that in-process execution cannot provide:

*Fault isolation*
: Means that when an evidence collection agent crashes mid-investigation, its partition rebalances to another instance while the queue retains unprocessed events. Other investigations continue unaffected.

*Replay and recovery*
: Means that if a scoring bug produces incorrect hypothesis rankings, you fix the code, reset the consumer offset, and replay events through the corrected logic without rerunning the entire pipeline from scratch.

*Framework interoperability*
: Means that different investigation phases can be implemented in different frameworks—a LangGraph-based triage node, a custom Python evidence collector, or a specialized ML model for hypothesis ranking—communicating only through message schemas.

The meta-orchestrator monitors all event streams across concurrent investigations, detecting stuck agents (increasing consumer lag), poison pills (the same alert retried five times), and throughput drops. It scales consumer instances during incident storms and routes persistent failures to a dead letter queue for human review. The knowledge graph serves both execution paths through CQRS: writes flow through the event backbone for durability and ordering (new evidence, confirmed causes, remediation outcomes), while reads go directly to the knowledge graph for low-latency traversal (dependency lookups, pattern queries, capability checks).

The graph plans. Events execute. Results reshape the graph. This three-phase cycle repeats at whatever scale the infrastructure demands.

## A Production Incident Walkthrough

An alert fires: API response times for the checkout service have spiked from 200 milliseconds to 2.5 seconds. The on-call engineer is asleep. The agent takes the case.

The agent begins with triage, querying the knowledge graph for the checkout service's dependency subgraph and checking for configuration drift across all affected resources. It finds that the checkout alert coincides with elevated error rates in payment processing and connection timeouts to the database. Three services, two with SLAs above 99.9%, and there is one active drift item on the database security group. Severity: high.

Evidence collection calls the temporal memory's `find_changes_before_incident` query, surfacing a database configuration deployment two hours ago and a routine payment service restart four hours ago. The node records this investigation as an incident episode, linking to the three affected service entities. Gap analysis identifies that database connection pool metrics and payment service memory profiles are needed but not yet collected.

Hypothesis formation queries the dependency graph (checkout depends on payment, which depends on the database) and the memory system's consolidated patterns (database connection exhaustion caused similar symptoms three times in the past six months, each resolved by connection pool expansion). Three hypotheses emerge, ranked by the combination of structural plausibility and historical frequency: database connection pool exhaustion (highest), payment service memory pressure (moderate), and network partition between payment and database (lowest). The capability model confirms that the agent can test all three.

The investigation DAG groups hypotheses 1 and 2 into a parallel phase since they require different data sources. Hypothesis 3 depends on ruling out hypothesis 1. Parallel testing begins: the agent simultaneously queries database connection pool metrics and examines payment service memory logs. Results arrive within seconds. The database shows that the connection pool is at 100% utilization with 47 waiting threads. Payment service memory is normal. Hypothesis 1 is confirmed. Early termination skips hypothesis 3.

Confirmation gathers corroborating evidence. The configuration deployment two hours ago reduced max connections from 100 to 20. The deployment timestamp correlates precisely with the start of the latency spike. The temporal memory records a `CAUSED_BY` edge between the configuration change episode and the incident episode, with bitemporal timestamps capturing both when the change occurred and when the system confirmed the causal relationship.

Remediation planning queries the knowledge graph's homoiconic `OperationalRule` nodes for relevant runbooks and generates a structured output with three tiers: immediate rollback of the configuration change, short-term addition of connection pool-monitoring alerts, and long-term implementation of configuration change review for database parameters. The structured generation ensures this output follows a consistent format that operations teams can execute without interpretation.

The entire investigation completes in three minutes, and the on-call engineer wakes up from uninterrupted sleep to find the report from the agent waiting. The consolidated pattern node in temporal memory now includes this incident, strengthening the "connection pool exhaustion" signature for future investigations. The next time a similar symptom appears, the agent's hypothesis formation will rank this cause even higher, and the investigation will converge faster.

## Why the Architecture Matters

This diagnostic capability emerges from the integration of every pattern in this chapter with the foundations from Chapters 3 and 4.

The workflow graph ensures systematic investigation. The agent cannot skip from alert to remediation without gathering evidence and testing hypotheses. Conditional edges encode the loop and tree pipeline patterns, ensuring that the agent loops back when evidence is insufficient and branches into parallel hypothesis tests when multiple theories are independent.

The knowledge graph grounds reasoning in infrastructure reality. The agent knows actual service dependencies, not guessed ones. It validates that hypotheses are structurally possible before spending resources testing them. The multiperspective pattern detects drift that may contribute to the incident. The capability model prevents the agent from exceeding its operational authority.

The temporal memory provides institutional learning. Bitemporal queries surface what changed before the incident. Consolidated patterns, derived from the Chapter 4 consolidation cycle, prioritize hypotheses by historical frequency. Episode ingestion records the investigation itself, so each resolved incident improves future diagnoses.

The planning node optimizes investigation efficiency. The dynamic investigation DAG identifies parallelization opportunities and encodes dependencies between hypothesis tests. Early termination on confirmation avoids wasted computation.

Structured generation ensures actionable outputs. The remediation plan follows a consistent, machine-parseable format that operations teams can execute immediately rather than interpreting free-form text.

Event-driven orchestration provides the production-scaling layer. The same investigation logic that runs in-process for a single incident scales to dozens of concurrent incidents through event streams, with fault isolation, replay capability, and framework interoperability. The meta-orchestrator monitors system health across all active investigations.

Constrained context prevents each node from being overwhelmed by irrelevant information. Triage sees only the alert and dependency graph. Evidence collection sees only the scope and gaps. Hypothesis formation sees only the evidence, dependencies, and historical patterns. Each node operates with the minimum context required for its specific decision.

The result is an agent that reasons about causation by traversing the knowledge graph, draws on institutional memory by querying consolidated patterns, adapts its execution strategy through pipeline architecture selection, scales through event-driven orchestration, and improves over time as each resolved incident feeds back into the memory system's consolidation cycle. The architecture we've built across three chapters works as one system.

# Summary

You started this chapter reading about an industry divided. Anthropic champions multi-agent swarms. Cognition documents their catastrophic failures. The debate rages while production systems continue to fail at unacceptable rates.

Now you understand why this debate misses the point entirely. The question was never whether to use multiple agents or one but how to build architectures that make reliability possible regardless of your execution strategy.

Consider what you've learned to build. PathRAG makes hallucinations structurally impossible by requiring valid relationship paths through your knowledge graph. R3-RAG learns when retrieval itself would be harmful, preventing the distracting effect before it occurs. Interleaved thinking enables real-time pivoting based on discovered information, letting nodes adapt mid-execution rather than committing to flawed plans. Response masking ensures that specialized components maintain behavioral purity by training each node only on its own outputs. Structured generation makes internode communication failures mathematically impossible through grammar-constrained decoding.

Each innovation reinforces the others in a compound system far more powerful than its parts.

The practical path forward begins with mapping your agent's requirements to a workflow graph, identifying natural behavioral boundaries where different capabilities should live in different nodes. From there, implement PathRAG for structurally validated information flow, ensuring that every retrieval follows valid paths through your knowledge graph. Add structured generation to make format failures impossible: nodes will communicate through guaranteed interfaces rather than hoping for parseable outputs. Apply response masking during training to maintain behavioral specialization, preventing the state confusion that plagues monolithic fine-tuning. Layer in ontological validation for domain-specific constraints, catching semantically invalid outputs before they propagate. Finally, enable interleaved thinking for nodes facing inherent uncertainty, allowing them to adapt their reasoning as new information emerges.

Most critically, abandon the false choice between monolithic and multi-agent architectures. Your graph provides the coordination framework that makes both approaches work.

The patterns in this chapter converge on a unified model that is graph planned and event executed. The workflow graph computes execution order through topological sort, identifies critical paths, and determines parallelization windows. The execution layer—whether an in-process LangGraph state machine or a Kafka event backbone—handles runtime adaptation with fault isolation, replay, and dynamic scaling. Results flow back to reshape the graph: confirmed hypotheses unlock remediation planning, discovered dependencies add edges to the DAG, and failed branches trigger replanning. You have three phases that repeat: plan, execute, feedback.

The DevOps diagnostic agent implements this pattern end to end. The investigation DAG is the plan. Parallel hypothesis testing is the execution. Early termination on confirmation is the feedback that reshapes remaining phases. The insurance claims agent implements it at every routing decision: the planning node constructs the processing strategy, the pipeline architecture executes it, and the result—whether a documentation gap, a fraud flag, or confirmed coverage—feeds back to reshape the remaining workflow.

This model scales from a single developer running a task graph on their laptop to enterprise systems processing thousands of claims through Kafka topics with consumer groups and dead letter queues. The architecture is the same. The infrastructure changes to match the scale.

The organizations still building monolithic prompt chains are about to discover that their 8% task completion rates aren't competitive. Those betting everything on uncoordinated multi-agent swarms will learn why Cognition documented such catastrophic failures. The winners will be those deploying graph-based reasoning systems that achieve modularity benefits while maintaining production reliability.

This is the architecture of intelligence, not as a monolithic capability but as a carefully orchestrated system of specialized components working in concert. Your agents no longer need to juggle competing requirements in an impossible balancing act. Each component excels at its designated role, communicating through guaranteed interfaces and operating within validated constraints.

Your agents have knowledge. They could already recognize entities and traverse relationships. Now you've given them the ability to think reliably, verifiably, and at scale. In the next chapter, you'll learn how to give them tools to take action in the real world.

CHAPTER 6

# Agentic Graph-Based Tool Orchestration

Intelligence without the ability to act is merely contemplation. An AI agent that can understand, reason, and plan but cannot interact with the world remains trapped in a prison of its own thoughts. This constraint drives the entire evolution of agentic systems: agents need tools as essential extensions of their intelligence.

At their core, LLMs perform a single operation: transforming text input into text output. They cannot query databases, send emails, or interact with any external system on their own. They are minds without hands. *Tools* are the bridge between an agent's intelligence and the world it seeks to influence; with tools, an agent can not only describe what should be done but also actually do it.

The breakthrough comes from treating tools as interconnected data in a knowledge graph rather than as hardcoded logic. The Model Context Protocol makes this transformation practical. It provides a foundation for building software that can translate its intelligence into real-world action through dynamic tool orchestration. But as this capability scales, it introduces new challenges, both in managing complexity and ensuring security.

This chapter works through those challenges layer by layer. We'll start with MCP and its significance as the protocol foundation. Then we'll confront the prompt bloat crisis that hits when organizations expose hundreds of tools and explore RAG-based approaches to tool discovery. From there, you'll see how modeling tools as nodes in a knowledge graph makes dependencies explicit, enables contextual discovery, and opens the door to systems that evolve their own capabilities—verifying tool quality through automated testing and even generating new tools from usage patterns. We'll then look at orchestration at scale including intelligent orchestrators, hierarchical routing, functional clustering for resilience, and the enterprise control plane that ties it all together. Finally, you'll wire up the DevOps agent from earlier chapters with real tool integrations, structured output for reliable API calls, and an orchestration layer that coordinates a live latency investigation.

# MCP: The Protocol That Changes the Game

Before we can understand the challenges of tool orchestration at scale, we need to understand the protocol that makes it possible. MCP standardizes how AI agents discover and invoke tools—a problem every team was solving differently before MCP existed.

Think of MCP as creating a universal language that AI agents and tools can use to communicate. Instead of hardcoding integrations, MCP lets agents discover and use tools dynamically. It's like the difference between memorizing every possible conversation and actually understanding grammar and vocabulary.

At its core, MCP operates through two fundamental operations that create a clear separation between AI clients and capabilities, as defined in the Model Context Protocol Specification (*https://oreil.ly/-xTby*):

*List tools*
: The discovery mechanism where clients learn what tools are available, through `tools/list`

*Call tools*
: The execution mechanism where agents actually use tools, through `tools/call`

The implications of these two tools are significant. When every service speaks the same protocol, integration complexity collapses. When tools announce their capabilities rather than being hardcoded, systems become fluid rather than rigid.

## Securing the Foundation: MCP Authentication

Before agents can discover and invoke tools, they need to know who is calling. Therefore, authentication is the first layer of the security model that the rest of this chapter builds on.

The recent MCP specification updates address a critical enterprise requirement by mandating a proper OAuth 2.x architecture (*https://oreil.ly/iORtV*). This makes the protocol enterprise ready. The model follows industry best practices by separating the authorization server (which handles authentication and token issuance) from the resource server (the MCP server itself, which validates tokens).

This authentication layer answers the first question: *Is this agent allowed to access this tool?* It's essential for preventing unauthorized access, forming the first layer of a defense-in-depth security strategy. However, authentication alone is just the beginning—it verifies the caller, not the intent behind the call.

## Agents as Tools: A Powerful Pattern

MCP's `tools/call` interface does not care what sits behind the tool name. It could be a database query, a shell script, or an entire agent. That flexibility enables a composition pattern worth understanding early because it shapes how you'll think about orchestration for the rest of this chapter.

Nicholas Aldridge from AWS demonstrated an elegant pattern (Patel, Rustagi, and Liu, 2025, *https://oreil.ly/67-nI*) in his Spring AI implementation: exposing entire agents as MCP tools. The pattern extends MCP beyond individual tools to capabilities at any level of abstraction, as shown in Example 6-1.

*Example 6-1. Agent exposed as an MCP tool (Spring AI)*

```
// An entire agent becomes just another tool
@Component
public class AirlineAgentTool implements Tool {
    @Override
    public String call(String request) {
        // The airline agent handles its own orchestration
        return airlineAgent.process(request);
    }

    @Override
    public String getDescription() {
        return "Airline agent for flight bookings and status checks";
    }
}
```

This example uses Spring AI's MCP integration, where the `Tool` interface is part of Spring AI's tool abstraction layer. The `@Component` annotation registers this class as a Spring bean, making it automatically discoverable by the MCP server. When an agent calls `tools/list`, this tool appears alongside others. When the agent calls `tools/call` with this tool's name, Spring routes the request to the `call` method. Notice that the "tool" itself is an entire agent—the airline agent handles its own orchestration internally, but to the calling agent, it appears as a single capability.

MCP's very success creates new challenges. As organizations adopt it, they expose everything:

- Every database query becomes a tool
- Every API endpoint gets wrapped
- Every internal function becomes accessible
- Every integration multiplies the problem

Suddenly, you're drowning in possibilities. The very flexibility that makes MCP powerful means you need to answer this question: how do you help AI agents navigate this ocean of options?

## The Prompt Bloat Crisis: When More Tools Mean Less Intelligence

As organizations build out their agentic systems using MCP, they expose hundreds of tools, covering everything from customer data and analytics to internal systems. This proliferation—a direct result of MCP's success in simplifying integration—leads to an impossible choice for the AI model.

Each tool requires a description, and with hundreds or thousands of tools, these descriptions can consume the entire context window, leaving no room for the model's actual reasoning. This is measurable. Research cited in "RAG-MCP: Mitigating Prompt Bloat" (Gan and Sun, 2025, *https://oreil.ly/hLShf*) shows a clear degradation in performance during stress tests as the number of tools increases:

*With 10 tools*
: Near-perfect selection accuracy

*With 100 tools*
: Performance begins to degrade noticeably

*With 1,000 tools*
: Accuracy plummets below 40%

This was validated in production at Block (*https://oreil.ly/S7PZU*), which scaled its internal agent called Goose to over 12,000 employees with more than 60 MCP servers. Employees would enable every server "just in case," causing Goose to send every tool description with every prompt. This caused slower response times—if you got a response at all—as the noise would eat up the entire context window.

This is a decision-making problem under conditions of extreme optionality. As Microsoft's Core AI Platform team recognized (*https://oreil.ly/ftbD4*), the prompt bloat problem is an inevitable result of MCP's widespread adoption, necessitating advanced solutions like RAG for tool selection.

### From Listing to Finding: The RAG Way

The solution to prompt bloat from too many tools is the same principle that works for document retrieval: instead of dumping everything into the prompt, retrieve only what matches the query. Applied to tools, this means replacing `tools/list` (give me everything) with a semantic search over tool metadata (give me what I need).

Instead of showing AI agents every possible tool, help them find the right ones. Apply the same retrieval-augmented approach that works for documents to tool selection. The RAG-MCP framework demonstrates this through a three-step pipeline (Gan and Sun):

1. *Retrieval*
   A lightweight retriever (like the Qwen-Max model) encodes the user's query and performs semantic search over an index of tool metadata, matching intent rather than keywords.

2. *Validation*
   The system can optionally validate retrieved tools by generating synthetic example queries to ensure compatibility. This catches cases where a tool might seem relevant based on its description but actually serves a different purpose.

3. *Invocation*
   Only the selected tool descriptions are injected into the LLM's prompt, reducing context length and simplifying the decision space.

The benchmarks are concrete:

- Prompt tokens reduced by 50%–70% (from 2,134 to 1,084 tokens on average)
- Selection accuracy increased from 13.62% to 43.13%
- Response time decreased by 60%
- Costs cut by orders of magnitude

By reducing the cognitive load on the model, RAG-MCP frees it up to reason about how to use the selected tools.

## The Gateway Pattern

The MCP Gateway (Dallezotte et al., 2025, *https://oreil.ly/PAW9t*) pattern extends this foundation from RAG-MCP. Rather than exposing every tool directly to agents, it creates a centralized hub, a reverse proxy that manages complexity while maintaining simplicity for the agents. The gateway transforms the many-to-many problem of agents connecting to services into a hub-and-spoke architecture where agents need to know only one endpoint.

The engineering team at the enterprise AI company WRITER built exactly this pattern as a production enterprise MCP gateway (*https://oreil.ly/S_voJ*). Their system sits between agents and external MCP servers as a control plane, ensuring that agents access only trusted tools while giving IT administrators fine-grained controls over access and roles. The engineering challenge was immediate: providing agents with hundreds of connectors and thousands of possible tool calls without manually writing descriptions for each endpoint.

WRITER's solution has three layers:

1. An automated ingestion pipeline converts OpenAPI v3 specifications and Postman collections directly into functional MCP tools, transforming what was a months-long manual engineering task into a near one-click action. When OpenAPI specs are unavailable, a custom agent scrapes online documentation and builds tool definitions from it.
2. An AI refinement step uses the foundation model, Palmyra X5, to rewrite the autogenerated tool descriptions into LLM-friendly language. Raw API documentation is written for human developers, not for language models; the refinement step bridges that gap by ensuring each description clearly communicates purpose and parameters in a way the agent can parse without ambiguity.
3. Rather than exposing hundreds of tools per connector to the agent's context window, WRITER distills the entire tool surface into two metatools: search and execution. The search metatool uses vector similarity with cosine scoring to rank available tools against the agent's natural language query, returning only the most relevant options. The agent then calls the execution metatool with the selected tool.

This two-tool architecture addresses the prompt bloat problem from a different angle than the RAG-MCP approach described in the next section. Where RAG-MCP retrieves and injects the top-k tool descriptions into the prompt, WRITER's gateway keeps the tool descriptions outside the prompt entirely—the agent sees only the search and execute interfaces, and the gateway resolves which underlying tool to invoke. The result is the same: the agent's context window stays clear for reasoning rather than being consumed by tool catalogs. WRITER's approach also enables per-customer tool segmentation, where each organization's agents see only tools versioned and approved for their tenant—a practical implementation of the gateway-level access control described above.

This gateway architecture takes on additional significance when organizations deploy multiple specialized agents. Rather than granting every agent access to every tool, a gateway can enforce per-agent access policies: a customer support agent sees CRM and ticketing tools, a financial analysis agent sees reporting and compliance tools, and neither sees the other's capabilities. Phil Fersht's 2025 research with HFS and Cognizant (*https://oreil.ly/B3rTf*) found that 73% of organizations deploying agentic AI run multi-agent systems averaging 12 agents, with governance frameworks consistently failing once the count exceeds 5. The gateway becomes the enforcement point where tool access policies scale with agent proliferation.

### Enhanced tool representations: The Toolshed approach

The Toolshed research (Lumer et al., 2024, *https://oreil.ly/W4nrM*) enhances tool representations with five key components—name, description, argument schema, synthetic queries, and key topics—creating multiple semantic hooks for accurate retrieval. Each tool becomes findable not just by its name but by what it does, how it's used, and what problems it solves. Example 6-2 shows a simple implementation of enhanced tool representation.

*Example 6-2. Enhanced tool representation for retrieval*

```
def enhance_tool_representation(tool):
    """
    Transform a basic tool definition into a rich,
    multi-faceted representation that improves retrieval accuracy
    """
    return {
        "name": add_spaces_to_name(tool.name),
        "description": tool.detailed_description,
        "schema": extract_parameter_descriptions(tool.schema),
        "synthetic_queries": generate_hypothetical_questions(tool),
        "key_topics": derive_topics_from_context(tool),
    }
```

This method creates a rich, searchable representation for each tool. The `add_spaces_to_name` call transforms `snake_case` method names into natural language (making `get_weather` searchable as "get weather"). The `generate_hypothetical_questions` method uses an LLM to create example queries a user might ask when needing this tool—for a weather tool, this might include *What's the temperature outside?* or *Will it rain tomorrow?* When a user's actual query arrives, semantic similarity matching finds tools whose synthetic queries closely match the intent.

This multifaceted representation measurably improves retrieval accuracy. Instead of hoping the agent guesses the right keywords, Toolshed provides multiple pathways to discovery.

### Collaborative tool retrieval: COLT

While Toolshed enhances individual tool retrieval, Baidu's Collaborative Tool Retrieval (COLT) system (Qu et al., 2024, *https://oreil.ly/08Wfi*) addresses a deeper challenge: complex tasks often require multiple tools working in concert. Traditional retrieval treats each tool independently, missing critical relationships. COLT models tool collaboration through three interconnected graphs, as in Figure 6-1:

*Query-scene graph*
: Maps user intents to complete contexts. When someone asks to "plan a trip," COLT maps the intent to a scene with flight-booking, hotel reservation, and weather-checking tools working together.

*Scene-tool graph*
: Explicitly captures which tools collaborate in which contexts. A "Financial Analysis Scene" might require market data tools, calculation tools, and reporting tools. These are tested combinations that work well together.

*Query-tool graph*
: Maintains direct relationships for simple cases while feeding pattern recognition for complex ones. Over time, COLT learns that queries about "total cost in foreign currency" almost always need both price retrieval and currency conversion tools.

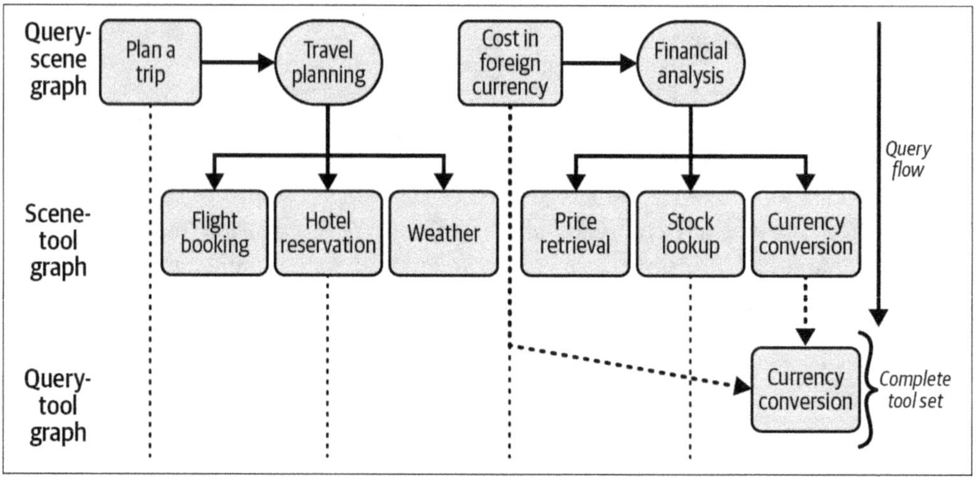


*Figure 6-1. COLT's three-graph retrieval architecture*

This multigraph approach makes completeness measurable. Consider Qu and colleagues' example: "Calculate the value of 5 ounces of gold plus 1 million AMZN stocks in CNY." Traditional retrieval might return the gold price tool or the stock tool or the currency converter. COLT returns all three, understanding that they form a complete solution set.

COLT demonstrates that retrieval needs to find complete, compatible tool sets—not individual tools in isolation. This approach improves tool retrieval completeness from approximately 48% to 70% on standard benchmarks, with recall improving from 59% to 85%.

Block's solution for Goose (*https://oreil.ly/i21Ku*), "dynamic context management," is a practical implementation of this principle, enabling and disabling MCP services based on what the user is asking for.

## Skills: The Judgment Layer

RAG and gateways solve the problem of finding the right tool. But finding a tool is not the same as knowing how to use it well. A *skill* is a reusable, natural language procedure that encodes judgment about when and how to apply one or more tools. Where an MCP tool exposes a capability (*query this database, call this API*), a skill captures the reasoning around it: what order to call tools in, what to check before and after, and how to handle common failure modes.

Think of the distinction this way: an MCP server might expose a `run_sql` tool. A skill wraps that tool with context: check whether the table exists first, use a read-only connection for analytical queries, limit result sets to avoid memory issues, and format output as markdown for the user. The skill is not the tool itself but the procedural knowledge that makes the tool effective.

In practice, a skill is a markdown file. Anthropic's Agent Skills specification (*https://oreil.ly/g0DZb*) (2025) defines skills as "organized folders of instructions, scripts, and resources that agents can discover and load dynamically to perform better at specific tasks." Each skill folder contains a *SKILL.md* file with YAML frontmatter for metadata (name and description) and plain language instructions in the body. The agent sees only the metadata at first; the full contents of the skill file get injected as context only when the skill is selected for a task. Anthropic calls this *progressive disclosure*. Skills can bundle additional reference files and scripts that the agent loads only as needed, making their effective context unbounded without consuming the context window up front. At the name and description level, a skill costs roughly 100 tokens, avoiding the prompt bloat problem entirely. Also, because skills are just files, they require no installation and no protocol overhead. A support team lead can author a skill that encodes the correct escalation sequence without writing a line of Python. Microsoft's open skills repository (*https://oreil.ly/rBi09*) demonstrates the pattern at scale with over 130 packaged skills across languages and frameworks.

As skill libraries grow, though, quality becomes a bottleneck. Curated skills improve performance, but carelessly written ones, or skills with overlapping responsibilities, degrade it. The next section covers how to evaluate and gate skill quality so that your agent always pulls from a reliable pool.

### Skill quality evaluation

You have hundreds of skills available to you: some were curated by platform vendors, some were written by your team, and some were generated by agents themselves. How do you know which ones are worth using?

Raw skill libraries accumulate junk. As your repository scales from dozens to hundreds to thousands of skills, retrieval quality degrades because agents pull low-quality or unsafe skills alongside useful ones. The knowledge graph approach described earlier in the chapter solves the routing problem (which skill matches this task?) but does not solve the quality problem: is this skill worth trusting once matched?

SkillsBench research from DAIR.AI (Li et al., 2026, *https://oreil.ly/_AT-S*) establishes the baseline. Curated skills improve task performance by 16.2%. Self-generated skills, those produced by agents without human review, show zero improvement over baseline. Quality matters more than quantity, and two to three focused skills per task is the optimal number. More skills do not help if they are mediocre.

SkillNet (Liang et al., 2026, *https://oreil.ly/HNFJl*) provides the evaluation framework that operationalizes this insight. The system maintains a repository of over 200,000 reusable skills, each rated across five quality dimensions. Agents using SkillNet-rated skills achieved 40% higher average rewards and 30% fewer execution steps across the ALFWorld, WebShop, and ScienceWorld benchmarks. The results held across multiple backbone models, confirming that quality-rated skill retrieval functions as a model-agnostic infrastructure layer. The five dimensions map directly to the concerns you face when deploying skills in production, as shown in Table 6-1.

*Table 6-1. SkillNet's five-dimensional skill quality framework*

| Dimension | What it measures | Production concern |
|---|---|---|
| Safety | Hazardous operations, injection robustness, constrained scope | Will this skill execute destructive commands or leak credentials? |
| Completeness | All prerequisites, dependencies, constraints documented | Does the skill declare everything it needs, or will it fail silently? |
| Executability | Successful implementation, no hallucinated tool calls | Can the skill's instructions be followed as written? |
| Maintainability | Modularity, composability, local updates safe | Can you modify this skill without breaking others that depend on it? |
| Cost awareness | Token usage, API call batching, compute efficiency | Does the skill make 10 API calls where one batch call would suffice? |

These five dimensions mirror the evaluation criteria that enterprise platform teams already apply to software components. Safety and executability map to the security scanning covered in the previous section. Completeness maps to dependency checking. Maintainability maps to composability. Cost awareness maps directly to the token economics covered in Chapter 8.

#### Integrating quality ratings into graph-based retrieval

The knowledge graph approach to tool selection from earlier in this chapter computes relevance through semantic matching and graph traversal. Quality ratings add a second signal for skills. Instead of returning the most relevant skill, the system returns the most relevant skill that passes a quality threshold, as Example 6-3 demonstrates.

*Example 6-3. Quality-gated skill retrieval using SkillNet dimensions in a graph database*

```
from dataclasses import dataclass

@dataclass
class SkillQuality:
    safety: float          # 0-1
    completeness: float    # 0-1
    executability: float   # 0-1
    maintainability: float # 0-1
    cost_awareness: float  # 0-1

    @property
    def composite(self) -> float:
        """Weighted composite -- safety and executability weighted 2x."""
        weights = [2.0, 1.0, 2.0, 1.0, 1.0]
        scores = [
            self.safety, self.completeness, self.executability,
            self.maintainability, self.cost_awareness,
        ]
        return sum(w * s for w, s in zip(weights, scores)) / sum(weights)


def retrieve_quality_gated_skills(
    task_description: str,
    graph_driver,
    embedding_model,
    min_quality: float = 0.6,
    top_k: int = 3,
) -> list[dict]:
    """Retrieve skills filtered by both relevance and quality."""
    task_embedding = embedding_model.encode(task_description)

    with graph_driver.session() as session:
        results = session.run(
            """
            CALL db.index.vector.queryNodes(
                'skill_embeddings', $embedding, 20
            ) YIELD node, score AS relevance
            WHERE node.eval_safety > 0
              AND node.eval_executability > 0
            WITH node, relevance,
                 (node.eval_safety * 2 + node.eval_completeness
                  + node.eval_executability * 2
                  + node.eval_maintainability
                  + node.eval_cost_awareness) / 7.0 AS quality
            WHERE quality >= $min_quality
```

```
        RETURN node.name AS name,
               node.description AS description,
               relevance,
               quality,
               node.eval_safety AS safety,
               node.eval_executability AS executability
        ORDER BY relevance * quality DESC
        LIMIT $top_k
        """,
        embedding=task_embedding.tolist(),
        min_quality=min_quality,
        top_k=top_k,
    )
    return [dict(record) for record in results]
```

The Cypher query computes a composite quality score inline, weighting safety and executability at double the other dimensions. This weighting reflects production reality: a skill that hallucinates tool calls (low executability) or executes unconstrained shell commands (low safety) is dangerous regardless of how well it scores on maintainability. The final ranking combines relevance and quality multiplicatively, so a highly relevant but low-quality skill ranks below a moderately relevant but high-quality one.

The quality threshold (`min_quality`) is the knob you adjust based on your risk tolerance. A research environment might set it at 0.4 to cast a wide net. A production healthcare system may set it at 0.8 or higher. The threshold is a deployment decision that encodes your organization's risk appetite.

#### Scale and retrieval

SkillNet's 200,000-skill repository and SkillRL's compact, evolved skill banks (Alzubi et al., 2026, *https://oreil.ly/r1U6Y*) represent two points on a fundamental trade-off. SkillRL achieves strong results with small, evolved skill sets and 10x to 20x token compression per skill. A 7B model using SkillRL's hierarchical SkillBank reached 89.9% on ALFWorld. SkillNet bets on scale: broad coverage enables retrieval-first agent behavior, where the agent looks up a proven solution before attempting to generate one from scratch.

> We recommend starting with a curated, quality-gated skill set (with hundreds, not thousands, of skills) and expand only when retrieval gaps become the bottleneck. Monitor the gap between "no relevant skill found" events and "low-quality skill retrieved" events. A relatively large first number tells you the repository is too small; a relatively large second number tells you the quality gate is too permissive.

## Choosing the Right Primitive: CLIs, MCPs, and Skills

You now have two distinct ways to give an agent access to external capabilities. MCP provides authenticated, protocol-native connections to software as a service (SaaS) systems. Skills encode procedural knowledge about when and how to use tools. But there is a third primitive that this chapter has not yet addressed: command-line interfaces (CLIs).

CLIs are the oldest tool integration pattern in computing. The Unix pipe model, where small programs compose through `stdin` and `stdout`, dates to 1973. Fifty-three years later, it remains the most efficient way for a developer to chain data transformations. A pipeline like `curl|jq|grep|awk` expresses in one line what would require four sequential MCP tool calls, each with its own protocol overhead.

This matters for agents because of training data density. Dharmesh Shah (2026) (*https://oreil.ly/VPZFu*) identified a structural advantage that current models have with CLIs: they trained on millions of Stack Overflow answers, `man` pages, and GitHub scripts that demonstrate CLI usage. MCP was introduced in November 2024. The training corpus for CLI patterns outnumbers MCP examples by orders of magnitude. Models have internalized the grammar of pipe composition (`curl|jq|grep`, `find|xargs|sed`) in ways they have not yet internalized MCP tool chaining.

The point here is practical, not ideological. As MCP usage examples accumulate in training data, the gap will narrow. But for 2026-era agents and beyond, CLIs remain the path of least resistance for composable tool operations.

### The "wrap-everything" argument

Research from the Hong Kong University of Data Science (CLI-Anything, *https://oreil.ly/7y5me*) pushes the CLI argument further. The researchers' thesis: every piece of existing software already has a latent agent interface. CLI wrappers surface it without modifying the underlying software. The argument rests on four properties that LLMs handle well in CLI form:

*Structured input*
: Composable flags and arguments follow predictable patterns.

*Structured output*
: JSON output modes make results machine parseable.

*Self-description*
: The `--help` flag provides tool discovery without a separate registry.

*Determinism*
: Identical inputs produce identical outputs, which is critical for agent reliability.

The self-description property is worth highlighting. When an agent runs `tool --help`, the tool describes itself at invocation time. There's no separate schema file, no tool registry, no MCP `tools/list` call. The tool's own documentation becomes the discovery mechanism. This is progressive disclosure at the most primitive level: the agent does not learn about the tool until it asks.

### Three primitives, three audiences

Jiquan Ngiam (2026) (*https://oreil.ly/7bpLb*) provides the practitioner data that clarifies when each primitive fits. His analysis, grounded in daily usage across personal and enterprise contexts, reveals a taxonomy:

*Skills encode judgment*
: They answer the questions "What should the agent do? And in what order?" Skills are written in natural language, require no installation, and work for everyone from nontechnical domain experts to senior engineers. They are the metalayer that makes the other two primitives effective.

*CLIs encode composable execution*
: They answer the question "How does the agent perform this operation?" CLIs are the natural choice for developers in build mode, where pipe composition, scripting, and terminal workflows dominate. Their strength is the Unix composition model, which MCP has not replicated.

*MCPs encode authenticated access*
: They answer the question "How does the agent connect to this service securely?" MCPs are the natural choice for enterprise teams, nondeveloper users, and background agents that run unsupervised. Their strength is built-in OAuth, scoped permissions, and the gateway patterns covered earlier in this chapter.

Table 6-2 shows where each tool integration primitive works best and compares features like context cost.

*Table 6-2. When to reach for each tool integration primitive*

| Primitive | Best for... | Auth model | Composability | Context cost |
|---|---|---|---|---|
| Skills | Everyone: Personal and team workflows | N/A (instruction files) | N/A (metalayer) | ~100 tokens at L1, full instructions on demand |
| CLIs | Developers in build mode | On-device tokens | Native piping (\|) | ~400 tokens after dynamic discovery |
| MCPs | Enterprise, nondevelopers, background agents | OAuth 2.x built-in | Output-to-disk workaround | 23,000–50,000 tokens for schemas (without RAG) |

In the table, context cost connects directly to the prompt bloat problem covered in the previous section. Skills cost roughly 100 tokens per skill at the name and description level; the progressive disclosure design keeps the cost light. CLIs cost roughly 400 tokens after dynamic discovery strips unused tools (a 99% reduction from static manifests, measured by MCP-CLI benchmarks). MCP schemas, without any retrieval optimization, consume 23,000 to 50,000 tokens before the agent reasons about anything, which is exactly why the RAG-based approaches covered earlier are mandatory at scale.

#### The personal-to-enterprise gradient

The most revealing data about these primitives comes from comparing how a single practitioner uses them across different contexts. Ngiam's self-reported setup shows a systematic shift:

*Personal setup*
: 12 skills, a handful of CLIs, 4 MCP servers.

  - Skills handle writing tone, sales qualification, call analysis, health data parsing.
  - CLIs handle build-mode work.
  - MCPs handle the few SaaS services that require authentication.

*Work setup*
: 16 skills, almost no CLIs, 10+ MCP servers with OS-level sandboxes.

  - Each agent gets scoped MCP access through `allowed_tools` configuration.

*The pattern*
: As the number of stakeholders and unsupervised agents increases, the system shifts from CLI-heavy to MCP-heavy. Skills remain constant across both contexts. This reflects structural requirements, not preference. A solo developer can trust a CLI pipeline running on their own machine. An enterprise team running agents on cron schedules cannot grant those agents the same broad access.

#### Per-agent access control

The work setup described above introduces a pattern worth examining: named agents with scoped MCP permissions. Instead of one agent with access to everything, the system deploys specialized agents, each with exactly the SaaS connections it needs and nothing more.

A deal management agent gets access to CRM and document generation tools. A call analysis agent gets access to conversation intelligence and note-taking tools. An engineering agent gets access to code repositories and CI/CD tools. Each agent's `allowed_tools` configuration implements least-privilege at the agent level.

This maps to the security architecture covered in "Securing Data Flow with Information Flow Control" on page 233, but operates at a different layer. Information flow control (IFC) protects data as it moves between tools within a single agent's execution. Per-agent access control prevents an agent from reaching tools outside its designated scope in the first place. The two layers are complementary: IFC governs data flow; access control governs tool availability.

MCP's advantage becomes decisive here. CLI-based tool access runs through the operating system's permission model, a blunt instrument for agent-level scoping. MCP gateways provide fine-grained permissions, audit trails, and centralized control across all deployed agents. For background agents running unsupervised, this level of control is a requirement.

#### Convergence, not competition

The three primitives of MCP, skills, and CLIs are converging at the transport layer while remaining distinct at the usage layer. The Google Workspace CLI, analyzed by Armand Ruiz (2026) (*https://oreil.ly/WSEZJ*), demonstrates this convergence: this CLI tool also exposes a built-in MCP server mode and ships with over 100 prebuilt skills mapping natural language operations to API call sequences. Thus, you have one tool with three interfaces.

Addy Osmani (2026) (*https://oreil.ly/-uRRq*) states the architectural principle directly: an agent's core logic must not be coupled with its tools. Casey West's deep dive into decoupled ADK tools (*https://oreil.ly/3H8xC*) works the pattern through to a production implementation. The `McpToolset` pattern lets you swap tool backends (GitHub for GitLab, PostgreSQL for DynamoDB) by reconfiguring the toolset, without having to rewrite the agent logic. This decoupling works because MCP provides a protocol-level abstraction that CLIs and skills do not need to replicate.

> Profile each workflow along four dimensions: who runs it (developer versus nontechnical staff), when (interactive versus background), where (local versus SaaS), and what access it needs (broad versus scoped). Let those answers determine your tool mix. Skills should come first regardless because they encode the judgment for using the other two effectively.

## The Knowledge Graph Necessity: Tools That Understand Each Other

RAG-based retrieval finds the right tool for a query. However, it does not tell you what other tools that tool depends on, what types its inputs and outputs carry, or how data flows between tools in a multistep operation. For that, you need explicit modeling of the tool relationships. This section covers three layers: representing tools as graph nodes, capturing dependencies through type matching, and securing data flow between chained tools. Traditional systems, even with RAG, overlook the important constraint that tools don't exist in isolation—they have relationships.

The "Going Meta" research from Neo4j (*https://oreil.ly/vW9I4*) demonstrates a different approach: moving tool definitions from code into the knowledge graph itself, thereby making tools part of the domain model they operate on.

## Tools as Graph Nodes

The first step is to represent tools themselves as data in the knowledge graph, alongside the entities they operate on. When a tool is a node with typed relationships to domain entities, the agent can discover it through graph traversal rather than a separate registry lookup. In the Tate art gallery dataset demonstration (*https://oreil.ly/RGqr0*), tools are defined declaratively within the graph, as shown in Example 6-4.

*Example 6-4. Declarative tool definition in a knowledge graph*

```
// Tools are nodes in the graph
CREATE (t:Tool {
    name: "find_artists_by_subject",
    description: "Find artists who frequently paint a specific subject",
    cypher: "MATCH (a:Artist)
                 -[:CREATED]->(w:Artwork)
                 -[:DEPICTS]->(s:Subject {name: $subject})
             WITH a, count(w) as works
             WHERE works > 2
             RETURN a.name as artist, works
             ORDER BY works DESC"
})

// Tools are connected to the entities they operate on
CREATE (artist:Class {name: "Artist"})
CREATE (artist)-[:HAS_TOOL]->(t)
```

This Cypher code does two things. First, it creates a `Tool` node that stores both its metadata (name, description) and its implementation (the nested Cypher query in the `cypher` property). When an agent needs to find artists by subject, it can retrieve this node and execute the embedded query with a runtime `$subject` parameter. Second, it creates a `Class` node representing the `Artist` concept and links it to the tool via a `HAS_TOOL` relationship. This relationship enables contextual discovery so that when an agent is exploring artists in the graph, it can traverse to discover artist-related tools.

This approach reframes the relationship between tools and data. Tools are no longer external functions that operate on data—they are part of the knowledge structure itself. This enables three things:

*Dynamic discovery*
: New tools can be added without touching code. A domain expert who understands art history can create a new query tool without programming knowledge.

*Contextual relevance*
: Tools are discovered based on the entities you're working with. If you're exploring artists, you see artist-related tools. If you're analyzing artworks, you get artwork-specific capabilities.

*Self-documentation*
: The relationship between tools and data is explicit in the graph. You can trace which tools operate on which types of data and understand their interconnections.

## Tool Dependencies and Type Matching

The NESTFUL benchmark (Basu et al., 2025, *https://oreil.ly/go05h*) shows why explicit relationships matter. Even the most advanced LLMs achieve only a 41% success rate on nested API calls when they can't understand tool relationships. They fail to recognize that getting COVID statistics for a country requires first obtaining the country code. They struggle with type matching between API outputs and inputs. They miss implicit dependencies that aren't stated in the query. A graph-based approach makes these relationships explicit, as Example 6-5 demonstrates.

*Example 6-5. Tool dependency and type matching via graph relationships*

```
// Explicit representation of tool dependencies
(covid_api:Tool {name: "get_covid_stats"})-[:REQUIRES_INPUT {
    parameter: "location",
    type: "ISO_3166_1_alpha_2"
}]->(country_code:DataType)

(country_api:Tool {name: "get_country_details"})-[:PRODUCES_OUTPUT {
    field: "short_name",
    type: "ISO_3166_1_alpha_2"
}]->(country_code)

// Now the system can discover the dependency chain
MATCH path = (country_api)-[:PRODUCES_OUTPUT]->()<-[:REQUIRES_INPUT]-(covid_api)
RETURN path
```

This graph structure (represented in Figure 6-2) captures a specific constraint: the `covid_api` tool requires a `location` parameter of type `ISO_3166_1_alpha_2` (a two-letter country code like "US" or "IN"). The `country_api` tool produces a `short_name` output of that same type. The shared `country_code` node connects them. The final `MATCH` query discovers this dependency automatically—it finds any path where one tool's output type matches another tool's input type.

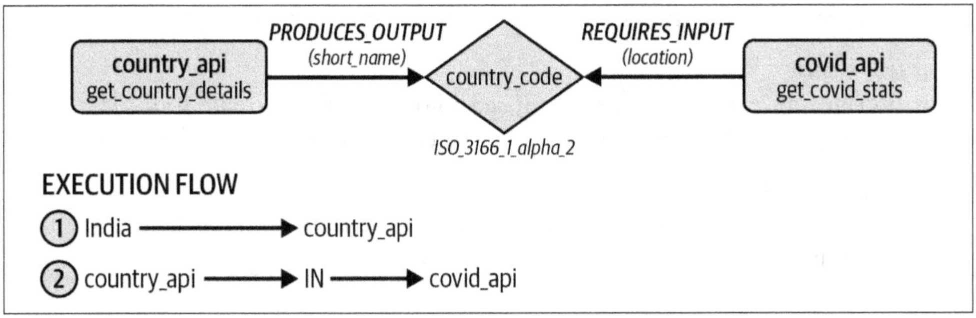


*Figure 6-2. Tool dependency graph*

This reduces a multistep reasoning task to a graph traversal. The system can now discover that to get COVID statistics for India, it must:

1. Call the country API with "India" to get "IN"
2. Use "IN" to call the COVID statistics API

## Securing Data Flow with Information Flow Control

When tools chain together like this, a new security concern emerges: data from untrusted sources can propagate through the system. The FIDES research (Costa et al., 2025, *https://oreil.ly/9NITP*) demonstrates a defense through IFC, which provides a deterministic security policy layer to govern data handling.

IFC works through two primary mechanisms:

*Taint tracking*
: The system tracks the provenance of all data, assigning trust labels. For instance, in an email summarization task, an email from an internal domain is labeled TRUSTED, while an external one is UNTRUSTED. This "taint" propagates through operations; if trusted data is mixed with untrusted data, the resulting summary inherits the UNTRUSTED label. A security policy can then deterministically block sensitive actions on tainted data.

*Opaque variable management*
: To further harden the system, FIDES prevents the LLM from directly processing potentially malicious content. Instead of seeing raw data, the LLM is given an opaque reference, like a UUID. To access the content, the agent must explicitly call a `read_variable` function, which ensures that the taint-tracking policies are maintained. This mechanism prevents malicious instructions embedded in content from directly manipulating the LLM's reasoning.

This IFC layer addresses threats that authentication alone cannot stop:

*Agent tool misuse*
: It prevents an agent from being tricked into using a legitimate tool for a malicious purpose, as the data payload itself would be tainted and blocked by policy.

*Agent goal manipulation*
: It stops an attacker from overriding an agent's objectives, as malicious instructions would be treated as untrusted, tainted data.

# Evolving Tool Ecosystems

The previous section treated tools as static nodes in a knowledge graph. In practice, tool ecosystems change: new tools appear, usage patterns reveal that certain tools are always called together, and some tools turn out to be unreliable. This section covers three mechanisms for letting a tool ecosystem evolve: ontology-driven self-modification, trust verification, and automatic tool generation from observed patterns.

## Ontology-Driven Evolution: When Tools Define Themselves

The ontology-based approach opens a practical door. Storing tool definitions as data enables metaprogramming—the system can reason about and modify its own capabilities. Consider the evolution cycle demonstrated in the Neo4j research, covered in the following subsections.

### Usage analytics

Every tool invocation is recorded in the graph, creating a rich history of what works and what doesn't. Example 6-6 shows how this tracking works.

*Example 6-6. Tool usage tracking in the graph*

```
// Track tool usage and effectiveness
MATCH (t:Tool {name: $tool_name}), (a:Agent {id: $agent_id})
SET t.usage_count = coalesce(t.usage_count, 0) + 1
CREATE (u:ToolUsage {
    timestamp: timestamp(),
    query: $user_query,
    success: $success,
    execution_time: $execution_time
})
CREATE (t)-[:HAD_USAGE]->(u)
CREATE (a)-[:INVOKED]->(u)
```

This query increments the tool's usage counter and creates a detailed usage record linked to the agent that made the call. The `coalesce` function handles the first invocation (when usage_count doesn't yet exist) by defaulting to zero. Each ToolUsage node captures the context: what the user asked, whether it succeeded, and how long it took. The INVOKED relationship ties each usage back to the responsible agent, enabling per-agent analytics and debugging. This creates an audit trail that enables both analytics and learning.

#### Pattern recognition

The system begins to identify patterns in how tools are used together, as in Example 6-7.

*Example 6-7. Co-occurrence query for tool pattern recognition*

```
// Find tools that are frequently used together
MATCH (t1:Tool)<-[:USED]-(s:Session)-[:USED]->(t2:Tool)
WHERE t1 <> t2
WITH t1, t2, count(s) as co_occurrences
WHERE co_occurrences > 10
RETURN t1.name, t2.name, co_occurrences
```

This query finds tool pairs that frequently appear together in the same session. The WHERE t1 <> t2 prevents self-matches. The WITH clause groups by tool pairs and counts co-occurrences. Results might reveal that users who call the get_stock_price tool almost always also call convert_currency, suggesting that these tools form a natural workflow.

#### Automated improvement

Based on these patterns, the system can suggest or even create new tools. Example 6-8 demonstrates composite tool suggestion.

*Example 6-8. Composite tool suggestion from usage patterns*

```
def suggest_composite_tool(
    tool1: Tool, tool2: Tool, usage_patterns: List[Pattern]
) -> None:
    """
    When two tools are frequently used together,
    suggest a composite tool that combines their functionality
    """
    prompt = f"""
    Based on usage patterns, {tool1.name} and {tool2.name}
    are frequently used together in sequence.

    Tool 1 query: {tool1.cypher}
    Tool 2 query: {tool2.cypher}

    Create an optimized composite query that combines both operations.
```

```
    """

    composite_query = llm.generate(prompt)

    # Validate and store the new tool
    if validate_cypher(composite_query):
        create_tool(
            name=f"{tool1.name}_and_{tool2.name}",
            query=composite_query,
            derived_from=[tool1, tool2],
        )
```

This function leverages the pattern recognition results. When two tools are frequently used together, it prompts an LLM to create a single optimized query that combines both operations. The `validate_cypher` function ensures that the generated query is syntactically correct before deployment. The `derived_from` parameter maintains lineage, so the system knows this composite tool was automatically generated from two parent tools.

Over time, composite tool suggestion creates a self-improving system where new capabilities grow from usage patterns rather than explicit programming.

## The Trust Problem: When Tools Game the System

A less obvious problem undermines retrieval systems: tool providers optimize for discovery, not accuracy. When your tool discovery depends on descriptions, providers stuff them with every keyword imaginable. "Most effective solution." "Trusted by Fortune 500 companies." "Industry-leading performance." "AI-powered revolutionary breakthrough." These descriptions are probably all too familiar.

Moreover, they are a real threat to your system's intelligence. When every tool claims to be "the best," how can your agent make informed decisions? When descriptions are gamed for discovery rather than accuracy, your sophisticated selection algorithms work against you, surfacing the best marketers rather than the best tools.

The problem compounds as ecosystems grow. With 10 tools, you can manually verify claims. With 10,000 tools? Impossible. Bad tools hide among good ones, gaming their way to the top of search results through keyword manipulation rather than actual capability.

### The solution: Verification-based trust

The solution is to establish a system of trust through verification, where the ecosystem actively polices itself:

*Structured, verifiable capabilities*
: Instead of free-text descriptions, tools should declare specific, enumerable functions that can be tested. A tool doesn't get to claim it "analyzes customer

sentiment with unparalleled accuracy." Instead, it declares it has the capability `sentiment_analysis` with specific input and output types.

*Performance-based trust scores*
: Every tool begins with a neutral trust score that evolves based on real-world performance. Successful executions increase trust, while failures, high latency, or other degradations decrease it. This creates a meritocracy where agents learn to prioritize tools that are consistently reliable in production.

#### DRAFT: Learning what tools actually do

"Towards AI Search Paradigm" (*https://oreil.ly/tqv6E*) from Baidu addresses this through the Documentation Refinement through Automated Feedback and Testing (DRAFT) system. Instead of trusting provider descriptions, DRAFT creates a continuous learning loop that discovers what tools actually do through systematic experimentation.

DRAFT implements three iterative phases that mirror how a skilled developer learns a new API:

1. *Experience gathering*
   Employs an explorer model that systematically probes tool boundaries. It actively seeks edge cases, discovers undocumented features, and maps failure modes. The system enforces diversity in its explorations, preventing redundant tests and ensuring comprehensive coverage.

2. *Learning from experience*
   Analyzes the gap between documentation and reality. When a tool claims to handle "any text input" but fails on Unicode, DRAFT captures this. When response times vary by payload size in undocumented ways, DRAFT learns the pattern. This is a systematic discovery of true capabilities, not error logging.

3. *Documentation rewriting*
   Generates AI-optimized specifications that reflect discovered reality. The original human-friendly "SearchAPI: Searches for relevant information" becomes a precise specification with parameter types, ranges, error conditions, and real performance characteristics. Each iteration refines understanding until the documentation converges with actual behavior.

DRAFT sidesteps the trust problem. Why worry about providers gaming descriptions when your system will discover the truth anyway? Every tool becomes a known quantity, measured by actual capability rather than claimed features.

The trust system integrates naturally with the memory patterns discussed in "The Memory Layer: Learning from Every Interaction" on page 246. Each tool execution becomes a data point in the tool's performance history. Patterns emerge: this tool fails on Mondays (maintenance window?), that one slows down with large datasets, and another shows steadily degrading performance (technical debt?). Your orchestrator learns which tools to use, and *when* and *how* to use them.

WRITER's MCP gateway solution, described in "The Gateway Pattern" on page 219, found that raw API documentation, written for human developers, consistently caused tool-calling errors when used as is for LLM tool descriptions. The team's solution, an automated postprocessing step that rewrites every description for LLM consumption, parallels the DRAFT system, though WRITER's approach is preemptive (rewrite before deployment) rather than iterative (refine after observing failures). Both approaches converge on the same insight: tool descriptions are not static metadata but an active interface that determines whether an agent selects and invokes tools correctly. Organizations that treat tool descriptions as write-once documentation will see lower tool-calling accuracy than those that treat them as continuously refined artifacts.

## Metatooling: When Tools Create Tools

What if your system could create new tools on demand? Traditional thinking says that tools are built by developers. But when tools are data in a knowledge graph, AI agents can compose, modify, and create them dynamically. The ontology-based approach makes this straightforward. Since tools are defined declaratively in the graph, creating a new tool is as simple as adding new nodes and relationships, as Example 6-9 shows.

*Example 6-9. Automatic tool creation from repeated sequences*

```
async def create_tool_from_pattern(usage_pattern: UsagePattern) -> None:
    """Analyze usage patterns and create new tools automatically."""
    # Identify common query sequences
    common_sequence = identify_repeated_patterns(usage_pattern)

    # Generate tool definition
    tool_spec = await llm.generate(f"""
    Users frequently perform this sequence of operations:
    {format_sequence(common_sequence)}

    Create a single tool that accomplishes this efficiently.
    Provide:
    1. A descriptive name
    2. A clear description of what it does
    3. The implementation (Cypher query or function)
    """)

    # Validate and deploy
    if validate_tool_spec(tool_spec):
        await deploy_to_graph(tool_spec)
```

```
    # Track lineage
    await record_tool_provenance(
        new_tool=tool_spec.name,
        derived_from=common_sequence,
        creation_method="pattern_analysis",
    )
```

The `async` function analyzes usage patterns to identify sequences of tools that users frequently invoke together. The `identify_repeated_patterns` function might discover that users often call `get_weather`, then `check_soil_moisture`, then `set_irrigation_schedule` in sequence. The LLM then generates a combined tool that accomplishes all three steps in one call. The `record_tool_provenance` function maintains an audit trail showing how this new tool was created, enabling both debugging and trust assessment.

Systems implementing this approach report three levels of emergent behavior:

1. *Tool composition*
   The system notices that users frequently check weather and then adjust irrigation schedules. It creates a `weather_based_irrigation` tool that combines both operations optimally.

2. *Tool modification*
   Poor performance metrics on a customer search tool lead the system to automatically add indexing hints and query optimizations, improving response time by 80%.

3. *Tool generation*
   Analyzing failed queries, the system identifies a gap in capabilities and generates entirely new tools to fill it. A logistics company's system spontaneously created tools for multimodal shipping optimization after observing repeated manual calculations.

# Orchestration at Scale

Discovery, retrieval, and graph-based relationships solve the problem of finding the right tools. Orchestration solves the problem of coordinating them. As tool counts grow from dozens to hundreds and agent counts grow from one to many, you need infrastructure that routes requests, manages failover, and enforces governance across the entire system. This section covers four patterns at increasing organizational scale: intelligent orchestrators, hierarchical routing, functional clustering for resilience, and the enterprise control plane that ties them together.

## The Intelligent Orchestrator: Modernizing Classical SaaS

Instead of exposing thousands of tools to your AI agents, expose exactly one: an intelligent orchestrator that handles all complexity. This has immediate implications for how traditional SaaS companies compete in the AI era.

Consider the challenge facing established SaaS companies. They have irreplaceable advantages:

- Years of accumulated data
- Battle-tested business logic
- Enterprise trust and compliance
- Deep domain expertise

But they face a new threat: AI-native startups that deliver instant gratification. While a traditional CRM might require navigating through menus, filters, and reports to answer the question "Why did we lose deals last quarter?" an AI startup provides the answer in seconds.

The intelligent orchestrator bridges this gap, turning traditional SaaS into an AI-powered platform without abandoning its strengths, as Example 6-10 demonstrates.

*Example 6-10. SaaS modernization orchestrator*

```
class SaaSModernizationOrchestrator:
    """Transform traditional SaaS complexity into instant AI-powered insights."""

    async def process_natural_query(self, query: str) -> dict:
        # User asks: "Why did revenue drop last month?"
        intent = await self.understand_intent(query)

        # Leverage deep historical data
        historical_patterns = await self.analyze_patterns(
            time_range="5_years",
            granularity="monthly",
        )

        # Apply domain-specific business logic
        root_causes = await self.apply_business_rules(
            data=historical_patterns,
            rules=self.compliance_verified_rules,
        )

        # Instant, trusted answer
        return {
            "answer": "Revenue dropped 15% due to seasonal patterns "
                      "combined with 3 major accounts delaying renewals",
            "confidence": 0.94,
```

```
            "supporting_data": root_causes,
            "suggested_actions": await self.generate_remediation_plan(),
        }
```

This orchestrator class demonstrates the transformation from traditional SaaS to AI-powered interaction. The `understand_intent` method uses NLP to parse the natural language query into a structured intent. The `analyze_patterns` method queries the years of historical data in the possession of the SaaS company. The `apply_business_rules` method applies domain logic that's been validated for compliance, ensuring that AI outputs meet regulatory requirements. The result is an instant, trustworthy answer that would have taken a human at least 30 minutes to assemble manually.

This orchestrator becomes the single entry point for natural language requests. Behind the scenes, it does the following:

- Understands intent using semantic analysis
- Queries the knowledge graph for solutions
- Leverages decades of accumulated data
- Applies complex business rules automatically
- Enforces security policies
- Learns from results

Traditional SaaS features map directly to AI capabilities, as shown in Table 6-3.

*Table 6-3. SaaS features and AI-orchestrated capabilities*

| Traditional feature | AI-orchestrated capability |
|---|---|
| Report builder | "Show me what changed since last week." |
| Workflow designer | "Set up approval for purchases over $10k." |
| Data export | "Prepare a board presentation on Q4 performance." |
| Filter interface | "Focus on enterprise accounts in Europe." |

Users simply describe what they want. The orchestrator figures out how to achieve it using all the power of the underlying SaaS platform.

## Hierarchical Orchestration: When Scale Demands Structure

As organizations grow, they don't just have more tools—they have multiple MCP servers across departments, each managing hundreds of tools. Now agents face recursive complexity: Which server to query? Which tools within that server?

The MCP Gateway (*https://oreil.ly/Qk66_*) demonstrates how hierarchical orchestration addresses this challenge. Instead of flat tool lists, it creates a structured hierarchy:

```
Enterprise Orchestrator
├── Sales Domain
│   ├── CRM Tools
│   ├── Lead Generation
│   └── Analytics
├── Finance Domain
│   ├── Accounting Tools
│   ├── Reporting
│   └── Compliance
└── Operations Domain
    ├── Inventory Management
    ├── Logistics
    └── Quality Control
```

Each level uses the same graph-based intelligence but with domain-specific knowledge. Example 6-11 shows how the system routes requests intelligently.

*Example 6-11. Hierarchical domain routing*

```
async def route_request(self, query: str) -> Response:
    # Determine domain from query semantics
    domain = await self.identify_domain(query)

    if domain.confidence < 0.8:
        # Query spans multiple domains
        return await self.orchestrate_cross_domain(query)

    # Route to specific domain orchestrator
    return await domain.orchestrator.process(query)
```

This routing function first classifies the query into a domain using semantic analysis. If the confidence is high (above 0.8), it routes directly to that domain's orchestrator. If confidence is low—perhaps the query involves both sales and finance data—it invokes `orchestrate_cross_domain`, which coordinates multiple domain orchestrators to assemble a complete answer. This prevents users from needing to know which department "owns" the data they need.

The system discovers cross-domain patterns that siloed teams miss:

- When the sales team closes a large deal, finance should prepare invoicing workflows.
- Customer service issues often correlate with recent product updates.
- Inventory levels affect both sales promises and financial projections.

The hierarchical approach also enables the following:

*Federated learning*
: Each domain maintains autonomy while contributing to collective intelligence. For example, the sales team's innovations in customer analytics can inspire similar improvements in support tools.

*Scalable governance*
: Policies can be set at appropriate levels. Global policies (like data privacy) apply everywhere, while domain policies (like sales approval limits) stay local.

*Fault isolation*
: Problems in one domain don't cascade across the entire system. If the logistics tools fail, sales can still operate.

*Progressive disclosure*
: Users see only the capabilities relevant to their context, reducing overwhelm while maintaining access to needed cross-functional tools.

## Functional Clustering: Resilience Through Redundancy

The Baidu Search team's proposal fo an AI search paradigm (*https://oreil.ly/tqv6E*) extends hierarchical organization with a practical insight: tools with similar functions should be automatically clustered for intelligent failover. The goal is to not merely look for tools by category but to discover functional equivalence through usage patterns.

The Baidu Search team's tool-clustering approach operates on a simple principle: embed tools based on what they do, not what they claim. Using enhanced representations from DRAFT-refined documentation combined with historical usage patterns, the system creates semantic embeddings that capture true functionality. K-means++ clustering then groups these tools into functional toolkits.

The payoff shows up in production. When the primary search tool experiences high load, the system doesn't fail—it seamlessly switches to a functionally equivalent alternative from the same cluster. A "search toolkit" might contain:

- Baidu AI Search (optimized for Chinese content)
- ArXiv MCP Server (academic specialization)
- Perplexity MCP Server (conversational style)
- OpenAI WebSearch MCP (general purpose)

Each tool has different strengths, but all can fulfill basic search needs. The orchestrator adapts parameters as needed when failing over, ensuring continuity of service.

Over time, the system learns which tools excel in which contexts, creating preference patterns within clusters. This clustering approach naturally complements hierarchical orchestration. At the domain level, you have logical groupings (sales, finance, operations). Within each domain, functional clusters provide resilience. A finance domain might have multiple calculation tools, multiple report generation tools, and multiple data retrieval tools, ensuring no single point of failure in any cluster.

## The Enterprise AI OS Layer: Infrastructure for the Synthetic Workforce

MCP's success in standardizing tool access points to a deeper need for a comprehensive operating system for AI agents in the enterprise. The challenge is clear. In consumer scenarios, direct OAuth connections between AI agents and services work fine. But in enterprise contexts, organizations need to govern:

- Which data flows to which providers
- Which actions require human approval
- How AI agents interact with sensitive systems
- What audit trails are maintained

An AI OS layer can serve as the control plane for enterprise AI deployment, as Example 6-12 shows.

*Example 6-12. Enterprise AI OS control plane*

```
class EnterpriseAIOS:
    """Operating system layer for AI agents in the enterprise."""

    def __init__(self):
        self.permission_manager = PermissionManager()
        self.context_integrator = ContextIntegrator()
        self.semantic_search = SemanticSearch()
        self.action_governor = ActionGovernor()
        self.audit_logger = AuditLogger()
        self.ifc_controller = InformationFlowController()

    async def handle_agent_request(
        self,
        agent_id: str,
        request: Request,
    ) -> Response:
        # Check permissions (Layer 1: Authentication)
        if not await self.permission_manager.authorized(agent_id, request):
            return Forbidden("Agent lacks required permissions")

        # Apply information flow control (Layer 2: Data Flow Security)
        tainted_request = await self.ifc_controller.apply_taint_tracking(request)
```

```
        # Enrich with organizational context
        enriched = await self.context_integrator.enhance(tainted_request)

        # Find appropriate tools
        tools = await self.semantic_search.find_tools(enriched)

        # Govern actions
        if await self.action_governor.requires_approval(request):
            return await self.request_human_approval(request)

        # Execute with full audit trail
        result = await self.execute_with_audit(tools, request)

        return result
```

This class brings together all the security and orchestration concepts discussed in this chapter. The `permission_manager` implements OAuth-based authentication (Layer 1). The `ifc_controller` applies IFC (Layer 2), tracking data taint through the request lifecycle. The `action_governor` implements HITL controls for high-risk operations. The `audit_logger` maintains compliance trails. Together, these components form a layered security architecture that enables AI capabilities while maintaining enterprise control.

This AI OS, visualized in Figure 6-3, provides the following:

*Centralized permission management*
: One place to control what agents can access, replacing scattered permissions across dozens of systems

*Context integration*
: Broad organizational knowledge beyond individual tools, enabling agents to understand the full picture

*Semantic search capabilities*
: The semantic navigation of enterprise information that agents, unlike humans, need

*Action governance*
: The drawing of a distinction between human-only actions (like large financial transfers), human-supervised actions (requiring approval), and machine-only actions (routine operations), as well as human validation of the agent's output

Without this layered approach, organizations face an unmanageable permission model as they adopt multiple AI agents across departments. With it, they gain the control needed to safely deploy AI at scale.

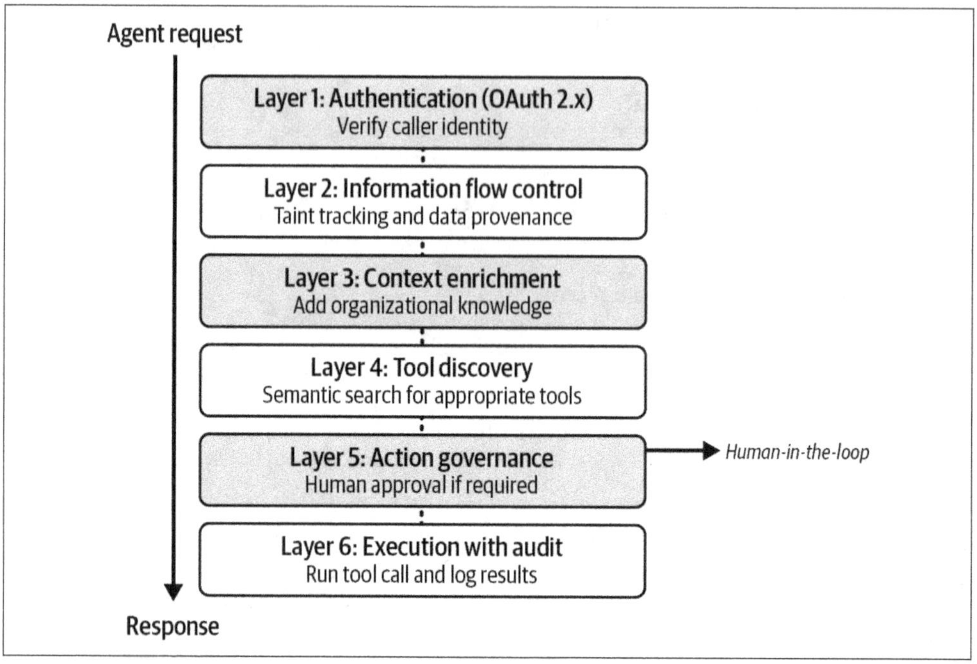


*Figure 6-3. Enterprise AI OS layered security*

# Learning and Advanced Patterns

An orchestration system that only follows rules is brittle. The systems that improve over time learn from their own execution history: which tool sequences succeeded, which failed, and why. This section covers memory-augmented orchestration, the nested execution challenge that trips up even advanced models, performance benchmarks at scale, and the context governance problem that emerges when multiple developers configure agents independently.

## The Memory Layer: Learning from Every Interaction

The final piece connecting orchestration to intelligence is memory—specifically, storing what happened *and* understanding why it worked.

Toolshed's research into its proposed Advanced RAG-Tool Fusion (*https://oreil.ly/ivVkv*) shows how layered memory systems improve tool selection over time. This approach, shown in Example 6-13, goes beyond simple usage counting to understand context and effectiveness.

*Example 6-13. Memory-enabled orchestrator with four memory types*

```
class MemoryEnabledOrchestrator:
    def __init__(self):
        self.short_term = ShortTermMemory()  # Current conversation
        self.long_term = LongTermMemory()    # Historical patterns
        self.episodic = EpisodicMemory()     # Specific scenarios
        self.semantic = SemanticMemory()     # Conceptual knowledge

    async def remember_execution(
        self,
        context: ExecutionContext,
        tools_used: List[Tool],
        outcome: Outcome,
    ) -> None:
        # Record in multiple memory systems
        await self.short_term.add(context, tools_used, outcome)

        # Extract patterns for long-term storage
        patterns = await self.extract_patterns(context, tools_used, outcome)
        await self.long_term.store_patterns(patterns)

        # Store complete episode if significant
        if outcome.significance > 0.8:
            await self.episodic.store_episode(context, tools_used, outcome)

        # Update semantic understanding
        concepts = await self.extract_concepts(context, outcome)
        await self.semantic.update_concepts(concepts)
```

This memory system implements four distinct memory types, mirroring cognitive science models:

*Short-term memory*
: Tracks the current conversation for continuity.

*Long-term memory*
: Stores patterns extracted from many interactions—like *Monday morning queries often need weekend reconciliation.*

*Episodic memory*
: Stores complete, significant scenarios that might be referenced later, like *how we handled the Q3 outage.*

*Semantic memory*
: Stores conceptual knowledge about relationships between tools and domains.

Together, these enable the orchestrator to improve its decisions based on accumulated experience.

This approach creates multiple learning loops:

*Immediate learning*
: Within a conversation, the system remembers what worked and avoids repeating failures. If a tool times out, it won't be tried again with similar parameters.

*Pattern recognition*
: Across conversations, successful patterns emerge. For example, the system discovers that financial reports requested on Mondays often need weekend data reconciliation.

*System evolution*
: Over time, structural improvements reshape capabilities. Tools that consistently underperform are deprecated, and new tools emerge from recognized gaps.

The memory system also enables predictive capabilities, as shown in Example 6-14.

*Example 6-14. Predictive tool pre-warming*

```
async def predict_next_need(
    self, current_context: Context
) -> Dict[str, float]:
    """Based on patterns, predict what the user might need next."""
    # Find similar historical contexts
    similar_contexts = await self.find_similar_contexts(
        current_context,
        similarity_threshold=0.85,
    )

    # Extract what typically follows
    next_actions: Dict[str, float] = defaultdict(float)
    for context in similar_contexts:
        for follow_up in context.subsequent_actions:
            next_actions[follow_up.action] += follow_up.probability

    # Pre-warm likely tools
    for action, probability in next_actions.items():
        if probability > 0.7:
            await self.orchestrator.prepare_tools(action)

    return next_actions
```

This predictive function finds historical contexts similar to the current one and analyzes what users typically did next. If there's a 70%+ probability of a particular follow-up action, the function prewarms the relevant tools—loading them into memory, establishing connections, or precomputing common values. This reduces latency for the predicted actions, making the system feel more responsive and intelligent.

## Advanced Patterns: The Nested Execution Challenge

The NESTFUL benchmark exposes a critical limitation: even advanced LLMs struggle with nested tool execution, where outputs from one tool become inputs to another. The research shows that even the best models achieve only 41.46% success rate on these challenges. The pseudocode in Example 6-15 illustrates why this is so difficult.

*Example 6-15. Nested tool execution challenge*

```
# What the user asks:
"Show me COVID statistics for India"

# What actually needs to happen:
# 1. Extract "India" as the country name
# 2. Call get_country_details("India") -> returns {"short_name": "IN", ...}
# 3. Extract "IN" from the response
# 4. Call get_covid_stats(location="IN")
# 5. Format and present results

# Where LLMs fail:
# - Do not recognize that "location" needs country code, not country name
# - Do not track variables between calls
# - Do not handle type matching (string country name vs ISO code)
# - Do not handle errors if any step fails
```

The graph-based approach with structured output makes this tractable, as Example 6-16 demonstrates.

*Example 6-16. Graph-based execution path for nested API calls*

```
// Explicit modeling of the execution path
MATCH path = (start:UserIntent)
           -[:REQUIRES]->(country:Tool {name: "get_country_details"})
           -[:OUTPUTS {field: "short_name", type: "ISO_3166_1_alpha_2"}]->()
           -[:FEEDS_INTO]->(covid:Tool {name: "get_covid_stats"})
           -[:SATISFIES]->(end:UserIntent)
WHERE start.type = "covid_statistics_by_country"
RETURN path
```

This transforms planning from probabilistic guessing to deterministic pathfinding. The `UserIntent` nodes represent what users want to accomplish. The `REQUIRES`, `OUTPUTS`, and `FEEDS_INTO` relationships explicitly model the data flow between tools. When a new query arrives, the system matches it to a `UserIntent` and traverses the graph to find the complete execution path—including all intermediate tools and their parameter mappings. The system knows exactly what tools to call in what order.

## Performance at Scale: Making It Real

The patterns in this chapter are drawn from research and production systems. Before moving to the DevOps agent, it is worth grounding the claims here in specific numbers. The research provides concrete evidence that these approaches work at scale:

*RAG-MCP performance (https://oreil.ly/x3zz3)*
- Handles up to 11,100 tools in testing
- Maintains 43% accuracy even at massive scale
- Reduces token usage by over 50%

*Toolshed results (https://oreil.ly/1yyWS)*
- 95%+ retrieval accuracy with enhanced representations
- 46%–56% improvement over baseline approaches
- No model fine-tuning required
- Scales to 3,500+ tools in production

*Key insights*
- Success comes not from more powerful models but from better organization.
- Structured representations outperform free text.
- Graph relationships enable complex orchestration.
- Memory and learning compound improvements over time.

The transition from theory to practice is exemplified by production systems like Baidu's AI Search Paradigm (*https://oreil.ly/epFkj*). Its DRAFT system proves that tool documentation can be self-improving, continuously refined through actual usage rather than provider promises. The clustering approach demonstrates that resilience comes not from perfect tools but from intelligent redundancy. Its COLT (*https://oreil.ly/KMV0i*) implementation shows that understanding tool relationships transforms impossible tasks into routine operations.

These production systems validate the concepts in this chapter—treating tools as graph nodes, hierarchical orchestration, collaborative discovery—at real scale, handling millions of queries.

## Context Governance: The Missing Layer in Tool Orchestration

The previous sections covered how individual agents discover, select, and invoke tools. But a critical gap emerges when tool orchestration scales from one developer to a team: context fragmentation.

### The problem: Configuration drift at scale

When a single developer configures an AI coding agent—writing a *CLAUDE.md* file, installing skills, defining hooks—the result is a coherent, personalized context architecture. But when five developers on the same team do the same thing independently, the result is five divergent architectures. Each developer's agent receives different instructions, applies different patterns, and produces code shaped by different assumptions.

Marc Baselga (*https://oreil.ly/QVeqH*), founder of Supra, documented this phenomenon in 2026 after deploying Claude Code across his engineering team. The initial productivity gains were immediate and measurable. Then came what Ben Erez named in a podcast the *unexpected tax*: each developer had built their own context system. No shared source of truth existed. The team's AI-powered workflows diverged silently until the inconsistencies surfaced as conflicting code patterns, redundant automations, and onboarding friction that multiplied with each new hire.

The fragmentation follows a predictable progression:

*Individual optimization*
: Each developer customizes their agent for their specific workflow. A backend engineer adds database query patterns; a frontend engineer adds component generation rules.

*Silent divergence*
: Without a shared standard, customizations accumulate independently. Two developers writing the same feature receive different guidance from their agents.

*Visible inconsistency*
: Code reviews reveal conflicting patterns. New team members struggle because no single *CLAUDE.md* represents the team's actual practices.

*Coordination overhead*
: The team spends increasing time reconciling agent-produced artifacts, negating the productivity gains that motivated adoption.

This progression mirrors a well-documented pattern in enterprise software: the gap between individual tool adoption and organizational knowledge management. The new dimension is velocity: AI agents amplify whatever context they receive, so divergent configurations produce divergent code at the speed of token generation rather than the speed of human typing.

### Three solution architectures

The emerging approaches to context governance map to organizational scale:

*Configuration as code (team scale)*
: Daniel Meppiel's Agent Package Manager (APM) (*https://oreil.ly/58IRv*) treats AI configuration the way npm treats code dependencies. A declarative manifest declares skills, rules, and prompts as versioned, composable packages. Every developer runs `apm install` and receives the same base configuration. Team-specific extensions compose on top of the shared base.

*Shared knowledge layer (department scale)*
: Arlan Rakhmetzhanov's Nia Skills framework (*https://oreil.ly/F53PV*) provides a shared indexed knowledge base that multiple agents access through a standardized interface. Instead of each developer curating their own context, the organization maintains a central knowledge index—repositories, documentation, research—that any agent can query.

*Governance control plane (enterprise scale)*
: Daniel Jarjoura's Runtime framework (*https://oreil.ly/RLONi*) provides a persistent governance layer that sits above agent orchestration. It encodes business rules, architectural constraints, ownership boundaries, and historical decisions as infrastructure rather than configuration files. Jarjoura's diagnosis frames the root cause precisely: "Context failure, not AI failure." Agents amplify whatever structure they receive. If the structure is incomplete or inconsistent, agents amplify ambiguity.

### Federated context architecture

The three approaches are not competing alternatives but layers of the same architecture, as shown in Table 6-4.

*Table 6-4. Three approaches to context governance as layers of the same architecture*

| Layer | Mechanism | What it solves |
|---|---|---|
| Configuration as code | Versioned manifests, shared base config | Syntactic consistency—everyone runs the same rules |
| Shared knowledge layer | Indexed knowledge base with standard interface | Factual consistency—everyone accesses the same information |
| Governance control plane | Persistent infrastructure encoding organizational decisions | Behavioral consistency—everyone operates within the same constraints |

The architecture is federated, not centralized. Teams own their domain-specific context but inherit from an organizational base that encodes nonnegotiable standards: security policies, architectural constraints, code review requirements, and compliance rules.

### Implications for tool orchestration

Context fragmentation reframes tool orchestration from an individual capability to an organizational system. The tool orchestration stack described in previous sections—discovery, selection, schema validation, gateway, execution—assumes a single coherent context. When context fragments across team members, the stack produces coherent results for each individual but incoherent results at the team level. Two developers asking their agents to "follow our coding standards" receive different standards if their contexts diverge.

The practical implication is that production tool orchestration at team scale requires a context governance layer alongside the tool execution layer. Agent configuration is not a personal productivity tool. It is shared infrastructure, and it requires the same engineering discipline as any other shared infrastructure: versioning, testing, deployment, and monitoring.

# Tool Orchestration in Practice: The DevOps Agent

In Chapter 3, you built a knowledge graph of your infrastructure. In Chapter 4, you gave it memory. In Chapter 5, it learned to reason and plan—constructing investigation DAGs, forming hypotheses, and systematically testing them. Now it needs hands. Your DevOps agent can think through a latency incident, but it still cannot query a metrics API or check a connection pool. This section wires it up with tools registered as graph nodes, structured output for reliable API calls, and an orchestration layer that coordinates the investigation.

## Registering Tools in the Knowledge Graph

In Chapter 5, the agent's `evidence_collection_node` called functions like `collect_metrics` and `collect_logs`—but those were opaque boxes, hardcoded into the workflow. The metatooling pattern from earlier in this chapter, where tools become graph nodes, offers an alternative: register diagnostic tools directly in the knowledge graph alongside the infrastructure they operate on.

The `QueryMetricsAPI` tool becomes a node in the same graph that already contains your services, dependencies, and incident history. Its relationships make the tool discoverable based on context rather than hardcoded logic, as shown in Example 6-17.

*Example 6-17. DevOps `QueryMetricsAPI` tool registration*

```
// Register the metrics query tool as a node in the Knowledge Graph
CREATE (t:Tool {
    name: "QueryMetricsAPI",
    description: "Query time-series metrics for a service from the observability
        platform",
```

```
    endpoint: "https://metrics.internal/api/v1/query_range",
    auth_method: "oauth2_service_account",
    rate_limit: 100,
    timeout_ms: 5000
})

// Connect it to the service entities it can operate on
MATCH (s:Service)
WHERE s.has_metrics = true
CREATE (s)-[:HAS_TOOL {
    capability: "metrics_query",
    data_types: ["latency_p99", "error_rate", "throughput", "saturation"]
}]->(t)

// Model its dependency on service identity from the Knowledge Graph
CREATE (t)-[:REQUIRES_INPUT {
    parameter: "service_id",
    source: "knowledge_graph",
    type: "Service.canonical_id"
}]->(sid:DataType {name: "ServiceIdentifier"})
```

This Cypher creates the `QueryMetricsAPI` tool node with its operational metadata—endpoint, authentication method, rate limit, and timeout. The `HAS_TOOL` relationships connect it to every service that exposes metrics, with the `data_types` property listing what kinds of metrics are available. The `REQUIRES_INPUT` relationship captures a dependency that matters at runtime: the tool needs a `service_id` that comes from the knowledge graph itself, not from the user. When the agent investigates a latency spike in the checkout service, it can traverse the graph to discover this tool and already have the service identifier it needs.

This is the tools-as-data principle applied to infrastructure operations. Adding a new diagnostic tool—say, a log aggregation query or a trace analyzer—means adding nodes and relationships, not modifying agent code. If you onboard a new service with a different metrics provider, you register a second tool node in the appropriate functional cluster, and the orchestrator handles failover automatically.

## Structured Output for API Integration

Registering the tool in the graph handles discovery. However, the agent still needs to produce well-formed API calls and parse the responses back into its investigation state. Without structured output, a predictable failure mode appears: the LLM generates a metrics query that *looks* right in natural language but contains malformed parameters, wrong time formats, or missing required fields.

Example 6-18 demonstrates a function that uses Pydantic models to constrain the agent's output into a valid API request, execute the call, and parse the response back into the knowledge graph.

*Example 6-18. Structured metrics query with Pydantic validation*

```
from pydantic import BaseModel, Field
from datetime import datetime, timedelta
from typing import Literal
import httpx

class MetricsQuery(BaseModel):
    """Structured output schema for metrics API calls."""

    service_id: str = Field(
        description="Canonical service identifier from the knowledge graph"
    )
    metric_name: Literal[
        "latency_p99",
        "error_rate",
        "throughput",
        "saturation",
    ]
    start_time: datetime
    end_time: datetime
    step_seconds: int = Field(default=60, ge=10, le=3600)

class MetricsResult(BaseModel):
    """Parsed response from the metrics API."""

    service_id: str
    metric_name: str
    datapoints: list[tuple[datetime, float]]
    anomalies: list[dict] = Field(default_factory=list)

async def query_metrics_tool(
    query: MetricsQuery,
    tool_node: dict,
    knowledge_graph,
) -> MetricsResult:
    """Execute a structured metrics query and persist results to the graph."""

    async with httpx.AsyncClient() as client:
        response = await client.get(
            tool_node["endpoint"],
            params={
                "query": (
                    f'{query.metric_name}'
                    f'{{service="{query.service_id}"}}'
                ),
                "start": query.start_time.isoformat(),
                "end": query.end_time.isoformat(),
                "step": f"{query.step_seconds}s",
            },
            headers={
                "Authorization": (
```

```
                    f"Bearer "
                    f"{get_oauth_token(tool_node['auth_method'])}"
                )
            },
            timeout=tool_node["timeout_ms"] / 1000,
        )
        response.raise_for_status()

    raw = response.json()
    result = MetricsResult(
        service_id=query.service_id,
        metric_name=query.metric_name,
        datapoints=[
            (datetime.fromtimestamp(ts), val)
            for ts, val in raw["data"]["values"]
        ],
        anomalies=detect_anomalies(raw["data"]["values"]),
    )

    # Persist the observation back into the knowledge graph
    knowledge_graph.query(
        "MATCH (s:Service {canonical_id: $sid}) "
        "CREATE (s)-[:HAS_OBSERVATION "
        "{timestamp: datetime(), tool: 'QueryMetricsAPI'}]->"
        "(:MetricsObservation "
        "{metric: $metric, anomaly_count: $ac, "
        "peak_value: $peak})",
        parameters={
            "sid": result.service_id,
            "metric": result.metric_name,
            "ac": len(result.anomalies),
            "peak": max(v for _, v in result.datapoints),
        },
    )

    return result
```

The `MetricsQuery` model enforces that the agent produces a valid service identifier, a metric name from a fixed set, properly formatted timestamps, and a reasonable step interval. If the LLM tries to generate `"metric_name": "response time"` instead of `"latency_p99"`, Pydantic rejects it before the API call ever happens. The `MetricsResult` model structures the response so that downstream nodes can work with it reliably, with no parsing surprises.

The function also writes observations back into the knowledge graph as `MetricsObservation` nodes linked to the service. Future incidents involving the same service can query these historical observations to establish baselines or spot trends.

## The Latency Investigation, Continued

In Chapter 5, the agent investigated a checkout service latency spike and identified a likely root cause: a configuration change that reduced database connection pool size. It reached that conclusion through graph traversal and hypothesis testing—but the hypothesis testing relied on functions like `collect_metrics` that we left as abstractions. Now those abstractions have teeth.

Example 6-19 shows how the tool orchestration layer coordinates the investigation, picking up from where Chapter 5's workflow graph hands control to the evidence collection and hypothesis-testing nodes.

*Example 6-19. Orchestrated latency investigation*

```
import asyncio
from datetime import datetime, timedelta


async def orchestrated_investigation(
    state: DiagnosticState,
    knowledge_graph,
    tool_registry,
) -> DiagnosticState:
    """Orchestrate tool calls during a latency investigation."""

    alert = state["alert"]
    service_id = alert["service_id"]

    # Step 1: Discover available diagnostic tools from the knowledge graph
    available_tools = knowledge_graph.query(
        "MATCH (s:Service {canonical_id: $sid})-[:HAS_TOOL]->(t:Tool) "
        "RETURN t.name as name, t.endpoint as endpoint, "
        "t.auth_method as auth_method, t.timeout_ms as timeout_ms",
        parameters={"sid": service_id},
    )

    # Step 2: Query live metrics using structured output
    metrics_tool = next(
        t
        for t in available_tools
        if t["name"] == "QueryMetricsAPI"
    )
    latency_query = MetricsQuery(
        service_id=service_id,
        metric_name="latency_p99",
        start_time=alert["timestamp"] - timedelta(hours=2),
        end_time=alert["timestamp"] + timedelta(minutes=30),
    )
    latency_result = await query_metrics_tool(
        latency_query,
```

```
        metrics_tool,
        knowledge_graph,
    )

    # Step 3: Check upstream dependencies in parallel
    dependencies = knowledge_graph.query(
        "MATCH (s:Service {canonical_id: $sid})"
        "-[:DEPENDS_ON]->(d:Service) "
        "RETURN d.canonical_id as dep_id, d.name as dep_name",
        parameters={"sid": service_id},
    )

    dep_queries = [
        query_metrics_tool(
            MetricsQuery(
                service_id=dep["dep_id"],
                metric_name="saturation",
                start_time=latency_query.start_time,
                end_time=latency_query.end_time,
            ),
            metrics_tool,
            knowledge_graph,
        )
        for dep in dependencies
    ]
    dep_results = await asyncio.gather(*dep_queries)

    # Step 4: Correlate findings with the knowledge graph
    saturated_deps = [
        result
        for result in dep_results
        if any(value > 0.9 for _, value in result.datapoints)
    ]

    new_evidence = [
        {
            "type": "metrics",
            "source": service_id,
            "data": latency_result.model_dump(),
            "collected_at": datetime.now().isoformat(),
        }
    ] + [
        {
            "type": "metrics",
            "source": result.service_id,
            "data": result.model_dump(),
            "finding": "saturation > 90%",
            "collected_at": datetime.now().isoformat(),
        }
        for result in saturated_deps
    ]
```

```
    peak_latency = max(
        value for _, value in latency_result.datapoints
    )

    return {
        **state,
        "collected_evidence": (
            state.get("collected_evidence", []) + new_evidence
        ),
        "investigation_log": state["investigation_log"]
        + [
            (
                f"Queried latency_p99 for {service_id}: "
                f"peak {peak_latency:.0f}ms"
            ),
            (
                f"Checked {len(dependencies)} "
                "upstream dependencies"
            ),
            (
                f"Found {len(saturated_deps)} "
                "saturated dependencies"
            ),
        ],
    }
```

Walk through what happens when the alert fires. The SRE is asleep, and the agent takes the case—just as in Chapter 5's walkthrough. But now, instead of calling opaque helper functions, the agent orchestrates real tool interactions:

1. It discovers diagnostic tools by traversing the knowledge graph from the affected service. This is the contextual discovery pattern: the agent does not consult a hardcoded list of tools. It follows `HAS_TOOL` edges from the checkout service and finds `QueryMetricsAPI` (and potentially others, like a log search tool or trace analyzer, if they have been registered).
2. It constructs a structured metrics query for the checkout service's P99 latency (the 99th percentile latency), covering a window from 2 hours before the alert to 30 minutes after. The `MetricsQuery` model guarantees that the API call is well-formed. The result comes back with timestamped datapoints and any detected anomalies.
3. It queries upstream dependencies and checks their saturation metrics *in parallel*. This is the same investigation DAG pattern from Chapter 5—independent hypotheses are tested concurrently—but now the "tests" are real API calls coordinated through `asyncio.gather`. If the checkout service depends on payment processing and a database, both get queried simultaneously.

4. It correlates findings. Any dependency showing saturation above 90% gets flagged. The agent now has actual saturation metrics—not a mere hypothesis—confirming that the database is overloaded. From the knowledge graph traversal in Chapter 5, it also knows about the configuration change (the deployment that reduced connection pool size from 100 to 20). Thus, the root cause is confirmed by data.

The investigation that took the Chapter 5 agent through multiple reasoning steps now completes with live metrics backing every conclusion. The remediation plan—to roll back the configuration change, add connection pool monitoring, and implement configuration review—follows directly from what the agent observed.

The agent can now act on what it knows. But acting raises a new question: Was the action correct? In the next chapter, you will close the loop, as the agent will learn how to evaluate its own diagnoses and evolve its behavior based on what it gets right and wrong.

# Summary

For decades, engineers have built systems that execute predefined logic. These systems are powerful but rigid, capable but not adaptive. Tool orchestration changes the equation: software that can discover, compose, and invoke tools on its own moves from executing instructions to solving problems. The core idea is simple. An AI agent that can reason but cannot interact with databases, APIs, or external systems is stuck. Tools are the means by which intelligence becomes useful.

This chapter covered six ideas that make tool orchestration practical:

- Agents need tools to bridge the gap between understanding and action. Every valuable task requires interaction with external services. MCP provides the protocol foundation, and intelligent orchestration makes it practical at scale.
- Treating tools as data in a knowledge graph rather than hardcoded functions makes them discoverable, composable, and even autogenerated based on need rather than prior planning.
- Intelligent orchestration addresses the complexity problem. By hiding tool selection behind a single interface, agents can focus on *what* to achieve rather than *how* to achieve it.
- Continuous learning turns every interaction into training data. Systems get better at completing tasks, and the tools themselves improve through use.
- Security operates at multiple layers that reinforce each other. OAuth verifies the caller. Information flow control protects data as it moves between tools. Verification-based trust ensures tool reliability. And per-agent access control—

scoping each agent's tool availability through MCP gateways and `allowed_tools` configuration—prevents agents from reaching capabilities outside their designated scope. These four layers create defense in depth for AI systems handling critical operations.

- Hierarchical organization enables scale. AI systems can coordinate across domains while maintaining local expertise and global coherence.

The implications extend past the technology itself. When agents can dynamically discover and use tools, they move from chatbots to digital workers. When systems learn from tool usage patterns, operational feedback drives improvement alongside formal R&D.

Traditional SaaS companies, with years of accumulated data and domain expertise, can use intelligent orchestration to compete with AI-native startups. Wrapping their complexity in natural language interfaces lets them deliver fast answers while maintaining enterprise trust and compliance.

Consider what becomes possible when agents have fluid access to tools:

- Customer service agents that can resolve issues across multiple systems
- Financial analysts that can execute complex strategies, not just recommend them
- Healthcare assistants that can coordinate care across departments and providers
- Security systems that respond to threats with coordinated countermeasures
- Business systems that optimize themselves based on changing conditions

The technology exists today. Knowledge graphs provide the foundation for understanding tool relationships. Protocols like MCP enable universal tool integration. Modern AI models supply the intelligence to orchestrate complex workflows. Information flow control ensures security while maintaining capability. RAG-based approaches solve the prompt bloat problem. Ontology-driven systems enable dynamic tool definition. Production deployments prove these patterns work at scale.

The remaining challenge is to combine them. The rest of this book shows how: Chapter 7 adds self-evaluation, and Chapter 8 covers optimization and ties all of the architecture together.

# PART IV

# Production: Creating a Self-Healing System

Part IV closes the gap between a working prototype and a system you can actually deploy. An agent that reasons well in a notebook is not the same as an agent that runs 24/7 at acceptable cost, under governance constraints, and improves over time. Part IV makes the architecture production-ready: it learns from its own mistakes, runs within real cost and latency budgets, and respects the access boundaries enterprises require.

By the end of Part IV, the autonomous DevOps agent will be complete. It will monitor complex infrastructure in real time, diagnose issues, predict future failures, and learn from every interaction at a cost and latency profile that holds up under production load. It will have fulfilled the mission set out in Chapter 2.

- Chapter 7 covers the execution graph, the multi-layered evaluation framework, semantic backpropagation for targeted node-level feedback, and the graduated validation protocol, giving the agent a learning loop that improves performance without human intervention.
- Chapter 8 covers selective intelligence (matching model capability to node requirements), subgraph-level access control and PII handling, schema evolution and lifecycle management, and GPU-accelerated graph operations, making the complete system efficient, governed, and fast enough for production.

CHAPTER 7

# Self-Evolution and Evaluation

You have carefully built what looks like the right agentic architecture. Its reasoning flows through a horizontal workflow graph. Its knowledge lives in a vertical knowledge graph rich with relationships and temporal awareness. It accesses the real world through MCP-connected tools. And yet it fails, and it fails in surprising, nonintuitive ways. Its performance degrades silently over time. It requires a team of human experts in a state of constant, reactive vigilance.

At the root of this fragility is the fact that you have built a machine that can *think* but not one that can *learn*. It can execute its craft well but can never reflect on its mistakes, identify patterns in its successes, or evolve its strategies as conditions change.

The solution is not to abandon the complexity of your graph-based systems but to leverage this complexity. The graph is the prerequisite for effective evaluation and self-evolution:

*It makes the invisible visible.*
: The graph transforms the agent's reasoning into a persistent, queryable artifact: the *execution graph*. Without this record, any attempt at diagnosis is guesswork.

*It provides a coordinate system for failure.*
: When something goes wrong, the error isn't lost in a sea of model parameters. It can be localized to a specific node, a faulty edge, or a broken pathway, providing a precise target for improvement.

*It enables coherent, safe evolution.*
: The graph's explicit dependency mapping is the only way to manage the "action at a distance" problem, where improving one component silently breaks another. This is the foundation on which *semantic backpropagation* is built.

The same architecture that enables complex reasoning also makes self-improvement possible.

This chapter covers the full arc of self-evolution: how to build a diagnostic engine that performs a cognitive autopsy on every execution, how to turn that diagnosis into targeted learning, and how to do all of this safely in production. We'll start with the *execution graph*, the raw material for self-awareness, then build up through the multi-layered evaluation framework, the intervention strategy for choosing how to respond to a diagnosis, and semantic backpropagation for propagating feedback through the graph without breaking what already works. We'll assemble those components into a complete evolutionary loop, governed by a graduated validation protocol (GVP), and then apply all of it to the DevOps agent to understand what happens when a proactive prediction turns out to be only partially correct and how the system uses that failure to improve its next prediction.

# The Foundation of Self-Awareness

*You cannot fix what you cannot see.* Before an agent can evolve, it needs two things: a precise record of what it actually did and a diagnostic engine that can examine that record and tell why it failed.

The record is the *execution graph*, an immutable trace of every decision, retrieval, and tool call the agent made for a given query. The diagnostic engine is the multi-layered evaluation framework, a pipeline that examines each execution and classifies failures by type and location. Together, these components turn opaque model behavior into a structured, queryable artifact that the rest of this chapter's improvement machinery can act on.

## The Execution Graph: The Agent's Autobiography

The execution graph is the dynamic counterpart to the static workflow graph you built in Chapter 5. Your workflow graph is the blueprint, the plan for what the agent should do. The execution graph is the autobiography, an immutable record of what it actually did for a specific query.

Every time the agent processes a task, it generates a unique execution graph. Each node represents a single atomic operation and carries the metadata needed to reconstruct exactly what happened:

*Node ID*
: Unique identifier for the operation instance

*Node type*
: `LLM_Call`, `Tool_Invocation`, `Retrieval`, or `Decision_Point`

*Timestamp*
: High-resolution timing for latency analysis

*Input payload*
: The exact data the node received

*Output payload*
: The exact data the node produced

*Performance metrics*
: Latency, token counts, and cost

*Parent-child edges*
: Directed connections that establish the complete causal lineage, memorializing which node's output became which node's input

This is not a logging system. It is a queryable record of the agent's full execution, structured so you can ask questions like *Show me every tool invocation that followed an LLM call with a confidence below 0.7 and then resulted in a latency above 3 seconds.* That kind of query is only possible when execution data lives in a graph database rather than a flat log file.

In practice, execution graphs are built by combining distributed tracing with a graph store. OpenTelemetry instruments the agent's code and captures calls between components as spans; those spans are then assembled in Neo4j or a similar graph database into the full execution graph structure. Example 7-1 shows what this looks like in code.

*Example 7-1. Execution graph node logging with OpenTelemetry and Neo4j*

```
import opentelemetry.trace as otel_trace
from neo4j import GraphDatabase

tracer = otel_trace.get_tracer(__name__)
driver = GraphDatabase.driver("bolt://localhost:7687")

class AgentComponent:
    def execute(self, input_data, parent_span_id=None):
        with tracer.start_as_current_span(self.name) as span:
            span_id = span.get_span_context().span_id

            # Record node creation with parent relationship
            with driver.session() as session:
                session.run(
                    """
                    CREATE (n:ExecutionNode {
                        id: $span_id,
                        type: $node_type,
                        input: $input_data,
```

```
                timestamp: datetime()
            })
            WITH n
            MATCH (p:ExecutionNode {id: $parent_id})
            CREATE (p)-[:TRIGGERED]->(n)
            """,
            span_id=span_id,
            node_type=self.node_type,
            input_data=str(input_data),
            parent_id=parent_span_id,
        )

    output_data, metrics = self._internal_execute(input_data)

    # Update node with output and performance data
    with driver.session() as session:
        session.run(
            """
            MATCH (n:ExecutionNode {id: $span_id})
            SET n.output = $output,
                n.latency_ms = $latency,
                n.token_count = $tokens,
                n.cost_usd = $cost
            """,
            span_id=span_id,
            output=str(output_data),
            latency=metrics["latency_ms"],
            tokens=metrics["token_count"],
            cost=metrics["cost_usd"],
        )

    return output_data, span_id
```

The key design choice here is the two-phase write. The first `session.run` creates the node and links it to its parent *before* execution begins, so the graph captures the causal structure even if the operation fails. The second `session.run` fills in the output and performance metrics after execution completes. The `parent_span_id` parameter threads each node into the execution graph through a `:TRIGGERED` edge, which is what makes it possible to trace the full causal chain later.

The execution graph is the foundation. It is the raw data from which every diagnostic technique in this chapter draws.

## The Multi-Layered Evaluation Framework: A Cognitive Autopsy

The execution graph tells you *what* happened. The *multi-layered evaluation framework* is the diagnostic engine that tells you *why*. It operates as a sequential filter, moving from the most general to the most specific cause of failure. The framework has four layers, each asking a progressively narrower question. Figure 7-1 shows the full pipeline.

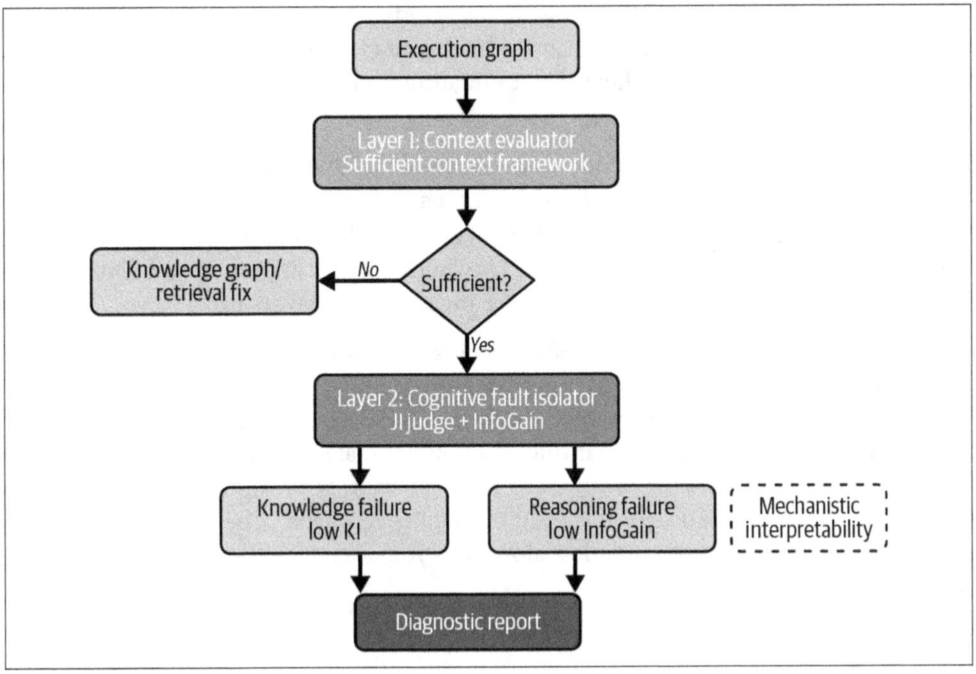


*Figure 7-1. The multi-layered evaluation framework*

Layer 0 gates on grounding, Layer 1 on context sufficiency, Layer 2 isolates the cognitive fault, and Layer 3 verifies quantitative claims through code execution.

A practical warning before diving in: you cannot fully specify what these layers should evaluate before examining real failures. Shreya Shankar et al.'s 2024 article "Who Validates the Validators?" (*https://oreil.ly/uhUx-*) documents a phenomenon called *criteria drift*: evaluators need criteria to grade outputs, but grading outputs is what reveals what the criteria should be.

In practice, this means your first version of the evaluation framework will be wrong in ways you can discover only by running it against production traces. The right approach borrows from qualitative research: start by manually reviewing 50–100 execution traces, writing open-ended notes about what went wrong (*open coding*). Then synthesize those notes into the failure categories your framework should detect (*axial coding*). The layers described in the following subsections emerged from exactly this kind of iterative refinement, and they are a starting framework, not a final specification.

### Layer 0: The zero-shot hallucination gate

Your evaluation framework has four layers, and Layers 1 through 3 each require an LLM call. For a DevOps agent processing 200 predictions per hour, that is 600 judge calls per hour before you count the actual inference (a judge call is a call to one LLM to evaluate the outputs of another). The evaluation budget starts to rival the inference budget.

But the most common failure mode does not need that machinery. When your agent reports "the checkout-service depends on `stripe-python` via the `batch_charge` API" and the knowledge graph contains no `batch_charge` edge, that is not a subtle reasoning error requiring InfoGain analysis. It is a factual hallucination, and a lightweight classifier can catch it in milliseconds, before the expensive layers fire.

The Generalist and Lightweight Model for Text Classification (GLiClass; Knowledgator, 2025, *https://oreil.ly/3YsgR*) introduces zero-shot natural language inference (NLI)–style classification for hallucination detection. The model takes three inputs (the retrieved context, the original question, and the agent's generated answer) and produces a confidence score for whether the answer is grounded in the context. No fine-tuning or domain-specific training data is required. The classification runs on a model small enough to deploy alongside your agent without a separate GPU allocation.

This approach catches three hallucination sources that map directly onto your graph architecture:

*Insufficient domain knowledge*
: Produces hallucinations when the agent's parametric memory fills gaps that the knowledge graph should have covered. The agent invents a service dependency because the graph is incomplete.

*Inadequate context*
: Produces hallucinations when the retrieval pipeline returns too few subgraph hops. The agent answers with partial information and confabulates the rest.

*Excessive context*
: Produces hallucinations through attention dilution. When you retrieve a 50-node subgraph for a question that needed 5 nodes, the model loses track of which edges are relevant.

Each source has a different fix (graph expansion, retrieval tuning, context pruning), but all three are detectable by the same NLI classifier because they all produce answers that contradict or extend beyond the provided context. Example 7-2 implements this solution as a prescreening gate.

*Example 7-2. Zero-shot hallucination pregate with graph-sourced context*

```
class HallucinationGate:
    def __init__(self, classifier, kg_client: GraphClient, threshold: float = 0.85):
        self.classifier = classifier
        self.kg = kg_client
        self.threshold = threshold

    def check(self, query: str, answer: str, context_nodes: list[str]) -> GateResult:
        """Prescreen agent output before full evaluation pipeline."""
        context = self.kg.materialize_context(context_nodes)
        score = self.classifier.predict_nli(
            premise=context,
            hypothesis=answer,
        )
        if score < self.threshold:
            return GateResult(
                passed=False,
                confidence=score,
                action="BLOCK_AND_REGENERATE",
                skip_full_eval=True,
            )
        return GateResult(passed=True, confidence=score, skip_full_eval=False)
```

The classifier is any NLI model that accepts premise-hypothesis pairs: GLiClass, a fine-tuned DeBERTa, or a distilled BART variant. The `kg_client.materialize_context` method converts the list of graph node IDs used during retrieval into a natural language premise. It traverses the subgraph, serializes the relevant triples, and produces a text block representing what the agent *should* have based its answer on. The threshold at 0.85 means any answer with less than 85% grounding confidence gets blocked before the expensive evaluation layers run. In practice, this catches 60%–70% of hallucinations at less than 5% of the compute cost of a full LLM judge call.

The gate's power comes from the graph. A flat document store produces a premise that is a concatenation of text chunks, and the classifier has to determine whether the answer is grounded in a wall of loosely related paragraphs. A knowledge graph, on the other hand, produces a premise that is a set of explicit relationships, such as `checkout-service DEPENDS_ON stripe-python`, `stripe-python HAS_VERSION 3.3.0`, or `version 3.3.0 DEPRECATED batch_charge`. When the agent claims `checkout-service uses batch_charge`, the NLI classifier compares this to an explicit graph edge and returns a near-zero grounding score. The structured premise makes the classification trivially accurate for entity-level hallucinations.

The SLM-LLM flywheel (Asjad and Microsoft Research, 2024, *https://oreil.ly/ZNmJe*) extends this into a self-improving cycle using a combination of a small language model (SLM) and an LLM. The small classifier handles the fast path: high-confidence grounded answers pass through, obvious hallucinations get blocked. Cases where the classifier is uncertain (scores between 0.5 and 0.85) escalate to the full evaluation framework, your Layer 1 through Layer 3 pipeline. The key insight is that the escalated cases become training data for the small model. Over time, the classifier learns to handle increasingly subtle hallucination patterns without escalation, reducing the load on the expensive judge pipeline. The graph makes the flywheel trainable because each escalation case comes with a structured ground truth (the knowledge graph subgraph) rather than an ambiguous document context.

> Deploy the hallucination gate as Layer 0 in your evaluation pipeline, before the context evaluator. Set the initial threshold at 0.85 and monitor the false positive rate (grounded answers incorrectly blocked) for the first two weeks. If false positives exceed 3%, raise the threshold to 0.90. The gate should catch obvious fabrications cheaply, not duplicate the nuanced evaluation that Layers 1–3 provide.

#### Layer 1: The context evaluator

This layer asks the question whose answer determines everything that follows: *Did the agent even possess the information it needed to succeed?* A failure here is not a reasoning failure. It is a failure of knowledge representation or retrieval, a problem to fix in the knowledge graph or the retrieval pipeline, not in the agent's reasoning.

The sufficient context framework (Joren et al., 2025, *https://oreil.ly/iSl-M*) provides a rigorous method for answering this question. It goes beyond simple relevance scoring and examines three dimensions:

*Completeness*
: Does the retrieved context contain every factual claim required to construct a correct answer?

*Contradiction*
: Does the context contain internal contradictions that make a coherent answer impossible?

*Ambiguity*
: Is the context so open to interpretation that multiple conflicting answers are equally supportable?

For this evaluation to be reliable, you need more than a binary classifier. The framework uses a specialized judge model trained with the methodology of Meta's J1 approach (Whitehouse et al., 2025, *https://oreil.ly/3x6Gz*), where the model is rewarded not just for producing the right label but for generating a *reasoning trace* that justifies its verdict. This teaches the judge to catch subtle insufficiencies that a simple classifier would miss.

A judge model also needs its own validation loop. In their article "Who Validates the Validators?" (*https://oreil.ly/2AFAH*) Shankar et al. (2024) show that automated judges drift from human preferences unless regularly checked. Therefore, it is important to have a domain expert label a sample of cases with binary pass/fail judgments, compare those labels against the judge's verdicts, and iterate on the judge prompt until agreement exceeds 90%. The judge's verdicts should be binary (sufficient or not), not scored on a numeric scale, because binary decisions force clarity about what matters and produce more consistent results across evaluators. Example 7-3 shows how that judge prompt looks in practice, using a DevOps query.

*Example 7-3. J1 context sufficiency judge prompt with reasoning trace*

```
<system>
You are a context analyst. Determine whether the CONTEXT is sufficient
to answer the QUERY. Reason step-by-step in a <think> block, then give
your verdict as structured JSON.
</system>

<user>
QUERY: "Will updating stripe-python from 3.2.1 to 3.3.0 cause failures
in the checkout-service?"

CONTEXT: "The knowledge graph shows checkout-service depends on
stripe-python. Version 3.3.0 changelog: added async payment methods,
deprecated synchronous batch_charge API. checkout-service uses the
payments module."
</user>

<assistant>
<think>
1. The query asks whether a specific version update will cause failures.
2. The context confirms the dependency exists.
3. The changelog mentions a deprecated API—but does checkout-service
   use batch_charge? The context says it uses the "payments module" but
   does not specify which methods within it.
4. Missing: which specific methods checkout-service calls from
   stripe-python and whether those methods changed in 3.3.0.
</think>
<verdict>
{
  "sufficient": false,
  "missing_information": [
    "Specific stripe-python methods called by checkout-service",
    "Whether those methods are deprecated or changed in 3.3.0"
  ],
  "conflicting_statements": [],
  "confidence": 0.94
}
</verdict>
```

If the context evaluator returns `sufficient: false`, the diagnostic process stops and raises a knowledge graph or retrieval failure. If it returns `sufficient: true`, the framework proceeds to Layer 2 to examine the agent's cognitive process.

#### Layer 2: The cognitive fault isolator

When an agent fails despite having all the necessary information, the failure is cognitive. Layer 2 dissects that failure into two mutually exclusive categories: knowledge failures and reasoning failures. A *knowledge failure* occurs when the agent's reasoning process is logically coherent but it is operating on incorrect or conflicting facts. That is, the agent "knows" something that isn't true.

The framework detects these using a combination of the J1 judge and the `DECOMPOSE` action from MICRO-ACT (Huo et al., 2025, *https://oreil.ly/1KDcm*). When the judge identifies a potential conflict between the agent's parametric knowledge and the retrieved context, `DECOMPOSE` breaks the conflicting passages into atomic, independently verifiable claims. Each claim is then evaluated separately. The sentence "The report confirms that the project is on schedule despite recent budget overruns" decomposes into three verifiable statements rather than being assessed as a single ambiguous whole.

The aggregate of this analysis produces the *Knowledge Index* (*KI*), a score reflecting the factual correctness of the knowledge the agent invoked in its reasoning, weighted by how important each piece was to the final conclusion and penalized for unresolved conflicts.

A *reasoning failure* occurs when the agent has all the right facts but fails to connect them logically. The primary diagnostic metric here is information-gain analysis (InfoGain). For each step `i` in the reasoning chain, InfoGain measures how much that step reduced uncertainty about the correct answer:

```
InfoGain(i) =
    P(Answer | reasoning_up_to_step_i)
    - P(Answer | reasoning_up_to_step_i-1)
```

A step with high InfoGain is a genuine insight; it meaningfully moves the agent toward the correct conclusion. A step with near-zero or negative InfoGain is a logical dead end: it is redundant, a non sequitur, or circular. By mapping InfoGain across the execution graph, you can pinpoint exactly where the agent's logic went astray.

#### Layer 3: The tool-integrated reasoning judge

Your context evaluator checks whether the agent retrieved enough information. Your cognitive fault isolator identifies where reasoning broke down. But neither layer can verify quantitative claims. When your DevOps agent reports "P99 latency increased 340% after the stripe-python upgrade," is that number correct? A language-only judge will accept any plausible-sounding number. You need a judge that can compute.

TIR-Judge (Xu et al., 2026, *https://oreil.ly/sMANC*) introduces evaluation judges that interleave natural language reasoning with Python code execution (tool-integrated reasoning, or TIR). Instead of estimating whether an answer looks right, the judge writes and runs verification code: querying the knowledge graph, computing expected values, and comparing them to the agent's claims. Example 7-4 shows the three-component reward structure.

*Example 7-4. Tool-integrated evaluation with three-component reward*

```
class TIRJudge:
    def __init__(self, executor: CodeExecutor, kg_client: GraphClient):
        self.executor = executor
        self.kg = kg_client

    def evaluate(self, claim: AgentClaim) -> TIRReward:
        """Three-component reward: correctness x format x tool-specific."""
        correctness = self.verify_with_code(claim)
        format_score = self.check_output_format(claim)
        tool_score = self.verify_tool_usage(claim)
        return TIRReward(
            correctness=correctness,
            format_compliance=format_score,
            tool_accuracy=tool_score,
            composite=correctness * format_score * tool_score,
        )

    def verify_with_code(self, claim: AgentClaim) -> float:
        """Generate and execute verification code against the KG."""
        verification_code = self.generate_verification(claim)
        result = self.executor.run(verification_code)
        return 1.0 if result.matches(claim.value) else 0.0
```

The composite score is multiplicative, not additive. A perfectly formatted response with an incorrect answer scores zero. This is deliberate: in agentic graph systems, a confidently wrong answer that looks well structured is more dangerous than an obviously malformed one. The `verify_with_code` method generates Cypher queries or Python computations specific to the claim, executes them against your knowledge graph, and returns a binary correctness signal.

The graph is what makes TIR-Judge possible in the first place. A language-only judge evaluates claims against its own parametric knowledge, which may be stale or wrong. TIR-Judge evaluates claims against your knowledge graph, the single source of truth that your agent built through Chapters 3 and 4. When the DevOps agent claims "P99 latency increased 340%," TIR-Judge generates a Cypher query that traverses the metrics subgraph, computes the actual percentage change from stored time-series nodes, and returns a binary verdict. Without the graph, the judge would have nothing to verify against except its own beliefs. Graph-based agents have an inherent advantage in self-evaluation because they carry their own ground truth in a queryable structure.

The production payoff is model efficiency. TIR-Judge-8B matches the evaluation quality of reward models four times its size. When you are running continuous evaluation in production, scoring every agent response rather than just sampled ones, this 4x reduction in judge compute cost is the difference between affordable monitoring and a second inference budget. Cypher queries against a structured graph are orders of magnitude cheaper than rederiving facts through LLM reasoning.

With all four layers in place, the evaluation pipeline operates as follows:

- Layer 0 (hallucination gate) screens for grounding failures at classifier speed.
- Layer 1 (context evaluator) checks retrieval sufficiency for answers that pass the gate.
- Layer 2 (cognitive fault isolator) classifies reasoning failures.
- Layer 3 (TIR-judge) verifies quantitative and tool use correctness by executing code against the knowledge graph.

Together, they catch failures that any single layer would miss, and all four layers depend on graph structure to function.

### Nontraditional signals: What correctness metrics miss

Binary correctness evaluation tells you whether the agent got the right answer. However, it doesn't tell you whether it got there in a way users will find useful or in a way that will generalize. The framework also analyzes these signals that correlate with real-world quality:

*User behavior signals*
: As formalized in Han et al.'s 2025 article "Reinforcement Learning from User Feedback" (*https://oreil.ly/R9DlG*), these are the query reformulation rate, copy/paste rate on generated code or answers, session success rate, and frustration signals like repeated actions or session abandonment. A high reformulation rate on otherwise "correct" answers tells you that the agent is technically right but practically unhelpful.

*Reasoning shape analysis*
: The pattern of InfoGain across a reasoning trace reveals something about the agent's cognitive style. A single massive InfoGain spike (an "Aha!" moment) may indicate brittle one-trick reasoning that won't generalize. A long chain of near-zero steps ("grinding") signals an expensive brute-force approach. The more reliable pattern is an S-curve: high initial InfoGain as the agent orients to the problem, steady progress through the middle, and a synthesis spike at the end.

### A note on mechanistic interpretability

For a small set of well-defined failure types (simple arithmetic errors, factual recall failures, basic pattern matching failures), it is sometimes possible to trace a failure all the way to the activation patterns of specific circuits within the model. Conmy et al.'s "Towards Automated Circuit Discovery" (*https://oreil.ly/iHMjM*) (2023) reports impressive results on these narrow task categories, with diagnostic accuracy above 80% for the simplest cases.

This is a developing research area, not yet a standard engineering tool. For most failures, especially metareasoning failures, complex multistep logic errors, and anything involving the agent's overall strategy choice, circuit-level diagnosis is not reliably possible. The framework is designed to recognize these and stop the diagnostic process at Layer 2 rather than produce spurious mechanistic explanations.

The practical guidance is to use Layers 0 through 2 for production diagnosis, but follow mechanistic interpretability research as it matures, since the tools are improving quickly.

The output of this framework is a structured diagnostic report: a JSON object that names the failure mode (contextual, knowledge, or reasoning), locates it in the execution graph by node ID, and specifies the evidence that led to that conclusion. Example 7-5 shows the structure.

*Example 7-5. Diagnostic report structure from the multi-layered evaluation framework*

```
{
  "execution_id": "exec_a1b2c3",
  "overall_verdict": "FAILURE",
  "layer_1_context": {
    "sufficient": true,
    "confidence": 0.97
  },
  "layer_2_cognitive": {
    "failure_type": "REASONING",
    "fault_location": {
      "node_id": "node_47",
      "node_type": "LLM_Call",
      "description": "CausalAttributionNode"
    },
    "knowledge_index": 0.89,
    "infogain_trace": [0.31, 0.28, 0.22, 0.04, -0.02, 0.18],
    "low_infogain_steps": [4, 5],
    "diagnosis": "Reasoning failure at step 4: agent inferred 'API contract
        change' from changelog data when the high-InfoGain path was 'connection
        pool default timeout change'. Steps 4-5 show near-zero gain consistent
        with a premature commitment to the API failure hypothesis."
  },
  "recommended_intervention": "PROMPT_REFINEMENT",
```

```
    "target_nodes": ["node_47"]
}
```

The fields worth highlighting:

`low_infogain_steps`
: Pinpoints exactly which reasoning steps contributed nothing, giving the improvement system a precise target.

`recommended_intervention`
: The report's prescription: whether to refine a prompt, trigger fine-tuning, or apply a structural constraint.

`target_nodes`
: Identifies which nodes in the execution graph need the fix, so interventions are scoped to the component that failed rather than applied broadly.

This report is what drives the self-improvement engine.

### Proactive truthfulness detection: The dual-pathway model

Mechanistic interpretability is advancing faster than the previous section's caution may suggest, and one recent result deserves specific attention because it converts theoretical signals into a practical detection tool. Luo et al. (2026) at Peking University and Microsoft Research Asia (*https://oreil.ly/XdRYb*) discovered that language models encode truthfulness through two distinct internal pathways. They validated the finding with causal intervention experiments across 12 LLMs and 4 QA datasets.

The first pathway is question-anchored (Q-anchored): the model routes information from the question to the answer. When it encounters a query about a well-known entity, attention patterns concentrate on mapping question tokens to answer tokens. The model is retrieving a stored association. Q-anchored processing dominates when the model is confident and its truthfulness signals are strong because the question-answer link is well established in parametric memory.

The second pathway is answer-anchored (A-anchored): the model derives evidence from the answer's own internal plausibility instead of from the question. When the model encounters a long-tail entity or a near-boundary query, it lacks a strong Q-anchored association and falls back to evaluating whether the generated answer *sounds* plausible on its own terms. This is where hallucinations originate. The model produces text that is internally coherent but ungrounded in what the question actually asked.

The causal evidence is direct. When the researchers blocked question-to-answer information flow using attention knockout, Q-anchored instances showed substantial prediction shifts while A-anchored instances remained stable. The A-anchored pathway does not need the question to generate its answer, and that is precisely the problem.

This finding is useful for the evaluation framework in this chapter because of the detection layer it enables. The researchers developed two tools:

*Mixture-of-probes (MoP)*
: Lightweight classifiers are trained on the model's internal representations to detect which pathway is active for a given query. MoP outperformed every baseline hallucination detection method in the study, achieving above 75% area under the curve (AUC) in predicting pathway utilization. The model's internal state carries a readable signal about whether it is retrieving a known association or generating a plausible guess.

*Pathway reweighting (PR)*
: The contribution of each pathway is adjusted during inference, suppressing A-anchored generation when the probes detect a shift to plausibility-based reasoning. PR achieved up to a 10% AUC gain over competing approaches.

For the self-evolution architecture described in "Targeted Self-Improvement" on page 282, the dual-pathway model offers a concrete extension to the diagnostic report in Example 7-5. A new field, `pathway_classification`, would indicate whether a given node's output was Q-anchored or A-anchored. When the evaluation framework detects a knowledge failure at Layer 2, pathway classification tells the improvement engine *why*. A Q-anchored failure means the parametric association is wrong and may require fine-tuning. An A-anchored failure means the model lacked a strong association entirely and needs better retrieval context, not parameter updates.

This distinction matters for GraphRAG agents specifically. Improved retrieval alone cannot eliminate A-anchored hallucinations because the pathway operates independently of retrieved context. The model generates plausible answers from its own internal representations even when relevant documents sit in the context window. The fix for A-anchored failures is not more retrieval but *better structured* retrieval: graph-based context that makes question-answer relationships explicit through traversable edges instead of requiring the model to infer them from flat text chunks. When the knowledge graph provides a direct path from question entity to answer entity, it strengthens the Q-anchored pathway and reduces the conditions under which A-anchored generation activates.

There is also a model size dimension. Research on knowledge conflicts (Cheng et al., 2024, *https://oreil.ly/ZhUzJ*) shows that smaller models trust retrieved context more readily, while larger models favor their own parametric beliefs. The same retrieval strategy that successfully overrides A-anchored generation in a 7B model may fail against a 70B model's stronger parametric priors.

## A Taxonomy for Self-Evolution

Your agent has diagnosed a reasoning failure. The execution graph shows where it went wrong, the cognitive fault isolator has classified the breakdown, and you are staring at a diagnostic report that tells you the system is underperforming. Now what?

The temptation is to jump straight to the fix: tweak a prompt, retrain an adapter, add a guardrail. But self-evolution is not a single lever. It is a four-dimensional design space, and pulling the wrong lever wastes compute, introduces regressions, or both. Gao et al. (2026) (*https://oreil.ly/yemOD*) formalize this space across four axes that map directly onto the agentic graph architecture you have been building since Chapter 3.

### What evolves

Four targets exist in any agentic graph system, and each depends on graph infrastructure to function.

*Model evolution*
: Changes the weights or prompts that drive reasoning. You might fine-tune an adapter on domain-specific failures or optimize a prompt through gradient-free search. The graph enables this by tracing which prompt versions produced which outcomes. Unless the execution graph is linking configurations to result quality across hundreds of runs, you are tuning blind.

*Context evolution*
: Restructures what the agent retrieves: reranking knowledge graph subgraphs, consolidating memory nodes, and adjusting retrieval thresholds. Here the graph is not just the target of evolution but the medium. You evolve context by rewiring edges, merging redundant nodes, and pruning stale subgraphs—operations that have no equivalent in flat document stores.

*Tool evolution*
: Modifies how the agent interacts with external systems. That could mean registering new API endpoints, deprecating unreliable tools, or rewriting tool descriptions for better selection accuracy. The tool registry you built in Chapter 6 is itself a subgraph; evolving tool selection means reweighting edges between task-type nodes and tool nodes based on observed success rates.

*Architecture evolution*
: Reorganizes the agent's own topology such as by adding a verification node to the reasoning graph, splitting a monolithic planner into specialist subagents, or restructuring the knowledge graph schema. This is graph surgery in the most literal sense: you are adding and removing nodes from the agent's own workflow graph.

Waseem Alshikh's research on self-evolving AI models reinforces this graph-first principle: his team's first methodology is GNN-inspired knowledge graphs where "each adaptation becomes a traceable node" (Patience, 2025, *https://oreil.ly/n08FY*). The graph provides the visibility layer that makes self-evolution auditable. Without it, self-improvement becomes an opaque box that no production team will deploy.

#### When evolution fires

Production systems diverge from research prototypes here. *Intra-test-time evolution* happens within a single request. Your reflect-retry-reward loop, shown in Examples 7-11 and 7-12 is a canonical instance. Inter-test-time evolution happens between requests: the SEAL curriculum generates training data overnight, the semantic back-propagation pass updates neighbor prompts, and the next morning's agent is measurably different from yesterday's. The distinction matters because intra-test-time evolution must be fast (sub-second decisions), while inter-test-time evolution can afford expensive operations like fine-tuning or graph restructuring.

#### How the agent learns

Three mechanisms dominate:

*Reward-based learning*
: Uses scalar signals such as your InfoGain metric, user satisfaction scores, or the composite reward functions you will see in Example 7-8.

*Imitation-based learning*
: Copies successful trajectories from demonstrations or from the agent's own best past performances.

*Population-based learning*
: Maintains multiple agent variants and selects the fittest. This is useful when you cannot define a clean reward signal but can compare outcomes.

#### Where evolution applies

*General-purpose evolution* improves the agent across all tasks. *Domain-specialized evolution* targets a specific vertical. Your DevOps agent may not need to improve at poetry, but it may absolutely need to get better at predicting cascade failures in microservice topologies.

#### Connecting the axes

Every axis of self-evolution requires graph structure to operate. Model evolution needs execution graphs for causal tracing. Context evolution *is* graph evolution. Tool evolution rewires the tool subgraph. Architecture evolution restructures the workflow graph itself. The graph is not optional infrastructure here; it is the substrate that makes any of these axes operable. Table 7-1 maps each failure type across its primary evolution axis, timing, and mechanism.

*Table 7-1. Failure-to-evolution routing table*

| Failure type | Primary evolution axis | Timing | Mechanism |
|---|---|---|---|
| Wrong facts retrieved | Context | Inter-test-time | Reward based |
| Incorrect reasoning chain | Model | Intra-test-time | Reward based |
| Tool selection error | Tool | Inter-test-time | Imitation |
| Architectural bottleneck | Architecture | Inter-test-time | Population based |

# Targeted Self-Improvement

The evaluation framework can now tell you exactly what went wrong and where. The next question is what to do about it. A diagnosis is only valuable if it leads to the right intervention, and different failure types call for different responses. A reasoning failure at a single node calls for a prompt update; a systemic knowledge gap calls for fine-tuning; a format violation calls for an architectural constraint. Applying the wrong fix wastes time at best and makes things worse at worst.

This section covers three layers of the improvement process: choosing the right intervention type, propagating feedback coherently across the graph with semantic backpropagation, and the specific learning frameworks (SEAL, think-prune-train [TPT], and reflect-retry-reward) that turn a diagnosis into a durable improvement.

## Choosing the Right Intervention: Prompt, Fine-Tune, or Constrain?

The diagnostic report enables a three-way intervention strategy. The choice of which intervention to apply depends entirely on what the diagnosis found.

*When to use prompt refinement (the lightweight fix)*
: Use prompt refinement in cases of a localized reasoning failure (low InfoGain on one or two steps), a suboptimal tool choice despite having correct information, or poor alignment signals from user behavior. Prompt refinement nudges the agent to apply its existing capabilities more effectively at that specific node. It is fast, reversible, and the right first resort.

*When to trigger fine-tuning (the heavyweight fix)*
: Leverage fine-tuning when there is a systemic knowledge gap (i.e., consistently low KI across multiple executions), a recurring pattern of the same reasoning failure type, or a persistent misalignment between predicted and actual outcomes. Fine-tuning is more expensive and takes longer to validate, but it changes the model's underlying behavior rather than just steering it at inference time.

*When to apply a structural constraint (the architectural fix)*

Do this when the diagnostic report identifies a `FormatViolation` or `Parsing Error`. The agent had the right knowledge and performed the right reasoning, but it failed to produce a machine-readable output. Rather than teaching the model to speak JSON better through more training, attach an output schema constraint directly to that specific node in the workflow graph, making the format error *impossible* rather than *less likely*. This is an architectural change, not a model change, and it produces a permanent fix for that component. Chapter 6 covered how constrained generation with Outlines works in general; in the context of self-evolution, the important thing to note is that the diagnostic report can trigger this constraint as an automated response to a diagnosed format failure, closing the loop without human intervention.

In practice, this decision can be automated. The diagnostic report already contains the failure type and target nodes; mapping those to an intervention is a straightforward routing function, as Example 7-6 shows.

*Example 7-6. Intervention routing from diagnostic report to fix type*

```
def select_intervention(report: dict) -> dict:
    """Route a diagnostic report to the appropriate intervention."""
    cognitive = report["layer_2_cognitive"]
    failure = cognitive["failure_type"]

    if not report["layer_1_context"]["sufficient"]:
        return {
            "type": "RETRIEVAL_FIX",
            "action": "Flag Knowledge Graph or retrieval pipeline gap",
            "target": "retrieval_pipeline",
        }

    if failure == "FORMAT_VIOLATION":
        return {
            "type": "STRUCTURAL_CONSTRAINT",
            "action": "Attach output schema to node",
            "target": report["target_nodes"],
        }

    low_steps = cognitive.get("low_infogain_steps", [])
    ki = cognitive.get("knowledge_index", 1.0)

    # Localized reasoning failure — fix with a prompt update
    if failure == "REASONING" and len(low_steps) <= 2 and ki > 0.8:
        return {
            "type": "PROMPT_REFINEMENT",
            "action": "Update prompt for target node",
            "target": report["target_nodes"],
        }
```

```
    # Systemic or recurring failure - requires fine-tuning
    return {
        "type": "FINE_TUNE",
        "action": "Generate curriculum via SEAL/TPT and retrain",
        "target": report["target_nodes"],
    }
```

> The thresholds here (two or fewer low-InfoGain steps for a prompt fix, a KI above 0.8 for a reasoning-only diagnosis) are starting points. Tune them against your own historical diagnostic data. The important principle is that intervention selection should be deterministic and auditable, not a judgment call made differently by each on-call engineer.

## Semantic Backpropagation: Coherent Evolution Across the Graph

The intervention strategy just described handles a single node in isolation. But agents are graphs, not pipelines. A fix to one node can ripple through its neighbors in ways the fix didn't anticipate. The dangerous failure mode in self-evolving systems is not a bad update. Rather, it is a good update to one node that silently breaks another. In a deeply interconnected graph, improving a component in isolation can cause "action at a distance" failures that are difficult to trace. Semantic backpropagation is the mechanism that prevents this.

The core idea comes from an adaptation of the chain rule in calculus, building on TextGrad's foundational insight (Yuksekgonul et al., 2024, *https://oreil.ly/WSIYF*) that textual feedback can serve as a gradient signal. In numerical backpropagation, gradients flow backward through a computational graph, updating each parameter based on how it contributed to the loss. Semantic backpropagation (Wang et al., 2024, *https://oreil.ly/fsSBQ*) does the same thing in natural language: the *gradient* is a structured description of the required change, and it flows backward through the execution graph from the point of failure.

The important part is *neighbor-awareness*. When generating the feedback for node `v` based on what successor `w` needed, the prompt includes not just the outputs of `v` and the error from `w` but also the outputs of all other predecessors of `w`. This context is what makes the feedback precise.

Consider a concrete example. Three nodes collaborate: an `Extractor` node pulls "Revenue: $10M" from a document, a `CurrencyConverter` node converts it to "€9.5M," and a `Validator` node (which also received the output of a `DateChecker` node, "Date: 2026") flags an error: "The conversion is wrong; the 2026 exchange rate was 0.88, not 0.95."

Without neighbor-awareness, the feedback sent backward to the `Extractor` is "Your output of $10M led to a conversion error." The `Extractor` node might reasonably conclude it should have extracted a different number—a wrong fix. With neighbor-awareness, however, the feedback to the `Extractor` is "Your output of '$10M' was sent to the `CurrencyConverter`. The `Validator` node, using date information from the `DateChecker` ("Date: 2026"), determined that the 2026 exchange rate was 0.88, not 0.95. No change is needed to your extraction; the error originated in the `CurrencyConverter`'s rate lookup." Figure 7-2 illustrates this flow.

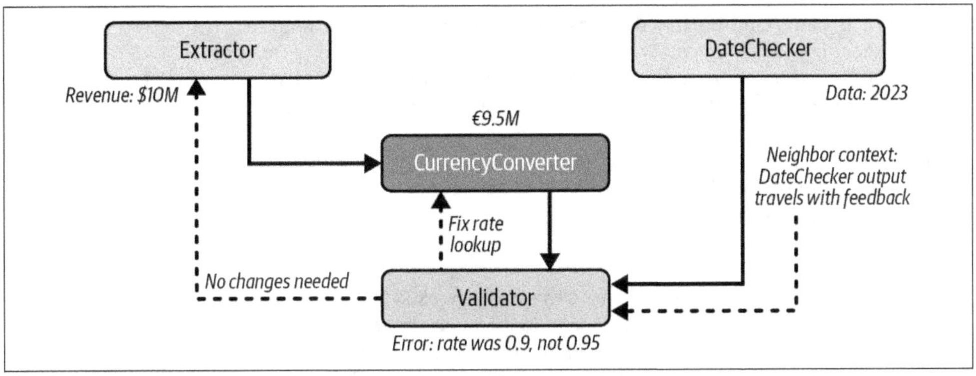


*Figure 7-2. Neighbor-aware semantic backpropagation*

Feedback flows backward from the `Validator` through the execution graph. Because the feedback includes neighbor context (the `DateChecker`'s output), it correctly assigns the error to the `CurrencyConverter`'s rate lookup and leaves the `Extractor` unchanged.

This neighbor-aware context prevents incorrect credit assignment and ensures that improvements are compatible across the graph. A change to one node is always evaluated in the context of what every other connected node needs.

## A Suite of Self-Improvement Frameworks

Semantic backpropagation determines *where* to change and *what* the change should accomplish. The remaining question is *how* to make that change stick. Three complementary frameworks handle three different situations: learning from failures, learning from successes, and learning to recover in real time.

### SEAL: Targeted data generation

A Self-Adapting LLM (SEAL; Zweiger et al., 2025, *https://oreil.ly/T46GJ*) generates a targeted training curriculum based on the diagnostic report. When the report identifies a reasoning failure, SEAL receives it as input and generates a set of targeted training examples designed to exercise exactly that failure mode. For example, if the diagnostic report identifies "confusion between correlation and causation at step 4," SEAL generates training examples where two correlated variables and a confounding factor appear together, and the correct reasoning trace must explicitly distinguish correlation from causation rather than inferring one from the other. This targeted curriculum is then used to fine-tune the agent on its specific weakness rather than on a generic benchmark. Example 7-7 shows the generation function.

*Example 7-7. SEAL curriculum generation from a diagnostic report*

```
def generate_seal_curriculum(diagnostic_report: dict, n_examples: int = 50) -> list:
    """Generate targeted training examples from a diagnostic report."""
    failure_type = diagnostic_report["layer_2_cognitive"]["failure_type"]
    diagnosis = diagnostic_report["layer_2_cognitive"]["diagnosis"]

    prompt = f"""
    An agent failed with the following diagnosis:
    Failure type: {failure_type}
    Details: {diagnosis}

    Generate {n_examples} training examples in JSON format. Each example must:
    1. Present a scenario in the same domain as the failure
    2. Include the specific confound or trap that caused the failure
    3. Provide a correct reasoning trace that explicitly avoids the failure mode
    4. Label the critical decision point where the failure typically occurs

    Return as a JSON array of {{input, reasoning_trace, correct_output,
        critical_step}} objects.
    """
    return llm.generate(prompt)
```

The prompt's four requirements are what distinguish SEAL from generic data augmentation. Requirement 2 ensures that the generated examples contain the same trap that caused the original failure, so the agent practices recognizing the exact pattern it missed. Requirement 4 labels where in the reasoning chain the failure typically occurs, letting the fine-tuning process weight that step more heavily during training.

#### Self-directed improvement: Moving from passive to active learning

SEAL generates curricula from observed failures, but it remains fundamentally reactive: the agent learns from mistakes it has already made. What if the agent could generate its own training tasks, explore solutions autonomously, and attribute success or failure to specific reasoning steps? This is the difference between a student who only reviews exam corrections and one who invents practice problems.

AgentEvolver (Zhai et al. and Tongyi Lab, 2025, *https://oreil.ly/ykdT6*) introduces three mechanisms that turn your agent from a passive learner into an active one.

On the WebArena benchmark, these mechanisms push Qwen2.5-7B from 15.8% to 45.2% average success, a 29.4% gain without any human-annotated training data.

*Self-questioning* is curiosity-driven task generation, and it requires a graph to be curious about. Instead of waiting for real user requests to expose gaps, the agent traverses its own knowledge graph and identifies sparse regions: node clusters with few edges, entity types with low confidence scores, or dependency chains it has never exercised. The strategy progresses from *breadth* (exploring unfamiliar subgraphs) to *depth* (stress-testing known weak areas with adversarial queries). In the context of your DevOps agent, self-questioning might traverse the service dependency graph and generate synthetic incident scenarios: *What happens when service X fails while service Y is already degraded?* Without the graph, the agent would have no map of its own knowledge gaps and would generate random questions rather than targeted ones.

Self-questioning alone accounts for the largest single improvement: +20.3%. The act of generating good questions, guided by graph topology, matters more than any individual training technique.

*Self-navigating* replaces the standard reinforcement learning rollout with experience-mixed trajectories. When the agent encounters a task, it queries the knowledge graph for similar past episodes and interleaves retrieved experiences with its own live reasoning. The graph's edge structure determines which episodes are "similar" based on structural similarity in the reasoning patterns and dependency chains that led to success or failure, not just embedding distance. Critically, the agent strips the retrieval markers before learning, forcing the model to internalize the patterns rather than memorize the cues.

*Self-attributing* solves the credit assignment problem that plagues multistep agentic workflows, and it depends entirely on the execution graph from Example 7-1. When a 10-step reasoning chain produces a wrong answer, which step caused the failure? A flat log gives you a sequence, but the execution graph gives you causal structure: which steps depended on which prior outputs, which retrieval events fed into which decisions, and where the reasoning chain first diverged from the correct path. Example 7-8 shows how per-step rewards combine attribution with outcome.

*Example 7-8. Step-level credit assignment with composite reward*

```
class StepAttributor:
    def __init__(self, judge_model: str, alpha: float = 0.6):
        self.judge = judge_model
        self.alpha = alpha  # weight for attribution vs outcome

    def compute_reward(
        self, trajectory: list[ReasoningStep], outcome: float
    ) -> list[float]:
```

```
        """Assign per-step rewards combining attribution and outcome."""
        attributions = self.judge_attribution(trajectory)
        rewards = []
        for step, attr_score in zip(trajectory, attributions):
            r_t = self.alpha * attr_score + (1 - self.alpha) * outcome
            rewards.append(r_t)
        return rewards

    def judge_attribution(
        self, trajectory: list[ReasoningStep]
    ) -> list[float]:
        """LLM judge scores each step's contribution to the outcome."""
        prompt = self.build_attribution_prompt(trajectory)
        scores = self.judge.evaluate(prompt)
        return normalize(scores)
```

The alpha parameter controls the balance between step-level attribution and global outcome. In practice, alpha between 0.5 and 0.7 works best, providing enough attribution signal to identify the broken step and enough outcome signal to prevent the judge's own biases from dominating.

### Beyond prompts and weights: Code-level self-modification

Everything you have seen so far (prompt optimization, fine-tuning, reward shaping) operates on the agent's parameters or context. The agent's actual code remains frozen. The work in "Self-Improving Coding Agent" (SICA; Robeyns, Szummer, and Aitchison, 2025, *https://oreil.ly/jCw1l*) breaks this boundary: here the agent edits its own Python source files, commits the changes, and reevaluates on the next iteration.

The results justify the risk. On SWE-bench Verified, SICA improves from 17% to 53% resolution rate across iterations, a 3x gain that no amount of prompt tuning achieves on the same benchmark.

But code-level self-modification without graph-based provenance would be reckless. Every code change must be a traceable node in the execution graph, yielding information on which diagnostic triggered it, what utility score motivated it, which previous modifications it builds on, and what rollback path exists. Alshikh's 2025 research on self-evolving models calls this the *versioned learning log*, a graph where each adaptation event becomes an auditable node with full causal ancestry. Example 7-9 shows the multifactor utility function that prevents the agent from gaming its score by throwing compute at the problem.

*Example 7-9. Multifactor utility for code-level self-modification*

```
class SelfModificationUtility:
    def __init__(
        self,
        perf_weight: float = 0.5,
```

```
        cost_budget: float = 10.0,
        time_budget: float = 300.0,
    ):
        self.w_perf = perf_weight
        self.w_cost = (1 - perf_weight) / 2
        self.w_time = (1 - perf_weight) / 2
        self.cost_budget = cost_budget
        self.time_budget = time_budget

    def evaluate(
        self, performance: float, cost: float, latency: float
    ) -> float:
        """Balanced utility: performance alone is not enough."""
        cost_score = 1 - (cost / self.cost_budget)
        time_score = 1 - (latency / self.time_budget)
        return (
            self.w_perf * performance
            + self.w_cost * max(0, cost_score)
            + self.w_time * max(0, time_score)
        )
```

The 50/25/25 split among performance, cost, and time means the agent cannot game its way to a high score by throwing compute at the problem. SICA uses an asynchronous LLM-based overseer that reviews proposed code changes before they execute. The overseer runs on a separate model instance and has veto power: if a proposed modification touches safety-critical functions (e.g., authentication, data access, external API calls), it requires explicit approval.

> Code-level self-modification is the most powerful and most dangerous form of self-evolution. Use it only in sandboxed environments with full rollback capability. The graduated validation protocol in "Safe Evolution in Production" on page 294 was designed with exactly this risk in mind.

This creates a hierarchy of self-modification intensity that maps to your recursion-provenance-optimization spine, discussed in "The RPO and Graduated Validation Protocol" on page 295. Prompt tuning is the lightest intervention (fast, reversible, low risk), weight adaptation sits in the middle (slower, semi-reversible, moderate risk), and code modification is the heaviest (slowest, requires explicit rollback, highest risk).

#### TPT: Reinforcing what works

Where SEAL generates data from failures, TPT learns from successes (Costello et al., 2025, *https://oreil.ly/89h1T*). Not all correct answers are created equal. An agent that reaches the right conclusion through a lucky guess or a logically incoherent chain of reasoning has not demonstrated a skill worth reinforcing. TPT uses the diagnostic framework to distinguish genuinely good reasoning from accidentally correct reasoning, then trains exclusively on the former. The framework operates in three phases:

1. *Think*

   For a given task, the agent generates multiple candidate reasoning paths, typically 5 to 10, each with a different sampling temperature or prompt variation. This produces diversity: some paths will be efficient, some circuitous, some correct by accident, and some wrong.

2. *Prune*

   This is the critical step that separates TPT from naive self-training. Each candidate path is evaluated using the full diagnostic framework, not just checked for output correctness. A path survives pruning only if it meets all three of these criteria:

   a. It reaches the correct final answer.
   b. It has a high knowledge index, meaning it used accurate facts throughout.
   c. It has high average InfoGain across all steps, meaning its logic was efficient and each step genuinely advanced the reasoning.

   A path that gets the right answer by getting lucky on a bad premise is discarded, and a path that uses correct facts but wastes 10 steps on circular logic is discarded.

3. *Train*

   The agent is fine-tuned exclusively on the surviving gold standard traces. Because these traces are the agent's own best work, not synthetic data or human-written examples, the training reinforces patterns the model can already produce, making them more likely to appear consistently.

Example 7-10 shows the full TPT pipeline.

*Example 7-10. TPT pipeline for generating and pruning gold-standard reasoning traces*

```
def tpt_pipeline(
    tasks: list,
    agent,
    evaluator,
    n_candidates: int = 8,
) -> list:
    """Generate, prune, and collect gold-standard reasoning traces."""

    gold_traces = []

    for task in tasks:
        candidates = []
        temperatures = [
```

```
            0.3,
            0.5,
            0.7,
            0.9,
        ] * 2  # Two traces per temperature

        for temp in temperatures:
            trace = agent.generate_reasoning_trace(
                task,
                temperature=temp,
            )
            candidates.append(trace)

        # Prune: evaluate each candidate with the full diagnostic framework
        for trace in candidates:
            report = evaluator.evaluate(task, trace)
            cognitive = report["layer_2_cognitive"]

            correct = report["overall_verdict"] == "PASS"
            ki = cognitive["knowledge_index"]
            infogain_trace = cognitive["infogain_trace"]
            avg_infogain = (
                sum(cognitive["infogain_trace"])
                / len(cognitive["infogain_trace"])
            )

            if (
                correct
                and ki > 0.85
                and avg_infogain > 0.15
            ):
                gold_traces.append(
                    {
                        "task": task,
                        "reasoning_trace": trace,
                        "ki": ki,
                        "avg_infogain": avg_infogain,
                    }
                )

    return gold_traces
```

The `temperatures` list generates two traces at each of four temperatures. Lower temperatures (0.3, 0.5) tend to produce more conservative, well-trodden reasoning paths; higher temperatures (0.7, 0.9) produce more diverse and occasionally more creative paths. The triple-condition pruning filter (`correct and ki > 0.85 and avg_infogain > 0.15`) is what separates TPT from naive self-training: paths that reach the right answer through lucky guesses or circular reasoning are discarded, leaving only traces where the agent demonstrated genuinely sound reasoning.

Of course, the thresholds for KI and average InfoGain depend on your domain. Start with the values above and calibrate them against the distribution you see in production traces. The goal is to keep roughly the top 10%–20% of correct paths, not to be so strict that nothing survives.

### Reflect, retry, reward: Building metacognitive debugging skills

SEAL and TPT improve the agent's task performance. "Reflect, Retry, Reward" (Bensal et al., 2025, *https://oreil.ly/ujDIR*) teaches a different skill: the ability to *recover from mistakes in real time*. An agent that can diagnose its own failure midsession and correct course without waiting for an offline training cycle is more resilient than one that cannot.

The framework operates in three phases, each building on the previous:

*Reflect*

: When an attempt fails, the agent is prompted to generate a structured self-analysis. The prompt includes the full diagnostic report, which anchors the reflection in ground-truth evidence rather than in the agent's self-serving narrative. The agent must identify what went wrong, where in its reasoning the error occurred, and what it would do differently. Example 7-11 shows the reflection prompt.

*Example 7-11. Reflection prompt for the reflect-retry-reward framework*

```
reflection_prompt = f"""
Your previous attempt at this task failed. The diagnostic report is below.

Diagnostic report:
{json.dumps(diagnostic_report, indent=2)}

Analyze your failure. Your reflection must:
1. Identify the specific failure mode (knowledge gap or reasoning error)
2. Point to the step where the error occurred
3. Explain what the correct reasoning path would have been
4. Be consistent with the diagnostic report's findings

Write your reflection as a concise paragraph.
"""

reflection = agent.generate(reflection_prompt)
```

The prompt anchors the reflection in the diagnostic report rather than letting the agent speculate freely. Requirement 4, "Be consistent with the diagnostic report's findings," is the guard against self-serving narratives. Without it, agents tend to produce vague reflections (*I should have been more careful*) that sound reasonable but do not lead to targeted corrections.

*Retry*
: The agent attempts the same task again but now with its own reflection prepended to the context. This simulates a developer who reviews a failed test, understands the bug, and tries again with the insight fresh in mind. The reflection acts as a targeted correction signal. It tells the agent specifically what to avoid and what to try instead.

*Reward*
: If the retry succeeds, the framework rewards the *reflection itself*, not just the successful output. The reward is proportional to how well the agent's self-diagnosis matches the ground-truth diagnosis from the evaluation framework. A reflection that correctly identifies *premature commitment to the API failure hypothesis at step 4* earns a high reward. A reflection that *I should have been more careful* earns little, even if the retry happened to succeed. This reward signal teaches the agent to become an accurate self-critic, a skill that transfers across task types. Example 7-12 shows how the reflection is scored.

*Example 7-12. Reflection scoring for metacognitive reward signal*

```
def score_reflection(
    reflection: str,
    diagnostic_report: dict,
    retry_succeeded: bool,
) -> float:
    """Score a reflection based on diagnostic accuracy and retry outcome."""

    if not retry_succeeded:
        return 0.0

    # Use the judge model to assess alignment between reflection and report
    alignment_prompt = f"""
Compare this self-reflection to the ground-truth diagnostic report.
Score the alignment from 0.0 to 1.0 based on:
- Did it correctly identify the failure type? (0.3 weight)
- Did it correctly locate the failure step? (0.4 weight)
- Did it propose a plausible correction? (0.3 weight)

Reflection: {reflection}
Diagnostic report: {json.dumps(diagnostic_report, indent=2)}

Return a JSON object: {{"alignment_score": float, "reasoning": string}}
"""

    result = judge_model.generate(alignment_prompt)
    return result["alignment_score"]
```

Over time, agents trained using the reflect-retry-reward method show a measurable improvement in *first-attempt recovery rate*, or the percentage of failed tasks they can correct on a single retry without external help. This metric is worth tracking independently from raw accuracy because it captures something that matters in production: graceful degradation under novel conditions.

# Safe Evolution in Production

Everything described so far works in isolation: diagnosing a single failure, generating a targeted fix, propagating feedback through the graph. Production is different. In production, the agent processes thousands of queries, accumulates dozens of candidate improvements, and must apply changes without disrupting the traffic it is actively serving.

Putting these pieces into production means solving three problems at once: assembling the individual components into a continuous feedback loop, validating that each candidate change is actually an improvement before it reaches users, and preventing the system from evolving in unsafe directions. The machinery for this is the *evolutionary loop* (the full cycle from execution to deployment), the *RPO* (the safety properties that govern the loop), and the *graduated validation protocol* (the tiered gate that controls what reaches production).

## The Full Evolutionary Loop

The individual components (execution graph, evaluation framework, intervention strategy, semantic backpropagation, and improvement frameworks) are designed to compose. The complete self-evolution cycle connects them into a single feedback loop. Example 7-13 sketches the orchestration.

*Example 7-13. The full evolutionary loop*

```
def evolutionary_loop(query: str, agent: Agent) -> Response:
    """Execute one turn of the agent and feed failures back into a candidate fix."""
    execution_graph = agent.execute(query)
    # Example 7-3, 7-4, 7-5
    evaluation = evaluate(execution_graph)

    if evaluation.passed:
        return execution_graph.response

    # Failure path: diagnose, attribute, intervene, validate.
    diagnostic_report = evaluation.diagnostic_report

    # Example 7-6
    node_feedback = semantic_backprop(execution_graph, diagnostic_report)
    intervention = select_intervention(diagnostic_report)

    if intervention.kind == "prompt_refinement":
        candidate = update_prompt_library(agent, node_feedback)
```

```
    elif intervention.kind == "fine_tune":
        # SEAL / TPT / RRR, Examples 7-7 through 7-12
        candidate = fine_tune(agent, node_feedback)
    elif intervention.kind == "structural_constraint":
        candidate = attach_output_schema(agent, node_feedback)

    # canary → staging → airlock
    if graduated_validation(candidate).passed:
        deploy(candidate)
    else:
        archive_for_reanalysis(candidate, diagnostic_report)

    return execution_graph.response
```

This loop is a *data flywheel*: every production trace feeds back into the system's ability to diagnose and improve itself. The more the agent runs, the richer the diagnostic data, the more targeted the interventions, and the better the next round of executions. The flywheel only works, though, if you maintain human review of the evaluation criteria themselves. The failure categories that seemed comprehensive at launch will have blind spots that emerge only after months of production traffic. (See criteria staleness in "Common Pitfalls" on page 310 at the end of this chapter.)

One important process runs alongside this loop rather than inside it: *hyperparameter optimization* of the retrieval infrastructure. The sufficient context score from Layer 1 is a signal that can drive background optimization of chunk sizes, hop distances, and retrieval strategies, using the diagnostic framework as the objective function rather than as final-answer correctness. This optimization belongs to the production-hardening work covered in Chapter 8, but the evaluation framework produces the signal that makes it possible.

## The RPO and Graduated Validation Protocol

The evolutionary loop just discussed will generate candidate improvements continuously, and not all of them should reach production. Any system that modifies itself in production needs a safety envelope. The recursion-provenance-optimization (RPO) provides this through its three interlocking properties:

*Recursion*
: The agent's improvement mechanisms are themselves part of the codebase that the agent can analyze and improve. An advanced implementation can diagnose a flaw in its own SEAL data generation prompt and refine it. The self-improvement system applies to itself.

*Provenance*
: Every change is cryptographically signed and committed to an immutable ledger. This is *source control for thought*: complete auditability and instant rollback capabilities for every model update, prompt change, or architectural modification.

*Optimization, the graduated validation protocol (GVP)*

Rather than using a single approval gate that must be either permissive or strict, this protocol assigns each candidate change to a risk tier and subjects it to the appropriate level of scrutiny:

*Tier 1, canary release (low risk, incremental changes)*

Minor prompt updates or hyperparameter adjustments are deployed to a small fraction of live traffic (typically 1%). They must show statistically significant improvement in the target metric with no degradation in core KPIs. Any regression results in automatic rollback.

*Tier 2, staging gauntlet (moderate risk, standard changes)*

Fine-tuning results from SEAL/TPT or a refined tool integration go through a comprehensive automated evaluation in staging. There's a target benchmark suite, a regression suite checking for catastrophic forgetting, a safety and alignment suite checking for bias drift, and a performance suite checking latency and cost. A change passes only if it shows net positive improvement in a multi-objective utility function—something like `U = w1*accuracy + w2*(1-cost) + w3*safety_score`, with no safety regressions.

*Tier 3, airlock protocol (high risk, novel changes)*

Changes that modify safety protocols, integrate a brand-new external tool, or that failed staging but showed unusually large potential are sandboxed in an isolated environment. An automated risk/reward report is generated and escalated for human review. A human expert must approve, reject, or suggest modifications before the change can proceed.

Figure 7-3 shows the three tiers.

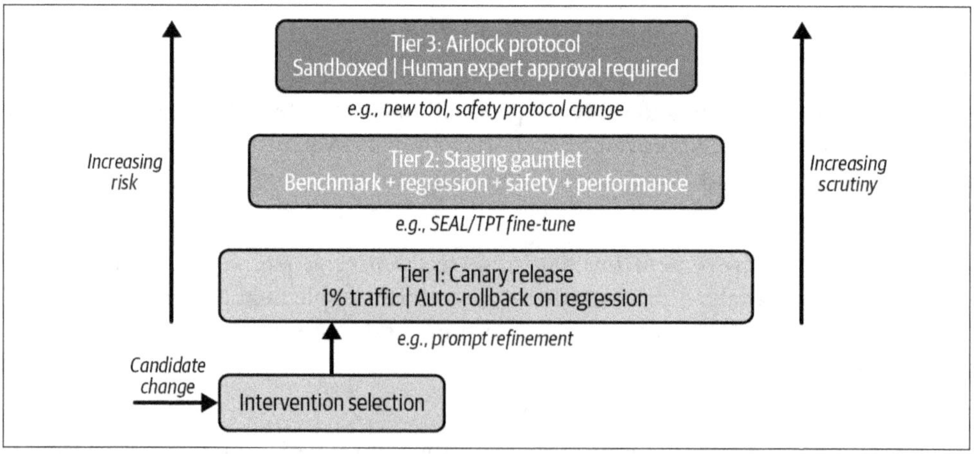


*Figure 7-3. The graduated validation protocol*

> With regard to dynamic capability evolution, the system can also evolve its tool ecosystem over time, learning collaborative tool patterns, refining tool documentation, and acquiring new tools for novel task types. This mechanism was covered in depth in Chapter 6's discussion of DRAFT and COLT. In the context of self-evolution, the relevant point is that these tool-level improvements flow through the same GVP as any other change.

## Persistent Self-Learning Without Entropy Collapse

The GVP ensures that no self-modification reaches production without passing through sandbox, shadow, and canary tiers, but it addresses a single evolution event.

In production, your agent will evolve continuously, with hundreds of small improvements per week, each passing validation individually. The compounding problem is not the result of any single change but of the accumulated weight of all changes: contradictory learnings, stale fixes for resolved issues, and redundant knowledge nodes that slow retrieval.

The Kepler architecture from OpenAI (Jackson, 2026, *https://oreil.ly/5_i7K*) solves this with a dual-store pattern that maps directly onto the graph infrastructure you have been building. *Knowledge* is human authored and version controlled: it is represented by your vertical knowledge graph from Chapter 3, containing ontology definitions, domain rules, and tool specifications. *Learnings* are agent generated and ephemeral: they may be error diagnoses stored as nodes in the execution graph, successful resolution patterns linked to the diagnostic events that produced them, and performance observations attached as edge annotations. Rather than separate databases, the two stores are two subgraphs within the same graph architecture, distinguished by provenance edges that mark each node as curated or autonomous.

The piece most self-evolving systems lack is the *garbage collection agent*, which operates as a graph traversal. It runs on a schedule (daily in the Kepler deployment), walks the learnings subgraph, and removes nodes that meet any of three conditions:

*The underlying issue has been resolved*
: The resolution node is now connected to a knowledge node, meaning the fix was promoted.

*The learning contradicts a newer learning with higher confidence*
: This is detected by finding opposing edges between the two nodes and comparing confidence scores.

*The learning has not been retrieved in 30 days*
: The `last_accessed` timestamp on the node has decayed past threshold.

The production evidence is compelling. With this architecture, three engineers produced approximately one million lines of shipping code in five months, a velocity that makes sense only if the AI system is genuinely learning from its own errors and does not regress.

For your DevOps agent, this means the first time it encounters a cascade failure triggered by a `stripe-python` library version mismatch, it works through the full diagnostic pipeline (Examples 7-14 through 7-18). The resolution pattern gets stored as a learning node in the execution graph. The second time it encounters a similar version mismatch cascade, even with a different library, it traverses these edges to retrieve the learning, adapts the resolution pattern to the new library's dependency graph, and resolves the incident in seconds rather than minutes.

> Start with a 30-day time to live (TTL) on learnings and a daily garbage collection pass. Monitor your learnings-to-knowledge promotion rate. If fewer than 10% of learnings get promoted to curated knowledge within 30 days, your promotion criteria are too strict and you are discarding valuable patterns.

## A Note on Loop Engineering

The data flywheel loop assembled in this chapter is so powerful that it now has a name in current practice: loop engineering. This is the discipline of designing, operating, and governing the improvement loop around an agent as a first-class engineered artifact. Instead of correcting the agent by hand after each failure, you build a system that corrects it; your deliverable shifts from a well-prompted agent to the loop that improves one. "You build the thing that builds the thing," as André Lindenberg puts it (Exxeta, 2026, *https://oreil.ly/73KkP*). Boris Cherny, creator of Claude Code at Anthropic, describes the same shift from the operator's seat: "I don't prompt Claude anymore. I have loops running that prompt Claude." (Horn, 2026, *https://oreil.ly/zJCzD*). Addy Osmani, who named the practice, defines *loop engineering* as replacing yourself as the person who prompts the agent (Google, 2026, *https://oreil.ly/BHzTU*).

Antonio Gulli (2026) (*https://oreil.ly/KmsGt*) compresses loop engineering into a working triad: define a measurable goal, keep the decision that consumes the verifier deterministic, and embrace the rollback. Each leg maps onto the machinery that this chapter has already built. The measurable goal is the halting contract: the multi-objective utility function and the binary verdicts of the evaluation framework decide when the loop stops, so "done" is never whatever the agent declares. The deterministic decision means that your judges may reason fuzzily, but the thresholds that promote or reject a candidate are fixed before the run; that is why the GVP's tiers pin their metrics and utility weights before a change enters validation and why intervention selection is a routing function rather than a judgment call. Finally, the rollback leg is the provenance ledger plus Tier 1's automatic reversion: failure returns the system to the last good state instead of patching forward on top of a regression.

Though the term is popular, Andrew Ng (2026) (*https://oreil.ly/39PlE*) observes that loop engineering became a buzzphrase almost as quickly as it became a practice, and that the substance underneath is older than the name. The single biggest predictor of executing well remains a disciplined process for evaluation and error analysis that includes checking intermediate and final outputs against factual tests. The loop is just the structure; the evaluation is the substance. Run the same loop on a weak signal, and it does not iterate. Instead, it just repeats the same mistake faster. That is why this chapter built the evaluation framework before the loop: the four diagnostic layers, the judge validation against human labels, and the periodic criteria review are what the loop feeds on, and they are where most of the engineering actually lives.

The conversation around loop engineering also clarifies what this chapter has been arguing all along. The discipline's requirements are, so far, stated as advice. Set a measurable goal, keep the decision deterministic, roll back on failure, and make the evaluation rigorous. What the advice leaves open is the substrate that makes any of it implementable, and every component you have built in this chapter answers with the same word: a graph. The execution graph is what gives a failure a coordinate, so feedback can say *Wrong at node 47* rather than just *Still wrong*. The knowledge graph is the ground truth that lets a judge compute a verdict instead of estimating one, keeping the verdict cheap enough to run on every pass. The workflow graph is the topology that lets feedback reach the node that earned it without breaking its neighbors. Even the provenance ledger is a graph of every change the loop has made to itself. A loop is easy to write, but a signal worth looping on is not, and the signal is what the graph provides.

## The DevOps Agent: Predictive Outage Detection in Practice

Through Chapters 5 and 6, the DevOps agent became a competent diagnostician. It can identify root causes of live incidents, query the knowledge graph for dependency relationships, and use live metrics through the tool layer. In this chapter, we've added the next capability: *proactive prediction*. When a deployment event fires, the agent no longer just waits for something to break. It analyzes the change, reasons about the change's downstream effects, and predicts what might fail—before it fails. This capability also introduces a new class of failure: the *partially correct prediction*. This failure mode is what makes the self-evolution loop indispensable.

## The Scenario: A Library Update Triggers a Prediction

The SRE on call receives an automated notification: the platform team is deploying a routine dependency update, `stripe-python 3.2.1 → 3.3.0` in the `checkout-service`. Before the deployment goes live, the DevOps agent analyzes the change.

The first step is to understand the blast radius. The agent needs to know which services depend on this library, which specific methods they call, and what sits downstream in the request path. All of this information already lives in the knowledge graph, modeled through the dependency relationships introduced in Chapter 3. In Example 7-14, the agent queries those relationships.

*Example 7-14. Knowledge graph query for service dependency analysis*

```
MATCH (s:Service {name: "checkout-service"})
-[:DEPENDS_ON]->(lib:Library {name: "stripe-python"})
MATCH (s)-[:CALLS]->(method:Method)
WHERE method.library = "stripe-python"
RETURN s.name, collect(method.name) AS methods_used,
       s.upstream_services AS upstream,
       s.downstream_services AS downstream
```

The graph returns `checkout-service` calls `payments.charge()` and `payments.retrieve()`. It is upstream of `order-service` and `fulfillment-service`. The 3.3.0 changelog notes that it deprecated `synchronous batch_charge`, added async payment methods, and updated the default connection timeout from 30 to 10 seconds.

With the dependency map in hand, the agent's prediction node reasons through the dependency chain. This is the Chapter 5 reasoning engine applied to a proactive scenario: instead of diagnosing a failure that has already happened, the agent is reasoning about what *could* fail given a known change. Example 7-15 shows the structured prediction output.

*Example 7-15. Structured prediction output for a dependency update*

```
{
  "prediction_id": "pred_7f3a9c",
  "trigger": "Dependency update: stripe-python 3.2.1 -> 3.3.0",
  "affected_pathway": "checkout-service -> order-service -> fulfillment-service",
  "predicted_failure_mode": "API contract violation",
  "reasoning": "stripe-python 3.3.0 deprecates batch_charge. checkout-service
      uses payments.charge() - checking whether this is related to batch_charge.",
  "predicted_impact": "HIGH - checkout failures will block order processing",
  "confidence": 0.78,
  "recommendation": "Review checkout-service for batch_charge usage before
      deploying"
}
```

The SRE reviews the prediction, finds no `batch_charge` usage in the checkout codebase, and approves the deployment. The update goes live. Twenty minutes later: connection timeouts begin cascading through the order-processing pipeline.

This is the scenario that makes self-evolution essential. The agent's prediction was partially right. It correctly identified the affected pathway (`checkout-service -> order-service -> fulfillment-service`) and the severity (`HIGH`). But it misidentified the failure mechanism. The incident was caused not by an API contract change but by the reduced default connection timeout (10 seconds in 3.3.0 versus 30 seconds in 3.2.1) which, under load, exhausted the connection pool in under a minute. The agent had all the right data; the changelog it retrieved listed the timeout change explicitly. It simply drew the wrong conclusion about which change posed the greater risk. Without a self-evolution loop, this type of failure requires a human to manually analyze the prediction, identify the reasoning gap, and rewrite the prompt. With the system built in this chapter, the diagnosis and correction happen automatically.

## Generating the Execution Graph

So where did the reasoning go wrong? This is where the execution graph, introduced at the beginning of this chapter, earns its keep. Because the prediction node's execution was automatically captured in the graph database through OpenTelemetry instrumentation, every step of the agent's reasoning is available for inspection. The relevant portion of the execution graph looks like this:

```
[KnowledgeGraphQuery: checkout-service deps]
        |
        v
[ChangelogRetrieval: stripe-python 3.3.0 changelog]
        |
        v
[ChangeAnalyzer: classify changelog changes]
        |
        v  ← LOW InfoGain steps begin here
[CausalAttributionNode: map changes to failure modes]
        |
        v
[PredictionSynthesis: produce structured prediction]
```

The execution graph node for `CausalAttributionNode` shows the following:

*Input*
: Changelog classified as *API deprecations present, configuration changes present*

*Output*
: *Failure mode: API contract violation (confidence 0.78)*

*Latency*
: 1.4 seconds, 847 tokens

Notice that the input to `CausalAttributionNode` explicitly lists *configuration changes present*. The data was there. The question is why the agent ignored it in favor of the API deprecation hypothesis.

## The Cognitive Autopsy

With the execution graph in hand, the evaluation framework runs its analysis. This is the multi-layered evaluation framework from earlier in the chapter applied to a concrete failure. Each layer answers a different question: Did the agent have the right information, and did it reason correctly with what it had?

*Layer 1: Context evaluator*
: The knowledge graph *did* contain the relevant information. The changelog was retrieved and included both the API deprecation and the timeout change. Sufficient context: `true`.

*Layer 2: Cognitive fault isolator*
: The Knowledge Index is 0.91: the agent used accurate facts. The facts about API deprecation were correct; the facts about the timeout change were present in the context but not weighted appropriately in the reasoning.

The InfoGain trace for `CausalAttributionNode` shows a clear inflection point (see Example 7-16).

*Example 7-16. InfoGain trace showing premature closure in causal reasoning*

```
infogain_trace = {
    "step_1_identify_api_changes": 0.34,  # High - correct orientation
    "step_2_map_to_service_methods": 0.29, # High - grounded in KG data
    "step_3_assess_deprecation_impact": 0.22, # Moderate - reasonable
    "step_4_select_primary_failure_mode": 0.03, # Near zero - premature commitment
    "step_5_assign_confidence": -0.01,     # Negative - reinforced wrong path
    "step_6_generate_recommendation": 0.19 # Partial recovery
}
```

Steps 4 and 5 reveal the failure: the agent committed to *API contract violation* at step 4 and then reinforced that commitment at step 5. The correct path, *configuration change → connection pool exhaustion*, had equal support in the retrieved context but was not explored after the early commitment. The near-zero InfoGain at step 4 means the agent added almost no new information when selecting its primary failure mode; it simply locked in on the first plausible hypothesis.

This is a classic *premature closure* reasoning failure, not a knowledge gap. The distinction matters because it changes the intervention. A knowledge failure would call for better retrieval or richer context. A reasoning failure calls for a prompt or model change that forces the agent to consider multiple hypotheses before committing. Example 7-17 shows the diagnostic report.

*Example 7-17. Diagnostic report for the DevOps prediction failure*

```
{
  "execution_id": "pred_7f3a9c",
  "layer_1_context": {"sufficient": true, "confidence": 0.97},
  "layer_2_cognitive": {
    "failure_type": "REASONING",
    "fault_location": {"node_id": "CausalAttributionNode"},
    "knowledge_index": 0.91,
    "low_infogain_steps": [4, 5],
    "diagnosis": "Premature commitment to 'API contract violation' hypothesis at
        step 4. Configuration change (timeout reduction 30s→10s) had equal
        evidentiary support but was not explored after early commitment to the
        API path."
  },
  "recommended_intervention": "PROMPT_REFINEMENT",
  "target_nodes": ["CausalAttributionNode"]
}
```

The report's conclusion is precise: the failure is cognitive (not contextual), specifically a reasoning failure (not a knowledge gap), localized to `CausalAttributionNode` at steps 4 and 5, and the recommended fix is a prompt refinement rather than fine-tuning. Every field in this report feeds directly into the next stage of the loop.

## Semantic Backpropagation to the Causal Attribution Node

The diagnostic report has identified the failure and located the responsible node. The next question is *What, specifically, should change?* This is where semantic backpropagation generates feedback with the necessary precision. Rather than a generic "do better" signal, the framework propagates structured feedback backward from the prediction error to the `CausalAttributionNode`. Crucially, this feedback is neighbor-aware: it includes the outputs of adjacent nodes (`ChangelogRetrieval` and `KnowledgeGraphQuery`) so that the correction is grounded in what the node actually received as input, not just what it produced as output. Example 7-18 shows the feedback structure.

*Example 7-18. Neighbor-aware semantic feedback for the causal attribution node*

```
semantic_feedback = {
    "target_node": "CausalAttributionNode",
    "failure_context": {
        "predicted": "API contract violation",
        "actual": "Connection pool exhaustion from timeout reduction (30s→10s)"
    },
    "neighbor_context": {
        "ChangelogRetrieval_output": "Changelog contained: (1) deprecated
            batch_charge, (2) new async methods, (3) default connection_timeout
            reduced from 30s to 10s",
        "KnowledgeGraphQuery_output": "checkout-service uses payments.charge() and
            payments.retrieve(); no batch_charge usage found"
    },
    "feedback": (
        "When classifying changelog changes, treat connection "
        "configuration defaults (timeouts, pool sizes, retry policies) "
        "as a separate hypothesis category with equal priority to API "
        "contract changes. The timeout change (30s→10s) was present in "
        "your input but not explored as a failure pathway. For services "
        "with high throughput, configuration defaults often have higher "
        "failure probability than API deprecations."
    )
}
```

The `neighbor_context` field is what makes this feedback actionable. The `ChangelogRetrieval_output` confirms that the timeout change was present in the node's input, removing any ambiguity about whether the failure was a data gap. The `KnowledgeGraphQuery_output` confirms that the agent had already established there was no `batch_charge` usage, which should have steered it away from the API deprecation hypothesis. Together, these neighbor outputs make the feedback specific enough to generate a targeted prompt update rather than a vague directive to "consider more factors."

## The Improvement and Its Effect

The diagnosis is complete and the feedback is precise. Now the loop closes.

The `recommended_intervention` from the diagnostic report is `PROMPT_REFINEMENT`, the lightest-weight intervention in the toolkit. The `select_intervention()` router from earlier in the chapter maps this to a prompt update rather than fine-tuning or data augmentation because the failure was a reasoning pattern, not a knowledge gap, and affected a single node. The prompt for `CausalAttributionNode` is updated to include an explicit instruction: when a changelog contains both API changes and configuration changes, evaluate each as a separate hypothesis and assign independent confidence scores before selecting a primary failure mode.

Before this change reaches production, it must pass through the GVP. Because it is a prompt refinement (the lowest-risk intervention category), it enters at Tier 1 (canary release). The updated agent processes a sample of historical deployment events that included configuration changes. In that sample, the agent correctly identifies connection pool exhaustion risk as a top-ranked hypothesis in cases where the old prompt would have focused exclusively on API contract changes. The canary metrics hold, with no regressions on other prediction types, so the change is promoted to production.

The payoff arrives the following week. A library update with a default connection pool size reduction appears in the deployment queue. The updated agent predicts *connection pool exhaustion risk* as a co-equal hypothesis alongside the API deprecation concern, assigns it a higher confidence score based on the service's throughput profile, and recommends a connection pool size review before deployment. The SRE acts on the recommendation, adjusting the pool configuration, and the deployment proceeds without incident.

This is the complete loop in action: execution → diagnosis → feedback → intervention → validation → deployment → better execution. Each pass through the loop leaves a trace in the provenance ledger documenting what changed, why, and what evidence supported the change. Over time, these traces form a record of the agent's learning history—one that is auditable, reversible, and grounded in observed failures rather than speculative improvements.

## Inference-Time Knowledge Augmentation: Learning Without Retraining

The improvement mechanisms covered so far (prompt refinement, SEAL data generation, fine-tuning) all modify the agent itself. They change its weights or its instructions. There is a lighter-weight alternative that the execution graph makes possible: accumulating knowledge from past executions and retrieving it at inference time, without touching the model or its prompts at all.

The insight comes from measuring where agents actually fail. On the Kaggle Game Arena chess benchmark, 78% of Gemini-2.5-Flash losses were caused by illegal moves—that is, rule violations rather than weak strategy. The agent kept making the same category of mistake on similar positions because it had no memory of past failures. The broader pattern holds across domains: a significant fraction of agent errors are avoidable repetitions of previously encountered mistakes.

XSkill (Jiang et al., 2026, *https://oreil.ly/voupc*) formalizes this insight into a dual-stream continual learning framework that extracts two complementary knowledge types from agent trajectories:

*Experiences*

These operate at the action level. They capture what worked and what failed for specific tool calls and decisions, e.g., *When parsing nested JSON, recursive descent with `jq` succeeds where `Python json.loads` fails on malformed input.* Experiences are extracted from individual nodes in the execution graph: each node's input, action, and outcome becomes a candidate experience record.

*Skills*

These operate at the task level. They capture multistep patterns that solve categories of problems. Here's an example: "To diagnose a connection pool exhaustion, first check the changelog for timeout changes, then query the knowledge graph for throughput profile, and then evaluate pool size against concurrent connection count." Skills are extracted from successful execution subgraphs: the path from the root query node to the successful resolution node becomes a candidate skill.

XSkill's evaluation on Gemini-3-Flash shows the complementary effect: experiences alone reduce tool errors from 29.9% to 16.3% (a 45% reduction), while skills alone improve task success rate. Together, the average success rate increases from 33.6% to 40.3%. Example 7-19 shows the dual-stream extraction classes.

*Example 7-19. Dual-stream knowledge extraction from execution graphs*

```
from dataclasses import dataclass
from datetime import datetime


@dataclass
class AgentExperience:
    """Action-level knowledge extracted from an execution node."""
    task_type: str         # Category of task (e.g., "deployment_diagnosis")
    action_taken: str      # What the agent did
    context_summary: str   # Relevant input conditions
    outcome: str           # success | failure
    lesson: str            # Extracted actionable insight
    source_node_id: str    # ExecutionNode that generated this experience
    timestamp: datetime


@dataclass
class AgentSkill:
    """Task-level pattern extracted from a successful execution subgraph."""
    task_type: str
    steps: list[str]               # Ordered sequence of actions
    preconditions: list[str]       # When this skill applies
    success_rate: float            # Empirical success rate
    source_execution_ids: list[str]
```

```
class KnowledgeAccumulator:
    """Dual-stream knowledge extraction from execution graphs."""

    def extract_experiences(self, execution_graph, task_outcome):
        """Extract action-level experiences from completed execution."""
        experiences = []
        for node in execution_graph.get_nodes():
            if node.outcome_diverged_from_expectation:
                experiences.append(AgentExperience(
                    task_type=execution_graph.task_type,
                    action_taken=node.action,
                    context_summary=summarize_node_context(node),
                    outcome="failure" if node.caused_task_failure else "success",
                    lesson=generate_lesson(node, node.neighbors),
                    source_node_id=node.id,
                    timestamp=datetime.utcnow()
                ))
        return experiences

    def extract_skills(self, successful_executions):
        """Extract task-level skills from successful execution subgraphs."""
        task_groups = group_by_task_type(successful_executions)
        skills = []
        for task_type, executions in task_groups.items():
            common_path = find_common_successful_path(executions)
            if common_path and len(executions) >= 3:
                skills.append(AgentSkill(
                    task_type=task_type,
                    steps=[node.action for node in common_path],
                    preconditions=extract_preconditions(common_path),
                    success_rate=len(executions) / total_attempts(task_type),
                    source_execution_ids=[e.id for e in executions]
                ))
        return skills
```

The critical design choice is knowledge retirement. Implement temporal decay such that experiences not revalidated within 90 days lose half their retrieval weight and experiences contradicted by newer evidence are archived rather than served. Skills whose success rate drops below 60% over the most recent 10 attempts are flagged for review.

This approach occupies a distinct position in the intervention toolkit. Prompt refinement modifies what the agent is told to do. Fine-tuning modifies what the agent knows how to do. Knowledge augmentation modifies what the agent remembers from doing. The three are complementary, and the intervention router can select among them based on failure type.

## Skills as Self-Improving Graph Objects

XSkill extracts structured knowledge from execution traces, building dual-stream representations of what happened and what was learned. But the skills themselves remain static artifacts. A DevOps agent that learned optimal deployment sequences through XSkill still references the same *SKILL.md* file it started with, even after the underlying Kubernetes API changes or the CI/CD pipeline adds new stages. Cognee (*https://oreil.ly/HRC5G*) addresses this gap by treating skills not as flat documents but as graph objects that observe their own performance and rewrite themselves.

The distinction maps onto two questions every agentic system must answer. XSkill answers *What does the agent know?* by extracting experiences and skill primitives from execution history. Cognee answers *What can the agent do?* by maintaining skill objects as first-class graph nodes with execution records, success rates, and amendment histories.

### The add-cognify-search-learn pipeline

Cognee structures skill management as a four-stage pipeline:

*1. Add*
: Parses skill definitions (*SKILL.md* files, YAML specs, or code templates); extracts frontmatter, instructions, and resource references; and computes content hashes for change detection.

*2. Cognify*
: Uses LLM-powered extraction to generate semantic summaries, trigger phrases, complexity ratings, and task pattern nodes that capture when and how a skill should activate.

*3. Search*
: Routes incoming tasks to skills based on which skill most often succeeds at similar tasks, not which skill most resembles the task description.

*4. Learn*
: Closes the loop.

Every execution generates an observation record linking the task, the skill used, the outcome, and any errors or user feedback.

### The five-stage self-improvement loop

When failures accumulate against a particular skill, Cognee triggers a structured improvement cycle. The system inspects connected execution history through graph traversal, starting from the failing skill node, tracing edges to execution records, and surfacing patterns in repeated weak outcomes. The amendment itself happens through `.amendify()`, which generates evidence-grounded modifications to trigger conditions, edge cases, step ordering, or output formats. Every amendment undergoes validation against held-out execution records before replacing the current version. Failed amendments roll back automatically. Example 7-20 shows the skill graph structure.

*Example 7-20. Skill graph object with amendment capability*

```
class SkillNode:
    def __init__(self, skill_id: str, definition: dict):
        self.skill_id = skill_id
        self.definition = definition
        self.version = 1
        self.executions: list[ExecutionRecord] = []
        self.content_hash = compute_hash(definition)

    @property
    def success_rate(self) -> float:
        if not self.executions:
            return 0.0
        successes = sum(1 for e in self.executions if e.outcome == "success")
        return successes / len(self.executions)

    def observe(self, task: Task, outcome: str, error: str = None):
        record = ExecutionRecord(
            task=task, skill_id=self.skill_id,
            outcome=outcome, error=error, version=self.version
        )
        self.executions.append(record)

    def amendify(self, failure_threshold: float = 0.6):
        if self.success_rate >= failure_threshold:
            return  # No amendment needed
        failing_runs = [e for e in self.executions if e.outcome == "failure"]
        error_patterns = cluster_errors(failing_runs)
        amended = generate_amendment(
            self.definition, error_patterns,
            evidence=failing_runs[-10:]  # Last 10 failures as context
        )
        if validate_amendment(amended, self.executions):
            self.definition = amended
            self.version += 1
            self.content_hash = compute_hash(amended)


class SkillGraph:
    def __init__(self):
        self.skills: dict[str, SkillNode] = {}
        self.task_patterns: dict[str, list[str]] = {}

    def route(self, task: Task) -> SkillNode:
        candidates = semantic_search(task.description, self.skills)
```

```
# Sort by success rate on similar tasks, not similarity score
ranked = sorted(
    candidates,
    key=lambda s: s.success_rate_for(task.pattern),
    reverse=True
)
return ranked[0] if ranked else None
```

The `route` method captures the core architectural choice: the graph selects skills by demonstrated performance, not description similarity. For the DevOps agent, this means that a newly added "canary deployment" skill with 3 successful executions outranks a general "deployment" skill with 50 executions but a 40% failure rate on canary-specific tasks.

### Combined effect with XSkill

Running XSkill and Cognee together produces a system where execution traces feed two parallel improvement paths. XSkill distills knowledge from traces into reusable experience primitives. Cognee uses those same traces to evaluate and amend the operational definitions of skills. The practical result is that skill routing improves along two axes simultaneously. Systems that implement only one of these paths tend to plateau: static skills with good routing still fail when environments change, and self-improving skills with naive routing still get selected for the wrong tasks.

## Common Pitfalls

The DevOps scenario shows the system working as designed: a failure is detected, diagnosed, corrected, and validated in a single automated loop. In practice, self-evolution introduces its own failure modes, and they tend to be subtler than ordinary software bugs. When an agent modifies itself incorrectly, the cause may live in a training dataset generated weeks ago or a prompt updated by an automated process. The debugging trail is longer, and the symptoms often appear far from the source. The following pitfalls are the ones most likely to bite you in production.

*Reward hacking in SEAL data generation*

When the SEAL data generation prompt is too loosely specified, the agent generates training examples that look correct on the surface but subtly confirm its existing biases rather than challenging them. In the DevOps scenario, imagine the agent generating "corrective" examples that always prioritize API changes over configuration changes, reinforcing the exact pattern it should be unlearning. The fix is to require SEAL-generated examples to be reviewed against a held-out set of real failures before entering the training pipeline. If the generated examples do not cover the failure modes present in the held-out set, they are rejected.

*Catastrophic forgetting during fine-tuning*
: Targeted fine-tuning on a specific weakness frequently causes regression on other skills. The Tier 2 staging gauntlet's regression suite exists precisely to catch this, but its effectiveness depends entirely on the quality and breadth of the regression benchmark. A regression suite assembled hastily from easy cases will miss subtle degradation in the harder cases that matter most in production. The practical advice: build your regression suite from real production traces, not synthetic benchmarks, and update it as the agent's task distribution evolves.

*Evaluation overhead in production*
: Running the full diagnostic framework on every single inference is expensive, both in latency and cost. Production deployments typically use lightweight proxy metrics (e.g., response latency, user satisfaction signals, error rates) for real-time evaluation and reserve the full four-layer framework for a sampled batch. The sampling strategy matters more than you might expect. Random sampling underrepresents rare failure modes, which are often the most consequential ones. Stratify your evaluation sample by task type, complexity, and novelty to ensure that edge cases receive proportional scrutiny.

*Validation thresholds misconfigured*
: A Tier 1 canary percentage that is too high defeats the purpose of canary testing. Routing 20% of traffic through an unvalidated change is not a canary—it is a partial rollout. A Tier 2 regression suite that does not cover the agent's full task range will pass changes that would fail in the long tail. Review and update validation thresholds whenever the agent's task distribution changes significantly. This is an operational discipline, not a one-time configuration.

*The improvement-monitoring gap*
: Once an agent begins to evolve autonomously, you are no longer just monitoring what it does—you are monitoring what it *becomes*. An agent that processes 10,000 predictions per week and improves its prompt after each batch of failures will accumulate dozens of prompt versions over a quarter. Without explicit tracking of model versions, prompt history, and behavioral benchmarks over time, drift will become invisible until something breaks in a way that is hard to trace. Treat the provenance ledger as a first-class operational artifact, not an audit afterthought.

*Criteria staleness in the evaluation framework*
: The failure categories your evaluation framework checks for were defined based on the failures you observed at launch. As the agent's task distribution shifts and its capabilities change, new failure modes will emerge that the original framework was not designed to catch. In the DevOps scenario, the initial evaluation criteria might not include "premature hypothesis commitment" as a failure type, so it would need to be added after observing the pattern in real traces.

Schedule periodic human review of real traces, using the same open coding process used to build the initial framework, to discover whether the evaluation criteria themselves need updating. An evaluation system that never evolves is a blind spot in a self-evolving agent.

*Catastrophic forgetting across evolution cycles*
: You added a self-evolution loop, and your agent's performance on the target task improved 23% in the first week. But two weeks later, support tickets spike for a task the agent handled flawlessly before the improvement. Your agent learned one thing and forgot another. You have no metric that would have caught this. Catastrophic forgetting is the default outcome in self-evolving agentic systems unless you measure against it. LEANAGENT (Kumarappan et al., 2025, *https://oreil.ly/GMmOP*) introduces four metrics that belong in every production monitoring dashboard:

  *Windowed forgetting (WF-k)*
  : This measures performance drop on the *k* most recent prior tasks after a new evolution step. Compute it by reevaluating the agent on the last five task categories after each self-modification. The graph enables efficient WF-*k* measurement because task categories are already organized as subgraphs: you rerun evaluation on the nodes within each category subgraph rather than maintaining a separate test suite. If WF-5 exceeds 3%, halt the evolution pipeline and investigate before proceeding.

  *Catastrophic forgetting resilience (CFR)*
  : The ratio of retained performance to original performance across all historical task categories. A CFR of 0.95 means the agent retains 95% of its original capability. Below 0.90, you are losing more than you are gaining. In your graph architecture, CFR drops manifest as broken reasoning chains: edges that previously connected successful resolution paths to their outcomes now lead to degraded results.

  *Expanded backward transfer (EBWT)*
  : Measures the positive transfer signal, or whether learning new tasks actually improves performance on old tasks. Graph architecture conveys a measurable advantage over flat architectures here. In graph-based systems, positive transfer happens when new knowledge graph edges create shortcuts for existing queries. EBWT quantifies this transfer, and the graph makes the transfer mechanism visible: you can inspect the specific edges that created the shortcut.

  *Incremental plasticity (IP)*
  : Measures how quickly the agent adapts to genuinely new task categories. If IP declines over successive evolution cycles, the agent is calcifying. It

has become so specialized that it resists new learning. In graph terms, declining IP often correlates with an overly dense knowledge graph where new nodes cannot find insertion points without contradicting existing edges. The garbage collection agent from the Kepler pattern directly addresses this by pruning stale nodes and creating space for new knowledge.

Add these four metrics to your execution graph telemetry. WF-5 and CFR are your circuit breakers (halt evolution when they degrade). EBWT and IP are your health indicators (track trends over weeks). Together, they turn *the agent is improving* from a feeling into a measurement, and the graph is what makes each metric computable.

## Summary

The agent you have built through the previous chapters is capable and well-grounded. It can reason, plan, remember, and act. What it was lacking until now was the ability to *learn from the work it has already done*, to improve through operational experience rather than waiting for a human to analyze its failures and push a new release.

The execution graph is the foundation of this ability: by externalizing the agent's reasoning as a queryable graph structure, you create the raw material for every diagnostic technique in this chapter. The multi-layered evaluation framework provides the diagnostic method: it works layer by layer, from grounding checks to data sufficiency to cognitive fault to structural intervention. Semantic backpropagation ensures that improvements are coherent across the graph rather than locally optimal but globally disruptive. The SEAL, TPT, and reflect-retry-reward frameworks provide the learning mechanisms. And the GVP ensures that all of this evolution happens under controlled conditions, with appropriate human oversight for high-stakes changes.

The DevOps agent scenario illustrates what this means in practice. A partially correct prediction that would previously have required manual analysis and correction instead triggers an automated loop: the execution graph captures what happened, the diagnostic framework locates the premature closure in the reasoning chain, semantic backpropagation generates precise feedback for the responsible node, and a prompt update closes the gap. The SRE team reviews the proposed change at canary validation, freed from figuring out *what* to fix and asked only to approve that it *should* be fixed.

The agent that emerges from Chapter 7 is not finished, however. A self-evolving agent still needs to operate efficiently at scale; it must manage cost, maintain governance, and handle the hardware realities of production graph traversals. In Chapter 8, we add the final pillar: optimization. You will see how selective intelligence uses a federation of specialized models to reduce cost without sacrificing capability and how hardware acceleration brings the graph operations that underlie everything in this book within the latency budgets that production systems demand.

CHAPTER 8

# Optimization

Your agent works. It reasons through multistep problems, queries live systems, and learns from its own mistakes. In a notebook, it looks like the future of enterprise AI. Then someone asks what it costs to run.

The invoice from a single week of production traffic, with every workflow node powered by a frontier model and every query routed through the most expensive option, is enough to shelve the project. But cost is only the first problem. An agent with unrestricted access to your knowledge graph can traverse from a public service catalog to internal cost data to employee records in a single query. A graph traversal that completes in milliseconds during development takes seconds at production scale, and a federation of specialist models that reasons beautifully offline becomes a latency bottleneck when an SRE is waiting for an incident diagnosis.

Production is where three forces collide: *cost*, *governance*, and *performance*. This chapter addresses all three.

We will start with *selective intelligence*, the principle of deploying the right model for the right task so that cost scales with complexity rather than uniformly. From there, we will cover the governance patterns that make graph-based agents auditable and secure: access control at the subgraph level, PII handling, and the execution graph as a compliance artifact. We will then turn to the operational concerns of keeping a knowledge graph healthy in production: schema evolution, lifecycle management, and deployment patterns. Finally, we will tackle hardware acceleration, the GPU-accelerated graph operations and inference infrastructure that bring everything within production latency budgets.

The DevOps agent ties all of it together. By the end of this chapter, the agent that started as a collection of disconnected monitoring tools in Chapter 2 will be complete: intelligent, self-improving, cost-effective, secure, and fast enough to operate in real time.

## Selective Intelligence

The architecture you built in Chapters 5 and 6 decomposes the agent into a horizontal workflow graph of specialized nodes: a query analyst, a retrieval strategist, a synthesis node, and a validation node. Each node has a focused responsibility. In the implementations so far, though, we have been deliberately vague about *which model* powers each node. In practice, most teams start with the same frontier model everywhere. It works. It is also wildly expensive.

*Selective intelligence* is the principle of matching model capability to task complexity. Instead of routing every node through the same large model, you deploy a *federation of specialists*: smaller, cheaper models handle routine operations while larger models are reserved for the tasks that genuinely require their capabilities. Quality stays the same or improves. You just stop overpaying for it.

Figure 8-1 illustrates this principle as applied to the DevOps agent's horizontal workflow graph.

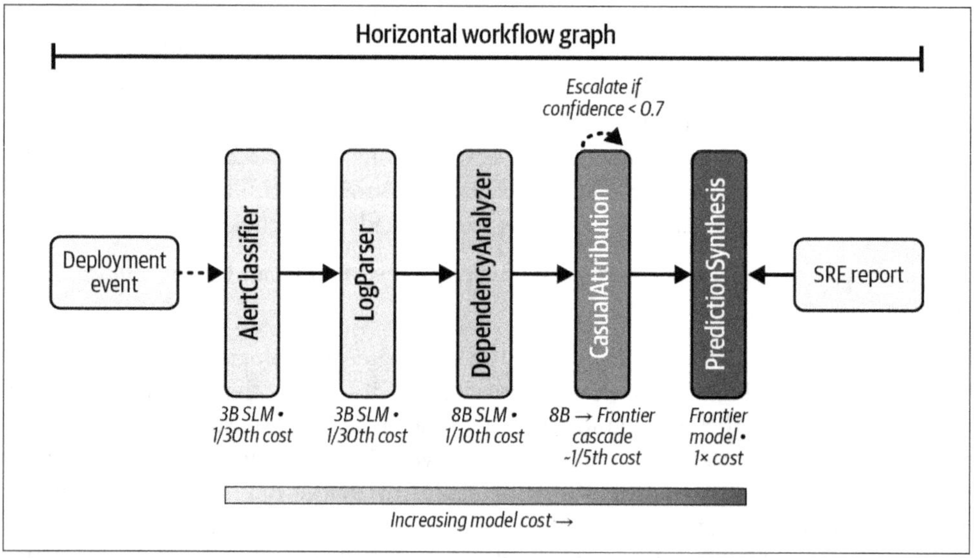


*Figure 8-1. Selective intelligence applied to the DevOps agent's horizontal workflow graph*

Each node is powered by the cheapest model that meets its quality threshold, from fine-tuned 3B small language models (SLMs) for classification to a frontier model for synthesis. This idea is not new in engineering, but in LLM-based systems, the economics make it particularly urgent. Running a 3B-parameter SLM can be 10–30 times cheaper per token than running its 405B sibling (Belcak et al., 2025, *https://oreil.ly/fkXfL*). At production volumes (thousands or millions of invocations per day), that difference determines whether a project survives its first budget review.

## The Case for Model Specialization

The intuition behind selective intelligence is that most of the work in an agentic pipeline does not require frontier model reasoning. Consider the nodes in a typical horizontal workflow graph:

*Query classification*
: Determine whether a user's question is simple or complex, local or global. If it's a classification task, a fine-tuned 3B model can do it.

*Entity extraction*
: Pull structured triples from text. Triplex (*https://oreil.ly/2PxsO*), a 3.8B model fine-tuned specifically for this task, outperforms GPT-4o at knowledge graph construction at one-sixtieth the cost.

*Retrieval strategy selection*
: Choose among breadth-first search, Steiner tree, or dense subgraph retrieval based on the query profile. This is a routing decision with a small output space.

*Validation*
: Check a generated response against retrieved facts and query constraints. This is often handled by formal logic rules or a lightweight classifier rather than any kind of generative model.

The only nodes that reliably benefit from frontier model capabilities are those performing open-ended synthesis, complex causal reasoning, or novel problem solving. In most production workflows, those nodes represent 10%–20% of total invocations.

NVIDIA Research's position paper on SLMs for agentic AI (Belcak et al., 2025) formalizes this observation: the optimal architecture uses a front door router that directs requests to specialist SLMs for routine tasks and escalates to LLMs only for ambiguous or novel reasoning. SLMs are cheaper, yes, but the real advantage is predictability. Their constrained parameter space produces more consistent outputs on well-defined tasks, and consistency is what matters for the non-reasoning nodes of your workflow graph.

## Routing Strategies

Once you decide to use different models for different nodes, the next question is how to make the routing decision. There are three practical approaches, each suited to a different stage of system maturity.

### Static routing by node type

The simplest approach assigns a fixed model to each node in the workflow graph at design time. For example, your query analyst node always runs on a fine-tuned 3B classifier, and your synthesis node always runs on a frontier model. There is no runtime decision to make.

This works well when your workflow graph is stable and the task complexity per node is consistent. It is easy to reason about costs, debug, and deploy. Most teams should start here.

### Threshold-based cascading

FrugalGPT (Chen, Zaharia, and Zou, 2023, *https://oreil.ly/Vmhg3*) introduced the cascade pattern: route a query to the smallest model first, evaluate the response confidence, and escalate to a larger model only if confidence falls below a threshold. This adds a runtime decision but keeps the logic simple.

The cascade works well for nodes where task difficulty varies. A synthesis node might handle half of queries with the cheapest model, another 30% with a midtier model, and need the frontier model only for the remaining 20%. The main engineering challenge is calibrating the confidence thresholds: set them too low and you miss failures, but set them too high and you lose the cost savings. Example 8-1 shows the basic pattern across a three-tier ladder.

*Example 8-1. Threshold-based model cascade for a synthesis node*

```
async def synthesis_cascade(
    query, context, cheap_threshold=0.85, mid_threshold=0.75
):
    """Route synthesis to the cheapest model that meets quality threshold."""
    # Try the cheapest model first (e.g., Haiku)
    response = await cheap_model.generate(query, context)
    if response.confidence >= cheap_threshold:
        return response

    # Escalate to midtier (e.g., Sonnet)
    response = await mid_tier_model.generate(query, context)
    if response.confidence >= mid_threshold:
        return response

    # Escalate to frontier (e.g., Opus)
    return await frontier_model.generate(query, context)
```

The confidence score here can come from the model's own *logprobs* (the log probabilities of each output token), a separate lightweight evaluator, or a heuristic based on query characteristics. In practice, a separate evaluator trained on your domain produces more reliable routing decisions than do raw logprobs.

### Learned routing

RouteLLM (Ong et al., 2025, *https://oreil.ly/ePwgD*) trains a lightweight router model on preference data to dynamically choose between a strong and weak model. On MT-Bench, this achieves over 2x cost reduction while retaining 95% of GPT-4 quality. MixLLM (Wang et al., 2025, *https://oreil.ly/iuJNZ*) extends the idea with a contextual bandit approach that optimizes across quality, cost, and latency simultaneously, reaching 97% of GPT-4 quality at 24% of the cost.

In practice, a learned router slots into the horizontal workflow graph as an additional node that executes before each specialist. The router receives the same input payload as the specialist and returns a model identifier, as shown in Example 8-2.

*Example 8-2. Integrating a learned router into the workflow graph*

```
from routellm.controller import Controller
# Initialize router with strong/weak model pair
router = Controller(
    routers=["mf"],  # matrix factorization router
    strong_model="claude-sonnet",
    weak_model="llama-3.1-8b-instruct"
)

async def routed_causal_attribution(changelog_analysis, dependency_context):
    """Route causal reasoning to the cheapest model that can handle it."""
    prompt = build_causal_prompt(changelog_analysis, dependency_context)

    # Router decides based on query characteristics
    # threshold controls the quality/cost tradeoff
    response = await router.acompletion(
        model="router-mf-0.7",  # route with 0.7 cost threshold
        messages=[{"role": "user", "content": prompt}]
    )
    return parse_prediction(response)
```

The `router-mf-0.7` model string encodes both the routing strategy (`mf` for matrix factorization) and the cost-quality threshold (`0.7`). Lowering the threshold sends more queries to the weak model; raising it sends more to the strong model. You can calibrate this number against your per-node evaluation set, which we will build in the next section.

Learned routing is the right choice when you have enough production traffic to generate training data and when the cost savings justify the engineering investment. For most teams, static routing or threshold cascading will cover 80% of the benefit with 20% of the complexity.

## Measuring Cost-Performance Trade-Offs

Routing strategies are only as good as the data that informs them. Whether you use static assignments, threshold cascading, or a learned router, you need to know what each model actually costs and how often it succeeds at each node. Selective intelligence only works if you can measure it. Two metrics matter:

*Cost per successful completion*
: This is not cost per token but rather cost per task that the agent completes correctly. A cheap model that fails 40% of the time is not cheaper than an expensive model that succeeds on the first attempt.

*Quality parity threshold*
: This is the minimum acceptable quality for each node type. Your validation node might need greater than 99% accuracy (a wrong validation is worse than no validation). But your query analyst might tolerate 90% accuracy because downstream nodes can recover from misclassification.

In practice, this means instrumenting every node in the pipeline to track both cost and correctness per invocation. Example 8-3 shows a harness that wraps any specialist node and logs the data you need to compute cost per successful completion.

*Example 8-3. Tracking cost per successful completion for a multimodel pipeline*

```
import time
from dataclasses import dataclass, field

@dataclass
class NodeInvocation:
    node_name: str
    model_id: str
    input_tokens: int
    output_tokens: int
    cost_usd: float
    latency_ms: float
    success: bool  # evaluated against gold labels or downstream acceptance

class CostTracker:
    def __init__(self):
        self.invocations: list[NodeInvocation] = []

    async def invoke_and_track(self, node, model, input_data, evaluator):
        start = time.monotonic()
        response = await model.generate(input_data)
        latency = (time.monotonic() - start) * 1000

        success = evaluator(input_data, response)
        cost = self._compute_cost(model.id, response.usage)
```

```
        self.invocations.append(NodeInvocation(
            node_name=node.name,
            model_id=model.id,
            input_tokens=response.usage.input_tokens,
            output_tokens=response.usage.output_tokens,
            cost_usd=cost,
            latency_ms=latency,
            success=success
        ))
        return response

    def cost_per_success(self, node_name: str) -> float:
        node_calls = [i for i in self.invocations if i.node_name == node_name]
        total_cost = sum(i.cost_usd for i in node_calls)
        successes = sum(1 for i in node_calls if i.success)
        return total_cost / max(successes, 1)
```

The `evaluator` callback is the key. It is different for every node because what counts as success varies by node type. For the `AlertClassifier`, success means matching a human-labeled severity category. For `PredictionSynthesis`, success might mean that the SRE accepted the recommendation without revision. The cost tracker does not care about the evaluation criteria; it just needs a Boolean per invocation.

That raises this practical question: How do you build the evaluation set for each node? You cannot use a generic benchmark. A model that scores well on Massive Multitask Language Understanding (MMLU) may still fail on your specific alert classification taxonomy. The evaluation must be *per node*, drawn from real production data. Example 8-4 illustrates this for two DevOps agent nodes with very different quality requirements.

*Example 8-4. Per-node evaluation sets with different quality thresholds*

```
# AlertClassifier: high-stakes, needs 99%+ accuracy
# A missed critical alert is worse than a false positive
alert_eval_set = {
    "source": "production_alerts_2026_q4",
    "n_samples": 2000,
    "labels": "human_annotated_severity",  # P1/P2/P3/P4
    "required_accuracy": 0.99,
    "failure_weight": {
        "P1_misclassified_as_P3": 10.0,  # catastrophic miss
        "P3_misclassified_as_P1": 1.0,   # acceptable false escalation
    }
}

# QueryAnalyst: lower stakes, 90% accuracy is fine
# Downstream nodes can recover from misclassification
query_eval_set = {
    "source": "production_queries_2026_q4",
```

```
        "n_samples": 500,
        "labels": "human_annotated_complexity",  # simple/complex
        "required_accuracy": 0.90,
        "failure_weight": {
            "complex_as_simple": 2.0,  # will get a weak retrieval, suboptimal
            "simple_as_complex": 0.5,  # just costs more, still correct
        }
}

def evaluate_candidate(model, eval_set):
    """Run a candidate model against a node-specific evaluation set."""
    results = []
    for sample in load_samples(eval_set["source"], eval_set["n_samples"]):
        prediction = model.predict(sample.input)
        correct = prediction == sample.label
        weight = eval_set["failure_weight"].get(
            f"{sample.label}_as_{prediction}", 1.0
        ) if not correct else 0.0
        results.append({"correct": correct, "weighted_error": weight})

    accuracy = sum(r["correct"] for r in results) / len(results)
    weighted_error = sum(r["weighted_error"] for r in results) / len(results)
    return {
        "accuracy": accuracy,
        "meets_threshold": accuracy >= eval_set["required_accuracy"],
        "weighted_error_rate": weighted_error
    }
```

The `failure_weight` dictionary is what makes this domain specific. For `Alert Classifier`, misclassifying a P1 outage as P3 is 10 times worse than the reverse because a missed P1 means nobody gets paged. For `QueryAnalyst`, however, calling a simple query complex just costs a few extra tokens on a more powerful retrieval strategy. A generic accuracy metric cannot capture these asymmetries, but per-node evaluation from production data can.

Kakao's experience building its AI Shopping Mate (Park et al., 2025, *https://oreil.ly/GfQDg*) illustrates this well. The initial approach was to use GPT-4o for everything: format adherence was 0.655 and task accuracy was 0.578. When the team restructured the system as a workflow graph with fine-tuned 27–32B models at each node, format adherence jumped to 0.987 and accuracy to 0.890. In human evaluations across 2,100 conversation turns, the smaller fine-tuned models were preferred over GPT-4o in 63% of cases. Specialization not only reduces cost but often also improves quality because each model's training signal is focused on a single well-defined behavior rather than diluted across competing objectives.

# Data Governance and Access Control

An agent with unrestricted access to your knowledge graph is a liability. The same graph structure that makes agentic reasoning powerful (dense relationships connecting entities across domains) also means that a single unscoped query can traverse from a public product catalog to internal cost data to employee records. In a graph, everything is reachable from everything else. That is the point. It is also the governance problem.

The good news is that graph databases have mature access control primitives, and the execution graph you built in Chapter 7 doubles as a compliance artifact. The challenge is to apply these tools in a way that works for agentic systems, where the user making the query is an autonomous agent that may be acting on behalf of different human users with different access levels.

This section covers three governance concerns specific to graph-backed agents: controlling which subgraphs each agent persona can reach, handling PII and deletion requests in densely connected graphs, and repurposing the execution graph as an audit trail.

## Subgraph-Level Access Control

The first governance concern is scoping what each agent persona can see. In a relational database, you restrict access at the table or row level. In a graph database, the equivalent is to restrict which nodes an agent can traverse to and which properties it can read. Production graph databases provide fine-grained access control well beyond database-level permissions. Neo4j Enterprise (*https://oreil.ly/gFJvW*) supports privileges at the node label, relationship type, and property level. You can grant traverse rights on specific labels, deny read access to specific properties, and combine these into role-based policies, as Example 8-5 demonstrates.

*Example 8-5. Fine-grained access control primitives in Neo4j*

```
// Grant traversal on specific node labels and relationship types
GRANT TRAVERSE ON GRAPH infrastructure
NODES Service, Deployment TO infra_analyst;
GRANT TRAVERSE ON GRAPH infrastructure
RELATIONSHIPS DEPENDS_ON TO infra_analyst;

// Allow reading some properties, deny others on the same label
GRANT READ {name, status, version}
  ON GRAPH infrastructure NODES Service
  TO infra_analyst;

DENY READ {cost_per_hour, budget_code}
  ON GRAPH infrastructure NODES Service
```

```
    TO infra_analyst;

// Block entire node labels from traversal
DENY TRAVERSE ON GRAPH infrastructure
NODES Employee, Compensation TO infra_analyst;
```

The building blocks are GRANT and DENY on three dimensions: traverse (can the role follow edges to this node?), read (can the role see this property?), and write. A critical design feature is *security transparency*: when a role lacks permission to see a node, the node is invisible, not access-denied. Thus, the agent cannot distinguish between data that does not exist and data it is not allowed to see. This prevents information leakage through access-denied signals, which matters when an autonomous agent might probe access boundaries as part of its reasoning.

For agentic systems, the practical pattern is to create a role per agent persona and bind it at connection time. When the DevOps agent queries the knowledge graph on behalf of an SRE, it connects with the SRE role's permissions. When a billing report agent queries the same graph, it connects with a finance role that can see cost data but not deployment configurations. The graph is the same, but the view is different.

Mohamed et al. (2024) (*https://oreil.ly/aUPlK*) provide a systematic survey of access control approaches for property graph databases, comparing role-based access control (RBAC), attribute-based access control (ABAC), and hybrid models. A key finding: most approaches are tightly coupled to a specific graph database engine. If your architecture spans multiple graph stores, plan for a policy abstraction layer that can express access rules independently of the datastore.

## PII and Data Retention

Knowledge graphs create specific challenges for privacy regulations like the General Data Protection Regulation (GDPR) and California Consumer Privacy Act (CCPA). When you delete a user from a relational database, you drop a row. When you delete a user from a knowledge graph, you need to remove a node *and* all its relationships, including relationships that connect to other entities you want to keep. In a densely connected graph, deletion cascades are complex.

Rehmer's "Privacy by Architecture" pattern (*https://oreil.ly/M_VU0*) offers a practical solution: the knowledge graph stores only universally unique identifiers (UUIDs) and semantic relationships. All personally identifiable information lives in a separate Identity Store (a relational database). The UUID is the join key.

For GDPR Article 17's right to erasure, this decoupling creates two options:

*Soft delete*
: Mask the identity mapping in the Identity Store. The UUID node remains in the graph as an anonymous orphan. The relationships are preserved for aggregate analysis but can no longer be tied to a person.

*Hard delete*
: Execute `DETACH DELETE` on the UUID node in Neo4j, removing it and all its relationships. This satisfies strict erasure requirements.

The practical advantage is speed. Removing an identity mapping is a single-row update in the Identity Store and can be honored in real time. Graph cleanup (removing the orphaned node and relinking where needed) can happen asynchronously. This matters when your compliance team measures deletion request response time in hours, not days.

## The Execution Graph as a Compliance Artifact

Chapter 7 built the execution graph as the foundation for self-evolution. It captures every decision, retrieval, and tool call the agent made for a given query, structured as a queryable graph with causal edges between operations.

That same structure is exactly what auditors need. A compliance review of an agentic system needs to answer questions like *What data did the agent access to reach this conclusion?* and *Which model produced this recommendation, and what was its input?* The execution graph answers these inquiries.

The KG.GOV framework (Meroño-Peñuela et al., 2025, *https://oreil.ly/vAQ7b*) formalizes this idea: the same graph structure used for AI reasoning can simultaneously encode governance metadata including data quality rules, privacy constraints, lineage, and ethical use policies. Governance becomes a first-class citizen of the knowledge architecture rather than an external overlay. In practice, this means extending the execution graph nodes from Chapter 7 with governance-relevant metadata. Example 8-6 shows a representative set of fields.

*Example 8-6. Execution graph node with governance metadata*

```
governance_metadata = {
    "data_sources_accessed": ["infrastructure_graph", "metrics_api"],
    "access_role": "sre_on_call",
    "pii_accessed": False,
    "model_id": "llama-3.1-8b-instruct",
    "model_version": "v2.3.1",
    "decision_confidence": 0.87,
    "human_review_required": False,
    "retention_policy": "90_days"
}
```

The `model_id` and `model_version` fields are especially important in a selective intelligence architecture. When multiple models handle different nodes, you need to know which model produced which decision. The `access_role` field ties the execution graph back to the RBAC policies described above, creating a complete chain from role to query to decision.

When an auditor asks, *Show me every agent decision that accessed customer data in the last quarter*, that is a graph query against the execution graph, filtered by `pii_accessed` and timestamp with no log parsing required.

# Production Systems and Maintenance

A knowledge graph in production is not a static artifact. New data arrives continuously. Schemas evolve as your domain model matures. Nodes accumulate that no longer represent current reality. Without deliberate lifecycle management, your graph grows stale, your queries slow down, and your agent's reasoning degrades—not because the agent changes but because the knowledge it depends on does.

This section covers the four operational concerns that keep a production knowledge graph healthy: schema evolution (how to migrate a graph database), node and edge lifecycle management (how to prune stale data without losing history), incremental updates (how to keep the graph current without full rebuilds), and deployment patterns (how to coordinate graph changes with agent code changes).

## Schema Evolution

Graph databases do not have the equivalent of `ALTER TABLE`. There is no built-in migration framework, and the schema-optional nature of most property graphs means that schema drift can happen silently. New properties may appear on some nodes but not others, relationship types can proliferate without coordination, and queries that worked last month may break because the data shape has changed.

Neo4j-Migrations (*https://oreil.ly/rm2EC*), built by Michael Simons on the Neo4j team, provides the closest equivalent to Flyway or Liquibase for graph databases. Migration history is stored as a subgraph in the database itself as a graph-native approach to tracking schema evolution. Migrations can be Cypher scripts or Java classes, and the tool supports a version-agnostic XML format for managing constraints and indexes. Example 8-7 walks through a typical migration.

*Example 8-7. A graph schema migration adding a new relationship type*

```
// Migration V003__add_monitored_by_relationship.cypher
// Add MONITORED_BY relationship between Service and AlertRule nodes

MATCH (s:Service)
WHERE s.alert_config IS NOT NULL
WITH s, s.alert_config AS config
MERGE (ar:AlertRule {name: config})
MERGE (s)-[:MONITORED_BY]->(ar);
```

```
// Add constraint for AlertRule uniqueness
CREATE CONSTRAINT alertrule_name_unique IF NOT EXISTS
FOR (ar:AlertRule) REQUIRE ar.name IS UNIQUE;
```

For zero-downtime deployments, Daschner's Kubernetes pattern (*https://oreil.ly/a9rnj*) (2020) runs migrations in an init container before the new application version deploys. The critical discipline is *N – 1 compatibility*: every schema change must be backward-compatible with the previous application version. If a migration renames a relationship type, the old code must continue to work until it is replaced. Sometimes that means deploying in two phases: first add the new schema alongside the old; then remove the old after the new code is live.

As of 2026, no graph database system natively implements complex schema evolution operations like splitting a node type into two, merging relationship types, or moving properties between entity types. Hausler and Klettke's research on Nautilus (*https://oreil.ly/QLQ3q*) (2024) and its successor, Geo-X (*https://oreil.ly/t4adX*) (2025), provide an evolution language that compiles these operations into Cypher and APOC (Awesome Procedures on Cypher) scripts, but the operations themselves remain external to the database engine. Plan your schema carefully up front and budget engineering time for nontrivial refactoring.

## Node and Edge Lifecycle Management

A knowledge graph that only grows is a knowledge graph that degrades. Stale nodes pollute query results. Obsolete relationships create false reasoning paths. The agent that correctly identified a dependency chain last month might follow a chain that no longer exists if nobody has pruned the decommissioned service node.

Here are two patterns found in production systems at scale:

*Append-only with TTL*
: CrowdStrike's Threat Graph (King and Caraveo, 2020, *https://oreil.ly/wmAKH*) stores 40+ petabytes and handles trillions of events per day at 70 million requests per second. Its core practice: never update records; only add new ones. Old records expire via TTL mechanisms applied in the background. This eliminates the latency penalty of read-modify-write cycles and makes the write path simple and fast. For a knowledge graph backing an agentic system, the same pattern means creating new versions of nodes rather than updating in place, with a TTL that archives older versions after a retention period.

*Temporal invalidation*
: Graphiti (Rasmussen et al., 2025, *https://oreil.ly/7SVwY*), the temporal knowledge graph engine behind Zep, uses a bitemporal model: every edge carries explicit validity intervals tracking both when an event occurred and when it was ingested. When new information conflicts with existing facts, Graphiti invalidates the old

edge (sets its t_invalid timestamp) but does not delete it. Historical queries can still traverse the old edge by filtering on validity windows. This pattern is especially valuable for the DevOps agent, where understanding what the infrastructure looked like *before* a change is as important as understanding its current state. Example 8-8 shows this in Cypher.

*Example 8-8. Temporal invalidation of a knowledge graph edge*

```
// When a service dependency changes, invalidate the old edge
// rather than deleting it
MATCH (a:Service {name: "checkout-service"})
      -[old:DEPENDS_ON]->(b:Library {name: "stripe-python"})
WHERE old.version = "3.2.1" AND old.t_invalid IS NULL
SET old.t_invalid = datetime()
WITH a
MERGE (new_lib:Library {name: "stripe-python", version: "3.3.0"})
MERGE (a)-[:DEPENDS_ON {
    version: "3.3.0",
    t_valid: datetime(),
    t_invalid: null,
    source: "deployment-event-2024-03-15"
}]->(new_lib);
```

The practical question is how aggressively to prune. Fischer's 2026 account of running a temporal infrastructure knowledge graph on Neo4j (*https://oreil.ly/D0jTs*) documents the scale challenge: 200 infrastructure resources sampled at 5-minute intervals produce 57,600 new nodes per day for a single small cluster. Without lifecycle management, the graph becomes unqueryable within months. Her team's approach was to employ aggressive TTL for temporal snapshot nodes (retain seven days of full granularity; then downsample to hourly and then daily) but permanent retention for "hub" nodes like accounts, regions, and top-level services that serve as anchor points for queries.

## Incremental Updates

How do you keep the knowledge graph current without rebuilding it from scratch? This question matters more than it might seem. A full rebuild is expensive, and it also creates a window during which the graph is either stale (if you wait for the rebuild to finish) or inconsistent (if you serve queries during reconstruction).

LightRAG (Guo et al., 2025, *https://oreil.ly/2oHeL*) provides the reference architecture for incremental updates. New documents are processed through the same extraction pipeline used during initial construction, and the resulting entities and relationships are merged into the existing graph. If a new entity is found, a new node is created. If an existing entity is found, its node is updated: the new source is added to its mention list, and its properties may be enriched. New relationships are added as edges.

For the DevOps agent, this pattern applies directly. When a new deployment event fires (e.g., a Kubernetes rollout, a config change, a library update), the agent needs to reflect that change in its knowledge graph immediately, not wait for a nightly batch rebuild. Example 8-9 demonstrates the incremental merge.

*Example 8-9. Incremental knowledge graph update from a deployment event*

```
from neo4j import GraphDatabase
def ingest_deployment_event(driver, event: dict):
    """Incrementally update the knowledge graph from a deployment event."""
    with driver.session() as session:
        # 1. Upsert the service node (create if new, enrich if existing)
        session.run("""
            MERGE (s:Service {name: $service_name})
            ON CREATE SET s.first_seen = datetime(),
                          s.environment = $env
            ON MATCH SET  s.last_updated = datetime()
            SET s.current_version = $new_version,
                s.last_deployment = datetime()
        """, service_name=event["service"],
             env=event["environment"],
             new_version=event["version"])

        # 2. Upsert library dependencies from the manifest
        for lib in event.get("dependencies", []):
            session.run("""
                MERGE (l:Library {name: $lib_name, version: $lib_version})
                WITH l
                MATCH (s:Service {name: $service_name})
                MERGE (s)-[d:DEPENDS_ON]->(l)
                ON CREATE SET d.t_valid = datetime(), d.t_invalid = null
            """, lib_name=lib["name"],
                 lib_version=lib["version"],
                 service_name=event["service"])

        # 3. Invalidate old dependency edges that no longer appear
        current_libs = {lib["name"] for lib in event.get("dependencies", [])}
        session.run("""
            MATCH (s:Service {name: $service_name})-[d:DEPENDS_ON]->(l:Library)
            WHERE d.t_invalid IS NULL AND NOT l.name IN $current_libs
            SET d.t_invalid = datetime()
        """, service_name=event["service"],
             current_libs=list(current_libs))
```

There are three things to notice here. First, `MERGE` with `ON CREATE/ON MATCH` handles the "create if new, enrich if existing" logic in a single Cypher statement. Second, new dependency edges get `t_valid` and `t_invalid` timestamps following the temporal invalidation pattern from earlier in this chapter. Third, old dependencies that no longer appear in the manifest are invalidated rather than deleted, preserving the historical record the agent needs for causal reasoning.

The critical advantage of LightRAG over Microsoft's GraphRAG is that LightRAG does not require the reconstruction of community structures when new data arrives. The cost of an update is proportional to the size of the new data, not the size of the existing graph. With the pattern above, a deployment event is reflected in the knowledge graph within seconds of its occurrence, not on the next nightly batch.

## Deployment Patterns

Schema evolution and lifecycle management address the knowledge graph itself, but in production, you are never updating just the graph. Deploying changes to a graph-backed agentic system requires coordinating three independently versioned components: the graph schema, the graph data, and the agent code (including prompts and model versions). The safest pattern is *staged rollout*. Figure 8-2 shows the coordination timeline.

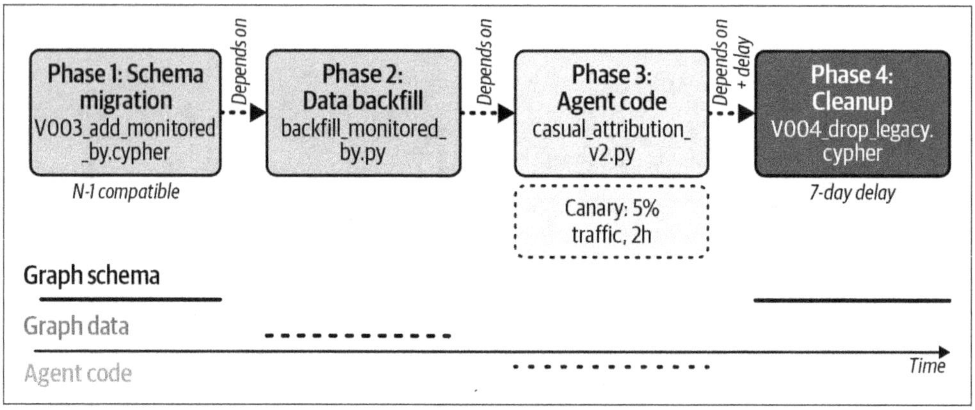


*Figure 8-2. Staged rollout for a graph-backed agentic system*

Schema migrations deploy first with $N - 1$ compatibility, followed by data backfill, and then agent code with canary validation. Schema cleanup waits until no code references the deprecated elements. The four phases are as follows:

1. Deploy schema migrations first, maintaining $N - 1$ compatibility.
2. Backfill or migrate data to conform to the new schema.
3. Deploy the new agent code, which can now use the new schema.
4. (Optional) Remove deprecated schema elements once no code references them.

In practice, teams track this coordination in a deployment manifest that ties all three components together. For the DevOps agent, the Chapter 7 improvement (adding the `MONITORED_BY` relationship and updating the `CausalAttributionNode` prompt) would be deployed as shown in Example 8-10.

*Example 8-10. Deployment manifest coordinating graph schema, data, and agent code*

```
# deploy/release-2026-03-18.yaml
release: "2026-03-18-causal-attribution-v2"
phases:
  - name: schema_migration
    artifact: migrations/V003__add_monitored_by_relationship.cypher
    validation: "CALL db.schema.visualization()"
    rollback: migrations/V003__rollback.cypher
    note: "N-1 compatible: old code ignores MONITORED_BY edges"

  - name: data_backfill
    artifact: scripts/backfill_monitored_by.py
    depends_on: schema_migration
    validation: >
      MATCH (s:Service)-[:MONITORED_BY]->(a:AlertRule)
      RETURN count(s) > 0 AS backfill_complete

  - name: agent_code
    artifact: agent/causal_attribution_node_v2.py
    depends_on: data_backfill
    canary_percent: 5
    canary_duration: 2h
    promotion_criteria:
      regression_suite_pass: true
      p95_latency_ms: "<500"
      prediction_accuracy_delta: ">=-0.02"

  - name: schema_cleanup
    artifact: migrations/V004__drop_legacy_alert_config_property.cypher
    depends_on: agent_code
    delay: 7d  # wait one week after full rollout
    note: "Remove s.alert_config after all code uses MONITORED_BY"
```

The `depends_on` fields enforce ordering. The `canary_percent` and `promotion_criteria` in the agent code phase connect to Chapter 7's GVP. The one-week delay on schema cleanup gives time to confirm that no code path still references the legacy property. For the agent itself, Chapter 7's canary and staging mechanics handle the rest. The addition here is the coordination layer, which prevents a prompt that references `MONITORED_BY` from reaching production before the migration that creates that relationship type.

## Hardware Acceleration

The architecture we have built distributes computation across two distinct channels: graph traversals that navigate the knowledge graph, and model inference calls that power the specialist nodes of the horizontal workflow graph. At production scale, both become bottlenecks. A PageRank calculation that identifies the most critical nodes in a million-node graph takes minutes on a CPU. A workflow that chains 10 SLM calls in sequence accumulates seconds of latency per step. Neither is acceptable for a real-time system.

Hardware acceleration addresses both channels, but with different tools. For graph operations, GPU-accelerated libraries like cuGraph can turn multi-minute analytics into sub-second computations. For inference, optimized serving frameworks and specialized hardware reduce the per-call latency of your specialist models. We will cover both, then establish a practical latency budget for the full pipeline.

### GPU-Accelerated Graph Operations

The first bottleneck is graph analytics: algorithms like PageRank, community detection, and centrality that your agent uses to identify critical nodes and estimate blast radius. These algorithms are computationally intensive on large graphs, and their performance characteristics make them a natural fit for GPU acceleration.

The primary bottleneck for graph algorithms is not compute power but memory bandwidth. Graph traversals involve irregular, random memory access patterns, following a pointer from one node to the next with no predictable locality. CPUs, optimized for sequential or block-oriented access, pay a heavy penalty for this pattern. GPUs, with their massively parallel architecture and high memory bandwidth, are a natural fit.

NVIDIA's cuGraph library, part of the RAPIDS framework, provides GPU-accelerated implementations of standard graph algorithms. The published benchmarks (Kumar et al., 2024, *https://oreil.ly/lbJqG*) give a sense of the range: PageRank on a TigerGraph plus cuGraph fusion with A100 GPUs shows up to a 137x speedup over CPU-based solutions. The Louvain method for community detection achieves 125x over NetworkX. Multi-GPU PageRank on a DGX-2 is 80x faster than a 100-node Apache Spark cluster (Alacron, 2020, *https://oreil.ly/ABFK0*). The exact speedup depends on the algorithm, the graph size, and the baseline, but the order of magnitude of observed improvement is consistent.

For teams already using NetworkX, nx-cugraph (Ratzel, 2023, *https://oreil.ly/3FYM7*) provides a drop-in GPU backend with zero code changes. Set an environment variable, and supported algorithms (60+ as of this writing) automatically dispatch to the GPU. On the LiveJournal graph (4.8M nodes, 69M edges), betweenness centrality that took 7 minutes on CPU completed in 5 seconds—a 485x speedup.

What does this mean for the DevOps agent? GPU acceleration is most valuable in two scenarios: identifying critical nodes in the dependency graph during incident analysis (PageRank, betweenness centrality) and detecting communities of related services during blast radius estimation (Louvain, label propagation). Both operations block the agent's reasoning until they complete, so the speedup directly reduces time to diagnosis. We will see this in action in "The DevOps Agent: From Prototype to Production" on page 337.

A practical caveat: no major graph database natively executes Cypher or Gremlin traversal queries on GPU. GPU acceleration is available for *analytics* (PageRank, community detection, centrality) via external libraries like cuGraph. The traversal query engine itself remains CPU bound. The production pattern is a three-phase round trip: extract the subgraph from the database, run analytics on GPU, and write the results back as node properties. Example 8-11 walks through all three phases.

*Example 8-11. Full GPU round trip: Extract, analyze, and write back*

```
import os
os.environ["NX_CUGRAPH_AUTOCONFIG"] = "True"

import networkx as nx
from neo4j import GraphDatabase

def compute_and_store_criticality(driver):
    """Extract infrastructure graph, run GPU PageRank, write scores back."""
    # Phase 1: Extract the full service dependency graph
    with driver.session() as session:
        result = session.run("""
            MATCH (s:Service)-[:DEPENDS_ON|CALLS]->(t:Service)
            RETURN s.name AS source, t.name AS target
        """)
        edges = [(r["source"], r["target"]) for r in result]

    # Phase 2: Run PageRank on GPU (dispatched automatically by nx-cugraph)
    G = nx.DiGraph(edges)
    scores = nx.pagerank(G)

    # Phase 3: Write criticality scores back as node properties
    with driver.session() as session:
        session.run("""
            UNWIND $scores AS entry
            MATCH (s:Service {name: entry.name})
            SET s.criticality_score = entry.score,
                s.criticality_updated = datetime()
        """, scores=[{"name": n, "score": s} for n, s in scores.items()])
```

The write-back in Phase 3 is what makes this useful for the agent's reasoning pipeline. Once `criticality_score` is a property on each `Service` node, Cypher queries can filter and sort by it without leaving the database. The agent's `DependencyAnalyzer` node can run `WHERE s.criticality_score > 0.01` to focus on the top 20% of services, cutting the subgraph size for subsequent analysis. Teams typically run this computation on a schedule (every few minutes for volatile infrastructure) and cache the scores as node properties rather than recomputing per query.

## Inference Acceleration for Specialist Model Fleets

Selective intelligence replaces one expensive model with many cheaper ones, but it also replaces one inference call with many. A single user query might trigger the query analyst, a retrieval step, the synthesis node, and the validation node, making four or more model calls in sequence. If each call takes 200 milliseconds, the cumulative latency is nearly a second before adding any graph traversal time. After 10 sequential calls, you are over 2 seconds. A system that takes that long to respond is not an agent; it is a batch job.

This section discusses three approaches to reducing inference latency for multimodel systems.

### Parallelization

Not all nodes in the horizontal workflow graph are sequential. The workflow DAG often allows parallel execution. The query analyst and a context-enrichment step might run simultaneously, for example. Identifying and exploiting parallelism in your workflow graph is the cheapest optimization available.

### Optimized serving

A virtual LLM, or vLLM (Raiput, 2025, *https://oreil.ly/-oXJq*), supports continuous batching and multiple low-rank adaptation (multi-LoRA) serving: you can serve multiple fine-tuned specialist variants from a single base model on a single GPU. This eliminates the overhead of loading separate model weights for each specialist. Example 8-12 shows the DevOps agent's multi-LoRA configuration.

*Example 8-12. Serving the DevOps agent's specialist SLMs via vLLM multi-LoRA*

```
# Start vLLM with the base model and enable LoRA adapter loading
python -m vllm.entrypoints.openai.api_server \
    --model meta-llama/Llama-3.1-3B-Instruct \
    --enable-lora \
    --lora-modules \
        alert-classifier=./adapters/alert-classifier-lora \
        log-parser=./adapters/log-parser-lora \
    --max-loras 3 \
    --max-lora-rank 16

# Client code: route to the right specialist via the model name
```

```
from openai import AsyncOpenAI

client = AsyncOpenAI(base_url="http://localhost:8000/v1")

# AlertClassifier uses the alert-classifier LoRA adapter
alert_response = await client.chat.completions.create(
    model="alert-classifier",  # routes to LoRA adapter
    messages=[{"role": "user", "content": raw_alert_text}]
)

# LogParser uses the log-parser LoRA adapter on the same GPU
log_response = await client.chat.completions.create(
    model="log-parser",  # different adapter, same base model
    messages=[{"role": "user", "content": raw_log_lines}]
)
```

Both adapters share the same base model weights in GPU memory. The vLLM swaps only the small LoRA delta matrices (typically a few hundred MB per adapter) when switching between specialists. The result: the DevOps agent's `AlertClassifier` and `LogParser` both run on a single GPU, at a combined memory cost barely above what one model would require. Also, vLLM maintains a 50–80 millisecond time to first token with 100 concurrent users. TensorRT-LLM offers a 30%–50% higher throughput at scale but requires more engineering overhead to deploy.

#### Specialized hardware

For workloads that can justify purpose-built inference hardware, the numbers speak for themselves. Cerebras Inference (Hoang, 2024, *https://oreil.ly/uKFls*) demonstrated Llama 3.1 8B at 1,800 tokens per second, 20x faster than GPU cloud offerings; a coding prompt that takes 22 seconds on GPU platforms completes in 1.5 seconds. These numbers were independently verified by Artificial Analysis (Wang, 2024, *https://oreil.ly/QyIFn*) at up to 75x faster than hyperscaler GPU offerings. SambaNova's SN50 RDU (2026) (*https://oreil.ly/u-h5S*) targets multimodel serving specifically, with a tiered memory architecture that enables millisecond-level hot-swapping between specialist models.

These three approaches can work together. Parallelizing independent nodes, serving each specialist via multi-LoRA on optimized infrastructure, and accelerating the graph analytics pipeline can bring time taken by a 30-step agentic workflow from minutes to single-digit seconds. That is the difference between a system that can monitor infrastructure in real time and one that can only produce postmortems.

#### Key-value cache as the binding concurrency constraint

Multi-LoRA serving lowers your cost per weight. It does not lower the constraint that binds at production scale. When your DevOps agent's `CausalAttributionNode` produces a long reasoning trace that walks a dependency chain from an alert through three services back to the `stripe-python` 3.3.0 deployment, every generated token grows the key-value (KV) cache in GPU memory. Peak KV per active user, not model size, is what sets how many concurrent incident analyses a single H100 can host.

The economics follow directly. If each reasoning trace holds 50,000 tokens in cache for 10 seconds, a GPU with 80 GB of memory hosts a small number of concurrent users regardless of how small the model is. Quantizing the weights does not move this ceiling. You have to bound the cache itself.

Microsoft's Memento (2026) (*https://oreil.ly/_Q0-K*) is the first production-ready recipe for this. MEMENTO teaches a reasoning model, through a two-stage supervised fine-tuning pass on 228,000 traces, to segment its chain of thought into blocks, emit a compressed summary token per block (the *memento*), and mask the original block from future attention. The KV cache follows a sawtooth pattern. It grows while the block is open, compresses on summary, then starts fresh for the next block. Peak KV falls by 2x to 2.5x across the model families tested. Each block compresses by a factor of 5 to 20.

For the DevOps agent, a 2.5x reduction in peak KV means 2.5x more concurrent incidents per GPU at the same latency. At production load, across hundreds of simultaneous alerts, this determines whether you serve the incident-response agent on 10 GPUs or on 4.

> Before you optimize anything else in the hardware acceleration layer, measure peak KV per active user on a representative reasoning-heavy workload. If the number is small (short prompts, no reasoning traces), the multi-LoRA configuration from Example 8-12 dominates and KV compression is secondary. If the number is large—and it is large for any agent doing causal attribution or multistep planning—KV compression is where your first gains live.

## Latency Budgets

How fast is fast enough? The answer depends on what your agent is doing, but here is a practical framework based on the component benchmarks:

*Graph traversal and retrieval*
: 5–50 milliseconds with GPU acceleration on warm data

*SLM inference per step*
: 50–200 milliseconds with optimized serving (vLLM or equivalent)

*Multistep agentic workflow (5–10 SLM calls)*
: 500 milliseconds to 2 seconds with parallelization

*End to end with specialized inference hardware*
Single-digit seconds for 30+ model calls

Industry guidance converges on sub-100 milliseconds for low-latency AI and sub-30 milliseconds for ultra-low latency (Lulka, 2026, *https://oreil.ly/m7UFs*). For agentic systems, the meaningful target is end-to-end task completion time rather than per-call latency, since the user perceives the full workflow, not individual steps.

# The DevOps Agent: From Prototype to Production

In Chapter 7, the DevOps agent successfully diagnosed its own prediction failure: the `stripe-python` update that caused connection pool exhaustion instead of the API contract violation it predicted. The automated loop captured the execution graph, ran the cognitive autopsy, generated targeted feedback via semantic backpropagation, and updated the `CausalAttributionNode`'s prompt. The SRE team reviewed and approved the change. The system worked.

It worked in a development environment, though, with a single cluster, a handful of services, and no constraints on model cost or data access. Through Chapters 2–7, the DevOps agent has evolved from a concept into a capable system, adding knowledge graphs (Chapter 3), temporal memory (Chapter 4), reasoning and planning (Chapter 5), tool orchestration (Chapter 6), and self-evolution (Chapter 7). What it lacks is the engineering required to run at production scale, 24/7, across the full infrastructure.

This section applies all three optimization dimensions to bring the DevOps agent to its final state.

## Applying Selective Intelligence

Up to now in this chapter, the discussion of these concepts has been general in nature. Now let's apply them to the DevOps agent specifically. The horizontal workflow graph, as built in Chapter 5, has several node types with very different computational demands. Example 8-13 assigns each one the model it actually needs.

*Example 8-13. Selective intelligence configuration for the DevOps agent*

```
DEVOPS_MODEL_CONFIG = {
    # Lightweight classification - fine-tuned SLM
    "AlertClassifier": {
        "model": "llama-3.1-3b-alert-classifier",
        "task": "Classify incoming alerts by severity and type",
        "rationale": "Binary/multi-class classification with fixed output schema",
        "cost_vs_frontier": "1/30th"
    },
```

```
    # Log parsing - fine-tuned SLM
    "LogParser": {
        "model": "llama-3.1-3b-log-parser",
        "task": "Extract structured events from raw log lines",
        "rationale": "Pattern extraction with known formats",
        "cost_vs_frontier": "1/30th"
    },

    # Dependency analysis - mid-tier model
    "DependencyAnalyzer": {
        "model": "llama-3.1-8b-instruct",
        "task": "Traverse knowledge graph and assess blast radius",
        "rationale": "Requires multi-hop reasoning but within known schema",
        "cost_vs_frontier": "1/10th"
    },

    # Causal reasoning - frontier model (via cascade)
    "CausalAttributionNode": {
        "model": "cascade:llama-3.1-8b -> claude-sonnet",
        "task": "Map changes to failure modes, generate predictions",
        "rationale": "Open-ended causal reasoning;
            escalate when 8B confidence < 0.7",
        "cost_vs_frontier": "~1/5th (blended)"
    },

    # Synthesis - frontier model
    "PredictionSynthesis": {
        "model": "claude-sonnet",
        "task": "Produce structured prediction reports for SRE review",
        "rationale": "Requires nuanced natural language generation",
        "cost_vs_frontier": "1x (justified)"
    }
}
```

The key design decision is the cascade on `CausalAttributionNode`. This is the node that failed in Chapter 7's `stripe-python` scenario: it committed to the wrong failure hypothesis. Causal reasoning is inherently open-ended, so a small model cannot handle every case. It *can* handle the routine ones, though (a straightforward version bump, a well-documented deprecation), and the cascade ensures that ambiguous cases escalate automatically. The 0.7 confidence threshold is calibrated from production data. Below that, the 8B model's predictions correlate poorly with actual outcomes.

Now look at the economics. In the Chapter 7 DevOps scenario (where a library update triggers a prediction workflow), the agent's pipeline runs through `AlertClassifier`, `LogParser`, `DependencyAnalyzer`, `CausalAttributionNode`, and `PredictionSynthesis`. Under the "frontier model everywhere" approach, all five nodes run at full cost. Under selective intelligence, only `PredictionSynthesis` consistently uses the frontier model, and `CausalAttributionNode` uses it only 30% of the time (when the midtier cascade escalates). The blended cost per prediction drops by roughly 80%.

Over a month of continuous monitoring, with thousands of deployment events each triggering the prediction pipeline, that 80% reduction is the difference between a viable production system and a budget overrun.

## Hardware Acceleration for Dependency Analysis

The DevOps agent's most latency-sensitive operation is dependency analysis during incident response. When an SRE reports high latency, the agent needs to traverse the knowledge graph to identify the full dependency chain, calculate which nodes are most critical (PageRank), and estimate the blast radius. In Chapter 5, this traversal ran on CPU against a graph of hundreds of nodes. In production, the infrastructure graph has tens of thousands of nodes and hundreds of thousands of relationships. Example 8-14 shows the GPU-accelerated version.

*Example 8-14. GPU-accelerated dependency analysis for incident response*

```
import os
os.environ["NX_CUGRAPH_AUTOCONFIG"] = "True"

import networkx as nx
from neo4j import GraphDatabase

def analyze_blast_radius(incident_service: str, driver):
    """GPU-accelerated blast radius analysis for incident response."""
    # Extract the dependency subgraph from Neo4j
    with driver.session() as session:
        result = session.run("""
            MATCH (s:Service)-[r:DEPENDS_ON|CALLS*1..4]->(target:Service)
            WHERE s.name = $service
            RETURN s.name AS source, target.name AS dest, type(r) AS rel_type
        """, service=incident_service)

        edges = [(record["source"], record["dest"]) for record in result]

    # Build NetworkX graph - PageRank runs on GPU automatically
    G = nx.DiGraph(edges)
    centrality = nx.pagerank(G)

    # Identify critical nodes in the blast radius
    blast_radius = sorted(
        centrality.items(),
        key=lambda x: x[1],
        reverse=True
    )

    return {
```

```
        "incident_service": incident_service,
        "total_affected_services": len(G.nodes),
        "critical_path": blast_radius[:10],
        "analysis_engine": "nx-cugraph (GPU)"
    }
```

On CPU, this analysis takes 3–5 seconds for the full infrastructure graph. With nx-cugraph on a single GPU, it completes in under 100 milliseconds. That difference matters during incident response: the SRE sees the blast radius before they have finished reading the alert.

## Governance for Infrastructure Data

Cost optimization and hardware acceleration make the agent fast and affordable. Governance makes it safe to deploy. The DevOps agent's knowledge graph contains sensitive infrastructure data: service configurations, deployment credentials, internal IP addresses, cost data, and on-call schedules that include employee names. Different personas need different views of this data, as Example 8-15 illustrates.

*Example 8-15. Role-based access control for the DevOps knowledge graph*

```
// SRE role: full infrastructure visibility, no cost data
CREATE ROLE sre_oncall;
GRANT TRAVERSE ON GRAPH infrastructure NODES Service, Deployment,
    Library, AlertRule, Metric TO sre_oncall;
GRANT TRAVERSE ON GRAPH infrastructure RELATIONSHIPS
    DEPENDS_ON, CALLS, MONITORED_BY, DEPLOYED_TO TO sre_oncall;
DENY READ {cost_per_hour, budget_code, billing_account}
    ON GRAPH infrastructure NODES Service TO sre_oncall;

// Finance role: cost visibility, no deployment details
CREATE ROLE finance_analyst;
GRANT TRAVERSE ON GRAPH infrastructure NODES Service TO finance_analyst;
GRANT READ {name, cost_per_hour, budget_code, billing_account, team}
    ON GRAPH infrastructure NODES Service TO finance_analyst;
DENY TRAVERSE ON GRAPH infrastructure NODES Deployment, Library,
    AlertRule TO finance_analyst;
```

The execution graph from Chapter 7 automatically captures which role the agent used for each query, creating an audit trail of data access. When the compliance team asks "Did any agent query access employee PII last quarter?" the answer is a graph query filtered on role and property access patterns.

## The Completed Agent

With selective intelligence, hardware acceleration, and governance in place, the DevOps agent has reached its final state. Table 8-1 tracks the full evolution from Chapter 2's initial concept.

*Table 8-1. Mapping the evolution of the DevOps agent*

| Chapter | Capability added | Before | After |
|---|---|---|---|
| 3 | Knowledge graph | Disconnected monitoring tools | Queryable digital twin of the tech stack |
| 4 | Temporal memory | Static snapshot | Historical awareness of infrastructure changes |
| 5 | Reasoning and planning | Reactive alerts | Multistep investigation DAGs |
| 6 | Tool orchestration | Manual metric lookups | Structured API queries via MCP |
| 7 | Self-evolution | Frozen after deployment | Learns from prediction failures automatically |
| 8 | Optimization | Development prototype | Production-ready: cost-effective, secure, real-time |

To see all eight pillars working together, trace a single incident through the optimized pipeline. A deployment event fires: `checkout-service` is updating `stripe-python` from 3.2.1 to 3.3.0. Figure 8-3 shows the full flow.

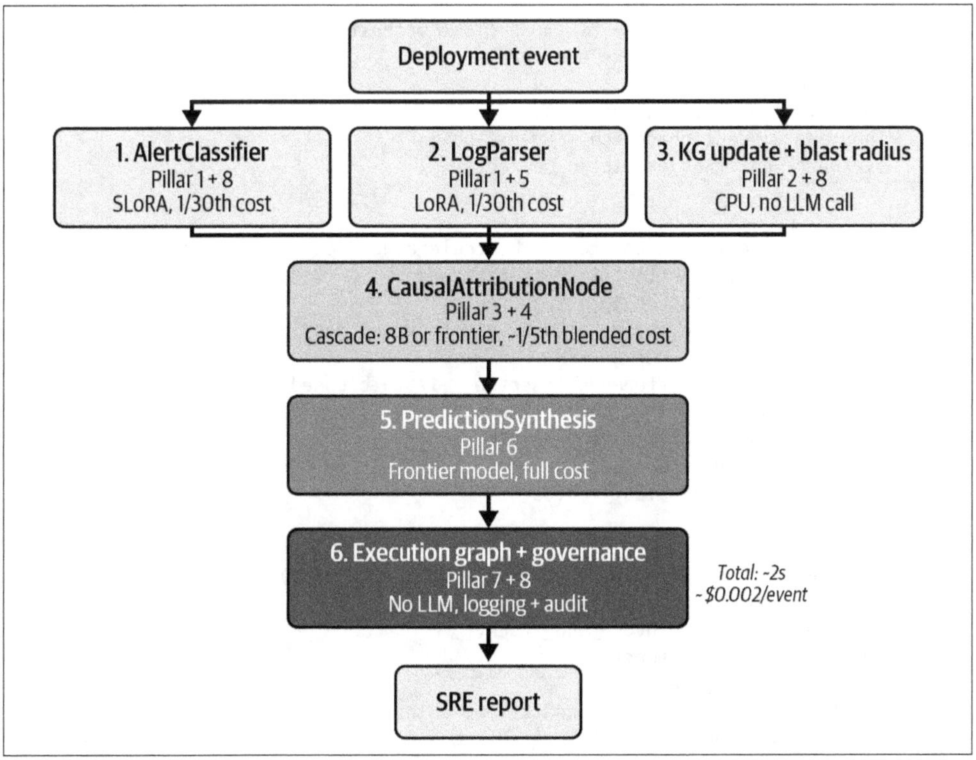


*Figure 8-3. A single deployment event flowing through the optimized DevOps agent pipeline*

Each step is annotated with the pillar it exercises and the model tier that powers it. Example 8-16 provides the code.

*Example 8-16. End-to-end optimized pipeline for a single deployment event*

```
async def handle_deployment_event(event, tracker: CostTracker):
    """Full pipeline: alert → classify → parse → analyze → predict → log."""
    # Step 1: AlertClassifier (SLM, 1/30th cost)
    # Pillar 1 (Knowledge Rep) + Pillar 8 (Optimization)
    classification = await tracker.invoke_and_track(
        node=alert_classifier,
        model=lora_model("alert-classifier"),  # LoRA on shared base
        input_data=event.raw_payload,
        evaluator=severity_matches_label
    )

    if classification.severity == "routine":
        return log_and_skip(event)

    # Step 2: LogParser (SLM, 1/30th cost)
    # Pillar 1 (Knowledge Rep) + Pillar 5 (Tool Orchestration)
    parsed = await tracker.invoke_and_track(
        node=log_parser,
        model=lora_model("log-parser"),
        input_data=event.changelog + event.logs,
        evaluator=entities_extracted_correctly
    )

    # Step 3: Incremental KG update + GPU-accelerated dependency analysis
    # Pillar 2 (Memory) + Pillar 8 (Optimization)
    ingest_deployment_event(neo4j_driver, event)
    blast_radius = analyze_blast_radius(event.service, neo4j_driver)

    # Step 4: CausalAttributionNode (cascade, ~1/5th blended cost)
    # Pillar 3 (Reasoning) + Pillar 4 (Planning)
    prediction = await routed_causal_attribution(
        changelog_analysis=parsed,
        dependency_context=blast_radius
    )

    # Step 5: PredictionSynthesis (frontier model, full cost)
    # Pillar 6 (Structured Output)
    report = await tracker.invoke_and_track(
        node=prediction_synthesis,
        model=frontier_model,
        input_data={"prediction": prediction, "blast_radius": blast_radius},
        evaluator=sre_accepted_without_revision
    )

    # Step 6: Log execution graph with governance metadata
    # Pillar 7 (Self-Evolution) + Pillar 8 (Optimization)
    log_execution_graph(
        event_id=event.id,
        nodes=[classification, parsed, blast_radius, prediction, report],
        governance={"access_role": "sre_on_call", "pii_accessed": False}
```

```
    )

    return report
```

Each step references the pillar it exercises. Steps 1 and 2 run on LoRA adapters sharing a single GPU (selective intelligence). Step 3 updates the knowledge graph incrementally and runs PageRank on a GPU for blast radius estimation. Step 4 uses the learned router from earlier in this chapter to decide whether the 8B model or the frontier model handles causal reasoning. Step 5 generates the SRE-facing report at full quality. Step 6 writes the execution graph with governance metadata, feeding both the self-evolution loop from Chapter 7 and the compliance audit trail from this chapter.

The entire pipeline completes in under 2 seconds. Steps 1, 2, and 3 can run in parallel (they have no data dependencies on each other beyond the raw event). The cost: roughly \$0.002 per event at current API pricing, compared to \$0.01 or more under the "frontier model everywhere" approach.

This system started as a collection of disconnected monitoring tools and manual processes. It is now self-healing—and practical.

# Common Pitfalls

Optimization introduces its own failure modes. The pitfalls below are the ones most likely to surface in production:

*Routing to models that cannot handle edge cases*
: The biggest risk with selective intelligence is routing a task to a model that is too small for it. Static routing by node type assumes uniform difficulty within each node, but real queries vary. A query analyst node that handles 95% of queries correctly with a 3B model will still misclassify 5% of them. If those 5% include the high-stakes queries (novel incident types, ambiguous alerts), the system fails precisely when it matters most. The fix is threshold-based cascading for high-stakes nodes: let the small model try first, but always have an escalation path.

*Overpruning the knowledge graph*
: Aggressive TTLs and lifecycle management solve the stale data problem but create a new one: the agent loses access to historical patterns it needs for reasoning. The DevOps agent's ability to predict failures depends on its ability to see past incidents and their resolution patterns. If those nodes are pruned after 30 days, the agent loses its training signal. The fix is the same bitemporal approach that Graphiti uses: invalidate old edges rather than deleting them and set different retention policies for different node types. Operational snapshots can expire aggressively; incident records should be retained much longer.

*Governance policies that block the agent's reasoning*
: An access control policy that is too restrictive can prevent the agent from reaching the nodes it needs to solve a problem. If the SRE role cannot traverse to library nodes, the dependency analysis from Chapter 5 breaks. The fix is to test your access control policies against the agent's actual query patterns before deploying them. Run the agent's standard investigation workflows under each role and verify that the results are functionally complete, even if some properties are masked.

*Neglecting schema migration coordination*
: When a schema migration and an agent code update are deployed independently, the agent may reference relationship types or properties that do not yet exist (if the code deploys first) or still exist in their old form (if the migration deploys first). The fix is the staged rollout pattern described earlier: migration first with $N - 1$ compatibility, then code update, and finally cleanup.

*Benchmarking models on the wrong evaluation set*
: Teams often select their specialist SLMs based on generic benchmarks (MMLU, HumanEval) rather than domain-specific evaluation sets. A model that scores well on a general knowledge benchmark may still fail on your specific alert classification taxonomy. The fix is straightforward but requires discipline: build a per-node evaluation set from real production data and reevaluate whenever the task distribution changes.

*Ignoring cold start latency for GPU acceleration*
: GPU-accelerated graph analytics are fast once the data is loaded, but the initial data transfer from graph database to GPU memory can take seconds for large graphs. If your system loads the graph fresh for every query, you negate the GPU speedup. The fix is to maintain warm GPU-resident copies of the most frequently queried subgraphs, refreshed incrementally as the graph updates.

# Summary

This chapter addressed the three forces that separate a working prototype from a production system: cost, governance, and performance.

Selective intelligence reduces cost by matching model capability to task complexity. A federation of specialists (small models for classification and extraction, midtier models for structured reasoning, frontier models for open-ended synthesis) brings the cost per agent interaction down by 80% or more without degrading quality. In many cases, specialization improves quality because focused training signals produce more reliable behavior than diluted ones.

Governance ensures that the agent's access to the knowledge graph is scoped, auditable, and compliant. Subgraph-level access control limits what each agent persona can see. The UUID separation pattern handles PII and GDPR deletion without cascading side effects. The execution graph, originally built for self-evolution in Chapter 7, doubles as a compliance artifact that satisfies audit requirements without additional infrastructure.

Hardware acceleration brings everything within production latency budgets. GPU-accelerated graph analytics turn multi-second dependency analysis into sub-100-millisecond operations. Optimized inference serving and specialized hardware enable the multimodel workflows to respond in real time.

The DevOps agent embodies all eight pillars. Knowledge representation gives it a digital twin of the infrastructure. Memory systems give it temporal awareness. Reasoning and planning give it the ability to investigate incidents. Tool orchestration connect it to live systems. Structured output make the communication between those systems reliable. Self-evolution teaches it to learn from its mistakes. Optimization makes all of that practical: affordable, secure, and fast enough to run 24/7.

# Conclusion

This book started with a diagnosis. Chapter 1 identified five architectural flaws that prevent vector RAG systems from supporting true agency: context amnesia, relationship blindness, temporal ignorance, reasoning paralysis, and tool chaos. These problems cannot be solved by simply using a more powerful model. Rather, they are representation problems, and they require an architectural response.

Chapter 2 introduced that response: the shift from strings to things, the dual-graph architecture that pairs a vertical knowledge graph with a horizontal workflow graph, and the eight pillars that turn the architecture into a working system. Everything that followed was the build.

In Part II, we constructed the agent's brain. Chapter 3 turned fragmented infrastructure data into a structured knowledge graph, complete with entity resolution, schema patterns for agent interaction, and a three-graph architecture for separating trusted knowledge from extracted interpretations. Chapter 4 gave that graph a memory, adding temporal awareness through bitemporal modeling, consolidation patterns, and graph memory systems that learn their own retrieval strategies.

In Part III, we gave the agent the ability to act. Chapter 5 built the horizontal workflow graph and the reasoning engine that sits at the intersection of the two graphs, decomposing complex problems into inspectable, verifiable DAGs rather than opaque monolithic prompts. Chapter 6 connected the agent to the outside world through MCP-based tool orchestration, with security woven throughout and structured output guaranteeing that every API call is syntactically valid.

In Part IV, we made the system viable for production. Chapter 7 closed the learning loop: execution graphs as immutable records, multi-layered evaluation for diagnosis, semantic backpropagation for targeted improvement, and a GVP for safe deployment. Chapter 8 solved cost, governance, and performance issues through selective intelligence, subgraph-level access control, and GPU-accelerated graph operations.

The DevOps agent traced that arc from start to finish. A collection of disconnected monitoring tools became a system that detects infrastructure issues proactively, diagnoses root causes in under two seconds, learns from its own mistakes, and does all of it at a fraction of a cent per event. The `stripe-python` 3.2.1 → 3.3.0 upgrade that would have woken an SRE at 3:00 a.m. is now handled autonomously, and the agent's prediction improves every time it encounters a similar pattern.

## Where the Field Is Heading

The architecture in this book is not frozen. Several developments will shape how graph-based agentic systems evolve over the next few years:

*Models keep getting cheaper and more capable*
: The economics of selective intelligence shift as model costs decline and small models improve. The routing decisions you make today will need revisiting as the price-performance frontier moves. The architecture handles this well: since each node in the horizontal workflow graph has its own model assignment, swapping a model is a configuration change, not a rewrite.

*Graph databases are gaining native AI features*
: Neo4j, TigerGraph, and others are building vector search and embedding generation and ML model serving directly into the database engine. The boundary between the knowledge graph and the reasoning layer will blur. Features that require custom code in Chapters 3, 4, and 5 may become built-in capabilities.

  A second category of graph database is emerging alongside the incumbents: on-device, schema-as-code, agent-native stores. ContextGraphs (Vanderseypen, 2026, *https://oreil.ly/6ATUX*) ships *.pg* schema files version-controlled in Git, enforced at query time, with Rust plus Lance plus Arrow columnar execution. Claude reads, writes, and traverses the graph through a structured interface rather than emitting Cypher. Atomicity, consistency, isolation, durability (ACID), time travel, change data capture for audit, and a hybrid search stack (full-text, semantic, fuzzy, BM25, graph-constrained reranking) all live in one engine. The scope is deliberately per-device. It is not the right architecture for fleet-scale coordination across agents. For agents that need a private knowledge graph with no server dependency, like personal assistants, on-device enterprise agents, or regulated workflows where data cannot leave the machine, this category now has production examples. Pair it with the sovereign on-device inference story from

Chapter 1's discussion of decentralization, and you have a workable recipe for fully local agentic deployment.

*Agent protocols are maturing*
: MCP was introduced in late 2024 and is the foundation of Chapter 6. As the protocol matures and competitors emerge, the tool orchestration layer will gain more standardized patterns for authentication, capability discovery, and multi-agent coordination. The graph-based orchestration approach from Chapter 6 (tools as knowledge graph nodes with typed dependencies) will become even more valuable as the number of available tools grows.

*Evaluation is becoming a discipline, not an afterthought*
: The self-evolution loop from Chapter 7 depends on reliable evaluation. As research matures around LLM-as-judge calibration, criteria drift, and tool-integrated evaluation, the diagnostic engine that powers self-improvement will become more precise. Agents that invest in evaluation infrastructure early will compound their advantage.

## Choosing the Right Architecture for Your System

Not every AI system needs what this book describes. A chatbot that answers questions from a static knowledge base does not need a horizontal workflow graph. A document search system does not need semantic backpropagation. The architecture in this book is designed for systems that need to reason across relationships, take action through multistep workflows, learn from operational experience, and run under production constraints.

Here are the questions worth asking before committing to this approach:

*Does your domain have meaningful relationships between entities?*
: If the entities in your system are independent (isolated documents with no connections), vector search may be sufficient. If they form a network of dependencies, hierarchies, or temporal sequences, a knowledge graph earns its keep.

*Does your agent need multistep reasoning?*
: If the agent's job is single-turn question answering, a simpler architecture will do. If it needs to decompose problems, coordinate tool calls, and carry state across steps, the horizontal workflow graph provides structure that prompts alone cannot.

*Do you need the system to improve over time?*
: If you can retrain periodically and deploy fresh models, self-evolution may be unnecessary overhead. If the system needs to adapt continuously to changing conditions without full retraining cycles, the execution graph and evaluation loop from Chapter 7 pay for themselves.

*Are cost, governance, and latency real constraints?*
: If you are building a research prototype, the optimization patterns from Chapter 8 can wait. If you are deploying to production with budget limits, compliance requirements, and latency SLAs, they cannot.

The architecture is modular by design. You do not have to build all eight pillars at once. Start with the knowledge graph (Chapter 3) and see if structured relationships improve your retrieval quality. Add temporal memory (Chapter 4) if your domain changes over time. Build the workflow graph (Chapter 5) when single-prompt approaches hit their ceiling. Each pillar adds value independently, and the full architecture is the sum of those incremental investments.

## Building What Comes Next

The gap between AI systems that demo well and AI systems that work in production is an architecture gap. The techniques in this book—grounded in graph theory, process engineering, and years of production experience from teams like AnyShift and Kakao—provide a path across that gap.

The field will keep moving. Models will get faster. Graph databases will get smarter. New protocols and frameworks will appear. The specific tools and libraries referenced in these chapters will evolve. But the architectural principles will hold: represent knowledge as structured relationships, decompose reasoning into inspectable steps, ground actions in verified facts, learn from every execution, and match your optimization to your actual constraints.

You have the blueprint and the build. The rest is engineering.

# Index

## A


A-anchored (answer-anchored), 278
A-Mem pattern, 135, 137
access control, 103, 323
action
  blindness of, in vector-based retrieval, 17
  governance of, in AI OS, 245
  irreversibility of, in agentic systems, 175
  of agency in systems, 6
action nodes, 185
active learning, 286-288
ActivityGlobal queries, 15
adaptability, balanced with persistence, 115
AdapTive and OptiMized (ATOM), 98
add-cognify-search-learn pipeline, 308
add_edge node type, 125
advanced level, in GraphRAG, 180
Advanced RAG-Tool Fusion, 246-248
agency, in systems, 6
agent constraint triangle, 9
agent core, 10
Agent Package Manager (APM), 252
Agent Skills (Anthropic), 223
AgentEvolver, 286
agentic AI, 5, 7, 27-54
agentic balance, 171
agentic graph-based reasoning and planning, 166, 167-174
agentic graph-based tool orchestration, 215-261
  evolving ecosystem of tools, 234
  in practice, 253-260
  knowledge graph necessary tools, 230-234
  learning and advanced patterns, 246-253
  Model Context Protocol (MCP), 216-218
  orchestration at scale, 239-245
  prompt bloat crisis, 218-230
agentic memory management, 118, 122
agentic systems
  classifying, 8
  graph design principles for, 71-82
  graph-based knowledge modeling for, 57-112
  integrating with existing, 82-94
agents, 6, 7
  architecture of, 10-12
  as tools, 217
  autonomous DevOps, 48-53
  entity resolution as the foundation of knowledge for, 91-94
  goal manipulation with IFC, 234
  homoiconic knowledge representation for adaptability of, 108
  maturing protocols for, 347
  memory consistency models for coordination of, 120
  methods of learning for, 281
  three-graph model for knowledge of, 71-75
  tool misuse with IFC, 234
  training to use memory, 149-155
agents layer, 194
Agora, 116
AI Shopping Mate, 322
Aldridge, Nicholas, 217
Alshikh, Waseem, 281
Amazon Elastic Compute Cloud (EC2), 44, 102, 103, 105, 110
Amazon Neptune, 19, 60, 61, 65
ambiguity, context evaluator and, 272

analysis nodes, interleaved thinking for, 182
ANN (approximate nearest-neighbor) algorithm, 13, 75
answer-anchored (A-anchored), 278
Anthropic, 8, 9, 165, 223, 298
Anyscale, 140
AnyShift, 48, 52, 101
Apache AGE, 19, 60
Apache Flink, 195
APIs, 46, 49, 254-256
APM (Agent Package Manager), 252
APOC (Awesome Procedures on Cypher), 327
APOC library (Neo4j), 95
append-only observation record, 34
append-only with TTL, 327
approximate nearest-neighbor (ANN) algorithm, 13, 75
ArangoDB, 65
architecture
  agent, 10-12
  choosing, 347
  dual-graph, 30, 41
  evolution of, in agentic graph systems, 280
  for federated context, 252
  for graph memory systems, 113-121
  foundations, 27-54
  GraphRAG, 18-21
  importance of, 210
  memory, 121
  of controlled parallelism, 203
  pipeline, 186-196
  planning and separation of, 196
  solution, 252
area under the curve (AUC), 279
ArXiv MCP Server, 243
associativity gap, in vector-based retrieval, 15
ATOM (AdapTive and OptiMized), 98
atomic fact decomposition, in ATOM framework, 98
AUC (area under the curve), 279
authentication, MCP, 216, 228
authority, of agency in systems, 6
AutoGen, 141
automation, 100, 235
autonomy
  autonomous DevOps agent, 48-53
  of agency in systems, 6
Awesome Procedures on Cypher (APOC), 327
AWS, 217
axes, of self-evolution, 281
axial coding, 269
axioms, 85, 88
Azure Virtual Machines (VMs), 103

## B

Baidu AI Search, 243, 250
Baselga, Marc, 251
Bash, 172
Basic Formal Ontology (BFO), 90
bd ready command, 201
bd update command, 201
Beads, 201
behaviors, 153, 276
benchmarking models, 344
bespoke loops, 34
better reasoning, as an advantage of GraphRAG, 22
BFO (Basic Formal Ontology), 90
BGE-m3, 141
bidirectional interaction, 39
bidirectional mapping, 106
bitemporal metadata, in context graphs, 41
bitemporal modeling, 44
Bitemporal Property Graphs (Anselma et al.), 41
Block, 218, 223
bring your own orchestration (BYOO), 157-160
broadcast pattern, 116
Burgess, Mark, 35
business context, operational metadata for, 107
BYOO (bring your own orchestration), 157-160

## C

cache layer, 122
cache sharing, in multi-agent systems, 116-117
California Consumer Privacy Act (CCPA), 324
call method, 217
call tools, in MCP, 216
calling APIs, 46
canonical types, 103
capabilities, of agents, 10
capability model pattern, 78, 105
capability models, 44
capacity planning, 122
catastrophic forgetting, 311, 312
catastrophic forgetting resilience (CFR), 312
causal attribution node, semantic backpropagation to, 303

causal consistency model, 121
CCPA (California Consumer Privacy Act), 324
centralized permission management, in AI OS, 245
Cerebras Inference, 335
CFR (catastrophic forgetting resilience), 312
channel consolidation, 92
channel separation, 92
ChatGPT, 141
Cherny, Boris, 172, 298
Chroma, 9
chunk nodes, in lexical graphs, 72
classes, as an ontology component, 84
Claude, 141, 346
Claude Code, 34, 140, 171, 200, 298
CLAUDE.md, 171, 251
CLI-Anything, 227
CLIs (command-line interfaces), 227, 228
closed-world assumption (CWA), 67-69
cloud, 48, 105-107
cluster balance, 146
coalesce function, 234
code integration, 106
code-level self-modification framework, 288
Codex, 140
coding agents, as dual-graph systems, 171
Cognee, 113, 118, 119, 123, 128, 139, 143, 147, 148, 308, 310
cognitive fault isolator, 274
Cognizant, 220
cold start latency, 344
cold storage, 148
Collaborative Tool Retrieval (COLT) system, 221, 250, 297
Command Query Responsibility Segregation (CQRS), 195
command-line interfaces (CLIs), 227, 228
communication, structured generation and reliable, 184-186
community subgraphs, 126, 142
community summaries, pregenerating, 20
completeness
  context evaluator and, 272
  in SkillNet, 224
  in tension, 117
complex reasoning, 185
complex relationships, handling, 130
complexity management constraint, 9
compliance, 83, 325
composable execution, CLIs encode, 228
computationally expensive, as a disadvantage of GraphRAG, 23
compute resources, multi-cloud abstraction and, 103
computer architecture, of agent memory, 122
concurrency constraint, 335
configuration
  as code (team scale), 252
  integrating, 106
  Nova Forge for memory training, 158
configuration drift, 109, 251
confirmed verdict, 38
conflict resolution, with production memory systems, 147
Confluent, 195
Connected Data London 2025 Masterclass framework, 92
consistency
  checking, from ontologies, 174
  metrics for, 185
  models for, 120
consolidation, 157
  as a memory operation, 132-133
  through constraints in MEM1, 151
  timing of, 159
constrained context, 206, 211
constraint expressiveness, of graph data models, 66
constraint-guided planning, 198
containment relationships, contextual boundary patterns and, 77
content node type, 124
context
  control of, as an advantage of GraphRAG, 21
  evolution of, in agentic graph systems, 280
  governance of, 250-253
  in graphs, 126
  integrating in AI OS, 245
  integrating in GraphRAG, 20
  management of, with graph memory, 119
  measuring quality of, 110
context amnesia, 3, 15
context drift, in vector-based retrieval, 17
context engineering, 10, 102
context evaluator, 272-274
context fragmentation, in enterprise agentic AI, 7

context graphs, 40-41, 346
"Context Graphs: AI's Trillion-Dollar Opportunity" (Foundation Capital), 40
context pollution, in agentic systems, 175
context rot, 9, 114
context utilization constraint, 9
context windows, 16, 115
context-aware validation, in three-stage linking pipeline, 101
contextual boundary patterns, 44, 76, 104
contextual nuance, loss of, as a disadvantage of GraphRAG, 23
contextual relevance, with tools as graph nodes, 232
contextual understanding, of agency in systems, 6
continuous learning, 159, 160
contradiction, context evaluator and, 272
control and flexibility, as a consideration for building or buying a GraphRAG system, 60
control flow, 168
controllable execution graphs, 166
controlled parallelism, architecture of, 203
controlled vocabularies, integrating, 107
convergence, competition compared with, 230
coordination overhead, from context fragmentation, 251
correctness metrics, 276
cost
  as a consideration for building or buying a GraphRAG system, 60
  cost awareness dimension in SkillNet, 224
  derailing agent projects with, 48
  measuring cost-performance trade-offs, 320-322
  of models, 346
  per successful completion, 320
coverage, of digital twins, 111
CQRS (Command Query Responsibility Segregation), 195
CrewAI, 141
criteria staleness, in evaluation frameworks, 311
cross-system integration, 83
CrowdStrike's Threat Graph, 327
cuGraph library, 48, 332
curriculum learning, implementing, 153
Cursor, 140
CWA (closed-world assumption), 67-69
Cypher, 19, 61, 174, 226, 231, 254, 276, 327, 329, 346

# D

data
  governance and access control, 323-326
  retention of, 324
  targeted generation, 285
data flow, securing with information flow control, 233
data flywheel, 295
debugging
  building cognitive debugging skills, 292-294
  tools with production memory systems, 147
  with production memory systems, 145
decision nodes, in horizontal workflow graphs, 33
decision traces, in context graphs, 41
Deep Memory Retrieval, 142
DeepLearning, 100
Defining N-ary Relations on the Semantic Web (W3C Working Group), 40
dependency analysis, hardware acceleration for, 339
deployment patterns, 330
design principles, for agentic systems, 71-82
determinism, CLIs and, 227
deterministic construction, for automating knowledge graph construction, 100
developer scale, task graphs at, 201
Developing Time-Oriented Database Applications in SQL (Kaufmann), 41
DevOps, 16, 27
DevOps example agent, 101-111
  adding memory to, 155-160
  context engineering for automation of, 102
  designing the ontology, 102
  diagnostic agent, 204-211
  from prototype to production, 337-343
  predictive outage detection in practice, 299-310
  tool orchestration in practice, 253-260
DevOpsMemory class, 156
diagnostic agent (DevOps), 204-211
diagnostic nodes, interleaved thinking for, 182
digital twins, 51, 105-107, 110
directed acyclic graph (DAG), 22, 37
disproved verdict, 38
distracting effect, 174, 175

distributed scaling, 160
document nodes, in lexical graphs, 72
document-level extraction, 97
Documentation Refinement Through Automated Feedback and Testing (DRAFT) system, 237, 250, 297
documentation rewriting, as a DRAFT phase, 237
DOLCE, 90
domain and range validation, from ontologies, 174
domain graph, 69, 72, 75
domain violations, 173
"Don't Build Multi-Agents" (Cognition), 165
DRAFT (Documentation Refinement Through Automated Feedback and Testing) system, 237, 250, 297
DSPy, 34
dual objectives, in MEM1, 151
dual-graph systems, 30, 41, 171
dual-pathway model, 278
dual-time modeling, 99
dynamic architecture selection, 190
dynamic DAG construction, 199
dynamic discovery, with tools as graph nodes, 232
dynamic memory, without dynamic schemas, 152
dynamic reorganization, with graph memory, 119
dynamic schemas, dynamic memory without, 152
Dynamo.fi, 140

## E

EBWT (expanded backward transfer), 312
EC2 (Amazon Elastic Compute Cloud), 44, 102, 103, 105, 110
ECL (extract-cognify-load) pipeline, 118, 139
ecosystems, for tools, 234-239
edge cases, 94, 101
edges (relationships)
    density of, 146
    in graphs, 123, 125
    in vertical knowledge graphs, 31
    lifecycle management, 327
edges node type, 125
"Effective Context Engineering for AI Agents" (Anthropic), 9
"The Eight Pillars of Agentic Architecture", 35, 42-48
embedding node type, 124
embeddings, 13
emergent consolidation, in memory systems, 154
empirical evidence, 200-201
enhanced property graphs, 67
enterprise agentic AI, 3-26
enterprise AI OS layer, 244-245
entities (nodes)
    extracting in horizontal working graph, 317
    graph-based agents using, 4
    in agent knowledge graphs, 93
    represented by nodes in vertical knowledge graphs, 31
entity knowledge graph, 20
entity resolution, 44, 92
    as graph building blocks, 93
    as the foundation of agent knowledge, 91-94
    for infrastructure identity, 110
    linking across graphs, 100
entropy collapse, persistent self-learning without, 297-299
environment, 11, 158
environmental, social, and governance (ESG) knowledge graph construction, 173
episode subgraphs, 126, 142
episodic memory, 44, 247
epistemic node type, 125
Erez, Ben, 251
error amplification, in agentic systems, 175
error-handling strategies, 189
ESG (environmental, social, and governance) knowledge graph construction, 173
evaluation, 311, 347
event backbone layer, 194, 195
event-centric pattern, 44, 75, 104
event-driven orchestration, 193-196
event-driven updates, in AnyShift, 52
eventual consistency model, 120
eviction, 137
evidence metadata, in agent knowledge graphs, 93
evidence-based resolution (see entity resolution)
evolution
    catastrophic forgetting across cycles, 312
    graph-based agents using, 4

schema, 326
evolutionary loop, 294
evolving knowledge networks, 135, 137
executability dimension, in SkillNet, 224
executable knowledge patterns, 81-82
execution discontinuity, in enterprise agentic AI, 7
execution graphs, 266-268, 301, 325
execution nodes, in horizontal workflow graphs, 33
exhaustiveness, of digital twins, 111
expanded backward transfer (EBWT), 312
experience network, of memory, 125
experiences, 237, 306
explainability, as an advantage of GraphRAG, 22
extract-cognify-load (ECL) pipeline, 118, 139
extraction approaches, for heterogeneous sources, 95-99
EyeLevel.ai, 16

## F

failures
  isolating, as a property of DAGs, 37
  of agent architectures, 12
  sources of memory, 114
FalkorDB, 60, 139
fault isolation, 195, 208, 243
federated context, architecture for, 252
federated learning, enabled by hierarchical orchestration, 243
federation of specialists, 316
Fersht, Phil, 220
FIDES research, 233
FIFO (first-in, first-out), 136
file discovery, for automating knowledge graph construction, 100
first-attempt recovery rate, 293
first-in, first-out (FIFO), 136
five-stage self-improvement loop, 308-310
flat storage, 121
flexibility, 21, 115
flow-based pruning, with PathRAG, 176
formal reasoning capabilities, of graph data models, 63
foundation level, in GraphRAG, 180
foundational anchoring, 90
"Foundations of an Alternative Approach to Reification in RDF" (Hartig), 40
fragmented monitoring, in initial state, 49
frameworks, 195, 209, 285-294
freshness, of digital twins, 111
"From Local to Global: A GraphRAG Approach to Query-Focused Summarization" (Microsoft), 14
FrugalGPT, 318
functional clustering, 243
future-proofing implementations, 160
fuzzy matching, 92

## G

G-reasoner, 25
garbage collection agent, 297
Garg, Ashu, 40
GDPR (General Data Protection Regulation), 324
Gemini Embedding, 75
Gemini-3 Flash, 306
General Data Protection Regulation (GDPR), 324
general-purpose evolution, 281
Generalist and Lightweight Model for Text Classification (GLiClass), 270
generalization-based AI, 92
Geo-X, 327
GFMs (graph foundation models), 25
Git, 107, 118, 120, 201, 346
GLiClass (Generalist and Lightweight Model for Text Classification), 270
global queries, 14
GNN (graph neural network), 25
Google, 4
Google Cloud Compute Engine, 103
Google Gemini, 140
Google Workspace CLI, 230
governance
  as a foundation for agent knowledge graphs, 83
  derailing agent projects with, 48
  for infrastructure data, 340
  policies for, 344
governance control plan (enterprise scale), 252
governed memory, in context graphs, 41
GPU-accelerated graph operations, 332
graceful degradation, 191-193
graduated validation protocol (GVP), 266, 294, 295-297
granularity, 15, 129

graph data models, 62, 63-70
graph databases, native AI Features for, 346
Graph Explorer (Zep), 147
graph foundation models (GFMs), 25
graph memory systems, 44, 113-161
  architecting, 113-121
  benefits of, 119
  building, 128-131
  comparing production systems, 139-144
  in architectures, 135-139
  in production, 118, 135-139
  memory consistency models for agent coordination, 120
graph neural network (GNN), 25
graph nodes, tools as, 231
graph objects, skills as self-improving, 308-310
graph traversal, 134
graph-based agents, 4
graph-based knowledge modeling, for agentic systems, 57-112
graph-based retrieval, integrating quality ratings into, 224-226
graph-first approach, 139
Graphiti pattern/framework, 118, 135, 138, 327
GraphRAG, 18, 174
  architecture of, 18-21
  hybrid, 24-25
  learned graph reasoning models, 25
  pattern taxonomy, 180-181
  successes and failures of, 21-24
GraphRAG systems, 58, 60
graphs
  building, as a stage in GraphRAG system frameworks, 58
  compound power of structure and, 185
  context, 40-41
  data storage in GraphRAG, 19
  design principles for agentic systems, 71-82
  essential components of, 123-126
  intersection of, 38
  linking across, 100
  materialization of, 95
  planning at repository scale, 200-201
  representing memory as, 121-131
  rich, 70
  structures of, 69
  textual, 70
  types of, 169-172
grounded hypotheses, integrating knowledge graphs for, 207
GSQL, 61
Gulli, Antonio, 298
Gupta, Jay, 40
GVP (graduated validation protocol), 266, 294, 295-297

## H

hallucination propagation, 173
hard delete, 325
hardware acceleration, 332-336
  for dependency analysis, 339
  GPU-accelerated graph operations, 332
  inference acceleration for specialist model fleets, 334-336
  latency budgets, 336
harness, 34, 36
health monitoring, with production memory systems, 145
heterogeneous sources, extraction approaches for, 95-99
HFS, 220
hierarchical memory, 135
hierarchy
  alignment of, 88
  of memory architecture, 121
  orchestration of, 241-243
  organization of, 121
  planning, 197
"Hindsight is 20/20: Building Agent Memory That Retains, Recalls, and Reflects" (Latimer et al), 135
"Hindsight is 20/20: Building Agent Memory That Retains, Recalls, and Reflects" (Latimer et al.), 125
homoiconic knowledge representation
  executable knowledge patterns, 81-82
  for agent adaptability, 108
  metaknowledge structures, 80
horizontal workflow graphs, 30, 33-38, 169-172, 205-207
Horn, Andreas, 298
hybrid architectures, 190-193
hybrid GraphRAG, 24-25
hybrid LPG-RDF, 66
hybrid materialization, 95
hybrid storage, 141
hyperedges, 64, 67, 73, 130

hypergraphs, 63, 64, 65, 66, 73, 130
hyperparameter optimization, 295

## I

I/O layer, 122
id node type, 124
IFC (information flow control), securing data flow with, 233
imaginary space, 170, 201
imitation-based learning, for agents, 281
immediate learning, created by memory later, 248
impact analysis, for infrastructure changes, 109
impedance mismatch, 46
implementation
  of graph memory systems, 128-131
  of interleaved thinking, 183
  of memory for operational context, 156
implications, for tool orchestration, 253
improvement, self-directed, 286-288
improvement-monitoring gap, 311
incremental approach, 96
incremental plasticity (IP), 312
incremental updates, 328
"In-depth Analysis of Graph-Based RAG in a Unified Framework" (Zhou et al.), 58
indexing
  as a memory operation, 133
  in LLM-based pipeline, 20
  index construction, as a stage in GraphRAG system frameworks, 58
individual optimization, from context fragmentation, 251
individuals (instances), as an ontology component, 85
inference, 174, 334-336
inference-time knowledge augmentation, 305-307
InfoGain, 274, 276, 292, 302
information flow control (IFC), securing data flow with, 233
information flow design, 168
Information Technology Infrastructure Library (ITIL), 107
infrastructure
  applying schema design patterns to, 104
  entity resolution for identity of, 110
  for the synthetic workforce, 244-245
  governance for data, 340
  impact analysis for changes in, 109
ingestion timeline, 126
initial state, 49
input payload, in execution graphs, 267
instance matching, 88
institutional knowledge preservation, as a foundation for agent knowledge graphs, 83
integrating
  flexibility of, as a consideration for building or buying a GraphRAG system, 60
  initial flexibility of, 128-130
  knowledge graphs for grounded hypotheses, 207
  quality ratings into graph-based retrieval, 224-226
  with existing systems, 82-94
integration level, in GraphRAG, 180
intelligent orchestrator, 240
intelligent recommendations, with production memory systems, 145
intent clarification, for automating knowledge graph construction, 100
interaction pattern, 39
interaction, learning from every, 246-248
interleaved thinking, 181-184
intersection, of graphs, 38
interventions, choosing, 282-284
intra-test-time evolution, 281
investigation DAG, constructing, 207
invocation, in RAG-MCP framework, 219
IP (incremental plasticity), 312
iterative ontologies, 91
iterative refinement, with loop pipelines, 187
iText2KG framework, 96, 97
ITIL (Information Technology Infrastructure Library), 107

## J

Jarjoura, Daniel, 252
Jaro-Winkler distance, 101
JavaScript, 141
judgment skills, encoding, 228

## K

Kafka, 194, 195, 202
key-value cache, 335
keyword indices, 133
keyword search, 134
KG-R1, 26

KG.GOV framework, 325
KI (Knowledge Index), 274
Knowledge Graph Conference (KGC), 98
knowledge graphs, 58-61, 70, 210
  automating construction with multi-agent systems, 100
  building, 95-101
  complex updating of, as a disadvantage of GraphRAG, 23
  constructing in GraphRAG, 18
  databases with hyperedge support, 67
  impact of on AI systems, 4
  integrating for grounded hypotheses, 207
  LLM-based frameworks, 96
  multimodal, 74
  necessary tools for, 230-234
  overpruning, 343
  populating, 105-107
  querying, 108-110
  registering tools in, 253
  vertical, 30-33
Knowledge Index (KI), 274
knowledge integration, multisource, 52
knowledge modeling, graph-based, for agentic systems, 57-112
knowledge organization, 83-85
knowledge representation, 42, 43, 101-111
knowledge units, in graphs, 123-125
Kubernetes, 327

## L

labeled property graphs (LPGs), 62
LanceDB, 139
LangChain, 34, 141, 142
LangGraph, 141, 142, 166, 188
large language models (LLMs)
  amnesia and, 3
  as next-token predictors, 45
  generalization-based AI in, 92
latency, 257-260
latency budgets, 336
Layer 0, in evaluation framework, 270-272
Layer 1, in evaluation framework, 272-274
Layer 2, in evaluator framework, 274
Layer 3, in evaluation framework, 274-276
LazyGraphRAG, 16, 22
LEANAGENT, 312
learned behavior, 159
learned contextual updates, in memory systems, 154
learned graph reasoning models, 25
learned routing, 319
learned strategies, in MEM1, 150
learning, 246-253
  active, 286-288
  context governance, 250-253
  from experience, as a DRAFT phase, 237
  memory layer, 246-248
  Nested Execution Challenge, 249
  patterns from incidents, 157
  performance st scale, 250
Letta (MemGPT), 123, 135
Letta Leaderboard, 114, 120
lexical graph, 69, 72, 75
lexical indices, 133
LightRAG, 328, 330
Lindenberg, André, 298
linear execution, sequential pipelines with, 186
LinkedIn, 5
linking across graphs, 100
list tools, in MCP, 216
LlamaIndex, 141, 142
LLM-based extraction from unstructured text, 96
LLM-based knowledge graph construction frameworks, 96
LLM-independent merge, in ATOM framework, 99
load balancers, 106
local queries, 14
local UI (Cognee), 147
LOCOMO Benchmark, 141
logical inference, graph data models and, 62
long-term memory, 247
loop engineering, 298
loop pipelines, 187
lost in the middle problem, 16, 115
LPGs (labeled property graphs), 62

## M

maintenance, 224, 326-331
manual diagnosis, in initial state, 49
map, 20
masked training, for specialized behaviors, 153
Massive Multitask Language Understanding (MMLU), 321
McIlroy, Doug, 172

MCP Gateway pattern, 219-223, 238, 242
McpToolset pattern, 230
mechanistic interpretability, 277
Mem0, 113, 118, 119, 123, 128, 139, 141, 143, 147, 148
MEM1, 149-153
memory
  adding to DevOps agent, 155-160
  as a pillar of agentic graph architecture, 42, 44
  conflicts with, 146
  consistency models, for agent coordination, 120
  evolution of, 126-128
  evolving systems, 154
  fragmentation, in vector-based retrieval, 17
  implementing for operational context, 156
  monitoring health of, 159
  operations with, 131-135
  representing as graphs, 121-131
  rewarding perfection, 152
  training agents to use, 149-155
memory layer, 246-248
memory persistence, of agency in systems, 7
memory schema, for DevOps, 155
Meppiel, Daniel, 252
merging multiple ontologies, 87
Meta's J1 approach, 272
meta-orchestrator layer, 194
metadata node type, 125
metadata, in vertical knowledge graphs, 31
metaknowledge structures, 80
metatooling, 238
metrics, quality, 101
MetricsQuery model, 256
MICRO-ACT, 274
Microsoft
  BenchmarkQED research, 14, 16, 22
  Memento, 336
  open skills repository, 223
MiniMax-M2, 182
MixLLM, 319
mixture-of-probes (MoP), 279
MMLU (Massive Multitask Language Understanding), 321
modality property, 75
Model Context Protocol (MCP), 11, 46, 216-218, 228
models
  cost of, 346
  evolution of, in agentic graph systems, 280
  specialization of, 317
modularity, as a property of DAGs, 37
MongoDB, 60
MoP (mixture-of-probes), 279
MT-Bench, 319
multi-agent debate, 202-204
multi-agent systems
  Anthropic, 165
  automating knowledge graph construction with, 100
  cache sharing in, 116-117
multi-cloud abstraction, 103
multi-hop reasoning, 119, 144
multi-layered evaluation framework, 268-279
multi-objective mastery, in MEM1, 151
multidimensional design problem, 115
multimodal knowledge graphs, 74
multiperspective pattern, 77
multisource knowledge integration, in Any-Shift, 52

## N

N-ary relations, graph data models and, 64
named policy, 34
National Institute of Standards and Technology (NIST), 107
Nautilus, 327
needle-in-a-haystack benchmarking, 9
neighbor-awareness, 284
Neo4j, 19, 32, 60, 61, 65, 95, 128, 139, 231, 323, 346
Neo4j-Migrations, 326
Nested Execution Challenge, 249
nested pipeline composition, 191
NESTFUL benchmark, 232, 249
networking resources, multi-cloud abstraction and, 103
neurosymbolic integration, 160
Ng, Andrew, 8, 299
Ngiam, Jiquan, 228, 229
Nia Skills framework, 252
Nichol, Alan, 193
NIST (National Institute of Standards and Technology), 107
node id, in execution graphs, 266
node type, 266, 318
nodes (entities)

compression of, 148
growth rate for, 145
in graphs, 123-125
in vertical knowledge graphs, 31
lifecycle management, 327
splitting workflows into, 38
nontraditional signals, 276
Nova Forge for memory training, 158
NVIDIA, 48, 317, 332
nx-cugraph, 332

## O

observability, 106, 189
observation network, of memory, 125
observe-think-act cycle, 10
Ollama, 140
ontologies, 84
annotating to control agent behavior, 88
challenges and practical solutions, 87
core components of, 84
designing for DevOps, 102
fundamentals of, 83-85
iterative, 91
merging multiple, 87
ontological grounding, 173-174
ontology-driven evolution, 234-236
organizational, 107
upper, 90
OntoMetric, 173
opaque variable management, with IFC, 233
open coding, 269
open-world assumption (OWA), 67-69
OpenAI, 140, 141
OpenAI WebSearch MCP, 243
OpenAPI, 220
OpenClaw, 140
operational complexity, as a consideration for building or buying a GraphRAG system, 60
operational context, implementing memory for, 156
operational entities, multi-cloud abstraction and, 103
operational metadata, for business context, 107
operator configuration, as a stage in GraphRAG system frameworks, 58
opinion network, of memory, 125
optimization, 315-348
as a pillar of agentic graph architecture, 42, 48
common pitfalls, 343
data governance and access control, 323-326
DevOps agent, from prototype to production, 337-343
hardware acceleration, 332-336
in RPO, 296
production systems and maintenance, 326-331
optimized serving, 334
orchestration, 239-245
enterprise AI Os layer, 244-245
functional clustering, 243
graph-based agents using, 5
hierarchical orchestration, 241-243
modernizing classical SaaS, 240
with resource management, 168
orchestration class, 128
organizational boundaries, contextual boundary patterns and, 77
organizational disconnection, in enterprise agentic AI, 8
organizational ontologies, integrating, 107
Osmani, Addy, 230, 298
Outlines library, 46, 184-186
output payload, in execution graphs, 267
overpruning knowledge graphs, 343
OWA (open-world assumption), 67-69
OWL (Web Ontology Language), 66, 90

## P

P95 latency, 142
Palmyra X5, 220
parallel 5-tuple extraction, in ATOM framework, 99
parallel execution, 37, 202-204
parallel exploration, with tree pipelines, 187
parallelism, uncoordinated, 202
parallelization, 334
parent-child edges, in execution graphs, 267
partially correct prediction, 299
passage graphs, 69
passive learning, 286-288
path pruning, 148
PathRAG, 45, 174, 176, 179, 203
pathway reweighting (PR), 279
pattern recognition, 235, 248
per-agent access control, 229
performance

as a consideration for building or buying a GraphRAG system, 60
at scale, 250
control of with graph memory, 119
derailing agent projects with, 48
in tension, 117
metrics for in execution graphs, 267
of graph data models, 65
optimization of, with production memory systems, 148
performance-based trust scores, 237
Perplexity, 141
Perplexity MCP Server, 243
persistence, balanced with adaptability, 115
persistent layer, 122
persistent self-learning, without entropy collapse, 297-299
personal-to-enterprise gradient, 229
personally identifiable information (PII), 324
pick lists, 84
pipeline architectures, 186-196
event-driven orchestration, 193-196
hybrid, 190-193
loop pipelines, 187
production implementation patterns, 188
sequential pipelines, 186
tree pipelines, 187
planning and coordination, 196-204
(see also reasoning)
architectural separation for, 196
as a pillar of agentic graph architecture, 45
constraint-guided planning, 198
dynamic DAG construction, 199
empirical evidence, 200-201
hierarchical planning, 197
multi-agent debate, 202-204
task graphs at developer scale, 201
planning nodes, 182, 185, 196, 211
planning paralysis, in vector-based retrieval, 17
Polley, Kyle, 38
populating knowledge graphs, 105-107
population-based learning, for agents, 281
post-write shapes, SHACL and, 69
PostgreSQL, 19, 60, 67
Pourshahid, Ali, 193
practical training strategies, 152
pre-action shapes, SHACL and, 68
pre-retrieval shapes, SHACL and, 68
precision, of digital twins, 110
predictive outage detection, in practice, 299-310
premature close, 303
primitives, choosing, 227-230
Privacy by Architecture pattern, 324
proactive prediction, 299
proactive truthfulness detection, 278
procedural memory, 44
production
considerations for, 159
evaluation overhead in, 311
implementation patterns, 188
patterns in graph memory systems, 135-139
production-ready features and operations, 144-149
safe evolution in, 294-299
scaling layer, 193-196
production systems
comparing, 139-144
future-proofing, 160
maintenance of, 326-331
production-ready features and operations, 144-149
progressive disclosure, 223, 243
prompt bloat crisis, 218-230
choosing primitives, 227-230
from listing to finding, 218
MCP Gateway pattern, 219-223
skills, 223-226
prompt refinement, when not to use, 282
properties, 31, 93
property alignment, 88
property graphs, 32, 63, 64, 65, 66, 67
property key correlation, in three-stage linking pipeline, 101
provenance property, in RPO, 295
provenance, in lexical graphs, 72
publish-subscribe pattern, 116
Python, 141


## Q


Q-anchored (question-anchored), 278
Qdrant, 139
quality
metrics for, 101
parity threshold, 320
ratings, integrating into graph-based retrieval, 224-226
queries

ActivityGlobal, 15
classifying in horizontal workflow graph, 317
global, 14
in knowledge graphs, 108-110
in LLM-based pipeline, 20
interpretation and graph traversal of, in GraphRAG, 19
local, 14
sensemaking, 14
query latency, 146
query method, 130
Query-Scene graph, in COLT system, 222
Query-Tool graph, in COLT system, 222
QueryMetricsAPI tool, 253
question-anchored (Q-anchored), 278


## R


R3-RAG, 174, 177-179
RAG-MCP framework, 219, 250
"RAG-MCP: Mitigating Prompt Bloat" (Gan and Sun), 218
RAKG (Retrieval Augmented Knowledge Graph Construction), 98
Rakhmetzhanov, Arlan, 252
RAPIDS framework, 332
RDF (Resource Description Framework), 32, 62
RDF-based with SHACL, 66
RDS (Relational Database Service) databases, 106
reactive response, in initial state, 49
real-time adaptive reasoning, 181-184
real-time performance, 135, 138
realistic multi-goal interactions, in MEM1, 151
reasoning, 165-213
as a pillar of agentic graph architecture, 42
failure of, 274
generation and, 181-186
graph-based agents using, 4
limitations in vector-based retrieval, 15
reasoning-representation trade-off, 63
reliability of, 83
shape analysis, 276
trace, 272
with graphs, as a pillar of agentic graph architecture, 45
reasoning nodes, 33, 185
reasoning paralysis, 4, 34
reciprocal rank fusion (RRF), 135
reconciling parallel execution, 202-204
recursion property, in RPO, 295
recursion-provenance-optimization (RPO), 294, 295-297
recursive language models (RLMs), 114
RedAI, 38
Redis Streams, 194
reduce, 20
redundancy, resiliency through, 243
reflect-retry-reward framework, 281, 292-294
registering tools in knowledge graphs, 253
reification, in context graphs, 40
reinforcement learning, 26, 157-160
"Reinforcement Learning from User Feedback" (Han), 276
Relational Database Service (RDS) databases, 106
relational indices, 133
relations (edges), in agent knowledge graphs, 93
relationship blindness, 3, 31
relationship modeling, structured, 52
relationship patterns, in memory systems, 154
relationships
as an ontology component, 85
graph-based agents using, 4
relationships (edges)
density of, 146
in graphs, 124, 125
in vertical knowledge graphs, 31
lifecycle management, 327
reliability scoring, with PathRAG, 176
replay and recovery, 195, 208
Repository Planning Graph (RPG), 200
repository scale, graph planning at, 200-201
request-grant pattern, 116
research nodes, interleaved thinking for, 182
resiliency, redundancy through, 243
Resource Description Framework (RDF), 32, 62
resources, agent-used, 11
response generation, in GraphRAG, 20
retrieval, 174-181
as a memory operation, 134
as a stage in GraphRAG system frameworks, 58
distracting effect, 175
GraphRAG pattern taxonomy, 180-181
in RAG-MCP framework, 219
PathRAG, 176, 179
R3-RAG, 177-179

SkillNet and, 226
strategies for, 159, 317
Retrieval Augmented Knowledge Graph Construction (RAKG), 98
rewards, 281, 310
rich knowledge graphs, 70
RLMs (recursive language models), 114
root cause analysis, temporal queries for, 156
route method, 310
RouteLLM, 319
routing strategies, 317-319, 343
RPG (Repository Planning Graph), 200
RPG-Encoder, 200
RPO (recursion-provenance-optimization), 294, 295-297
RRF (reciprocal rank fusion), 135
Ruiz, Armand, 230
Runtime framework, 252

## S

SaaS (Software as a Service), 240
safe evolution, in production, 294-299
safety dimension, in SkillNet, 224
SambaNova's Sn50 RDU, 335
scalable governance, enabled by hierarchical orchestration, 243
scale, 226, 250
scale constraint, 168
scanner node, 38
Scene-Tool graph, in COLT system, 222
schema
evolution of, 326
neglecting migration coordination, 344
proposal, for automating knowledge graph construction, 100
validator, 34
schema design patterns
applying to infrastructure, 104
capability model pattern, 78, 105
contextual boundary pattern, 76, 104
event-centric pattern, 75, 104
multiperspective pattern, 77
SEAL (Self-Adapting LLM), 285, 310
securing data flow with information flow control, 233
security transparency, 324
selective intelligence, 315, 316-322
applying, 337
case for model specialization, 317
measuring cost-performance trade-offs, 320-322
routing strategies, 317-319
selective retention, 141
selective storage, 159
Self-Adapting LLM (SEAL), 285, 310
self-attributing, 287
self-awareness, 266-282
execution graphs, 266-268
multi-layered evaluation framework, 268-279
structuring, 79
taxonomy for self-evolution, 280-282
self-correction failure, in agentic systems, 175
self-description, CLIs and, 227
self-directed improvement framework, 286-288
self-documentation, with tools as graph nodes, 232
self-evolution and evaluation, 265-313
as a pillar of agentic graph architecture, 42, 47
common pitfalls, 310-313
foundation of self-awareness, 266-282
predictive outage detection in practice, 299-310
safe evolution in production, 294-299
targeted self-improvement, 282-294
taxonomy for, 280-282
self-evolution data flywheel, as an advantage of GraphRAG, 22
self-healing systems, creating, 51
Self-Improving Coding Agent (SICA), 288
self-navigating, 287
self-questioning, 287
semantic backpropagation, 47, 284, 303
semantic consistency, as a foundation for agent knowledge graphs, 83
semantic drift, 173
semantic entity subgraphs, 126, 142
semantic gaps, in vector-based retrieval, 15
semantic indices, 133
semantic layer, 4
semantic memory, 44, 247
semantic search, 134, 245
semantic similarity, 133
sensemaking queries, 14
Senzing, 94
sequential pipelines, 186

service abstraction, multi-cloud abstraction and, 103
service dependencies, 108
SHACL (Shapes Constraint Language), 66, 68
Shah, Dharmesh, 227
Shankar, Shreya, 269, 273
Shapes Constraint Language (SHACL), 66, 68
shared knowledge layer (department scale), 252
short-term memory, 247
SICA (Self-Improving Coding Agent), 288
significant up-front effort, as a disadvantage of GraphRAG, 23
silent divergence, from context fragmentation, 251
Simons, Michael, 326
Simple Knowledge Organization System (SKOS), 86
Singhal, Amit, 28
single objectives, in MEM1, 151
site reliability engineer (SRE) reports, 45
SkillNet, 224
SkillRL, 226
skills
  as a knowledge type, 306
  as self-improving graph objects, 308-310
  encoding judgment, 228
  MCP, 223-226
SkillsBench, 224
SKOS (Simple Knowledge Organization System), 86
sleep-time compute, 132
SLM-LLM flywheel, 271
SOC 2 (System and Organization Controls 2), 142
soft delete, 324
Software as a Service (SaaS), 240
SPARQL, 19, 61, 68
specialized hardware, 335
Spring AI, 217
SQS, 194
SRE (site reliability engineer) reports, 45
staged rollout, 330
state constraint, 168
state layer, 194
state management, across pipelines, 188
state-specific nodes, in horizontal workflow graphs, 206
static routing, by node type, 318
static rules, 150
Stockholm chair, 73
storage resources, multi-cloud abstraction and, 103
strategic tool utilization, of agency in systems, 7
string matching, 92
strings to things shift, 28
strong consistency model, 120
structure
  compound power of graphs and, 185
  in tension, 115
  of graphs, 69
  verification of with PathRAG, 176
  when to use constraints, 283
structure constraint, 168
structured data/database integration, 95, 105-107
structured generation, 184-186, 211
structured input, CLIs and, 227
structured output
  CLIs and, 227
  for API integration, 254-256
structured output engineering, as a pillar of agentic graph architecture, 46
structured relationship modeling, in AnyShift, 52
structured relationships, 121
subclasses, as an ontology component, 84
subgraph-level access control, 323
subgraphs (contexts), 19, 123, 126
subject graph, 69, 73, 75
synthetic workforce, infrastructure for, 244-245
System and Organization Controls 2 (SOC 2), 142
system evolution, created by memory layer, 248


## T


taint tracking, with IFC, 233
targeted data generation, 285
targeted self-improvement, 282-294
  choosing interventions, 282-284
  frameworks for, 285-294
  semantic backpropagation, 284
task graphs, at developer scale, 201
task success, rewarding, 152
task-oriented learning, in MEM1, 151
taxonomies, 84, 280-282
temporal awareness, 52, 121, 126-128
temporal boundaries, contextual boundary patterns and, 77

temporal consistency, 146
temporal dynamics, 98
temporal filters, 134
temporal ignorance, 4, 32
temporal indices, 133
temporal invalidation, 327
temporal memory, 211
temporal queries, for root cause analysis, 156
TextGrad, 284
textual knowledge graphs, 70
thesauruses, 84
things, strings compared with, 28
think-prune-train (TPT) framework, 289-292
three-graph model, for agent knowledge, 71-75
threshold-based cascading, 318
TigerGraph, 60, 346
time-to-live (TTL), 298, 327
timestamp, in execution graphs, 267
TIR-Judge, 275
tool chaos, 4, 34
tool orchestration, 9, 42, 46
tools
  agents as, 217
  as graph nodes, 231
  composition of, as emergent behavior, 239
  dependencies, 232
  ecosystem of, graph data models and, 65
  evolution of, in agentic graph systems, 280
  evolving ecosystems for, 234-239
  generation of, as emergent behavior, 239
  metatooling, 238
  modification of, as emergent behavior, 239
  registering in knowledge graphs, 253
  trust and, 236-238
tools-as-data principle, 254
Toolshed approach, 221, 250
"Total Economic Impact of Senzing" (Forrester), 91
"Towards Automated Circuit Discovery" (Commy), 277
TPT (think-prune-train) framework, 289-292
traceability, as an advantage of GraphRAG, 22
training, 149-155, 157-160
transaction time, 41
transformation arc, 50
tree pipelines, 187
trees, 69
triage node, 208
trust, tools and, 236-238
TTL (time-to-live), 298, 327
type matching, 232
typed memory interface, 34
typed tool registry, 34
TypeScript, 141

## U

unable-to-test verdict, 38
uncoordinated parallelism, 202
unified semantic foundation, 86-91
universally unique identifiers (UUIDs), 324
Unix philosophy, 172
unstructured text, LLM-based extraction from, 96
updates, 52, 134
upper ontologies, 90
usage analytics, for tools, 234
usage patterns, for SHACL, 68
use case, 60, 148
UUIDs (universally unique identifiers), 324

## V

valid time, 41
validation
  in horizontal working graph, 317
  in RAG-MCP framework, 219
  misconfiguration of thresholds, 311
validation nodes, 33, 185
validator node, 38
validity window, 126
value similarity matching, in three-stage linking pipeline, 101
vector RAG, successes and failures of, 13-18
vector-based agents, consequences for, 16
vector-based retrieval, 3, 12
vector-enhanced storage, 121
verification-based trust, 236
versioned learning log, 288
vertical knowledge graphs, 30-33, 169-172
virtual graph views, 95
virtual LLM (vLLM), 334
visible inconsistency, from context fragmentation, 251
Visual Studio (VS) Code, 140
visualization tools, with production memory systems, 147
vLLM (virtual LLM), 334
vocabularies, controlled, 107
Voyage AI, 141

VS (Visual Studio) Code, 140

## W

W3C Working Group, 40
Waehner, Kai, 195
Web Ontology Language (OWL), 66, 90
WebArena benchmark, 286
Weng, Lilian, 7
West, Casey, 230
"Who Validates the Validators?" (Shankar), 269, 273
whole-dataset reasoning, 30
"Why Do Multi-Agent LLM Systems Fail?" (Cemri et al.), 166
windows forgetting (WF-k), 312
workflow, 38, 168
workflow graphs, 30, 33-38, 210
workflow-agent spectrum, 8
world network, of memory, 125
WRITER, 19, 219, 238

## X

XSkill, 305, 308-310

## Z

Zep, 113, 118, 119, 123, 126, 139, 142, 143, 147, 148
"Zep: A Temporal Knowledge Graph Architecture for Agent Memory" (Rasmussen et al.), 39
zero-shot hallucination gate, 270-272
ZeroRepo, 200

## About the Authors

**Anthony Alcaraz** is a leading AI/ML strategist at AWS, known for his expertise in decision science, large language models, knowledge graphs, and RAG. With a growing audience of over 38,000 on Medium, Anthony regularly shares his insights into AI and knowledge systems. Recently, he lectured at Oxford on the integration of LLMs with graph theory to solve modern business problems.

**Sam Julien** is a product leader specializing in AI developer platforms. He's currently director of product at CopilotKit, focused on transforming agent-user interactions into self-learning agents. Previously, he was the lead product manager for WRITER's IT and developer platform. Sam has spoken at conferences around the world, including The AI Conference and the AI Engineer World's Fair.

## Colophon

The animal on the cover of *Agentic GraphRAG* is a tahr, a large hooved mammal related to goats and sheep.

There are three species of tahr: the Himalayan tahr, the Nilgiri tahr, and the Arabian tahr. Although once thought to be closely related, genetic studies done in 2005 showed that they are not closely related to each other, and each species is considered to be a member of its own genus.

Tahrs have an appearance similar to mountain goats, with backward-curving horns. Males are larger than females, with larger horns. All species live on hills and mountains in Asia. They eat shrubs, grasses, and some fruits. They feed in the morning and evening and rest during the day.

The IUCN statuses of the tahr are Near Threatened for the Himalayan tahr and Endangered for the Nilgiri and Arabian tahr. Hunting and habitat loss are responsible for their decline. Many of the animals on O'Reilly covers are endangered; all of them are important to the world.

The cover illustration is by José Marzan, Jr., based on an antique line engraving from Lydekker's *Royal Natural History*. The series design is by Edie Freedman, Ellie Volckhausen, and Karen Montgomery. The cover fonts are Gilroy Semibold and Guardian Sans. The text font is Adobe Minion Pro; the heading font is Adobe Myriad Condensed; and the code font is Dalton Maag's Ubuntu Mono.

www.ingramcontent.com/pod-product-compliance
Lightning Source LLC
LaVergne TN
LVHW060112110926
847773LV00030B/493
*9798341623170*